THE CRIMEAN WAR BRITISH IMAGINATION

The Crimean War (1854–1856) was the first to be fought in the era of modern communications, and it had a profound influence on British literary culture, bringing about significant shifts in perceptions of heroism and national identity. Stefanie Markovits explores how mid-Victorian writers and artists reacted to an unpopular war: one in which home-front reaction was conditioned by an unprecedented barrage of information arriving from the front. This history had formal consequences. How does patriotic poetry translate the blunders of the Crimea into verse? How does the shape of literary heroism adjust to a war that produced not heroes but a heroine, Florence Nightingale? How does the predominant mode of journalism affect artistic representations of "the real"? By looking at the journalism, novels, poetry, and visual art produced in response to the war, Stefanie Markovits demonstrates the tremendous cultural force of this relatively short conflict.

STEFANIE MARKOVITS is Associate Professor of English at Yale University.

CAMBRIDGE STUDIES IN NINETEENTH-CENTURY
LITERATURE AND CULTURE

General editor
Gillian Beer, *University of Cambridge*

Editorial board
Isobel Armstrong, *Birkbeck, University of London,*
Kate Flint, *Rutgers University,*
Catherine Gallagher, *University of California, Berkeley,*
D. A. Miller, *University of California, Berkeley,*
J. Hillis Miller, *University of California, Irvine,*
Daniel Pick, *Birkbeck, University of London,*
Mary Poovey, *New York University,*
Sally Shuttleworth, *University of Oxford* and
Herbert Tucker, *University of Virginia*

Nineteenth-century British literature and culture have been rich fields for interdisciplinary studies. Since the turn of the twentieth century, scholars and critics have tracked the intersections and tensions between Victorian literature and the visual arts, politics, social organization, economic life, technical innovations, scientific thought – in short, culture in its broadest sense. In recent years, theoretical challenges and historiographical shifts have unsettled the assumptions of previous scholarly synthesis and called into question the terms of older debates. Whereas the tendency in much past literary critical interpretation was to use the metaphor of culture as "background," feminist, Foucauldian, and other analyses have employed more dynamic models that raise questions of power and of circulation. Such developments have reanimated the field. This series aims to accommodate and promote the most interesting work being undertaken on the frontiers of the field of nineteenth-century literary studies: work which intersects fruitfully with other fields of study such as history, or literary theory, or the history of science. Comparative as well as interdisciplinary approaches are welcomed.

A complete list of titles published will be found at the end of the book.

THE CRIMEAN WAR IN THE BRITISH IMAGINATION

STEFANIE MARKOVITS
Yale University

CAMBRIDGE
UNIVERSITY PRESS

CAMBRIDGE UNIVERSITY PRESS
Cambridge, New York, Melbourne, Madrid, Cape Town,
Singapore, São Paulo, Delhi, Mexico City

Cambridge University Press
The Edinburgh Building, Cambridge CB2 8RU, UK

Published in the United States of America by Cambridge University Press, New York

www.cambridge.org
Information on this title: www.cambridge.org/9781107412644

© Stefanie Markovits 2009

This publication is in copyright. Subject to statutory exception
and to the provisions of relevant collective licensing agreements,
no reproduction of any part may take place without the written
permission of Cambridge University Press.

First published 2009
First paperback edition 2012

A catalogue record for this publication is available from the British Library

Library of Congress Cataloguing in Publication Data
Markovits, Stefanie, 1971–
The Crimean War in the British imagination / Stefanie Markovits.
p. cm. – (Cambridge studies in nineteenth-century literature and culture ; 68)
Includes bibliographical references and index.
ISBN 978-0-521-11237-6 (hardback)
1. English literature–19th century–History and criticism. 2. Crimean War, 1853–1856–Literature
and the war. 3. Crimean War, 1853–1856–Influence. 4. War and literature–Great Britain–
History–19th century. 5. Literature and society–Great Britain–History–19th century.
6. Crimea (Ukraine)–In literature. I. Title. II. Series.
PR468.W37M37 2009
820.9´358–dc22

2009022582

ISBN 978-0-521-11237-6 Hardback
ISBN 978-1-107-41264-4 Paperback

Cambridge University Press has no responsibility for the persistence or
accuracy of URLs for external or third-party internet websites referred to in
this publication, and does not guarantee that any content on such websites is,
or will remain, accurate or appropriate.

For Ben

Contents

List of illustrations	*page* ix
Acknowledgements	xi

	Introduction	1
	I The blossom of war	1
	II A brief history of the war	6
1	Rushing into print: journalism and the Crimean War	12
	I "The *Times* war"	15
	II "Mr. Russell's 'War'"	25
	III "The people's war"	42
2	From Amyas Leigh to Aurora Leigh: gender and heroism in the novels of the Crimean War	63
	I Eastward Ho?: the Kingsleys and heroic manliness	69
	II From East and West to *North and South*	86
	III "Heroic womanhood"	98
3	"The song that nerves a nation's heart": the poetry of the Crimean War	123
	I The poetic (battle-) field	125
	II Giving voice to the war: Tennyson's "Charge" and *Maud*'s battle-song	148
4	Painters of modern life: (re)mediating the Crimean War in the art of John Leech and John Everett Millais	168
	I "Nothing like knowing the country"	173
	II Playing at war	183
	III *Peace concluded*?	192

Afterword: Elizabeth Thompson, Lady Butler, *The Roll Call*,
and the afterlife of the Crimean War 210

Notes 219
Bibliography 265
Index 277

Illustrations

1. Roger Fenton, *William H. Russell, Esquire, The Times Correspondent* (1855). Gernsheim Collection, Harry Ransom Humanities Research Center, The University of Texas at Austin. — page 34
2. [Edward Linley Sambourne], "W. H. Russell, Esq., L.L.D," *Punch* 81 (1881), 166. Courtesy of the Yale University Library. — 35
3. Edward Pearce, "The Weather in the Crimea," letter to the editor, *The Times*, January 24, 1855, 10. Courtesy of the Yale University Library. — 52
4. "Right Against Wrong," *Punch* 26 (1854), 144. Courtesy of the Elizabethan Club, Yale University. — 105
5. John D'Albiac Luard, *A Welcome Arrival* (1857). Courtesy of the Council of the National Army Museum, London. — 171
6. [Constantin Guys], "Turks Conveying the Sick to Balaclava," *Illustrated London News*, March 17, 1855, 260. Courtesy of the Watkinson Library, Trinity College, Hartford, CT. — 174
7. [John Leech], "How Jack Makes the Turk Useful at Balaclava," *Punch* 28 (1855), 4. Courtesy of the Yale University Library. — 175
8. [John Leech], "One of the Horrors of the Chobham War," *Punch* 25 (1853), 24. Courtesy of the Yale University Library. — 177
9. [John Leech], "A Little Dinner at the Crimea Club," *Punch* 27 (1854), 200. Author's copy. — 178
10. [John Leech], Untitled, *Punch* 28 (1855), 64. Courtesy of the Yale University Library. — 179
11. "Our Artist in the Crimea," *Punch* 28 (1855), 12. Courtesy of the Yale University Library. — 181

12	[John Leech], "A Trump Card(igan)," *Punch* 27 (1854), 209. Author's copy.	185
13	[John Leech], "Enthusiasm of Paterfamilias," *Punch* 27 (1854), 213. Author's copy.	187
14	James Collinson, *Home Again* (1856). © Tate, London, 2008.	190
15	John Everett Millais, *Peace Concluded, 1856* (1856). Minneapolis Institute of Arts, The Putnam Dana McMillan Fund.	193
16	John Everett Millais, *L'Enfant du Régiment* (1854–55). Yale Center for British Art, Paul Mellon Fund.	201
17	[Henry R. Howard], "Sketching from Nature," *Punch* 29 (1855), 130. Courtesy of the Yale University Library.	206
18	Elizabeth Thompson, Lady Butler, *Calling the Roll after an Engagement, Crimea* (1874). The Royal Collection © 2008, Her Majesty Queen Elizabeth II.	211
19	Elizabeth Butler, *An Autobiography* (1922), tailpiece engraving. Courtesy of the Yale University Library.	217

Acknowledgements

Numerous friends and colleagues gave generously of their time and intelligence to this project, in its various stages and elements; I would like to thank in particular Ruth Yeazell, Linda Peterson, Claude Rawson, Pericles Lewis, Nicole Rice, David Quint, Joseph Bristow, Andrew Miller, and Steven Pincus. I also want to thank the anonymous readers at various journals and at Cambridge University Press who gave such useful comments on the book and its constituent parts. Linda Bree has been wonderful to work with; her support has been much appreciated. But my greatest thanks, as always, go to my family, who have encouraged me throughout: Inga and Dick, Daniel and Sarah, Ben and Caroline, Julia and Jeff, Rebecca and Asher, Nelly and Florence (whose name owes something to her great Crimean predecessor), and especially Ben, to whom I dedicate this book, and who was its inspiration.

A version of parts of chapter 2 first appeared as "*North and South*, East and West: Gaskell, The Crimean War, and the Condition of England," in *Nineteenth-Century Literature* 59.4 (March 2005), 463–93; © 2005, The Regents of the University of California. Thanks to the University of California Press for permission to republish this material. A version of chapter 1 first appeared as "Rushing Into Print: 'Participatory Journalism' During the Crimean War," in *Victorian Studies* 50.4 (2008), 559–86. Thanks to Indiana University Press for permission to republish this material. Finally, very special thanks go to the West Virginia Press and John B. Lamb for agreeing to publish a version of part of chapter 3 as "Giving Voice to the Crimean War: Tennyson's 'Charge' and Maud's Battle-song" in the Fall 2009 volume of *Victorian Poetry*.

Introduction

I THE BLOSSOM OF WAR

> For the long, long canker of peace is over and done
> And now by the side of the Black and the Baltic deep,
> And deathful-grinning mouths of the fortress, flames
> The blood-red blossom of war with a heart of fire.
> Tennyson, *Maud* (1855)

In 1854, Britain entered into a full-fledged war for the first time in forty years. The nation had, in Matthew Arnold's words, been "[w]andering between two worlds, one dead, / The other powerless to be born."[1] The Crimean War served as midwife to the age. Led by an army composed of "the old men of the past," as *The Times* called survivors of the Napoleonic wars, Britain marched into an uncertain future.[2] Historic foes stood together, as Britain's imperial interests led it to ally itself with France, in defense of an "infidel" nation (Turkey), against a Christian enemy (Russia). The telegraph was used for the first time in British military operations, while trench warfare during the siege of Sebastopol prefigured the fighting conditions of World War I. The first war correspondents, both writers and photographers, reported the action for a news-hungry nation. And the businesslike idea of the management (and mismanagement) of war dictated public opinion, as initial popular support gave way to disillusionment and then outrage – enough to topple a government – when those same correspondents described the bureaucratic bungling at the front. This book examines responses in word and image to the two-year-long Crimean War. As the predominant topic of public and political discourse during the day, the war can be used to shed light on social questions. The Crimean War created and crystallized trends in cultural development, and contemporary reactions to it were guided by expectations shaped by literature and art. Representations of the war show the strains of a nation negotiating ideas of heroism and patriotism during a campaign distinguished more by blunder than by glory.

When Karl Marx, writing for the New York *Tribune*, wanted to pinpoint what was typically British about the parliamentary debate leading up to the war, he turned to Shakespeare: "A singularity of English tragedy . . . is its peculiar mixture of the sublime and the base, the terrible and the ridiculous, the heroic and the burlesque." Yet while the mix of high and low modes might have been characteristic, Marx proceeded to recognize the novelty of the current situation: "All great historical movements appear, to the superficial observer, finally to subside into farce, or at least the commonplace. But to commence with this is a feature peculiar alone to the tragedy entitled 'War With Russia.'" Lamenting the Aberdeen government's style of leadership, he noted that even Shakespeare never gave to "the Clown the task of speaking the prologue of a heroic drama. This invention was reserved for the Coalition Ministry."[3] Marx's invocation of Englishness through literature suggests how culture enshrines national identity. He also brings up two key issues that Crimean War literature would have to negotiate: voice (who was "speaking" the drama, and in what tone?) and mode (how should one treat events that tragically combined "the heroic and the burlesque"?).

The fact that Marx's comments were published in a newspaper makes them a particularly appropriate place to begin a study of the cultural impact of the war, for the press played a central role in creating this impact. Indeed, when the curtain finally came up on the tragic farce that was the Crimean War, it revealed a stage that was set with a newspaper every bit as prominent as one of Ibsen's guns: Czar Nicholas first received the British ultimatum that led to the declaration of war by reading it in *The Times* (of London), which broke the story before the statement had traversed its official diplomatic path. And throughout its course, the war was processed by means of words and images appearing in the press and moving rapidly between the Eastern front and the home front. Thus the most famous cultural product of the war – Tennyson's "The Charge of the Light Brigade" (1854) – was stimulated by a *Times* report from the Crimea (printed a mere three weeks after the disastrous events), and the poem itself was first published in a newspaper (the *Examiner*) a few weeks thereafter. Soon, the soldiers in the East were recorded to be "singing" it aloud and were requesting more copies of the verses (a request Tennyson rapidly granted). In a review of the war poetry written from the front for *Blackwood's Edinburgh Magazine*, E. B. Hamley commented on the odd consequences of such rapid transmission: "Fancy . . . the white-haired

Nestor, and the sage Ulysses, reading, towards the close of the first year of their sojourn before Troy, the first book of the *Iliad*, to be continued in parts as a serial."[4] Hamley's awareness of the strange effects on consumers, subjects, and producers of writing about the war must have been underpinned by his own triple role as critic, active officer, and author of an ongoing *Story of the Campaign* (then being published serially in *Blackwood's*).

This was what we would now call a "media war": a war that was experienced through cultural documentation not only after the fact but as events were transpiring. No doubt bureaucratic confusions during the Napoleonic wars had resulted in pointless deaths, too, but now the deaths were reported almost as soon as they occurred, and the reports were being read at home by an increasingly large and powerful British middle class. The back and forth of information between the East and Britain resulted in an imaginative interpenetration of home front and battlefront, heightened by the fact that most of the deaths in the Crimea occurred from the same disease (cholera) that was currently devastating British communities. Visual tributes to the war frequently point to the merger of East and West – and the role played by the media in this merger: the monument to the Coldstream Guards in St. Paul's depicts on its front an image of a monument already constructed to them in the Crimea; J. D. Luard's painting *A Welcome Arrival* (1857; figure 5) shows a Crimean officer's hut plastered with engravings from British illustrated magazines of both domestic and Crimean scenes.[5] The ascendancy of journalism (the subject of my first chapter) had consequences for practitioners of artistic representation in other modes (which I treat in subsequent chapters); what might be called the pressure of the press changed the shape of novels, poems, and paintings about the war, either through oppositional reaction to the dominant form, or by an attempt to accommodate its forces.[6]

Such a climate was bound to test conceptions of the heroic. Of course, writers always struggle with the question of what makes someone a worthy hero; this struggle was particularly evident in the early 1850s in Britain, when literary journals of the day were hotly debating the proper role for the heroic in literature and the relationship of this issue to concerns about genre. But war compels a reconsideration of ideas of heroism. And during the Crimean War, these ideas were undergoing significant alterations. Initial enthusiasm for engagement in the Crimea depended in part on the belief that it would unify a threateningly mercantilized nation, divided in the aftermath of the "hungry 'forties," behind a new cadre of aristocratic and knightly heroes. Contemporary references to Carlyle's *On Heroes*,

Hero-Worship and the Heroic in History (1841) and to chivalry abound; indeed the renewed interest in the chivalric can be attributed in part to the war. As the heroic devolved into what Marx had characterized even from the start as burlesque, though, such a faith in heroes was replaced – or at least offset – by an ethos of middle-class practicality, as when governmental incompetence resulted in calls in Parliament for contracting out the war effort. Views of the military changed, too. Before the war, the stereotypical soldier was an aristocratic fop. After it, he was a brave private (eulogized in countless poems in *Punch* to "Private Smith" and his kin). These conflicting beliefs about heroism become manifest in responses to the charge of the Light Brigade, in which the traditionally aristocratic cavaliers appear both as reinvigorated figures of English chivalry and as proof of their own outmodedness, even their evolutionary unfitness.

But if the charge of the Light Brigade stands as one lasting reminder of the Crimean War, the other remaining cultural touchstone from the conflict must also be considered in relation to ideas of the heroic. While the abstract common soldier was newly lauded, the great and remembered individual hero of the war is instead a heroine: Florence Nightingale. Nightingale's extraordinary rise to fame sits at the intersection of the "Woman Question" and the "Eastern Question." In *Cassandra*, written a few years before the war, Nightingale had bewailed the opportunities for female action: "Why cannot we make use of the noble rising heroisms of our own day, instead of leaving them to rust?"[7] She herself demonstrated what modern "[h]eroic womanhood" (as Longfellow called it in his paean, "Santa Filomena" [1856]) might look like.[8] Indeed, images of Britannia were scattered throughout the illustrated newspapers of the day, sensational heroines pervade the war novels, and the war produced a much-lionized female military painter in Elizabeth Thompson, Lady Butler. Yet at the same time, Coventry Patmore was presenting the first two parts of his influential vision of domesticated womanhood in *The Angel in the House* (1854, 1856). Thus alongside heroism, what has come to be called "heroinism" became a topic of debate in the culture wars of the war years.

So this war can be considered as presenting a particularly revealing case study in the fate of epic action in the period, an example of a process I and others have described elsewhere whereby epic ambitions are caught up in the quagmire of nineteenth-century realities and become feminized and bureaucratized as a result.[9] But it can also shed light on the role literature and art play in these developments, and in the process whereby a Nation revises its sense of self. Winston Churchill once remarked to Siegfried Sassoon that "War is the normal occupation of man," before qualifying his claim slightly: "War – and gardening!"[10] While he was thinking of one form of cultivation (or "blossom"), he could as easily have been thinking of another. And in fact, the occupations of war and art are connected: war forces a culture to memorialize itself, to see itself in the present as a historical artifact, as something that is set in stone – or in words on a page or paint on a canvas. Linda Colley has shown how the culture of war contributed in the eighteenth and early nineteenth centuries to the creation of British national identity.[11] Even as early as Shakespeare's *Henry V*, representative proto-Britons – English, Welsh, Irish, and Scottish – come together (albeit uneasily) in King Harry's "band of brothers" in order to defeat the French at Agincourt. But as Richard Helgerson has pointed out in describing the cultural construction of Englishness in Elizabethan times, a "second great period of English national and imperial self assertion" arrived with "the reign of Queen Victoria."[12] In *Westward Ho!* (1855), written in the midst and in support of the British efforts in the Crimean War, Charles Kingsley tried to use an Elizabethan setting to "rally the troops," military and civilian, at home and abroad. As Kingsley's pointed invocation of the past suggests, mid-nineteenth-century Britain was acutely aware of different models of historical change, and contemporary thinking about the conflict in the East was central to Victorians' awareness of themselves as historical subjects. Yet if the Crimean War represents the first large-scale instance of British self-assertion in a reign that was to be defined by it, it also sets an ambiguous precedent. Current history indicates how war can highlight and exacerbate not only the things that bring a people together but also the things that divide us. Because the Crimean War was accessible to and unpopular with the public in a completely new way, it illuminates mid-Victorian attitudes about national identity.

By looking at the war literature and art, I track the presence of a more modern reaction to war, one in which a sense of general futility accompanies the recognition of valor, in which the heroic and the burlesque intermingle uneasily. In *The Great War and Modern Memory*, Paul Fussell has shown how irony is the determining mode of responses to World War I. Malvern Van Wyk Smith has argued that the poetry of the Boer War first introduced concepts of irony to British war poetry; he calls Tennyson's "Charge" "the last great battle piece that could be written in English."[13] Yet while the Crimean War does represent a watershed moment, it cannot be so easily equated with the past. Mid-Victorian earnestness generally precluded irony in favor of outrage, but since various forms of "blunder" dominate the experience in the Crimea, imaginative reactions to the war show nascent signs of ironic technique in a kind of bewilderment that registers both on the level of form and of content. Critics such as Fussell and James Chandler have demonstrated how rich a story can be told about a nation's cultural life by focusing on its response to a traumatic period, how much can be gained by identifying, in Chandler's words, "a moment in the history of a literary culture."[14] The Crimean War, for all its brevity and blunder (actually, because of its blunder), provides fertile terrain for such investigation.

If the Crimean War plays a crucial role in mid-nineteenth-century cultural developments, it also foreshadows many concerns stemming from our present "stupid quarrel about great-power stewardship" (Christopher Hitchens's words, used in comparing the past Eastern Question to today's one[15]) – as an early example of "Grand Strategy" politics at work, as a window on to how public disillusionment over a war can create a climate for cultural production, as a study in the role played by the media in the process. There has been significant and ongoing historical interest in the war, and two excellent books have been published on the visual art of the conflict (by Ulrich Keller and Matthew Lalumia). But while recent attention to imperialism in literary studies has spawned books on responses to the so-called Indian Mutiny and to the Boer War,[16] because the Crimean War has fewer obvious connections to imperial discourse, it has garnered less sustained consideration in the field.[17] *The Crimean War in the British Imagination*, the first book to be devoted to the wider cultural effects of the conflict, seeks to offer a more comprehensive view of these effects than can be gleaned from attending to the war's impact on a single writer or through a single generic lens. Literary critics of the 1850s often concentrate on the implications of the Great Exhibition of 1851 (again, an important moment of imperial culture). But if Alexander Smith and Sidney Dobell opened their *Sonnets on the War* (1855) with a poem called "The Crystal Palace" (the site of the Exhibition), they did so only to recognize that the transparency promised by this clear edifice had given way to a far murkier atmosphere, in which the disembodied voices of the war poems that follow also appear as through the fog of war. I will delve into this fog to trace its consequences for the shape of the British imagination.

II A BRIEF HISTORY OF THE WAR

In addition to the fog of war, though, we face the fog of memory. An odd assortment of names and objects emerge from this fog: Nightingale and the charge of the Light Brigade, of course, but also the idea of the thin red line and a few bits and pieces of clothing (the cardigan, named after the earl who led the charge; the balaclava, worn to protect the soldiers' faces against the bitter Crimean cold). These remnants are significant; as a character remarks in Brian Friel's *Translations*, "it is not the literal past, the 'facts' of history, that shape us, but images of the past embodied in language."[18] Yet while what follows is predicated on belief in Friel's observation, it nevertheless helps to have some sense of the "facts" – especially those facts to which writers and artists of the day were responding – when trying to come to grips with how "images of the past" become "embodied" not only in language itself but in more concrete cultural productions.

As a gauge of what has remained of the war, we can turn to W. C. Sellar and R. J. Yeatman's 1930 comic history, *1066 and All That*, which might be called a cousin of Frielian history in its basic premise that "History is not what you thought. *It is what you can remember.*" Yet *1066 and All That* recognizes that the difficulty in remembering how Britain got into the "exceptionally inevitable" Crimean War is paradoxically the first of its memorable aspects (perhaps a less surprising fact if one recalls the muddle Marx described even at the time).[19] In fact, the war grew out of what was known as the Eastern Question: the problems connected with the long, slow withdrawal of the Ottoman Empire.[20] The immediate spark was given when a squabble broke out between Catholic (French) and Orthodox (Greek and Russian) Christians over possession of the keys to the Church of the Nativity in Bethlehem; the disagreement fueled an ongoing debate about who had sovereignty over Christians living within the Ottoman Empire. But for the British, the most significant reason for war was the fear of Russian imperial expansion. It was this fear that led Britain to put historic prejudice to the side and take up arms with the French after Russia encroached on Turkish territory in July of 1853.

By then, the nation was eager to go to war to save the beleaguered Turks from being absorbed under Czar Nicholas's authoritarian rule. Yet the Prime Minister, Lord Aberdeen – head of a coalition government that included the strongly anti-Russian Palmerston – was less excited by the prospect. The slow diplomatic shuffle up to war was wittily characterized by the secretary of the British ambassador in Constantinople: "When everyone else is dead I intend to write an Oriental romance to be called *Les mille et une notes.*"[21] His comments hinted forward to the bureaucratic red-tape that would scar the Crimean campaign even while acknowledging an exotic backdrop that should have offered a contrasting form of excitement. Nevertheless, war was eventually declared, on March 28, 1854, creating allegiances that resonate strongly with the global politics of the twentieth century. Indeed, the Crimean War stands almost midway between the great conflicts of what is called the long nineteenth century: as more than one commentator has noted, 1815–1854–1914 suggests a satisfyingly symmetrical view of historical development.

The chronology of the war can be divided roughly into five major phases. The initial phase saw a buildup of troops in the East throughout the spring and summer of 1854, first at Constantinople, and then at Varna (in modern Bulgaria), where significant losses to cholera began to be reported. (At the same time, naval conflict erupted in the Baltic. This was to continue throughout the war, with the Allies even threatening to bombard Kronstadt – a strategy that would have left St. Petersburg defenseless.[22]) After much deliberation, the decision was made to attack Sebastopol, Russia's great Black Sea naval port, and troops departed to the Crimea.

Hereupon followed the second major phase of the war: a rapid series of relatively traditional battles. First came the Battle of the Alma (a river crossed by Allied armies on their approach to Sebastopol) on September 20. The Battle of Balaklava (named for the nearby port town, used by the British to transport men and goods during the siege of Sebastopol) soon followed on October 25; it was here that the charge of the Light Brigade occurred. Finally, on the already historically burdened 5th of November, Russians attacked British and French siege positions before Sebastopol at what was called the Battle of Inkerman.[23] While these battles all contained their portions of blunder (including, of course, that leading to the famous cavalry charge at Balaklava), they could be construed as Allied victories, and the war was generally popular throughout this period.

Nevertheless, of the three engagements, only two figure in the short list of memorable events of the war compiled in *1066 and All That*: Inkerman is recalled for the fog in which it was fought (thus becoming an emblem of the age in line with Matthew Arnold's "ignorant armies clash[ing] by night"[24]), and Balaklava is remembered entirely through the lens of Tennyson's ballad's vision of the charge, ignoring the more successful British effort on the day (the charge of the Heavy Brigade). Alma, the clearest British military victory of the war, does not receive mention. One can see how the Crimean War has been made to fit neatly – and indeed helped create – what James Morris has called "the British mystique of splendour in misfortune."[25]

Yet the greatest source of misfortune came not from the Russians but from the weather. While these battles were fought, winter descended on the Crimea. Phase three of the war began on November 14, 1854, when a severe storm hit Balaklava, sinking twenty-one British transport ships (including the *Prince*, carrying 40,000 winter uniforms and 150 men, only six of whom were saved). The losses both presaged and contributed to the disasters of the season, as British soldiers found themselves without adequate housing, clothing, provisions, or medical care. Enter item four in Sellar and Yeatman's list of memorable "facts" of the war: Florence Nightingale, who arrived in Constantinople on November 4 to help administer the military hospital at nearby Scutari. In spite of efforts by Nightingale and others to contain the organizational chaos that had sent an army to war with little thought of a winter campaign – it was all supposed to have been over by then – thousands succumbed to cold and disease. Indeed, by the end of the war, only 10 percent of the almost 20,000 British servicemen who died in the East had died in action, the vast majority of the deaths occurring during the winter of 1854–55.[26] This disaster – reported on by journalists at the front – led to the public outrage that caused the fall of the Aberdeen Government at the end of January 1855 (Aberdeen was replaced by Palmerston after protracted negotiations). The perception of governmental incompetence also fueled the creation of entities like the so-called Roebuck Committee in Parliament, formed to investigate the state of the army before Sebastopol, and the Administrative Reform Association (with which the likes of Dickens and Thackeray were connected), with its mission "To bring up the public management to the level of private management in this country."[27]

But while conditions for the troops improved throughout the spring, and while the much-maligned Commissariat Department initiated a series of reforms that ensured that the winter troubles would not be repeated the following year, these changes for the better did not translate into glory on the battlefield. In fact, the nature of warfare had shifted over the course of the season, as the fortifications of Sebastopol, engineered by the brilliant Todleben, discouraged any rapid attempts to take the town. Instead, the Allies put their energies into the construction of a system of trenches from which they could bombard the defenses, hoping to weaken them in advance of an attack. Tolstoy, who was with the Russian army in Sebastopol, captures wonderfully the discomfort, dreadful anticipation, and sheer monotony that characterized such warfare in his *Sebastopol Sketches*, written at the time. (While it was and is customary to speak of the "siege" of Sebastopol, technically this is a misnomer since open supply routes to the north were maintained throughout.)

A slow and anticlimactic summer of attempts to take Sebastopol ensued, with a major bombardment taking place in April, and then three times in June. These bombardments, however, failed adequately to prepare the ground for the infantry attack that was to bring the fall of the town. While the French made some headway in early June, capturing the advance Russian defenses, the next assault, on June 17, was disastrous for both the British and the French; the death soon thereafter of the much-maligned British Commander-in-Chief of the Forces in the East, Lord Raglan, was attributed to a heart broken by repeated disappointments. Compounding their frustrations, the British were conscious of their increasingly minor role in the proceedings, as the absence of forced conscription (although they did turn to mercenaries) prevented the replenishment of depleted troop numbers, even as the French army gained in size. The result was malaise in the camps and war-weariness at home. And when Sebastopol finally fell on September 9, 1855, reports made clear that the victory was French; British troops botched their part of the effort (the goal had been to take the fortification known as the Great Redan), the troops succumbing to ignominious "confusion, panic and terror."[28] Indeed, so tainted was the victory that Palmerston refused to allow the usual celebratory ringing of the church bells throughout the land; the Queen exclaimed how she could not "bear the thought that 'the failure on the Redan' should be our last *fait d'Armes.*"[29]

Not surprisingly, *1066 and All That* distorts the memory of this event almost beyond recognition: while the entry for "*Flora MacNightshade*" crowns the chapter on the war, "*The Siege of Sir Pastobol* (the memorable Russian General)" must relinquish its climactic position not only to her, but also to the relatively extensive account of the Tennysonian-inflected Balaklava, which in this version of history, comes last of the battles. In contrast, Sir Pastobol (we are concisely informed) "was quite besieged, and the English were very victorious." This is not a place where national memory would be disposed to linger.

Officially, the campaign was not yet over, although the armies in the Crimea ceased to play a significant role. In its final phase, the war again became a matter of diplomacy (the combatant nations had talked even as the bombs fell during the "Vienna Conference" of 1855), accompanied by some military baring of teeth as Britain amassed her strongest force yet in anticipation of a possible naval attack on Kronstadt. Negotiations – and Sweden's threatened entrance for the Alliance – led eventually to the declaration of an armistice on February 28 and the signing of the Peace in Paris on March 30, 1856. The war ended in what has been described as a stalemate: "each side claimed a victory of sorts."[30] This conflict, which was to have been "one of the great events in the history of the world,"[31] concluded "not with a bang but a whimper" – unless one counts the explosions of celebratory fireworks in London, the expression of a relieved nation. By the end of July, the last British troops had left Crimean soil. Queen Victoria greeted them on their homecoming.

CHAPTER I

Rushing into print: journalism and the Crimean War

In the middle of January 1855, during the heart of the first, ravaging winter spent by British troops on Crimean soil – and only a few short weeks before public outrage at the mismanagement of the war effort toppled the Aberdeen Government – Captain Fred Dallas sent a letter home:

> I must give you an instance while I think of it, of the clever way in which everything connected with the Army is done, at home as well as here. We got up at last about 20 pair of boots per company, a great want as the men were all in a wretched state. Would you believe that they are all too small! & except for a very few men useless! How curiously the vein of Incapacity seems to wind about thro' everything, not omitting even the humble boot. With endless wealth, great popular enthusiasm, numberless ships, the best material for Soldiers in the World, we are certainly the worst clad, worst fed, worst housed Army that ever was read of.[1]

Dallas's letter is remarkable on a number of fronts. The student of literature may be struck first by the elaborate construction of its sentences, in which the motif of the central "vein of incapacity" seems to find a grammatical correlative in a manner both recalling Dickens's fog of Chancery at the start of the recently published *Bleak House* (1852–53) and anticipating the frustrations of his Crimean-born "Circumlocution Office" in *Little Dorrit* (1855–57). Dallas's sarcasm (note that "clever") might also surprise; but while it runs counter to our expectations for the tone of a young Victorian war hero's description of his experiences to his family, such sarcasm pervades his letters home, which frequently refer to the siege as "farce."[2] In general, the missive provides evidence that, at least as regards the issue of mismanagement, perceptions of the war on the battlefront were very close to those on the home front. But it also – and to me even more remarkably – indicates the reason for this correspondence. Because in some ways the most surprising part of the passage is its final two words: what Dallas notes is not his membership in the "worst housed Army that ever *was*," but "that ever *was read of*."

It seems a slight difference, but in what follows, I wish to argue that these words contain the crux of what made the British experience of the Crimean war such a novel one, both for the army in the East and for people at home – and what makes it so interesting a topic for someone concerned with British literature to consider. Because to an unprecedented degree, the experience of this war was filtered through print – not just, as with past wars, after the fact, as poets, novelists, and historians memorialized the conflict – but in what clearly struck those caught up in its events as "real time," and by an extraordinary range of writers. Dallas gives an example of the major reason for this shift earlier in the same letter, when he comments that "Lord Raglan, who I think must have read *The Times*, came up here today, & is going to send the 63rd to Balaklava."[3] He is referring to complaints made in *The Times*'s editorial columns and the reports sent home by William Howard Russell, the "Special Correspondent" to the newspaper, that Raglan was not helping his popularity by being so little seen among the overworked men in the trenches. But more significant to me than any military adjustments is Dallas's conviction that his general's actions were spurred by reading the newspaper. And one week before, Dallas had attributed his own tone to the same cause: "I am very glad to see that you seem thoroughly to understand my all letters," he remarks, "I thought & still think it an unworthy thing to write cheerful letters & say nothing of facts that you must know sooner or later by the papers."[4]

Dallas describes here typical moments of the war, moments in which reading and writing play central roles. The cycle often begins with Russell, who has been dubbed the first real "war correspondent."[5] Virtually unknown at the start of the conflict, Russell's was a household name by its conclusion, although the reports were published anonymously, usually under the sobriquet "from our Special [i.e., not just 'Own'] Correspondent." His columns were read by hundreds of thousands of Englishmen and women whenever they appeared. The letters, detailing not only military action but also the day-to-day life of the army and its appendages, made him into a hero and (at times) a villain. Russell's acknowledged dominance caused Henry Kingsley to defer to him when, in writing the novel *Ravenshoe* (1862), he was faced with the need to describe Sebastopol: "I could do it capitally by buying a copy of Mr. Russell's 'War' [the two-volume compilation of his reports to *The Times*, published in 1855–56], or even by using the correspondence I have on the table before me [i.e., the original newspaper reports]. But I think you will agree with me that it is better left alone. One hardly likes to come into the field in that line after Russell."[6] As Dallas himself admitted, in one of the many mentions of British newspaper accounts of the war that punctuate his letters home, "I am sick of telling you . . . all the ills and wrongs that the 'Special Correspondent' tells you so much better."[7] According to the memoirs of the Jamaican Creole Mrs. Seacole, renowned "doctress" and owner of a popular store in Balaklava, Russell was so vital a part of the war that it stopped during his brief absence from the scene in the summer of 1855: "Nothing of consequence was done in the front for weeks, possibly because Mr. Russell was taking holiday, and would not return until August."[8]

But if Russell's voice was the loudest, it was backed by a chorus in the newspapers of the day. Indeed, the papers provided a forum in which public and private voices mixed, as official "dispatches" were printed alongside personal letters from soldiers at the front, and in which institutionally backed "leading" editorials were surrounded by an unprecedented barrage of letters to the editor on the topic of the war, even as "hard" news took the shape of letters from "own correspondents." It is the joint effect of all these voices that I wish to consider here, before turning in the following chapters to secondary accounts, like Kingsley's – or like Tennyson's "Charge of the Light Brigade," also drawn from Russell's columns – that built upon them. And while my focus will be on the newspapers, such confusion persisted after the war, as writers like Mrs. Seacole – with no official status in the army, an outsider by virtue of her racial and national background – jostled with soldiers, camp-followers, and historians in a marketplace flooded by Crimean memoirs (often taking the form of published correspondence or journals). In *The Structural Transformation of the Public Sphere*, Jürgen Habermas declared "[t]he world fashioned by the mass media" to be "a public sphere in appearance only":

The mass press was based on the commercialization of the participation in the public sphere on the part of broad strata designed predominantly to give the masses in general access to the public sphere. This expanded public sphere, however, lost its political character to the extent that the means of "psychological facilitation" could become an end in itself for a commercially fostered consumer attitude.[9]

But while no doubt the product of commercialization, the world fashioned by the mass media during the Crimean War seems to have functioned as a public sphere in reality as well as in appearance. Early on, *The Times* christened the conflict in the East "the people's war."[10] This claim – to the extent that it is true – depended upon the role of the newspapers.

I "THE 'TIMES' WAR"

The newspaper press occupies a central and undisputed place in the British experience of the Crimean War. In an essay in the *Edinburgh Review* of October 1855, W. R. Greg declared the phenomenon of the increasing power of the fourth estate to be the "greatest Fact" of his times.[11] And the fact was widely recognized: for example, Matthew Lalumia notes that genre paintings about the war frequently incorporated newspapers, as often as not – as in John Everett Millais's *Peace Concluded* (1856) (figure 15) – *The Times*.[12] The dominance of the press was based on a variety of technological and historical causes: the growth of newspapers in the period leading up to the war, improvements in the technology of information transmission (mail and telegraph), changes in the role and nature of foreign correspondents, and the unusual lack of censorship in Britain.

By the time of the Crimean War, newspapers had become the acknowledged primary vehicle for the dissemination of political opinion.[13] As Greg observes, "One of the most remarkable features in the history of political literature in England is the change of form, – the substitution of newspapers for pamphlets." Given how easy it was to write a letter to the editor – or even a series of such letters – and given the readiness with which editors published such correspondence, there was no need for non-professional writers to resort to the more complicated procedures of private pamphlet publication that had been used during the French Revolution and in its wake. And for the professionals, newspapers and periodicals also offered a range of outlets:

Daily and weekly journals, monthly magazines, and trimestrial reviews, have not only absorbed the talent, the mental activity, and the polemical temper which formerly found vent in short isolated publications, but offer to the writers the attractions of a far more certain, extensive, and immediate circulation than mere pamphlets, except of the most extraordinary and startling merit, could ever hope to attain.[14]

While newspapers increasingly became the preferred forum for the publication of domestically produced opinion pieces, they also made great strides in their ability to publish accurate and speedy reports from abroad. Accuracy depended on the relatively recent "invention" of the professional foreign correspondent. During the Napoleonic wars, foreign news had mostly been transmitted by amateur "agents" – usually diplomats or local British expats – who had generally limited themselves to translating and/or amalgamating reports in the local press. Occasionally, an agent would deliver a first-hand account of events he happened to witness, but no real attempts were made to pursue stories. War reporting was done in the same fashion, with the odd letter from a junior officer thrown into the mix (over Wellington's strong objections). Even a professional correspondent like Henry Crabb Robinson (sent out by *The Times* to cover the Battle of Corunna) tended to rely on second-hand accounts and translation.[15] This scenario started to change in the late 1840s and early 1850s, as newspapers began actively to recruit foreign correspondents in important locales to write their own independent reports on regional affairs, both political and more broadly cultural. Thus, for example, at the time the Crimean War erupted, *The Times* already possessed one knowledgeable regional voice in Thomas Chenery, its political and diplomatic correspondent at Constantinople (the future author of the notorious reports on hospital conditions at Scutari that would lead to Florence Nightingale's mission). The paper's early realization of the potential of the story of the war – of its possible narrative pull – appears in a letter written by its manager to Chenery in July of 1854, during a brief Russian siege of the Turks at Silistria and two months before British troops had so much as landed in the Crimea, in which he admits that "The idea of a newspaper correspondent keeping the journal of a siege till the affair is over has driven me wild."[16] Of course, the siege in question would be not of Silistria but of Sebastopol, and its journalist would be not Chenery but Russell, whose own mission turned out to be a lucky stroke on the part of *The Times*'s editor, John Thadeus Delane. It had been Delane's idea to send the young parliamentary reporter and lawyer, who had drawn some attention with dispatches from his native Ireland in 1845, to accompany the Guards when they were sent as a precautionary measure to Malta in February of 1854. "You will be back by Easter," Delane had asserted.[17] The rest, as they say, was history – or at least it was journalism. Russell's dogged pursuit of the truth in the face of considerable difficulty set him apart from his predecessors (while the authorities never sent him home, they certainly worked hard to make his life miserable by, for example, initially refusing him the rations and passage he had been promised and taking down his tent in his absence). His methods of combining an on-the-spot perspective with carefully weighed accounts from a wide range of participants and eyewitnesses (with his great social charm, he was particularly skilled at befriending junior officers) made his reports the new standard for accuracy.

If accounts from abroad became more reliable as a result of these innovations, foreign reports also arrived on British soil with increasing speed. Julius Reuter had established a telegraph agency in London in 1851, allowing brief official dispatches from the Crimea and unofficial translations from the foreign presses to arrive within days. While mail boats took longer, Russell's semiweekly correspondence would generally appear a mere two weeks after the fact, in comparison to the months needed to transmit news from the East during the Napoleonic wars.[18] The two modes of information transmission could coexist awkwardly, especially given that when war broke out, the telegraph line from London had reached only as far as Belgrade.[19] For example, in late September of 1854, when reports of the British victory at the Alma began to trickle in over the wires, they were so imprecise as to give the impression of a victory at Sebastopol, as well. When (like other newspapers) *The Times* actually announced the fall of Sebastopol on the 2nd of October – on the basis of the latest telegraphic dispatches, both British and foreign – the bold headlines and transcriptions of the wired messages were followed not by detailed reports of the battle but by Russell's letters covering the initial landing of the troops in the Crimea on the 14th of September. Russell's correspondence about the Alma did not arrive until the 10th of October, by which time (as telegraph messages had failed to confirm a victory at Sebastopol) the newspaper had realized its mistake.[20] Russell often complains about this phenomenon of time-lag in his letters. So, to give one instance, towards the beginning of his report of the storming of the Malakoff and Redan fortifications that brought about the final fall of Sebastopol, and following the proclamation that "The contest on which the eyes of Europe have been turned so long is nearly decided – the event on which the hopes of so many mighty empires depended is all but determined," he goes on to lament:

How trite all these announcements appear! How disheartening it is to the writer to feel that all he is describing is known in England, and has been discussed and canvassed in every homestead ere he can sit down to tell the story, and that by the time his letters reach those for whom they are intended all that to him appears as novel, and recent as it is interesting and important, will be a twice told tale![21]

Still, the uncertainty attending the telegraphed messages undoubtedly also contributed to the thrill of reading the papers, as the wired dispatches served almost as advertisements for the more detailed reports that would follow. Thus a leader in *The Times* on November 6, 1854 (that is, before full reports of the battle of Balaklava, fought on the 25th of October, had arrived) opens by declaring: "The suspense of the country during the absence of authentic information from the seat of war has been but partially relieved by the imperfect, and, at first sight, inconsistent telegraphic accounts which have at length found their way to us from the Crimea."[22] Russell's report would not be published until the 14th.

Finally, the dominance of newspapers in Britain during the war was conditional on an extraordinary freedom in reporting that allowed journalists like Russell to comment extensively on British failures, both organizational and strategic. The right was well established by the time war broke out: Arthur Aspinall points to the general perception that "A free Press was 'the birthright of Britons,' the most valuable of all their privileges, 'the great palladium of British freedom.' It was, said Blackstone, 'essential to the nature of a free State.'"[23] Moreover, as Aspinall adds, "It is surely remarkable that during the Napoleonic wars there was neither an official nor a voluntary censorship" in Britain, while "[o]n the Continent [as during the Crimean War], the freedom of the Press was non-existent."[24] Olive Anderson notes that throughout the Crimean War, "The principle that the Press should not disclose information of military value was enunciated by the Government and accepted by the Press, although its application was left to the patriotism of individual editors and correspondents."[25] And perhaps unsurprisingly, these editors showed little desire to limit their correspondents – especially given how lucrative the reports from the war were proving to be. Nevertheless, the freedom of the press did not go uncontested. Indeed, it spurred much debate, both political and (appropriately) journalistic. Countless leaders and letters to the editor speak to the issue, as does Russell's correspondence.

Significantly, the right to a free press becomes conflated in the debate with another major force of the war years: public opinion. Habermas posits that "The self-interpretation of the function of the bourgeois public sphere crystallized in the idea of 'public opinion.'"[26] And since newspapers – and especially *The Times* – were mere organs for the expression of public opinion, freedom of the press meant freedom for the expression of public opinion. For example, a letter to the editor of *The Times* argues that "the course of the last six months has too unmistakably shown the advantage of a free press in stimulating the activity of our

Ministers to allow us to withhold our gratitude from the unfettered organs of public opinion."[27] In fact, the debate about a free press also encompassed a debate about publishing private letters from the front – letters that gave unfiltered access to the people's views. Consider, for example, *The Times*'s leader of December 7, 1854:

> Strong objections have been expressed in quarters that claim our highest respect to the free publication of letters from the East containing news likely to be serviceable to the enemy. That we have gone to the verge of prudence in satisfying the curiosity or the scientific interest of our readers we cannot deny, and on a cursory perusal of our columns it might seem, at first sight, that we had conveyed a dangerous amount of information. We have described the positions of the camps of the different divisions, and of the head-quarters, the number of the guns mounted in the several batteries, the unexpected and untoward diminution of our forces by disease, the difficulty of getting up ammunition, the roads, and the various speculations afloat as to the manner and success of the siege. We have even remarked on the fact that the distinguishing uniforms of our officers had drawn upon themselves, and particularly on the staff, the fire of the enemy . . . We say we have told all this, but the fact is, the letters of private correspondents contain quite as much detail, and in some instances more detail, of a military character than the more picturesque descriptions of our own correspondent [Russell]. Moreover, it is not only we, but the whole newspaper press, that has done the same . . . Indeed, when every mail from the East brings many thousand letters, when not only every subaltern pretends to be a tactician, but every corporal has his budget of military gossip, and when there are several hundred newspapers in this country ready to pick up every stray scrap of information that they can call their own, it is evident that the evil complained of is gigantic – that is, it is commensurate with the whole British public and people. In fact, it is nothing more nor less than that publicity which is the life not only of freedom, but equally of all political action in this country.[28]

The ostensibly private correspondence of soldiers and the public voice of the press merge in the concept of public opinion.

Nevertheless, the very technological advances that had spurred the success of the newspapers rendered the information they were divulging increasingly dangerous. While not much might have been gained from hearing of British weapons and positions months after the event, it was a different matter for the enemy to hear of them within weeks or even days. Consider Fred Dallas's account of how a captured Russian revealed that Sebastopol received copies of *The Times* as soon as the British camp:

> Just conceive the infinite mischief the ample accounts in it from here must do us! . . . Tho' one of course knew that they got the *Times*, yet few of us knew how late a one they have in Sebastopol, & yet the *Times* & the *Vox Populi*, one and the

same thing in England, will persist that their minute revelations can do no harm! I don't wonder at the French being indignant with our allowing the presence of "Special Correspondents" . . . ![29]

So predictably, the freedom of the press that had so constituted the experience of the Crimean War was also a victim of it: when General Codrington took over as Commander-in-Chief in the final days of the war, he issued an order that "forbade the publication of details of value to the enemy, authorised the ejection of a correspondent who, it was alleged, had published such details, and threatened future offenders with the same punishment." Codrington's order ensured the uniqueness of the written experience of the Crimean War; as Phillip Knightley records: "When Britain next became involved in a major war – against the Boers – censorship was accepted as necessary and just, and it became the dominating feature of the reporting of the First World War, crushing correspondents into virtual silence."[30]

As the preceding account of the newspaper industry has already intimated, *The Times* – or "The Thunderer," as it was already known – stood securely on top of the mountain of newspapers of the day; Trollope records its power (as the *Jupiter*) in *The Warden* (1855) and *Barchester Towers* (1857). The stage for the paper's dominance was set early: before he had received the official copy, the Czar had already read the British ultimatum to Russia in *The Times*.[31] The real impact of *The Times* on the trajectory of the war is a matter open to dispute. As Olive Anderson puts it,

It may well be doubted whether *The Times* influenced the actual course of events as much as its contemporary readers believed or its twentieth-century historians have claimed. To assert, as the official history of the paper does, that it "made the war; it had been largely responsible for the Crimean campaign, that had brought victory in the end; it had saved the remnant of an army; it had destroyed one Ministry and forced important changes in another; and it had caused the removal of a commander-in-chief," among other great things, is obviously to exploit the official historian's license.

"Yet," she adds, "in 1855 these claims would not have seemed grotesque to most practical men outside the inner circle of politicians. To them the thunderings of *The Times* and the public's response were among the wonders of the age."[32]

What Greg called the paper's "dangerous eminence" came from the unprecedented circulation it had achieved by the time war erupted, an eminence only enhanced by the popularity of Russell's correspondence.[33]

In 1855, *The Times* had a daily print order of 61,000 copies; its biggest rival, the Peelite *Morning Chronicle*, had a circulation of only around 5,000.[34] As a result, *The Times* could claim a public role unavailable to other journals, as it did in a leading article of October 13, 1854, in which the paper defended its right to receive official government news before its competitors. "Considerable dissatisfaction has been expressed by some of our contemporaries at what they term the partiality shown by the Admiralty in the communication of intelligence to the organs of public information," the leader opens. And it goes on to declare its own voice the new chief of such organs: "The *London Gazette* [the authorized source of military news] is, no doubt, the genuine old-fashioned organ of such communications, and on certain occasions it answers the purpose tolerably well." But, *The Times* asks, "How many of our readers . . . have ever seen or handled a single copy of that publication in the course of their lives?" As for its other competitors, one might ask the War Department to send reports simultaneously to all the national papers, and

> [v]ery likely such a course might equal the advantages, in a single respect, of *The Times* and the *Morning Chronicle*, but we think the people of England will hardly be disposed to endure 24 hours' unnecessary suspense [which would be occasioned, the paper argues, by the more complicated distribution of the information] for the sake of such a result . . . The only businesslike course is to select as a recipient of intelligence that organ which can perform the public service best; and the selection falls upon us, not certainly, as our contemporaries are fain to admit, because we are more complaisant to the authorities than they are [*The Times* was already well advanced in its campaign against the mismanagement of the war effort by this date], but simply because we print 60,000 copies where they print 5,000, and are read by five hundred households where they are read by one.[35]

But while *The Times*'s dominance owed much to its circulation even before the war, it was enhanced by the writing in the paper. For one thing, as this leader suggests, its management had amassed an enormously talented stable of "media-savvy" editorial writers who made the best possible use of catch-phrases – Anderson cites as examples "[t]he System," "the cold shade of Aristocracy," and "routine,"[36] and I would add words like "mismanagement" and tags like the "the people's war" and "public opinion." Consider, for example, how in the leader quoted above, the paper intimates its backing by "the people of England" and labels its own objectives "businesslike," thus hinting at the distinction between this well-run organ and the mismanaged affairs of its more "old-fashioned" competitors – not to mention of the government. Indeed, at times leaders can read as little more than the overwhelming amalgamation of such terms. Take this diatribe of December 1854: "The noblest army ever sent from these shores has been sacrificed to the grossest mismanagement. Incompetency, lethargy, aristocratic hauteur, official indifference, favour, routine, perverseness, and stupidity reign, revel, and riot in the Camp before Sebastopol."[37] It may not be subtle, but one can see why it worked.

Moreover, the leader-writers' brandishing of the editorial "we" allowed them to speak fluently and unanimously for the nation as a whole. This ability was bolstered by the popular perception that *The Times* did indeed "speak" for the people, that it was the true *vox populi*; as a leading article puts it when defending the paper's decision to take Queen Victoria to task for going on her usual Highlands holiday in spite of the present crisis: "We have but written that which is publicly uttered everywhere, and in far more explicit terms."[38] While many objected to the resultant power of the paper, few denied its facility at giving voice to public opinion. So, for example, a man styling himself "A West Country Gentleman" begins a letter to the editor of the *Morning Chronicle* by calling *The Times* "The Czar of the newspaper press" – that is, a ruthless enemy dictator. He proceeds to explain the cause for the paper's power: "this success has in part arisen from adroitly studying and expressing, without the smallest regard to consistency, the fluctuating passions of the upper and middle classes of this country. People like to see their confused and shadowy prejudices thrown into a clear and tangible shape." Such embodiment is the leader-writers' forte, and even this angry reader accepts that the results yield documentary attractions: "Certainly, it is interesting, in a psychological point of view, to study so sensitive an index of the various emotions of English human nature; a photographic likeness of the passions and prejudices, nay, it must be admitted, at times the generous impulses of the people."[39] Others also had sinister views of *The Times*. As W. R. Greg remarked, while the normal role of the fourth estate may be benign, matters change "when from any cause one single journal has so far distanced its competitors as virtually to have extinguished them, when it has so completely monopolised the public ear, and filled the public eye, that other organs can scarcely be seen or heard." Then "[t]he 'republic of letters' . . . becomes a despotism [the implication is, like Russia], and menaces us with the evils which attach to autocracy in all its forms." Such power had accrued to *The Times* during the war: "It of itself forms, and is, the public opinion of the country."[40] David Urquhart put the matter succinctly: "The *Times* gave to the present war the name of 'the people's war.' A contemporary replied by calling it 'the *Times* [sic] war.'"[41] Perhaps the paper was not just expressing public opinion but also (literally) dictating it. Indeed, one writer to the paper made precisely this point in discussing the popular silence in response to the failure, after the fall of the Aberdeen Ministry, to form a new administration quickly:

> Common-sense people cannot understand this, but they are neither indifferent nor unimpassioned observers . . . [Rather] they are not factitiously disposed – however some of our statesmen may be – because they have but one desire, to see a vigorous War Administration, and are not as yet able clearly to see the proper combination of parties to carry out a proper policy, and because the recent Administration has so compromised and neutralized political leaders. Let *The Times* dictate such a policy, and point out the men, and I venture to say the country will rally round them.[42]

As Urquhart put it – less sanguinely – "Heretofore the people had 'leaders' whom at least they knew; now they have columns of anonymous type [i.e., editorial 'leaders']."[43]

A benign example of such dictation (or proof of the "generous impulses" referred to by "A West Country Gentleman") occurs in one of the most famous leaders of the day: the one setting up what became known as *The Times*'s Fund, the charitable offshoot of the paper that collected public donations and not only sent them east, but actually distributed them under the direction of a newspaper employee at Scutari. Appearing in the same edition of the paper as one of Thomas Chenery's first explosive reports on the terrible hospital conditions at Scutari, the leader adroitly maneuvers pronouns in a manner anticipating Tennyson's similarly adept manipulations in "The Charge of the Light Brigade," written a month later.[44] It begins with a particularly ostentatious use of the editorial "we":

> Every man of common modesty must feel, not exactly ashamed of himself, but somehow rather smaller than usual, when he reads the strange and terrible news of the war. Here we are sitting by our firesides, devouring the morning paper in luxurious solitude, lazily tracing the path of conquest on one of Arrowsmith's best maps, counting the days of Sebastopol, and imagining the look of the Czar as he finds the key of the Euxine is wrenched from his hands. To us war is a spectacle, and, if we happen to have no friends engaged in it, a very amusing spectacle. It is true we are paying a double income-tax, and it is quite as well that we should be pinched somewhere; but, on the whole, the suffering is sadly vicarious.

Note how the writer of the editorial has used the "we" to enfold himself in his audience's situation: his pen is nowhere to be seen; rather he participates in the reader's cozy armchair experience of the war as "spectacle," experience mediated, one might add, through the very article he is himself writing. This position is maintained throughout a long paragraph, culminating in a litany of what "we," in our position, are unable to do for "the exhausted soldier": "All this is beyond our power, but, if we only wish to do something, we have no doubt that something may be found to be done."

Now the leader-writer has "us" thinking! So what is to be done? But rather than tell us outright, he takes a step back. The next paragraph essentially recaps the most searing points of Chenery's article of the same day: "The wounded were carried to the ships and transported to the barrack at Scutari," it begins, setting the scene. It goes on to describe the conditions at the hospital, including the famous observation that "There are no nurses at Scutari; at least, none for the English, though the French are attended by some Sisters of Mercy from a neighbouring convent" – thus putting in motion Florence Nightingale's mission with the oft-used (both by the leader-writers and by Russell and other correspondents) argumentative tactic of fueling British rage through unflattering comparisons with the French. From the insistent "we" of the preceding paragraph, the writer has moved back to a distanced – although angry – reportorial "they"; only once does "we" reenter in this paragraph, in an offhand reminder of Chenery's role ("Thus we are told") that confirms the leader-writer's claim to share the position of reader with his audience.

It is only in the next and final paragraph, though, that the leader-writer pulls out his full range of pronominal weapons. He begins by reintroducing the "we" of the opening paragraph:

Now, here is happily provided an occasion for that sympathy which, as we observed above, the terrible details of warfare ought to awaken. If it is the mysterious order of PROVIDENCE that others must go to the war for us, must hunger and thirst, expose themselves to the pest, suffer dreadful wounds, and die in our cause . . . the remedy consists in doing what we can, and we can do a good deal. Here, then, good citizens of London, is the opportunity you profess to desire for showing how your hearts beat for your fellow-countrymen and your noble allies.[45]

That "you" is almost unprecedented in the leader-columns, and its rhetorical force is all the greater for its rarity. It appears only momentarily and is soon swallowed up again into the embrace of the editorial "we": "We have now an opportunity . . . So as we let these fellows fight for us, let us send to them also the means for celebrating the victorious union of our armies." One can compare its effect to the difference between the stern face and demanding outwardly pointed finger of the iconic "Uncle Sam Wants You" poster first used in World War I and the more genial (albeit still determined) "We Can Do It!" of World War II's Rosie the Riveter, with her profiled bicep. The first gesture commands participation as a combatant; the second announces a united and involved home front. But the leader's grammar works to confuse the categories: it is as if Rosie momentarily took on Uncle Sam's position, turning that arm out at us. Of course here, instead of the government's doing the asking, it is the major newspaper of the day.

The leader ends by drawing attention to an aspect of journalism the papers are often eager to point out: its immediacy. Just as the correspondence, dispatches, and editorials published in *The Times* reflect the most up-to-date knowledge of events, so *The Times*'s "sick and wounded" Fund (as it was christened in full) addresses not future needs, but present ones: "Surely the gallant chiefs of the two armies will deserve the most handsome testimonials that taste and good feeling can devise from the wealthy British public. But that admits of postponement, – not so the sufferings of the sick and wounded in the hospitals of Constantinople and the Black Sea."[46] This is not about memorializing but about doing, and if the paper considered itself a protagonist in the war, it was also working to allow the people it represented an active role, and not merely a "voice." The people responded: by the time of the next day's printing, editors were already prepared to include in their pages letters from four generous citizens offering a considerable range of help (conveniently representing the considerable class range of the paper's subscribers): from £200 donated by Robert Peel, the former Prime Minister's son, to "£5 in money and some old sheets" from "A.D." A couple weeks later, when Nightingale and her staff of nurses were dispatched for the Crimea, they were also accompanied by a Fund overseer empowered to distribute over £7,000 as he saw fit.[47] The contributions would continue to flow in.

II "MR. RUSSELL'S 'WAR'"

While the leader-writers of *The Times* exerted considerable influence, William Howard Russell's voice was even louder. His dominance appears in the extraordinary space he was granted for his correspondence; it was not unusual for his letters to take up an entire page of newsprint: six columns, often encompassing more than ten thousand words. To appreciate fully the impact of such prolixity, it helps to have some sense of what the papers of the day looked like. They were remarkably "patchwork" affairs. At twelve pages, *The Times* was the longest of the dailies (the *Morning Chronicle*, for example, ran to eight). Much of this length was due to its outsized advertising section, comprising the first four and last two pages of the paper. Page five would cover a mix of mostly financial news, and the paper's masthead would generally not appear until page six, to be followed by three leading articles, each occupying about a column. What followed on the leaders varied: it could be the court circular or official intelligence reports from the war (telegraphic dispatches, military statements, lists of killed and wounded, etc.); it could be Russell's correspondence (which usually appeared somewhere on pages six through eight); it could be a letter to the editor (these were interspersed throughout the paper rather than aggregated in proximity to the editorials, as they normally are today). And the rest of the paper was similarly diverse, often including reports reprinted from foreign or regional newspapers as well as letters from "own correspondents" in various locales. But what is visually striking about this layout is how many contributions are short – thus appearing indistinguishable. The leaders, following the masthead, are easy to spot. But Russell's longer letters look like coherent blocks (albeit subdivided by dates; they are written in journal format) within the patchwork in a manner that makes them feel generically distinct from the rest of the news.

Russell's columns also gained narrative thrust from being published in what one might call "serialized" form, with ongoing headings reading like chapter titles ("The British Expedition," "The Battle of the Alma," "The Siege of Sebastopol"). And while it would be going too far to say that he intentionally milked the opportunity for "cliff-hangers" provided by this arrangement – in combination with the time-lag occasioned by the distance to London – he often notes rushing his composition so as to meet the mail even as events around him are thickening. Indeed, in the same letter about the fall of Sebastopol quoted above in reference to the phenomenon of time-lag, Russell records how

In my last letter, a portion of which was written ere the mail started on Saturday, I was so confused by the accumulation of events that I made a serious mistake in my dates, which I trust has been rectified at home. It is rather hard to have to sit down to save the post when one knows that in 15 minutes from the time of his writing he will be the witness of a general assault on one of the strongest places in the world.[48]

Nevertheless, this frustration was no doubt matched by his readers' suspense: the letter he refers to, printed on the 21st of September, had been prefaced by an editorial comment emphasizing that what followed would "only bring down the narrative of events before Sebastopol to noon on the 8th of September, the hour in which the French and English storming columns were in the very act of rushing to the assault against the city." And Russell had ended his own report with this terse and tense comment on the state of affairs:

SEPT. 8, 11 A.M.

All comers from Balaklava and the rear of the camp are stopped by a line of sentries. Another line of sentries in front prevents anyone going as far as Cathcart's Hill or the picket houses, except staff officers or men on duty. The fire is exceedingly heavy. The assault takes place at noon. The 4th division is now under arms.[49]

One can understand why readers would have been willing to pay for the "next instalment" detailing that assault, even if they already knew the official results.

Such material distinctiveness was bolstered both by the distinctiveness of Russell's prose and by his unusual sense of agenda. Put simply, for the father of war correspondents, he doesn't seem to spend much time discussing combat. As John Peck notes,

Traditional war writing sees events as an epic struggle, a play, where opposing forces led by exemplary generals engage in dramatic confrontations; at the same time there is, of course, an implicit sense of boys playing games.[50] Russell, however, does not offer us dramatic confrontations and heroic leadership . . . What Russell offers, by contrast, is a largely static plot, where the fighting is almost incidental; what is of interest is what he sees in the details behind the fighting. And essentially, in the manner of a realistic novelist, what Russell sees is a social problem.[51]

In light of Peck's claim, it is instructive to compare Russell's columns with those published by the *Morning Chronicle*. Consider the account of that newspaper's "Special Correspondent" (Captain Blakeley[52]) of the Battle of the Alma. Here is Blakeley's report:

The river once crossed, the men dashed into some vineyards which flanked the high road; but these having been cut down, afforded no shelter. The fire here was fearful, for now the British were within grape range. The men here gave one of those surprising examples of coolness and contempt of danger which forms one of our national characteristics. In the midst of the most tremendous fire which an army has ever encountered, with comrades falling around them, the men commenced seeking for and plucking the half-ripe grapes, which were hanging temptingly on the hewn vines.[53]

The *Chronicle*'s editors' appreciation of their agent's powers of description appears in the opening to their first leader of the same day, which begins not with the victory itself, but with a "puff" of their special correspondent's column (offering also further proof of public interest in the novelty of such war reporting):

> The account given of the Battle of the Alma by our Special Correspondent, who was an eye witness of that memorable engagement, will abundantly satisfy the curiosity which the official reports serve rather to excite than to allay. Simple and clear as is Lord RAGLAN's narrative, the limits of a despatch necessarily precluded a detailed notice of many highly interesting points; and, besides, the province of a general is, not to gratify the public, but to give information to his Government. In the communication, however, which we now present to our readers, it will be seen that the skill of the penman has been combined with the eye of the soldier . . . The achievements of the army of the East have not to wait for the tardy pen of the annalist, but are proclaimed on the instant, wherever newspapers are read.

The leader then goes on to admire the passage I singled out above (drawn, no doubt, by the availability of a pun on "grapes" almost as tempting to its writer as the real things had been to the soldiers). The editors comment that

> The incident recorded by our Correspondent, of the men of the light division, who, when within grape-range, and "in the midst of the most tremendous fire which an army has ever encountered," commenced calmly seeking in the vineyards for grapes of a more harmless nature, places this marvellous intrepidity in a far stronger light than any general description [is there another pun here, on General Raglan's prose style?], however eloquent.[54]

The two-fold grapes are an example of what Paul Fussell has called "ironic vegetation"; they instance the peculiarly British understanding of a pastoral inflected by death (identified also in the British double-take on the classical tag, *Et in arcadia ego*).[55] Yet here the emphasis is on the comforting role that such comparison can provide, rendering "harmless" – even attractive – what is in fact deadly. While Russell was not above spouting patriotic platitudes like those employed in the rival newspaper, his tendencies were very different, much closer to the ironizing habits of thought that Fussell recognizes as characteristic of the best writing to come out of the Great War. To Russell, instead of being harmless evidence of British bravery, these grapes were acknowledged to be every bit as deadly as their metal counterparts; he thrives on using such details to underscore the incompetence of the authorities and to highlight the suffering caused by such incompetence. The point is not one that he makes in his initial treatment of the Battle of the Alma, which mentions the vineyard only in passing; as many commentators have noticed, this account is the most "Boy's Own Paper" description of war we get from Russell (who was no doubt intoxicated by the fact that finally, after long months, he had not only a real battle to describe, but a genuine British victory).[56] But in the extended description he gives in *The British Expedition to the Crimea* (1858), his revised final published version of the columns, Russell notes the moment that the *Morning Chronicle* had focused on to very different effect:

grape, canister, round and shell tore through their ranks, and the infantry on the flanks of the battery advancing at an angle to it, poured in a steady fire upon them from point-blank distance. It must be confessed that this advance was very disorderly . . . The men had not only got into confusion in the river from stopping to drink as I have related, but had disordered their ranks by attacks on the grapes in the vineyards on their way.[57]

Certainly, the mentions of "disorder" and "confusion" and the "attack" upon grapes instead of Russians entail a measure of critique.

Yet to contemporary readers of Russell's columns, these comments would have had greater resonance than they hold for us today. The soldiers' thirst – in consequence of their inadequate supplies and inappropriate dress – had been a staple topic of the correspondence. After all, Russell had needed to fill his columns for months before the fighting began, and he had soon realized the narrative potential of analyzing such "social problems," to use Peck's term. Indeed, in the same report in which he first described the Battle of the Alma, in detailing the previous day's march, Russell had noted "a small stream," the "object of delight to our thirsty soldiers, who had now marched more than eight miles from their camp."[58] And the idea of "deadly fruit" had come in for discussion during the attack of cholera at Varna (in Bulgaria, where the British had encamped before departing for the Crimea), when Russell had lamented the "recklessness which verges on insanity" of many of the men (fruit was thought to carry the disease): "You might see them in stupid sobriety gravely paring the rind off cucumbers of portentous dimensions, and eating the deadly cylinders [more "ironic vegetation"?] one after another . . . or frequently three or four of them will make a happy bargain with a Greek for a large basketful of apricots, 'killjohns,' scarlet pumpkins, water melons, wooden pears, and green 'gages' and plums."[59]

An expression of this theme had actually occasioned early proof of Russell's potential influence. In describing the march of British troops under Sir George Brown (who had a reputation as a stickler in matters of dress-code) from one camp to another in the neighborhood of Gallipoli, Russell noted the suffering caused by the uniforms:

> Leaving the baggage to its fate, let us climb up one of the hills, near the scene of the French review, and watch the march of our regiments. They came on solid and compact, as blocks of marble, the sun dancing on their polished bayonets and scarlet coats with congenial fierceness. The gallant " – th" halt close by – all the men are as red in the face as turkeycocks – they seem gasping for breath – they are indeed sorely distressed, for a rigid band of leather rendered quite relentless by fibres and buckles of brass is fixed tightly round their throats, and their knapsacks are filled to the pitch of mortal endurance, so that it requires the aid of a comrade for each man to get his on his back; while the Frenchman, unassisted, puts his knapsack on in an instant . . . [A]nd if one follows them, he will see how men drop out, exhausted and half-smothered, and at what a vast amount of physical inconvenience all this solidity and rigidity of aspect are acquired. Take one fact: – In a single company which left Bulair 45 file strong – 90 men – so many men fell out on the march to Soulari, a distance of six miles or thereabouts, that the Captain reached the camping ground with only 20 men – the rest straggled in during the forenoon. The halts were frequent for so short a march, and the rush to every well and fountain showed how the men suffered from thirst.[60]

This is hallmark Russell: the acknowledgement of his own witnessing eye, but used to draw the reader into the scene, the nod towards the expected patriotic blazon (polished bayonets, etc.), the dramatic move to the present tense (also utilized during battle accounts), the nationalistic comparison to the French, the sympathetic detail of the soldiers' suffering, and the bolstering of the whole with businesslike statistics. And it was effective; shortly after Russell drew public attention to the detrimental consequences of the "stocks" (those leather and brass neckbands mentioned here), the Secretary at War announced their abolition.[61] Thus a reader coming upon those soldiers eating grapes while being barraged by enemy fire would have had much with which to compare the moment. The effect of the columns is (intentionally, as in a book) cumulative, as Russell points time and time again to related phenomena in order to show the pervasiveness of a given problem.

If initially Russell doesn't quite take advantage of the thematic opportunities offered by the Battle of the Alma, a masterly account of the week following the engagement, occupying more than a full page of the paper on October 20, displays his ability to use his medium to advantage. He begins by detailing the "painful labour" of removing the dead and injured from the battlefield and of burying the dead. In describing the horrifying aftermath of battle, his language becomes particularly extravagant:

> It was a sad sight to see the litters borne in from all quarters hour after hour – to watch the working parties as they wandered about the plain turning down the blankets which had been stretched over the wounded to behold if they were yet alive, or were food for the worms, and then adding many a habitant to the yawning pits which lay with insatiable mouths gaping on the hillside, or covering up the poor sufferers destined to pass another night of indescribable agony. The thirst of the wounded [once more, this thematic touchstone] seemed intolerable, and our men – all honour to the noble fellows! – went about relieving the wants of the miserable creatures as far as they could.

The letter returns repeatedly to such agony. For example, on the following day Russell draws his readers into a single instance of suffering – his own version, in a way, of Wilfred Owen's "Strange Meeting" (1918). The episode opens with a detached statement of fact: "Many men died of cholera last night." But we quickly descend into more personal nightmare:

> My sleep was disturbed by the groans of the dying, and on getting up in the morning I found that the corpse of a Russian lay close to the tent in which I had been permitted to rest. He was not there when we retired to rest, so that the wretched creature, who had probably been wandering about without food upon the hills ever since the battle, must have crawled down towards our fires and then expired in the attempt to reach them.

Here his own first-person experience helps bring the reader into the macabre quasi-encounter; Russell's position in the tent, listening, but crucially separate from the misery, mirrors that of his audience but also intensifies it, even as it mirrors and intensifies the guilt of the noncombatant that the passage covertly expresses (a difference, of course, from Owen's poem, in which the guilt of the combatant is the issue). Still, the language moves in part by being comparatively unemotional; a more gruesome and bombastic description appears later on, when Russell sets the scene of the flank march to Balaklava:

> But what is that grey mass on the plain, which seems settled down upon it almost without life or motion? Now and then, indeed, an arm may be seen waved aloft, or a man raises himself for a moment, looks around, and then lies down again. Alas! that plain is covered with the wounded Russians still . . . [W]e must leave them as they lie. All this nameless, inconceivable misery – this cureless pain – to be caused by the caprice of one man!

Yet while he may try to lay the blame comfortably at the feet of the Czar, it is "we" who are now "leav[ing] them as they lie."

But not everyone has gone:

In order to look after their wounds an English surgeon was left behind with these 750 men. This most painful and desolate duty devolved upon Dr. Thomson, of the 44th Regiment. He was told his mission would be his protection in case the Cossacks came, and that he was to hoist a flag of truce should the enemy appear in sight, and then, provided with some rum, biscuit, and saltmeat, he was left alone with his charge.[62]

Since suffering is the problem, the hero will be not a soldier but a doctor. While the situation seems laden with dramatic possibility, Russell characteristically does not focus further on Dr. Thomson. Rather, Thomson, who goes completely without individuation, serves as much as a marker for a type as do the many representative "portraits" – of a Greek, of a Zouave, of a British private in winter dress, of a Sardinian – that punctuate Russell's letters and allowed readers in Britain better to visualize the scenes he was rendering. Indeed, Russell generally lacks interest in psychology – one way (for all Peck's claim) he differs from a realist novelist. Dr. Thomson's role is thematic: in his singleness, he instantiates the failure of the British government to provide sufficient medical staff (another recurring subject of Russell's correspondence). And instead of following Thomson to his end (sadly, this was death from cholera, not long after[63]), Russell marches on with the troops.

Nevertheless, he does not allow his readers entirely to forget the abandoned doctor, either; the theme reenters in a different register, as he takes advantage of a striking coincidence:

The road now assumed the character of an English byway in Devonshire or Hampshire. Low walls at either side were surmounted by fruit trees laden with apples, pears, peaches and apricots, all ripe and fit for use, and at their foot clustered grapes of the most delicate flavour. The first villa we came to was the residence of a physician or country surgeon. It had been ruthlessly destroyed by the Cossacks. A verandah, laden with clematis, roses, and honeysuckle in front, was filled with broken music stools, work-tables, and lounging chairs . . . Everything around betokened the hasty flight of the inmates. Two or three side saddles were lying on the grass outside the hall door, a parasol lay near them, close to a Tartar saddle and huge whip . . . No pen can describe the scene within. Mirrors in fragments were lying on the floor, the beds had been ripped open, and the feathers littered the rooms a foot deep; chairs, sofas, fauteuils, bedsteads, bookcases, picture frames, images of saints, women's needlework, chests of drawers, shoes, boots, books, bottles, physic jars, all smashed or torn in pieces, lay in heaps in every room . . . The physician's account-book lay open on a broken table; he had been stopped in the very act of debiting a dose to some neighbour, and the entry remained unfinished. Beside his account-book lay a volume of *Madame de Sévigné's Letters* in French and a *Pharmacopoeia* in Russian. A little bottle of prussic acid lay so invitingly near a box of bonbons that I knew it would be irresistible to the first hungry private who had a taste for almonds, and I accordingly poured out the contents to prevent the possible catastrophe.

The tone is elegiac, almost after the manner of Wordsworth's "Ruined Cottage" (albeit a bourgeois version of it) – a comparison strengthened by Russell's invocation of a pastoral English countryside at the beginning. And the elegy being said is as much for Thomson (who must also fear Cossack raiders, as we have just been told) as for the physician owner of the villa. Simultaneously, Russell provides British readers with a feminized, domestic correlative to the scenes he had just been detailing on the battlefield: a rape of the home, a proof that war destroys all that is civilized, cultured, and sacred. Notice that this "still life" – or *nature morte* – can be more easily described than the confusing action of battle, during which Russell frequently laments his inability to be witness to the whole scene. Notice also, though, how in the final lines of the passage, Russell himself enters to break the stillness with his own small act of heroism, a prevention of "possible catastrophe" that turns him into a benign parody of the looting Cossacks and a replacement for the absent physician.

When comparing Russell to a novelist, Peck argues convincingly that what emerges over the course of the letters is the implication that "Russell's real hero is himself":

the resourcefulness he demonstrates in acquiring the facts, processing them and reporting home is just the kind of professionalism that is lacking in the conduct of the war . . . [W]hat he offers his middle-class readers, in the manner of a mid-Victorian novelist, is both a position with which they can identify and an individual perspective from which the incomprehensible and disturbing can be controlled and given meaning.[64]

We see such skill manifested, for example, in an early letter in which Russell announces that "The life of an 'Own Correspondent' is not all *couleur de rose* here," before detailing the difficulties he had faced and overcome when the promise of his passage to shore at Gallipoli had been reneged upon.[65] And Russell's heroism appears also in contemporary representations of the journalist, as in Roger Fenton's photograph portraying him in a thoughtful, seated pose (in his strangely hodge-podge, quasi-military garb, bearing traces of a rough-and-ready life among the troops), leaning slightly forwards as if towards his audience. A cartoon from *Punch* in 1881 makes the point more obviously, showing him

Figure 1 Roger Fenton, *William H. Russell, Esquire, The Times Correspondent* (1855)

precariously astride a charging horse, pen and paper in hand, even as he avoids the explosions and gunshot surrounding him (figures 1, 2).

Still, Russell's "heroic" self-portrayal strikes me as somewhat more problematic than Peck implies, as his role in the scene quoted above suggests, where even while playing the hero, he is tainted both by his affiliation with the Cossacks and by the contrast with the bravery of Dr. Thomson. And if Russell lacks the realist novelist's concern for action or plot, he also (as I have noted) lacks concern for the portrayal of

Figure 2 [Edward Linley Sambourne], "W. H. Russell, Esq., L.L.D," *Punch* 81 (1881), 166

character, including his own. Actually, in many ways the letters (especially the early ones, when the inactivity of the British troops forced Russell to look elsewhere for subject-matter) are closer to travel writing than they are to novels, with their descriptions of exotic foreign locales and national dress. And indeed, travel literature hovers behind much writing on the war; Kinglake, its great historian, gained his fame as the author of *Eothen; or, Traces of Travel Brought from the East* (1844),[66] and *Blackwood's*

Edinburgh Magazine noted how interest in the Crimea had stimulated a vogue for travelers' tales.[67]

Nevertheless, Peck rightly points to Dickens as the model for Russell's style, offering as example the detailed picture of Gallipoli the journalist gives in one of the first letters from the expedition, which takes the form of a single, paragraph-length sentence that grammatically renders the town's bewildering disorder.[68] Peck compares the sentence to the opening view of Marseilles in *Little Dorrit* (a novel also displaying the fashion for travel writing), noting that in both cases, loco-description anticipates the grander themes of the narrative. The connection makes sense: after all, while Peck speaks of "traditional war writing," no one had really done what Russell was doing. He needed a "father" himself, and, as an orphan, he knew the benefits (including financial ones) that would accrue from hanging on to Dickens's overwhelmingly popular stylistic coattails.

Dickens and Russell were actually friendly acquaintances: the novelist was present (along with Thackeray[69] and Wilkie Collins) at a farewell dinner given in honor of the journalist, anticipating his departure for the East. And it was Dickens who recommended to Russell that he cash in on his Crimean celebrity by going on a lecture tour after his return to England.[70] But journalism, with its zest for all that is new – or *novel* – was also crucial to the development of the fictional genre in Britain in the 200 years or so preceding the Crimean War. As J. Paul Hunter has shown, "the consciousness that made the present moment the center of human attention and led to the directions of modern journalism helped prepare the cultural context for novelists' preoccupations, too, and the crucial dimensions of the modern novel seem unimaginable without the peculiar combination of 'News, and new Things' that obsessed English culture at the turn of the eighteenth century";[71] this obsession was brought to a pitch by the media frenzy of the Crimean War.

Hence the curious closeness manifested between Russell's reports and Dickens's novels; one might recall as well that Dickens began as a parliamentary reporter (1831–34) and wrote for the *Morning Chronicle* for two years. Peck's comparison of Russell's prose to *Little Dorrit* is underscored by Russell's influence on Dickens's novel, with its Circumlocution Office (where the art of 'HOW NOT TO DO IT' is practiced to perfection) reflecting the bureaucratic bungling to which the journalist's reports had drawn attention.[72] Indeed, Dickens would later write admiringly to Russell: "I have always followed you closely, and have always found new occasions to express my sense of what England owes you for your manly out-speaking and your brilliant description."[73] Russell seems particularly keen to draw attention to the connection, which he must have recognized as flattering. When he revised his columns for *The British Expedition*, he alluded to Dickens's novel:

Admiral Boxer arrived to assume the command of the harbour of Balaklava; and that gallant and energetic old sailor, by his incessant personal exertions, succeeded in carrying out many improvements, and in introducing some order in the internal economy of that focus of feebleness, confusion, and mismanagement, where the head-quarters of the Circumlocution office were for a long time established.[74]

Of course, many other writers echoed Dickens in their attempts to make sense of events in the Crimea. So, for example, Fred Dallas (with whose Dickensianism I opened this chapter) invokes the idea of "muddle" from the recently published *Hard Times* (1854) when describing the injustice of the system of military promotion:

The misfortune of the system is that perhaps nine out of ten Colonels do well enough, & the 10th is in every way incapable & unworthy, and this is only known to those who have the misfortune to be under him, & this 10th man is made a C.B. [Commander of the Most Honourable Order of the Bath] in the crowd . . . [W]hen I think of the many good fellows out here who have never missed a day's duty since the Army came out, who have on every occasion behaved splendidly, whose self devotion, whose bravery, and whose talents those only who have known & associated with them (and the private soldiers who adore them) could bear witness to – when I look at many of these sort of men, still Captains and Subalterns as they came out, and then at the Hon[ble] Percy Herbert, Queen's A.D.C., C.B., and I know that he came out here the same time that they did, a Captain, & that instead of risking his life twice a week in the trenches & freezing "on Picquets" for numberless days and nights all through the horrid Winter, he has led a comparatively easy life on the Staff, and perhaps been "under fire" as it is called 5 or 6 times for all these honours – when I look on cases of this kind, (& thank God such very disgusting cases are rare) I begin to think with some character of Dickens (I forget who) that all human institutions and laws are "in a great muddle" & I don't see how it can be put to rights.

Even for us out here on the spot, it is almost impossible to get at the truth of things that take place out here. We hear one day that "A. behaved very well at the Sortie last night". Next day it appears that "A. couldn't be found on that occasion" & that B. was the man, & perhaps next day we find out that B. was not there at all! Just conceive of the difficulty of "an authority" getting at the truth of anything. [Examples follow, and then . . .] – isn't it all "a muddle"?

How utterly valueless history, tho' written by the most eloquent & truthful men, will always seem to me, when on the spot where events daily are taking place, I can't tell you the whole truth of them, do what I can to fish it out.[75]

Note how Dallas calls upon the novelist not only in relation (predictably) to the "system," but also in the context of the difficulty of reporting facts accurately, of writing history – or journalism, for that matter. Thus, Dickens's grammar seems the only appropriate one in which to chronicle this war, its fabulous twists and turns simultaneously reflecting the reality of the experience and offering a consoling hope of eventual Providential (i.e., Dickensian) disentanglement. Consequently, when Mrs. Seacole wants to describe her early efforts to "become a Crimean *heroine*" by going out as a nurse, her pains inevitably bring to mind those of Arthur Clennam in *Little Dorrit*:

So I made long and unwearied application at the War Office, in blissful ignorance of the labour and time I was throwing away. I have reason to believe that I considerably interfered with the repose of sundry messengers, and disturbed, to an alarming degree, the official gravity of some nice gentlemanly young fellows, who were working out their salaries in an easy, off-hand way. But my ridiculous endeavours to gain an interview with the Secretary-at-War of course failed, and glad at last to oblige a distracted messenger, I transferred my attentions to the Quartermaster-General's department. Here I saw another gentleman, who listened to me with a great deal of polite enjoyment, and – his amusement ended – hinted, had I not better apply to the Medical Department; and accordingly I attached myself to their quarters with the same unwearying ardour. But, of course, I grew tired at last, and then I changed my plans.[76]

Yet while it sounds like Dickens, a complimentary introduction by Russell prefaced the memoir on its publication in 1857. Like the passages from Dallas's letters home, Seacole's description demonstrates the degree to which Dickens's and Russell's prose intertwined to form the voice of authority in the war.

Curiously, though, for all his admiration, Russell's only novel, *The Adventures of Doctor Brady* (published in 1868, but begun ten years earlier[77]), shows his sense of the genre to have been largely un-Dickensian – and even more unlike the social realism to which Peck compares the correspondence. Intensely autobiographical, *Doctor Brady* does begin like *Great Expectations*, with a confession of deep-seated childhood guilt on the part of its young protagonist, the Irish Terence Brady, orphaned son of a British Indian officer: "But I was full of sin and shame; my youthful life was stained with them; and conscience frowned at many undetected crimes, in regard to cream and sugar, which never came to light."[78] Yet the novel quickly leaves such realism behind, turning rather towards adventure and sensation fiction for inspiration. The plot is too complicated to rehearse here – the first volume alone contains a naval chase after pirates, two schoolboy narratives, a train crash, and, behind it all, a deep mystery about the protagonist's bewitching mother, who was supposed to have died in a shipwreck on the voyage to Ireland that brought the infant Terence over from India.[79] Russell's interest in politics shows in his sensitivity to small-scale abuses (as when a rich man jumps the queue in a fancy doctor's waiting room by offering his receptionist a bribe) and in a backdrop of Irish nationalism in the time of O'Connell. But the heart of the plot concerns Terence's ever-present desire to meet his mother, who, we learn, is still alive and living as the "Rani of Auripore." Actually, in its post-"Mutiny" use of British affairs in India, *Doctor Brady* bears comparison to *The Moonstone*, which was published in the same year. When at the end of the second volume Russell reveals the true fate of Terence's mother since the shipwreck, Terence exclaims, "Was I in the flesh, listening to the words of a sensible, reputable country gentleman in an Irish country-house in the middle of the nineteenth century?" (II:268). The resemblance to Gabriel Betteredge's oft-quoted expression of astonishment is striking: "Here was our quiet English house suddenly invaded by a devilish Indian diamond – bringing after it a conspiracy of living rogues . . . Who ever heard the like of it – in the nineteenth century, mind, in an age of progress, and in a country which rejoices in the blessings of the British constitution?"[80] Either passage could be cited in defining the "sensation novel." So while Peck is right to point out the novelistic aspects of the letters, Russell's actual novel demonstrates the limits of the comparison.

Nevertheless, the Crimean episodes of *Doctor Brady* – covering roughly the first 200 pages of the third volume of this thousand-page novel – stand apart stylistically from the rest. John Sutherland suggests that the book failed to live up to its publishers' high hopes (they paid him £1,300) because it took so long for Russell (whose fame rested on his Crimean reports) to get his hero to the East.[81] But to my mind, the Crimean scenes themselves appear to engender a peculiar authorial discomfort; in them, Russell cannot figure out how to blend fact with fiction, realism with romance. At first, Russell follows his columns quite closely, repeating (for example) his own argument with Sir George Brown about the soldiers' dress in Terence's voice (III:33–34) and offering a description of the troops' landing at Gallipoli that – in its light-hearted use of British soldiers' and sailors' exchanges – takes up one of the most novelistic techniques of the letters, where such "characteristic" dialogues offer frequent comic relief. And his account of the Alma includes a moving, almost cinematic, sketch of the ballet of the battlefield (singled out by

The Times's reviewer as a "passage in which he seems to speak less as the novelist than as the historian"[82]):

> To see a man fall gently forward on his face and hands as though he had tripped on a stone and would get up immediately, and yet to know he would never stir more . . . – to see a man pirouette and reel and drop, and try in vain to rise, – to see a man tumble and roll over again and again like a rabbit shot in full run, – to see a man stagger, lean against his musket, slowly incline himself to the ground and there lean on his arm whilst one hand pressed the wound, – to see a man topple abruptly and then crawl away, dragging a broken leg behind him, – to see a body stand for a second ere it fell, without a head, or the trunk and head lying legless, – to see in the line of a rush of grape a track of dead and dying, just as small birds are cut down in winter-time by boys in a farm-yard – this was in a few minutes quite familiar to me, and was far less terrible than one glimpse of some terror-stricken wretch as, in fear of being trodden to death, he sought to creep away to a quiet place to die; or the mute imploring faces of the wounded who all at once felt their part in the day was over. (III:120–21)

The passage strangely combines two forms of gaze: the artist's aesthetic sensibility and the witness's guilty memory.

But Russell's more sensational understanding of the novel (shared by *The Times*'s reviewer when he called the preceding passage historical) coexists awkwardly with the subject of the Crimea. In these chapters, and only here, Russell resorts to the journal form that had structured the correspondence, as though the scenes themselves placed generic demands upon his writing: "I was ordered to go down to Scutari with a detail of wounded and sick . . . And now, as the best record of what happened, I shall take a few pages out of my diary, omitting trivial and unimportant details, and dealing only with the matters which affect my own story" (III:180). Still, it is just those seemingly "trivial and unimportant details" that realism (like Russell's correspondence) exalts, often even to the detriment of "story" or plot. So while the first date-heading appears to promise a "journalistic" or realist description of work in the wards, by the next day, Russell (or Terence) has reverted to sensation: "Who would credit what happened last night if he read it in a novel? and yet it is true, every word" (III:181). Terence records recognizing one of the nurses as Rose Prendergast, the sister of an old school friend who had since become an Irish radical; thereafter the journal form, Terence's voice, and the Crimea disappear from the chapter, as its remaining thirty-five pages are taken over by Rose's account of meeting (back in Ireland) a mysterious woman whom we later discover to have been Terence's mother. And while the novel's action generally stagnates on Crimean soil, Rose's own story offers an exception, for reasons that should become clearer in the following chapter.[83] Russell seems more at ease when the tale moves to the hot and thick atmosphere of the India of the "Mutiny," where the central plot concerning Terence's mother finally achieves resolution, with her help ("The secret passion of her life – the only affection she has – is in a plot" [II:265]). Suggestively, though, a diatribe against the kind of sensationalist journalism that the "Mutiny" had elicited anticipates the move to India: "But how many lives have the ignorant or terrified scribblers to answer for, who filled the press with hideous inventions, and drove our soldiers wild with fury and passion?" (III:256). Such muck-raking is as much the journalistic correlative to sensation as Russell's Crimean war coverage is to realism.[84]

The Adventures of Doctor Brady also manifests generic discomfort with the Crimea in its search for a properly heroic male lead. Russell's main character is a doctor, but Terence's heroism (such as it is) seems oddly divorced from this fact: instead of showing us Doctor Brady at work, saving the dying troops, Russell repeatedly reminds us that Terence would rather have been a soldier – as though reflecting the journalist's own guilt about his noncombatant status. Nevertheless, Terence's ability to play hero in the Crimea suffers most from comparison with Russell's stronger avatar in these scenes: Staples Standish, war correspondent for the *Hercules*. Standish relives many of Russell's experiences, and wherever he is allowed a say, his urgent voice usurps the narrative. It does so literally, for example, when Terence himself begins to describe the Allied positions before Sebastopol:

The British gunners reduced the Redan to eloquent silence . . . But the French, whose trenches were on the lower ground . . . and whose batteries were nearer, more lightly armed, and less scientifically made, were simply snuffed out.

'Yes, indeed, snuffed out,' repeated Standish, 'and the assault can't take place for ever so long.' (III:140)

Thus Standish wrests narrative power from Terence, continuing to draw his own "very gloomy picture," as Terence puts it (III:143), for several pages more.

Standish quotes Milton in describing his vocation as a war correspondent (perhaps also defending Russell's reinterpretation of epic):

This is my post. I am a soldier of the pen, and here I am on guard –

> "Not sedulous by nature to indite
> Wars, hitherto the only argument
> Heroic deemed – "

here I stick, nevertheless; and if death comes he shall find me with my pen and my note-book in my hand. (III:218)

Standish's death – his "heroic martyrdom" – comes soon. Terence describes a sentimental scene in which the correspondent's wife and young children visit his Crimean tomb, a "humble memorial" erected by the doctor (III:222). Only when Standish dies can Russell finally leave the troubling realism of the Crimea behind and continue on to sensational India, where Terence becomes the active hero he wants to be. But Russell's decision to kill the journalist also manages to secure his avatar's heroism: while a noncombatant, Standish gave his life for the nation.

III "THE PEOPLE'S WAR"

As I have argued, Russell's heroic self-representation in the columns was compromised by his recognition of the distance between him and the men whose lives – and more troublingly, deaths – he was describing. But it was affected, too, by his awareness that he was but one writer among many describing the war – including many who also fought. So just as Fred Dallas had to accept that his mother would be reading Russell's correspondence and adjust his tone accordingly, Russell had to write under the burden (or on the foundations) of the thousands of private letters arriving from the front. For example, in the midst of describing the Battle of Inkerman, Russell comments that "No doubt, there will be abundance of private letters full of similar details."[85] Rather appropriately, Inkerman had been christened "the soldiers' battle" because the fog in which it was fought (meteorological as well as figurative, this time) meant that the leaders of the army could not see enough to command the action, leaving combat decisions to the soldiers. As he details, in his efforts to put together a complete narrative Russell labored under the same difficulties as the generals:

The Battle of Inkermann admits of no description. It was a series of dreadful deeds of daring, of sanguinary hand-to-hand fights, of despairing rallies, of desperate assaults . . . No one, however placed, could have witnessed even a small portion of the doings of this eventful day – for the vapours, fog, and drizzling mist obscured the ground where the struggle took place.[86]

Soldiers would step in to remedy the situation here, too.

And in some ways, the most interesting trend brought about by the war concerned not the professional newspaper correspondence but the less official correspondence published alongside it. A *Times* leader describes the phenomenon (again in the context of the debate over freedom of the press):

> Are we, or are we not, to publish the letters that pour in from the Crimea? The question no longer concerns the graphic narratives of "our Own Correspondent"... The question now concerns letters long and many, some original, from sergeants and privates, some copied by fair and anxious hands, from officers of all ranks in the army, from old colonels to youthful lieutenants, – from everybody, in fact, excepting only the members of that faithful cordon that surrounds each General. Two months ago we could not have seen the letter of an officer containing some trifling reflections on the inevitable mishaps of an army on the march or in the field without being laid under the most solemn obligation not to publish it... Now the whole army rushes into print. Parents, wives, brothers, the whole family circle... urge us to publish, and tell the whole truth.[87]

Writing to his family in England, Fred Dallas records proof of this rush into print:

> People at home seem certainly greedy of any information from here, and in many instances having been lent letters to read, have most unwarrantably published them. To my astonishment, I saw in a Liverpool paper, a note of mine to a poor Sergeant's wife, whom I think I told you I had written to, about her husband. As it merely stated that her husband had been wounded and was unable to write, in a very few lines, I cannot conceive what interest anybody could have taken in publishing it. It is hardly safe to write an order to one's Tailor now.[88]

Dallas registers both distaste and astonishment at the occurrence, which he clearly takes to be a breach of privacy. And that "order to one's Tailor" reminds me of the laundry list in *Northanger Abbey* (1818) upon which Catherine Morland pounces with such potentially dangerous interest, thinking it to be the incriminating document that will prove General Tilney a murderer; both scraps of paper provide instances of a greedy desire not just to search through people's "closets" but to do so in the context of an unreasonable hunger for new (novel?) reading material, whether it be gothic or quotidian. Of course, as readers of Austen's novel have been arguing for years, her ultimate point is that the gothic (the evidence of Tilney's guilt) and the quotidian (the laundry list) are often indistinguishable: Tilney may not be a murderer, but by the end of the novel, he has revealed himself to be a domestic tyrant. And as a matter of fact, during a war in which the inadequate uniforms of soldiers became a *cause célèbre*, an officer's tailor's bill might indeed have held an almost gothic interest.

Actually, for all his derisiveness, in an earlier letter Dallas had (with predictably Dickensian humor) described – not publicly, perhaps, but still to a wider circle than the intended audience – not only writing the note that would be published but also the letter from his Sergeant's wife to which he was responding:

> He himself told me that she was "a first rate woman", but that her spelling was indifferent, & then showed me a letter from her, & insisted on my reading it from one end to the other, smoking a little pipe on his stretcher & making the quaintest comments on it. "Have you come to the part, where she says, Captain, she doesn't care if I come home with no limbs?" She spelt it, poor dear woman, "lims", & seemed to have a sort of idea that her husband would return a "torso". I shall be quite sorry to part with him, when he goes, & he asked me if he might write to me when he goes away.[89]

The passage provides evidence of the increasingly literate population that helped create the flood of correspondence about the war. There were limits to this trend, and large portions of the soldiers' experience of the war must have remained unrecorded. A "lady volunteer" serving as nurse in the East tells of her encounters with such voicelessness in describing what happened when she offered to write letters home for injured soldiers: "very often they had not a word to say, but trusted entirely to the lady. 'What shall I say?' we began with. – 'Just anything at all you like, Miss – just the same as you writes your own letters home. You knows how to make up a letter better than I do!'"[90] Nevertheless, some of the published letters were "private" in both senses of the word (that is, they were from *privates*),[91] and they seem at least to be authentic expressions (they were clearly taken as such) of what had hitherto remained silent sufferings.

But the circumstances surrounding the publication of Dallas's response remind us that war always forces a confrontation between public and private perspectives and responsibilities. As Tricia Lootens has argued in relation to war poetry, the most reactionary Victorian patriotic fervor becomes interesting in its attempts "openly to unite developing conceptions of subjective identity, at its most intimate, private, and inescapable, with shifting definitions of the powers and duties of public political subjects."[92] The sergeant's wife must have believed that Dallas's note belonged not only to her, but in some sense to the British public: as acknowledgement of her husband's heroism and his officer's kindness, as evidence of what was happening in the East. Even in Russell's case the distinction between public and personal writing broke down at times: the substance of Russell's "private" letters to Delane often made their way into the editorials, and the letters were perhaps published even against his wishes on occasion. After having raged against a particularly harsh report from "Our Special Correspondent" accusing British military brass of incompetence in the final disastrous attack on the Redan, Dallas records two weeks later how "Russell . . . has the decency to avow (with I don't know what amount of truth) that the low personalities about Simpson, Airey & others in the trenches on the 8th were written in a private letter & not intended for publication."[93] But presumably, Delane felt that the public deserved to know the contents of that letter, also.

Indeed, published private letters like Dallas's to his sergeant's wife served in the papers as supplementary narratives to those given by Russell and other "own" correspondents.[94] They were often grouped under headings like "Private Letters from the Crimea," and editors appear to have striven to assemble these groups to represent some range of military experience. Thus, for example, a collection published by *The Times* on November 28, 1854 consisted of missives from "a Scotch sergeant of artillery to his wife," from "a young officer of the 'Royal' Regiment to his sister," and from "a private soldier of the 63d [sic] Regiment . . . to his mother." The letters would be introduced either by notes from the individuals who had sent them in or by brief editorial comments that would set the tone for what followed. For instance, the letter from the private in the 63rd, George Evans, was prefaced by a moving endorsement from the older gentleman who had initially urged Evans to enlist, the young man's "having fallen into some of those youthful errors so common among our rural population." The army has transformed him, and the proof comes in the private's letter, which touchingly recounts the death of the endorser's own son, a standard-bearer for the regiment. But this private moment is offered up to the public not only as a memorial to his son's bravery but also "as showing that the British private soldier, while he entirely appreciates the gallant bearing of the officer who cheers him into action, is deeply influenced by early local attachments, and is not insensible of those sympathies which must render him capable of becoming a good citizen no less than a courageous and admirable soldier." A most personal of letters – one describing the death of a son – has public significance. It has also condensed the narrative of a sentimental novel written under the aegis of Wordsworth.

Other letters offer private perspectives on the public events of the war. Thus the officer whose letter appears in the same grouping describes one man's experience of the chaos of Inkerman, beginning with the admission, "I can tell little more of it than what I was actually concerned in":

I and some others, with about 200 men, had just come in from being 24 hours in the trenches, during the most of which it rained, and I was just getting warm in bed when we heard the bugles sound the assembly. We were marched over to where the fighting was going on, and were told to advance immediately and support the Guards, who were skirmishing in front, and to drive the Russians down the hill ... We killed numbers of them, and as we had no orders to halt, we continued keeping along the hill side, about half-way down, and firing at the retreating enemy. I then heard the bugle sound to retire, and set about trying to get the men back – no such easy matter, as by this time, from several regiments having been sent after each other, they were all mixed up. [A renewed Russian attack interrupts this effort.] Our soldiers returned their fire, but were at a disadvantage from being exposed at such a short distance. At this time Sir George Cathcart [Commander of the 4th Division, who died during the battle] rode up within a few steps of where I stood, but I heard no order given, and began to have visions of being shot through the head or going prisoner into Sebastopol, as we could scarcely muster a company, and the enemy had a large force above us ... They stopped firing at us and began to stone us, as it seemed to me with very large stones; but I don't now understand what it could be, as one struck a man just in front of where I stood, knocked his head to pieces, and sent him back with such force as to knock over the man behind him. I saw that something was clearing the way in that line, and stepped aside, so as to give it a chance of passing me, and had scarcely done so when an officer who came into my place was killed at my elbow. I then saw we could do nothing where we were.[95]

The letter both confirms and personalizes the details of Russell's report, serving in the supplementary manner the "Special" correspondent had predicted. It shares Russell's focus on the disorder of the engagement, but it adds a note of individual horror, especially in describing how the officer died, quite literally, in the writer's place. The tone of the private correspondence could vary widely, though. A letter in the *Morning Chronicle* introduced as coming "from a young man who, a few years since, was one of the singing boys at Rye church" ends an opening paragraph detailing experiences at the Alma and the deprivations of the march with: "Tell mother I shall want a stunning beef-pudding, with all the vegetables in season."[96] Such homely touches abound in the published private correspondence. The aforementioned "Scotch sergeant," for example, worries about his wife's finances: "How do you get your money; it is always in my mind?"[97] These very private moments in the letters are perhaps their most affective ones – again, one can see how they would have appealed to a reading public educated in the sentimental language of the realist novel.

Indeed, one thing that comes out in much of the correspondence (especially, predictably, that of officers like Dallas) is the degree to which reading has influenced members of the British public in their own writing. That is to say, one is frequently made aware of the fact that one is reading the writing of readers, and in particular, of novel- and newspaper-readers. Paul Hunter has noted how the practice of what were known as "Occasional Meditations" – in which "Diarists learned to 'meditate' on earthly objects by imitating the printed meditations of figures like Robert Boyle" – had consequences for the rise of the novel: "every reader becomes, in effect, his or her own writer."[98] During the Crimean War, the interpenetration of the "voice" of the novel with that of the foremost journalist of the day had a similarly empowering effect on the British public. And that all of this published writing was taking the form of the most ubiquitous and democratic of genres, the letter (itself, of course, a forerunner to the novel), only eased the rush into print. As Habermas reminds us, "the private activities of reading novels and writing letters" are "preconditions for participation in the public sphere."[99] The letter-writers of the newspapers of the war years were well primed for such participation.

Thus Russell's columns were subject to public commentary and amendment in the very newspaper in which he wrote, in a manner that translated them into part of a broader, interactive phenomenon – what Hunter has called "participatory journalism."[100] As a *Times* leader of November 5, 1855 declared for the people of Britain: "We are intelligent and self-respecting races, and require to have our interest and sympathy fed and sustained by constant participation in the history and even the conduct of the war."[101] So, to cite one example of such public nourishment, an "F. Flyers" sent a letter to the editor of *The Times* in which he enclosed "an extract of a letter . . . from a near relation now serving with the army in the East, which fully confirms the justice of your remarks in *The Times* [a leader written in support of Russell's columns, discussed above] a few days ago relative to the inexpediency of the soldiers being obliged to wear the tight and unbending stock." The fragment that follows in evidence is substantively very much like Russell's report: "instead of making a good appearance to the French officers, we had the ground dotted over with men who could not remain in the ranks . . . that horrid collar and stock, which our martinets are so fond of, are as much the cause of this as anything else."[102] In effect, Russell's correspondence merges with the editorial leader supporting it, a letter to the editor citing a corroborating eyewitness report, and the letter containing that "private" corroboration. The shared epistolary nature of the documents (even the leader uses a related first-person format), the editorial "titles" often given to the letters, and the absence of a set position for the letters to the editor in the newspaper's layout aided the conflation of voices.

Such exchanges are paradigmatic of the way in which "the story of the war" was pieced together in the newspapers of the day. Indeed, where no documentary letters were available to record the particular deeds of an individual, an original narrative – a kind of supplement to Russell's correspondence and the official dispatches – could be written. So "An Old and Sincere Friend of Captain Maude's" submits a character portrait to *The Times* (including Maude's family history and details of his gallantry at the Alma and at Balaklava), noting that "It appears to be the fashion of the day to publish in the papers any facts connected with persons that may be considered interesting to their relatives and their friends, and I therefore see no reason why the gallant officer above alluded to should not have the gratification."[103] Still others wished to correct mistakes in Russell's columns. Thus a reader in Balaklava writes to rectify a misattribution to himself of the command of a regiment at Inkerman.[104]

A particularly interesting example of such correction comes in a letter published in the same batch of correspondence from Captain Edward Bruce Hamley, the author of his own anonymously written *Story of the Campaign* (then running in the pro-war *Blackwood's*). Hamley complains of what he intimates to be Russell's layman-like errors: "Your correspondent states that the Russians brought 32-pounders into the field. These were not 32-pounder guns, but 32-pounder howitzers – by no means a match for 18-pounder guns," to give one example in a catalogue of inaccuracies disclosed.[105] His *Story of the Campaign* is by implication free from such mistakes, emphasizing its author's experience. But like Russell's columns, it demonstrates the interplay of "private" correspondence and public expression in the war journalism. Its first monthly part (of eleven) was introduced by the editors with "extracts from the private letter of our correspondent, dated 'Camp before Sebastopol, October 27,' [which] will explain the circumstances under which 'The Story of the Campaign' has been written" – the letter then details delays caused both by illness and by "[a]larms of attacks, mostly false." The editorial preface of the second installment again proves Hamley's active involvement in the conflict with extracts from a letter, this time telling of his sergeant's loss of a leg during Inkerman, sustained in the act of rescuing Hamley himself.

Hamley's account, though, is generally far less personal than Russell's reports (he uses the first person more sparingly, for example), with the probably unintentional exception of his tendency to linger about scenes of gore, especially of amputations and battlefield dismemberment. Even here, the contrast with Russell is suggestive: Hamley almost never mentions illness. Presumably, he considers the topic to be tangential to the real "story" of war, which concerns events of the battlefield. Hamley is also much less critical than Russell of the generals' management of the war. But he is forced to make some adjustments in the face of circumstances; he opens Part v (entitled "Exculpatory" and published in April of 1855) with the remark,

In the earlier chapters I have rather avoided comment, confining myself to a plain narrative of the course of events as they flowed one into another. The public had been more than content with the campaign, and demanded only an intelligible and detailed account of the occurrences which had led to such pleasing results. But opinion had begun to exercise so large an influence on the war, that a record of its progress would be defective in which this new element should be left unrecognised.[106]

Still, the belated publication of this notice – itself a preface to a defense of many of the army's moves – suggests Hamley's general attitude towards the criticism of people like Russell: his sense that non-military men should stay away from matters they do not and cannot understand. Russell himself responded to such and other accusations, periodically defending his columns where he thought he was right and demonstrating his willingness to correct any genuine mistakes; as he often admits, war is a difficult thing to report perfectly on the spot.

Yet members of the army were not the only ones rushing in the direction of the newspapers. The British public at home also showed its eagerness to participate in the war by writing to give both opinions and advice. As "One Who has a Relative in the Crimea" put it in a letter to the editor of *The Times*, in response to the general "abhorrence of the conduct of those professing to have the management of affairs," "The eyes of all England were turned upon the expedition, and suggestions poured in from all quarters as to the best and most efficient course to be adopted in order to insure their comfort in a foreign land."[107] People seem to have felt it to be both within their capacity and a matter of duty to add their "two bits" to the war effort, not only in terms of pounds but in terms of expertise. Indeed, the letters to the editor during the war reveal Britain to have been a nation of self-proclaimed experts.

For example, one of the most prominent debates of the winter of 1854–55 concerned the question of the weather in the Crimea: what it would be like and how the soldiers could best protect themselves against it. The topic – which would spawn hundreds of letters in *The Times* alone – begins to appear in that paper in October under the heading "The Climate in the Crimea," with letters like that from "J. B. D.," who, in place of a report from a soldier in the East, sends in a quotation from a book introduced by a scholarly note: "The volume of *Clarke's Travels* from which I quote contains the most interesting accounts of the Crimea of any book ever published, except that of Professor Pallas" – just in case another reader wants to study the matter in more detail.[108] By November, the subject has gained in urgency. "One Who has Been in the Crimea in Winter" submits a brief but typically pressing appeal: "Sir, – What has been done, or what is about to be done, about clothing our troops in the Crimea? Are our people at home aware that a night or two in the clothing in which they are now clad may leave them stiff enough in their tents, without any trouble on the part of their numerous foes?"[109] Three days later, *The Times* publishes a collection of letters on the topic under the heading "The Winter in the Crimea," in which a series of correspondents give recommendations on the basis of their experiences of various northern locales. "H. R." describes the tricks acquired during a residency "on the shore of Lake Huron," while "A Practical Man in a Question of Cold" (many readers chose to emphasize their "practicality" in selecting their *noms de plume*) tells of the benefits of using animal skins for robes and gloves, like the native tribes of North America.

But the next day, another reader objects to the wishy-washy nature of such personal observations (he also signs his name, as though to emphasize his own straightforwardness), calling them "mischievous" "random assertions." To counter such emotional language, he submits "facts," the first in a string of meteorological tables to appear, this one documenting (among other things) that the average temperature in Sebastopol is above freezing, and warmer than that of Dijon.[110] Of course statistics do not always speak the truth. Soon a further table appears (citing Count Demidoff's book of travels), submitted with the observation that the problem is not so much the average temperature, as "the alteration of temperature in the winter months below and above the freezing point, which is shown by this table, and which I hear adverted to on the spot by an intelligent person of long experience in the Crimea."[111] Curiously, "A Meteorologist" who enters the lists a few days later provides no charts but rather bases his observations on the fact that the vineyards noted in so many reports could not survive in mean winter temperatures below 33 degrees.[112] By the 14th of December, the newspaper itself feels ready to weigh in on the matter, observing that "The state of the weather in the Crimea is at this moment the most important fact connected with the progress of the siege," before giving its own carefully measured conclusion: "From the best information that has been obtained, there seems but little reason to anticipate the rigour of a Siberian winter . . . but the changes of the season . . . are even more trying to the patience and health of the army."[113] Still, ten days later an apotheosis of statistical detail submitted from a reader actually in the Crimea (figure 3) takes the subject to new heights.[114] Perhaps the editors decided enough was enough; in any case, no such further tables appeared. The debate finally closed on a comic note, with a poem submitted in April (by which time spring had arrived, and the focus could shift from survival to tactics), entitled "Lord Raglan and the Weather":

> Lord Raglan might in September have taken
>   Sebastopol duly and truly;
> But the weather (he raves about weather!) was warm,
>   And he wished to take it – coolly!
>   . . .
> October, November, December came on,
>   As if missioned his army to kill off:
> "The weather is now too cold," quoth he,
>   "I'll take it – with the chill off!"
>
> For three months more despatches he wrote
>   In meteorological form,
> 'till the storms had passed; "'tis too late now,"
>   Quoth he, "to take it – by storm!"
>
> Thus, whether the weather be foul or fair,
>   Sebastopol 'scapes the blow –
> Then, down with the weatherglass! – give us a man
>   Who will take it – whether or no!"[115]

This account, though, fails to register the full extent of the correspondence, because a series of related debates accompany the question of the numbers throughout: about the best clothes to wear (as already mentioned, with an off-shoot debate about what is actually termed "the 'frozen toe' question"[116]), the warmest houses to build, the best forage to feed the horses, the best recipes to concoct from the rations. As a result, more or less everyone has something to contribute, and the letters reflect this fact. Of course, letters from medical men were legion. But "A Practical Farmer" explains that all that is needed to give sound advice is common sense and real day-to-day experience in some line or other: "Now, being a farmer myself, and working 30 horses regularly, I feel that, as a practical man, I may venture to give an opinion."[117] And an even more modest "W." writes to recommend using a flour paste to apply

THE WEATHER IN THE CRIMEA.

TO THE EDITOR OF THE TIMES.

Sir,—I beg to forward you a few extracts from my meteorological journal, which a friend of mine, one of your correspondents, has informed me may perhaps, at the present time, prove interesting to your general readers. In all probability, I shall be stationed at Balaklava during the winter. I shall be happy to send you a table by every post, provided you consider it worthy of your attention.

I remain, Sir, your most obedient servant,
EDWARD PEARCE.

Her Majesty's ship Diamond, Balaklava, Jan. 5.

METEOROLOGICAL REPORT FROM BALAKLAVA FROM THE 1ST TO THE 5TH OF JANUARY, 1855:—

Date.	Thermometer (Self-registering) Observations Taken at 8 a.m. for the Preceding 12 Hours. Min. Deg.	Max. Deg.	Observations Taken at 8 p.m. for the Preceding 12 Hours. Min. Deg.	Max. Deg.	Temperature of the Open Air in the Shade. 8 a.m. Deg.	3 p.m. Deg.	8 p.m. Deg.	In the Sea. Deg.	Barometer. Minimum. Deg.	Maximum. Deg.	Medium. Deg.	Winds. General Direction and Force. a.m.	p.m.
Jan. 1	42	46	43	48	45	46	48	48	29·30	29·60	29·43	4 to 6 S.S.W.	6 to 7 S.S.W.
2	46	48	42	50	47	45	46	47	28·68	29·0	28·82	7 S.S.W.	3 S.S.W.
3	34	45	34	39	35	35	44	45	29·0	29·5	29·1	1 N.E.	1 N.N.E.
4	29	37	26	35	30	28	27	42	29·15	29·55	29·42	2 N.	2 N.
5	19	33	20	29	19	22	27	40	29·50	29·55	29·52	N.	N.

GENERAL REMARKS.

Jan. 1.—Cloudy and overcast; 10 a.m. began to rain. Showers all day.

Jan. 2.—Overcast. Commenced to rain 4 a.m.; showers all day; night, heavy rain; rain up to 5 a.m.; 8 a.m., snow falling, but thawing as it fell.

Jan. 3.—12 n., raining; rain, snow, and hail showers all day.

Jan. 4.—Ground covered with snow; overcast; snow showers all day.

Jan. 5.—Very fine day, with passing clouds.

The 4th is the first day, for the winter, in which the snow has remained on the ground for any length of time.

EDWARD PEARCE, Assistant-Surgeon,
Her Majesty's ship Diamond.

Her Majesty's Ship Diamond, Balaklava, Jan. 5.

Figure 3 Edward Pearce, "The Weather in the Crimea," letter to the editor, *The Times*, January 24, 1855, 10

paper over the cracks of the wooden huts that housed the soldiers, adding, "Pardon the suggestion of so trivial a thing; but it sometimes happens that, in the hurry and excitement of great efforts, the omission of some small but obvious matter greatly reduces the value of the exertions made."[118] Again the "trivial" detail – the domain both of the novel and Russell's letters – becomes elevated to a new level of importance by the war. And again, the "everyman" becomes a potential hero, a private soldier in "the people's war."

Still the ordinary and the famous mixed in the columns of the paper: the cookery suggestions came from Alexis Soyer, the well-known chef for the Reform Club. He states in the anonymous note accompanying his recipe that he has sent it in response to a request mentioned in a letter from the Crimea that had appeared a few days previously.[119] This correspondence progressed into something more extensive when Soyer decided to go to the East himself, together with a camp stove he had invented that proved so successful that the British Army continued to use a version of it for the next hundred years. Soyer subsequently recorded his experiences in a memoir-*cum*-cookbook, in which he tells how his mission began with reading the newspapers – Russell's letters and the private correspondence – and in which he also reprints both this first letter to the editor and several more (that had been published under his own name) following it. Indeed, when he left the East, he sent another letter to the editor, beginning with the assertion that "As my mission is drawing to a close, it will probably interest you to learn that I shall be able to terminate my culinary campaign to the general satisfaction of, I hope, yourself and all persons." And he finished with a well-placed compliment: "I should not have trespassed upon your valuable time were it not again to acknowledge that the good effected is entirely due to your fearless and patriotic exposure of the truth in your unique and powerful journal."[120] While Soyer was no doubt acting patriotically and fearlessly, too, he was well aware of the luster his *Culinary Campaign* (as the title of his 1857 memoir would also put it) would add to his already well-burnished name.[121]

For all Soyer's fame, his memoir – like others produced by this war – exhibits a democratic approach reminiscent of the newspaper correspondence. Many of the popular memoirists are themselves very different from the military heroes whose recollections chronicled previous conflicts. Consider Mary Seacole. And Elizabeth Davis, the spirited Welsh servant-turned-Crimean-nurse, famous for her disagreements with what she saw as Nightingale's overly bureaucratic manner of distributing "free gifts" (the cartloads of goods that the British public had sent to the Crimea).[122] Such

Crimean celebrities portrayed a kind of "knowable community" where authors of dubious social stature could brush shoulders with each other and with the great and mighty. (The two women suggestively replace novelistic courtship plots with narratives reaching toward professional satisfaction and security.) Curiously, these writers were not only of lower class but also racial or national "outsiders": the Jamaican Seacole, the Welshwoman Davis, the Frenchman Soyer (Russell's Irishness comes to mind here as well). Collectively, their books give a surprisingly wide-ranging picture of the sense of "Britishness" that emerged from the war: Seacole, for example, writes repeatedly of her soldier "sons" and of the way they call her "mother." But they simultaneously make clear that such integration as was achieved under wartime duress would have a hard time surviving the peace: both wartime "heroines" wrote in part to relieve the poverty into which they had fallen on their return "home" to England.

Still, in their range and number, the letters to the editor during the war were truly extraordinary. To give some indication of their novelty, a search through *The Times* during the Napoleonic wars (I focused on the discussion surrounding the battles of Trafalgar and Waterloo) elicited only a smattering of comparable letters.[123] The closest thing I found to the public debate about the Crimean War concerned the erection of a monument to Nelson following Trafalgar.[124] As the leader setting up *The Times*'s charitable Fund claimed, though, now the present, not the future, was the issue. Indeed, that very leader met a typical response in a letter written by a British woman who called herself "A Sufferer by the Present War?" (the question mark presumably referring to the uncertain status of her family member in the East). She wrote specifically to "entreat" the editor's continued support for increased medical aid to the army, in the process demonstrating an adroit manipulation of the very pronouns the leader-writer had used to such good effect:

You cannot, perhaps, adequately conceive the deep solicitude felt in the matter by mothers, wives, and children at home, in the humbler as well as in the higher classes.

We sit at home trying to picture the last moments of those dear to us, and our agony is increased by the fear that all was not done that might have been done to relieve their suffering, or, may be, to save their lives. The question will arise with regard to someone who has fallen – "Was there no one near to relieve his sufferings, to speak a word of kindness or hope, to receive some last message, perhaps, for some dear ones at home, or even to support his head or give him a drink of water?"

The strongest man becomes helpless and dependent like a child in his hour of need, and we all know how, in such a case, a humble nurse, with no other recommendations than a kind heart and skilful hands, appears to the sufferer as a saving angel.

The leader's all-inclusive home front "we" is thus – respectfully – declined, and in its place appears a different domestic contingent, of women whose interest in the cause is less detached, who do not sit comfortably in their armchairs following the war on maps and in the papers. And these women, the writer insists, would "joyfully and with alacrity go out to devote themselves to nursing the sick and the wounded, if they could be associated for that purpose and placed under proper protection."[125] This letter was among the forces that would send Florence Nightingale to the East.

But the writer's claim actually reaches far beyond Nightingale's mission: she argues that her status as an emotionally involved and "able-bodied" woman gives her the professional qualifications – the expertise – necessary to contribute to the war effort, both through her letter and, potentially, through going out to nurse. And women clearly felt empowered – to write and to act – by the conditions of this war. Thus "A Yorkshirewoman" sending in a letter on the matter of "Mits and Socks for the Army in the East" dispenses with the usual formality of submitting requests through the intermediary of the paper's editor, instead addressing her note "To the Women of England." Her brief missive is a jewel of practical advice. After giving the directions to which the said articles should be sent, she adds:

Crochet work is quicker than knitting, perhaps not more effective. At the joining of the thumb with the hand the thickness should be double to prevent wear. The best division of labour is for the mits to be done by ladies, while (the yarn being furnished) the poorer women of the town or village do the socks at 4d. a pair for labour, and others do it cheerfully gratis as their mite in this great cause. The brown drab yarn is about 2s. a-pound, which will make eight or nine pairs of mits.[126]

Here is a woman speaking with authority, proving that while the source of the science of *oeconomics* is in the home, it need not rest there. After all, her tone sounds much like that Florence Nightingale herself was already using to such effect.[127]

In addition to the many one-off contributions from the public, the war created a new kind of private editorialist to vie with both Russell and the leader-writers. This development arose when correspondents to the paper began to make such frequent appearances (both through their own letters and through references to them in letters to the editor written by others) as to gain "name-recognition." So, for example, E. Elers Napier, a military man and member of a great military family (which included his stepfather, Admiral Charles Napier, commander of the Baltic fleet during the war) had had nineteen letters published in *The Times* on the topic of the war by its conclusion. Before the war, he had submitted the occasional military-themed letter to the editor (a total of six, beginning in 1848), but the Crimean experience seems to have struck him as demanding a new (and unrepeated) level of such involvement (no doubt brought on also by his rather surprising inability to find active duty during the conflict, in spite of his efforts).

Coming from an army man, though, Napiers's contributions make a certain kind of sense. And he tends to write in a manner drawing attention to his military expertise and experience (several letters also address the topic of the fund for warm clothing and newspapers for the East that he started). More surprising is the case of the man who styled himself "A Hertfordshire Incumbent." It is under this sobriquet that Joseph Williams Blakesley, a former member of the Cambridge Apostles (like Tennyson and Nightingale's admirer Richard Monkton Milnes), became famous. As the *DNB* records,

As vicar of Ware he became widely known as the Hertfordshire Incumbent, whose letters in *The Times* newspaper examined social and political subjects of the day. The letters greatly increased his reputation, and in 1863 he received a canonry at Canterbury from Lord Palmerston, with whose political views he fully sympathized. In 1860 Palmerston had offered Blakesley the regius professorship of history at Cambridge in preference to Dr Woodham of Jesus, despite Blakesley's lack of credentials as a modern historian.[128]

The entry testifies to the degree to which Blakesley owed his success to the name he earned as a writer of letters to the editor; these letters seem to have stood in place of other "credentials." But it fails to note that the letters came out of his response to a particular event in "modern history": the Crimean War. While Blakesley had long served *The Times* as an anonymous reviewer of books (including writing a notorious review of Brougham's *Demosthenes* in 1840[129]), the first letter by "A Hertfordshire Incumbent" was not published until November 30, 1854. It was on the favorite public theme of "The Climate in the Crimea."[130] A total of thirty-three more letters on the war, many of them well over a thousand words in length (not coincidentally, roughly the same length as most of the leaders in *The Times*), were to follow. They covered a broad range of topics: the weather, road construction, hut construction, troop movements, geography, and mosquitoes, to name a smattering. But the correspondence did not end with the conflict. Initially, the "Hertfordshire Incumbent" expanded his reach to other matters Russian. Yet as the war retreated into history, he proved himself willing and able to contribute on any number of subjects, among them India, wages, the militia, education, and religion. In all, eighty-four letters are ascribed to him in *The Times*'s searchable database, the final one published in April of 1872.

Thus Blakesley turned himself into a popular modern historian – as modern as it gets. He demonstrated such wide expertise of matters Crimean that other writers would turn to him (rather than to the newspaper's "leaders") for advice. So "A. T." concludes a letter addressed to the editor offering suggestions concerning the political fate of the Crimea in the wake of the Russian defeat with the comment: "I confess I shall be glad if this communication should affect the notice of your excellent correspondent, the 'Hertfordshire Incumbent.'"[131] In effect, the Incumbent became an additional (and presumably unpaid) leader-writer for the newspaper, and over the course of the war, his letters assume the attending tone, minus the editorial "we." "I observe that the attention of the public is beginning to be turned to the changes which may take place in the wants of our forces in the Crimea on the approach of spring," one letter begins, before sounding a warning against precipitate optimism on this front.[132] Yet popular should not be mistaken for populist. A scholarly quality pervades his correspondence throughout: the Incumbent never shies away from demonstrating book-learning, and frequent references to events in modern history ("When Munnich invaded the Crimea in 1736 he established posts all along his route from the lines of the Ukraine"[133]) help explain Palmerston's feeling that he would make a suitable candidate for the Cambridge professorship. Indeed, he pits his scholarship against personal experience in a rather heated exchange with "G. D. N." (another repeat-correspondent to the editor) about the implication of the winter topography of the Crimea for Russian troop reinforcements. In response to a long letter by the Incumbent about the possibility that the Russians could take advantage of winter freeze in moving troops and supplies across certain straits, "G. D. N." declares, "From the information I gathered personally on both shores of the Sea of Azoff I think it impossible for our enemy to do so."[134] But the Incumbent will not be so easily brushed off: "He appears to have been at Azoff. But has he been at Arabat? And can he speak from his own knowledge of the means of access to that place?" "I am not aware of any traveller who has described Arabat except Pallas," the

Incumbent continues, and thus declares a victory to book-learning before proceeding with his account.[135]

And if *The Times* had the ability to change the course of the war through its leader columns (as it did with the creation of the Fund), so, in his own smaller way, did the Incumbent, as he demonstrated in a remarkable exchange that takes place in the pages of the newspaper in the spring of 1855. It begins when he addresses a question directly to the British public on the basis of a fear Chenery had expressed in a column about summer water supplies for the troops (no doubt itself more noticeable for the many reports of thirst Russell had contributed in the previous summer). The question might be seen as an early example of what has recently been termed "crowdsourcing":

Can any practical engineer among your readers inform the public whether it would be feasible to set up speedily an apparatus for distilling the sea-water on such a scale as to render the failure of the springs in the neighbourhood of the camp an unimportant matter? In these days of steam-engines, gutta-percha tubing, and energetic contractors, I should fancy this might be done, and the fluid distributed to any part of the plateau occupied by the allies, without the necessity of withdrawing a single soldier from his proper duty.[136]

The Incumbent thus uses the newspaper as a public clearinghouse for ideas. And it works. By the following day, the paper had already published a reply, in which a Henry Williams states the possibility of erecting the suggested apparatus (and that he has enclosed a testimonial about the effectiveness of the equipment from a ship already using it in the Crimea). Two days after this, the aforementioned E. Elers Napier confirms the validity of the Incumbent's fear by quoting from Rabbe's *History of Russia*. And another two days later, "J. A." sends in a letter from an officer in the East, written on the 30th of March, in further confirmation of the problem: "I am afraid we are likely to run short of water . . . Some one ought to write up to *The Times* and propose to send out some of the distilling engines that they have on board of most of the steamers, so that we could use sea water in case we are hard pressed." The next day, though, the crisis appears to have been resolved. Henry Williams writes back:

I think it will be satisfactory to you, and to those of the public who take an interest in this matter, to know that the Admiralty yesterday sent an officer to inspect one of the machines while in operation, and that the gentleman devoted many hours to a careful examination of it. It seems, therefore, probable that the Government will take prompt measures to insure a supply of pure, wholesome, aerated water at Balaklava.[137]

Through the combined voices of the paper's "own" correspondents, its "leading" private correspondent, and the British public, both at home and in the Crimea, potential disaster had been averted.

Benedict Anderson has argued for the genesis of an "imagined community" – otherwise known as the Nation – in the experience of reading the daily newspapers. He himself imagines an

> extraordinary mass ceremony: the almost precisely simultaneous consumption ("imagining") of the newspaper-as-fiction ... It is performed in silent privacy, in the lair of the skull. Yet each communicant is well aware that the ceremony he performs is being replicated simultaneously by thousands (or millions) of others of whose existence he is confident, yet of whose identity he has not the slightest notion.[138]

Nevertheless, the sense one gets from reading about the influence of the press during the Crimean War is that this representation of newspaper-reading as solitary and private, while no doubt often strictly true, fails to recognize those communal aspects of the experience that did not depend entirely upon the imagination. In fact, illustrations of the day often show groups gathered around a newspaper, much as we fantasize about families huddled around radio broadcasts during World War II. The distinction matters because it suggests that the dialogue fostered by the newspapers was not just "in the lair of the skull," but that it also took place in the outside world in a manner that could easily be translated into the back and forth I have been detailing in the pages of the press.

Consider a couple of John Leech's cartoons for *Punch*, both of which indicate that the papers entered into dialogues as soon as they were read.[139] The later sketch, written after the "Crimean Correspondence" had erupted in the press, shows a domestic scene of two ladies at tea. One holds up a newspaper. The caption reads:

YOUNG LADY (READING CRIMEAN CORRESPONDENCE): "I MUST TELL YOU THAT I HAVE QUITE ABANDONED POOR BROWN BESS, AND THAT WITH MY BEAUTIFUL MINIÉ – "

ELDER LADY (INTERRUPTING HASTILY): "THERE – THERE – MY DEAR, GO ON TO THE NEXT LETTER. WE DON'T WANT TO HEAR ABOUT HIS BESSIES AND MINNIES – THESE SOLDIERS ARE ALL ALIKE"[140]

The joke lay in the fact that Brown Bess and Minié were the respective names for the older and newer styles of gun (musket and rifle) used by the army. But the sketch also demonstrates how the newspapers were appropriated by their readers and made to conform to their own imaginings about war – and it hints that the prevalence of the familiar letter format (perhaps filtered here through a slightly risqué French epistolary novel?) helped make accessible (even if only through misreading) the most "foreign" correspondence.

An earlier Leech cartoon, composed just as the debates in the press were beginning to emerge, also emphasizes newspaper reading as directly constitutive of community. A "big cut" entitled "Enthusiasm of Paterfamilias, On Reading the Report of the Grand Charge of British Cavalry on the 25th" (figure 13), the picture (which I will discuss in more detail in chapter 4) shows a British middle-class "Paterfamilias" surrounded by his family, reading aloud what one assumes to be Russell's famous account of the glorious but foolhardy charge of the Light Brigade from a *Times* newspaper that he holds in one hand.[141] In his other hand, he brandishes a poker. His excitement is shared by many of the younger members of his family, although a woman appearing to be his eldest daughter centers the composition, her tear-marked face indicating her displeasure (in which she is joined by her lamenting mother). In a wonderful discussion of the sketch (in the context of her reading of Tennyson's famous poem about the charge), Trudi Tate shows how it demonstrates what she calls the "*fantasy* investment in war": how people at home can turn the reports in the papers into a form of participation, whether by joining in with the action or by opting out of it.[142] Leech's sketch reminds us that the war abroad was fought in part to feed the fantasies of those at home; as George Eliot would wryly remark in *The Mill on the Floss* (1860), "It is doubtful whether our soldiers would be maintained if there were not a pacific people at home who like to fancy themselves soldiers. War, like other dramatic spectacles, might possibly cease for want of a 'public.'"[143] Yet while Leech makes fun of his "Paterfamilias," he does so affectionately: he wants us to recognize that such fantasizing is constitutive of national identity. And of course our recognition of this fact is aided by the way in which we ourselves are pulled into the experience of reading, the cartoon itself appearing in the magazine we hold before us.[144]

But in the Crimean context, the newspapers played a novel role in the process, offering "Paterfamilias" an entrance into the public sphere even from within the confines of his home; the printed map of the Crimea centered on the wall behind the assembled family – a pictorial analogue to the printed paper in Pater's hand – occupies the compositional space in which one would otherwise have expected to see a literal (rather than a "literary") window out to the world. And the Paterfamilias – or his daughter – could pick up a pen as easily as a sword or poker. He soon would. As Karl Marx noted derisively in complaining of the British bourgeoisie's decision to oust Aberdeen from his seat as Prime Minister and replace him with their hero, Palmerston, "The truly English Minister! His rule of conduct, his source of information, his treasury of new measures and reforms, were the interminable letters of 'Paterfamilias' in *The Times*."[145]

When Habermas declared "[t]he world fashioned by the mass media" to be "a public sphere in appearance only," he based his conclusion in part on what he saw as the troublingly unidirectional modes of communication of what he then (in the 1960s) called the "new media": their "Don't talk back!" attitude.[146] During the Crimean War, though, letters to the editor allowed the newspapers to function (at least to some extent) as a real public sphere, in which voices were brought into communication – more like what we today would call a part of the "new media": the blogosphere. Indeed, I think it fair to say that because of the role of the press, the degree of public participation in the media saw as exponential an increase during the Crimean War as has been attributed to internet technology during the present conflict in the East, in which (to cite an interesting analogue to the publication of soldiers' letters I have detailed) videos shot by troops in Iraq and uploaded by them on to YouTube are then collected and rebroadcast as documentary specials on television.[147] Even William Howard Russell seems to have recognized that the papers were dissolving distinctions between private and public voices of the war; after he had finished his duties as Crimean point-man for *The Times*, he responded to a critical letter from "A Guardsman" by submitting his own "letter to the editor," from the "Late Special Correspondent in the Crimea": "I beg to reiterate my former statement, and to deny the accuracy of the 'Guardsman's' assertion," Russell insists.[148] He was acknowledging his participation in the free-flowing, democratic medium of the newspapers of the day.

Given the impact that reading – both of journalism and (behind it) novels – had on the writing of the war, it seems appropriate that one continuing area of public correspondence in *The Times* concerned the establishment and maintenance of reading rooms for the soldiers in the East, places where even privates could access newspapers, journals, and books. Most of the letters on the topic address practical issues of collection and distribution. But occasionally, a correspondent embellishes a little. Thus H. P. Wright, Principal Chaplain in the Crimea, uses a letter to the editor of *The Times* to make a request concerning the nature of the public's contributions. Discussing the need for "a well-filled box" to make its way over, the chaplain specifies:

> When I say well-filled, I do not mean crowded, as some were last year, with old annual reports of the many religious societies, almanacks of 1817, dark mysterious divinity, heavy controversial tracts, last volumes of novels, Armenian bibles, trigonometrical tables, Loo-choo grammars, pamphlets on turnpikes, &c., but nicely packed with tales, novels, biography, Chambers's many publications, Dickens's works, and such like, all which are read with intense pleasure.[149]

And some of the works of literature to which I will turn in the following chapters actually did land in the hands of the soldiers, so becoming part of the back and forth between readers and writers, between the Crimea and the home front, that I have been describing here. Thus, for example, Florence Nightingale wrote to a friend in England asking for an edition of Elizabeth Gaskell's *North and South* for the hospital reading room in Scutari,[150] while comments from a chaplain's private letter to a friend of Tennyson's about the troops' clamorous enthusiasm for "The Charge of the Light Brigade" led the poet to print and send East two thousand copies of the ballad, in what he called "the soldier's version."[151] In a review of the poetry of the war, E. B. Hamley even remarked on the strange phenomenon: "Fancy . . . the white-haired Nestor, and the sage Ulysses, reading, towards the close of the first year of their sojourn before Troy, the first book of the *Iliad*, to be continued in parts as a serial."[152]

Wright's letter indicates his belief that the soldiers desired to have "novel" reading materials – in both senses of the word that I have discussed here. But it also implies that the impulse to use literature to forget is as strong as the impulse to use literature to remember: "the worst clad, worst fed, worst housed Army that ever was read of" would no doubt sometimes like to escape the fact in reading fiction. As the war passed into history, this complex negotiation between forgetting and remembering would become a topic for the authors of fiction, too, in their struggle to make sense of events so recently transpired and to translate journalism – writing of the *day* – into material that could not only outlast it but also memorialize it. Faced with a war that had so undermined the British understanding of military heroism, writers would have to engineer their own "novel" arsenal with which to manage this especially challenging process of translation, as I shall argue in the next chapter.

CHAPTER 2

From Amyas Leigh to Aurora Leigh: gender and heroism in the novels of the Crimean War

The novel events of the Crimean War might have been expected to generate a slew of novelistic responses, especially as the subject of the unprecedented public uproar at the mismanagement of the war was added to the potentially heady mix of military heroics. Henry Clifford, a bored officer who was reading *Hard Times* from his position in the East, wrote of Dickens: "I wish he could sit, with my pen and paper, and write a book, 'Hard Times' in the Crimea . . . Only just what is passing in front of the door of my comfortable little tent would give him plenty of matter."[1] But his wish was not fulfilled; in fact, relatively few novelists engaged with the events of the war directly, and Dickens himself (for all his involvement in the conflict through his work with the Administrative Reform Association and his editorship of *Household Words*) kept his novelistic response to the portrayal of bureaucratic bungling associated with the Crimea in the Circumlocution Office of *Little Dorrit*.[2] As I argued in chapter 1, journalism dominated during the war years; Arthur Hugh Clough recorded in January of 1855 how "Our literature, at present, is the war column in the newspaper."[3] Demand for novels went down so noticeably as to compromise new methods of publication: Richard Bentley's attempt in 1854 to produce cheap editions of novels "foundered when the Crimean War caused a slump in book sales."[4] Elizabeth Barrett Browning noted the phenomenon, remarking that the Newcomes, the family at the center of Thackeray's current offering (1853–55), were "not strong enough to resist the Czar": "I understand that literature is going on flaggingly in England just now, on account of nobody caring to read anything but telegraphic messages."[5] "What can any novelist write," Thackeray himself admitted, "so interesting as our own correspondent?"[6] This ranking is made manifest in his friend John Everett Millais's painting *Peace Concluded, 1856*, showing a British officer at home with his family on the day the war was declared to be over (figure 15). While the picture includes both a copy of *The Times* and the latest installment of *The Newcomes*, the latter is pushed as if forgotten to the edge of the canvas, while the former occupies a central position.

The radical journalist and novelist George W. M. Reynolds, as always keenly aware of popular trends, took advantage of the war-fever by churning out a Crimean potboiler for his *Miscellany* even as the conflict raged on. *Omar: A Tale of the War* appeared in the weekly magazine from January 6, 1855 (vol. 13, no. 339) to January 5, 1856 (vol. 15, no. 391), and while Reynolds gave himself a head start on history by beginning with Omar Pasha's rise (from his humble origins as a Croatian youth suffering under Austrian oppression) to his position as top commander of the Turkish army, events soon caught up with the narrative.[7] By March, the story had moved to the Crimea, where the tale frequently gives way to battle description that reads remarkably like William Howard Russell's, even as Reynolds is forced to figure out what to do with his titular hero, whose real-life equivalent had remained behind in the Danubian provinces when the French and British troops embarked for what was to become the primary theater of action before Sebastopol. As the novel progresses, it manifests its generic confusion in the way the illustrations beginning each installment cease to function descriptively; rather, they start to take the form of *colportage*, imaginary scenes not from the novel but from the war itself. Thus while a picture of "Lord Raglan, General Pelissier, and Attendant Officers" in a presumably Crimean landscape illustrates the installment published on August 11, 1855, its narrative mentions none of these figures, following instead the fortunes of a Wallachian family oppressed by the Austrians.

Yet in some ways, as I began to suggest in my discussion of Russell's own attempt at fiction, the novel is the genre best suited to displaying the complex negotiation with ideas of the heroic that came out of the war experience. So in Reynolds's novel, for example, the promise of a real hero in Omar Pasha gives way as the history of the war fails to provide him with adequate outlet for his energies. Early scenes describe a true man of action, a world-historical figure worthy of an epic role. But when he shows a young Omar engaged in battle against his arch-enemy (the head of the Austrian army), even Reynolds must admit the nostalgia attached to the scenario: "So unusual a thing is it in modern warfare for the chiefs of two opposing armies thus to meet hand to hand, that those around paused for a few minutes from the terrific work of carnage, to view the carnage – and with a presentiment likewise on both sides that on its issue depended the fortune of the day" (ch. 7, 13:404). And as the narrative shifts to the

Crimea, Omar is pushed to the side. While Reynolds frequently remarks on Omar's superiority over his English and French counterparts, his actual influence on events is small.

Various contenders for the title of hero assume Omar's narrative place: English, French, Polish, and Turkish officers. The most convincing of them, though, turns out to be a woman: Catherine Volmar, the daughter of a Polish revolutionary. Catherine disguises herself as a Zouave in order to nurse her husband – an English officer stationed in the Crimea, by whom she had previously been abandoned; her skills are required to make up for the woeful inadequacy of the British medical staff. Reynolds keeps Caroline's sex secret until she is injured on the battlefield in the act of saving her husband. But while the reader probably detects the truth before this moment, the realization comes slowly (at least it came slowly to this reader), and not before some rather bizarre "love scenes" between the Zouave and "his" unfeeling "master," who (we are told) looks "on the Zouave . . . as a menial who in the first instance had a duty to perform, but who by some caprice had learnt to make that duty a labour of love" (ch. 38, 14:226). Thus until we intimate the Zouave's sex, the issue reads as one of class rather than gender, so allowing for an overlap between these categories that also (as we shall see) operates in Elizabeth Gaskell's *North and South* (1855). Nevertheless, Caroline's gender is crucial to her role in the novel. And she does more than nurse: the supposed Zouave makes "his" way into Sebastopol, where "he" discovers the Russian plan for attack on Inkerman and warns the Allied troops just in time to save their chances in the battle. When Omar Pasha finally returns to the story, it is only to reunite the heroine with her rather undeserving husband, and to do so by unveiling Catherine's role as spy and declaring to her former patient: "you who possess the bravery of a hero, – can you not admire the valour of a heroine?" (ch. 51, 14:354).

George Whyte-Melville, author of *The Interpreter: A Tale of the War* (1858), bears yet another relationship to journalism: unlike any other Crimean War novelist I know of, Whyte-Melville served in the war, enlisting as a volunteer major in the Turkish cavalry. As a result, his novel offers a fair amount of "travel-guide" description common to the news reports and memoirs discussed in chapter 1; it also displays some of the horror of war, including accounts of civilian casualties, of beaten women and murdered babies.[8] Yet the work's first-person protagonist, Vere Egerton, is hardly a war hero. Rather, as his position of interpreter suggests, he is more remarkable for his powers of sympathetic understanding – and an attendant "womanly nature" (303).

Nevertheless, Vere (like Whyte-Melville and Reynolds) seems to spend much of the novel searching for heroes to worship – a somewhat fruitless search, calling to mind Fred Dallas's comment: "I am sorry to hear poor Whyte-Melville is coming out; he would be much better writing songs at home."[9] As in Reynolds's work, Omar Pasha initially appears a promising figure: the novel opens with Vere's romantic childhood encounter with the young Croat who was to become the famous general. But both the war and his place in the Turkish army stymie Omar's efforts, denying him the greatness he might have achieved. As Vere remarks, "As he rode away in his long dark overcoat and crimson fez, I looked after his manly, nervous figure, and thought to myself what a commander would that have been in any other service in the world" (209). So Vere continues his hunt, as chapter after chapter lines up the usual suspects as candidates for the honored role, privates and officers alike, but all unnamed and soon forgotten. In fact, Vere's dog offers the novel's best model of bravery: in a failed attack on the Redan, Vere merely looks on, while the aptly named Bold meets a hero's death. Still, the book does not entirely escape the pressures of formulaic conceptions: its one conventional "hero-plot" shows its scheming and socially ambitious villain being "converted" by the war:

It was indeed Ropsley, – Ropsley the Guardsman – Ropsley the dandy, but how altered! The attenuated *roué* of former days had grown large and muscular, his face was brown and healthy, his forehead frank and open, the clear grey eye was brighter and quicker than it used to be; it had caught the ready, eager glance of those who look death habitually in the face, but had lost much of the cruel, calculating, leaden expression I remembered so well. (226–27)

Something of the problem of heroism can be gleaned from Whyte-Melville's attempts to come to grips with the significance of the charge of the Light Brigade (about which I will say much more in chapter 3). He reverts to the events of the charge twice, and at length. The subject first arises in Constantinople, where

[t]wo cavalry officers, both wounded on the fatal day, recapitulate once more the *pros* and *cons* of the immortal charge at Balaklava – a question that has been vexed and argued till the very actors themselves in that most brilliant of disasters scarcely know how they got in, and still less how they ever got *out*. Though struck down by the same shell, within ten yards of one another, each takes a diametrically opposite view of the whole transaction. (231)

But Whyte-Melville can't accept such inconclusiveness, and when Vere reaches the "classic ground" of the charge, he imaginatively reenacts the event (beginning with the necessary quotations from Tennyson's ballad).

Still, at the end of this reenactment, even as Vere exults in his eulogy of the dead ("Weep, England, for thy chivalry! mourn and wring thy hands for that disastrous day; but smile with pride through thy tears, thrill with exultation in thy sorrow, to think of the sons thou canst boast"), the already converted Ropsley cuts in with the deflating remark, "That was a stupid business" (255).

The topic of the endangered status of the heroic addressed by both Reynolds and Whyte-Melville had been of concern at least since 1840, when Carlyle had presented the influential series of lectures that would become *On Heroes, Hero-Worship and the Heroic in History*. In the novels of the day, the debate blended with contemporary debates about the demise of epic and the contest between novels of plot and those of character, between masculine adventure fiction (also called *romance*) and the more inwardly driven (and, typically, more feminine) realist domestic novel. By the 1850s, realism, with its concern for the quotidian and the psychological, was increasingly dominant in fiction, and the novel had become "feminized," with a corresponding restriction of its sense of the possibilities for heroism.

But the war novel would seem to offer an opportunity for change, for a shift towards action and plot. Ernest Baker argued in the 1930s (no doubt recalling the First World War, too) that the Crimean War altered the domestic focus:

It is not straining the point to trace some of the most striking contrasts between the literature before and after the eighteen-fifties to the immense moral force of this event. The note of strenuousness, the sense of struggle, the feeling of the deep significance of action, are conspicuous by their absence from the prose and poetry of the earlier period.[10]

Baker's comments fail to acknowledge the degree to which the Crimean War was different from the wars that had preceded it – and that the perception of the war at home was different. Nevertheless, he gestures towards a prominent literary offspring of the war: the movement that came to be known as "muscular Christianity," and the related burgeoning of boys' adventure stories. The tag was coined in reference to Charles Kingsley's *Two Years Ago* (1857), a novel set in England during the Crimean War, and the war novels of both Charles and Henry Kingsley explore heroism in response to pressures exerted upon the concept of "manliness" during the war years.

But while Carlyle's hero, "with his free force direct out of God's own hand," promised to enkindle the "common languid Times, with their unbelief, distress, [and] perplexity," *Omar: A Tale of the War* suggests the possibility of aid from a different source: not a Great Man, but a Great Woman.[11] Margaret Oliphant linked the development of the sensation novel to the after-effects of a decade of war (both the Crimean War and the Indian "Mutiny" of 1857): "it is only natural that art and literature should, in an age which has turned out to be one of events, attempt a kindred depth of effect and shock of incident."[12] She thus pushes together two conflicts that had struck William Howard Russell as exerting very different generic demands, as I argued in chapter 1. But as what follows should indicate – and as my comments on Rose Prendergast's plot-line in Russell's novel and my reading of Caroline Volmar's role in *Omar* hint – a shift of focus from the male to the female protagonist can allow the Crimean War to be represented sensationally. E. S. Dallas described how "sensation" derives not just from any action but specifically from the action of women: "The life of women cannot well be described as a life of action. When women are thus put forward to lead the action of a plot, they must be urged into a false position . . . This is what is called sensation."[13]

The great female sensation of the war was Florence Nightingale. In *Cassandra*, written a few years before the war, she had bewailed the opportunities for female action: "What else is conventional life? *Passivity* when we want to be active."[14] Nightingale lamented the ensuing waste of moral energy: "Why cannot we *make use* of the noble rising heroisms of our own day, instead of leaving them to rust?"[15] The Crimean War had promised to regenerate masculine chivalry: G. A. Lawrence described how "Europe woke up, like a giant refreshed, from the slumber of a forty years' peace, and took down disused weapons from the wall and donned a rusty armour."[16] But it produced as its most memorable figure Nightingale herself – instead of a soldier-knight, a woman carrying a lamp rather than a shield, a lancet rather than a lance. As a poem published in *Punch* in 1855 put it, while "hero-worship's hungry haste" may have briefly made "meanest idols, tawdriest shrines" out of the likes of the Earl of Cardigan (who led the benighted charge of the Light Brigade), the people's "noble instincts" soon recognized in Nightingale – "a young and saintly volunteer" – a more suitable focus for their adoration.[17] "The lady with the lamp" thus provided novelists with a model of what "heroic womanhood" (as Longfellow called it in "Santa Filomena") might look like when liberated from the bonds of conventional life.

So it is in their portrayals of the hero – especially in relation to gender, as I have been intimating – that the novels of the war years most reflect the experiences of the war. Charles and Henry Kingsley's tales of boyish adventure attempt to redefine male heroism by engaging relatively directly with events of the war. But for all the brothers' insistence on a version of manliness allowing room for aggression ("muscular"), the Kingsleys' heroes end up surprisingly domesticated ("Christian"). Similarly, their novels about the war have a tendency to become novels about the state of things at home in England. Conversely, novels about the state of things at home can turn out to be about the war. Elizabeth Gaskell's *North and South* links the apparently masculine world of the Kingsleys' fiction to the purportedly feminine world of the domestic novel. While occluding the foreign conflict raging as it was being composed, it takes advantage of aspects of that conflict to tell its story of the "civil wars" in England. Most significantly, Gaskell's heroine, Margaret Hale, demonstrates the literary impact of Florence Nightingale on conceptions of heroic womanhood. Indeed "Heroinism" – and its connection to Nightingale's role in the war – also concerns Elizabeth Barrett Browning in her epic novel-in-verse from the period, *Aurora Leigh* (1856). Gaskell and Barrett Browning had different reservations about Nightingale. But for both, the traditional shape of the domestic novel had to be expanded to accommodate the new model of heroism she offered. Thus as the war consolidated changing ideas of the heroic, novelists reshaped existing subgenres (the Condition-of-England novel, the domestic novel) and developed new subgenres (the fiction of muscular Christianity, sensation fiction) to accommodate the changes.

I EASTWARD HO?: THE KINGSLEYS AND HEROIC MANLINESS

Westward Ho!

Perhaps the most thorough "war novel" about the Crimean campaign is among its earlier literary fruits: Charles Kingsley's *Westward Ho!* (1855). Kingsley's apparent embrace of the form may reflect the fact that the book was mostly composed before criticism of the war became fashionable (he began it in the spring of 1854, as hostilities were commencing, and had finished writing by Christmas). Nevertheless, he seemed nervous about his work's generic status, suggesting that his subject was "fit rather to have been sung than said, and to have been proclaimed to all true English hearts, not as a novel, but as an epic."[18] This, however, was impossible under current historical conditions; as Kingsley had speculated in reviewing Arnold's *Poems* (1853) – the volume to which the famous preface declaring the demise of epic poetry was attached – "the emasculating tendencies of our Mammonism" may well "have abolished martial song."[19] Still, in its attempts faithfully to novelize epic, *Westward Ho!* also attempted to reinvigorate British manhood.

Thus *Westward Ho!* has little to do with the realistic fare that shapes our sense of the Victorian novel (such as the socially conscious books that had made Kingsley famous: *Alton Locke* [1850] and *Yeast* [1851]), belonging rather to the category of romance. With its tale of Elizabethan heroics against the Spanish at home, in Ireland, and in the New World, it shares the historical bent of Kingsley's *Hypatia* (1853). But this book was composed for the present: copies were sent to the troops in the East, and the story was easily translated into contemporary terms by seeing Spain as Russia and the Irish and/or American Indians as the Turks. Kingsley's correspondence shows his awareness of this fact, as do comments in the novel; indeed the phrase "Eastward Ho!" rings through the period.[20] And Kingsley thought of his work as propaganda, as a tale that would "make others fight."[21] The novel is rabidly anti-Catholic and jingoist – its very title, complete with colonizing imperative and exclamation point, demonstrates its author's desire to motivate his readers through the promise of action and excitement.[22] John Peck, in an excellent reading of the book, describes *Westward Ho!*'s unusual engagement with war and the real needs of warriors, the mentality of fighting, and both the poetics and the economic underpinnings of nationalism and imperialism.[23] Kingsley would probably have agreed; he himself wrote of it as "a most ruthless bloodthirsty book . . . (just what the times want, I think)."[24]

The frontispiece in my turn of the century edition of *Westward Ho!* uses as its epigraph, "If I have a boy's age, sir, I have a man's fist."[25] The novel as a whole also foregrounds a vision of boyishness that drives its conception of manliness. In fact, one quality shared by almost all of the novels that treat the war directly is that they ask the question: what will make a boy into a man? While not exactly *Bildungsromane*, they concern themselves with education: many uphold the importance of good socialization through proper schooling. So *Westward Ho!* begins with its hero's schooldays, and in Henry Kingsley's *Ravenshoe* (1862), we are told that our protagonist "had not been drilled into habits of application early enough . . . It is possible that Eton in one way, or Rugby in another, might have done for him what Shrewsbury certainly did not."[26] But when *Ravenshoe* describes a "happy, innocent schoolboy day" of idyllic romping through the Turkish countryside (331), it becomes clear that the focus is on the education schoolboys receive from each other, not on matters of the classroom. And many of these war novels were written not just about but also for boys, with their tales of adventure in which combat and play take turns. Tellingly, G. A. Henty, the Franklin W. Dixon of the Victorian era (he wrote countless tales of adventure featuring brave English lads in exciting foreign realms), began his career in this war. As a young man, he served in the hospital commissariat in the Crimea and sent home letters that were published regularly in the *Morning Advertiser*. His experiences were later translated into the popular boy's novel, *Jack Archer, Or, The Fall of Sebastopol* (1883).

Thus these books present boyhood (not childhood, but scampering, mischievous, male boyhood) as a blessed and useful state – also a core tenet of the core text of the muscular Christian movement: Thomas Hughes's *Tom Brown's Schooldays* (1857). Hughes's novel's notorious Ode to Fighting declares its position on violence in the context of the war with Russia and the need to end the forty years' peace: "From the cradle to the grave, fighting, rightly understood, is the business, the real, highest, honestest business of every son of man ... I am dead against crying peace when there is no peace, and isn't meant to be."[27] As he was finishing *Westward Ho!*, Charles Kingsley had written to his good friend Hughes to anticipate a rabbit hunt with the schoolboy enthusiasm born (or reborn) of the Crimean War: he wishes the rabbits Russians and himself in the Crimea, "tin-pot on head and musket in hand! – oh for one hour's skirmishing in those Inkerman ravines ... !"[28] Between composing his two war novels, Kingsley wrote *The Heroes; or, Greek Fairy Tales for My Children* (1856), an indication of his growing interest in literature for children. Reflecting his fascination with events in the East, this book claims that the highest form of patriotism is such as sends young men "out to the war, leaving wealth, and comfort ... to face hunger and thirst, and wounds and death, that they might fight for their country and their Queen."[29]

So *Westward Ho!* wants to educate a race of warriors in manliness. It centers on the stalwart figure of its hero, Amyas Leigh, "a symbol, though he knows it not, of brave young England longing to wing its way out of its island prison, to discover and to traffic, to colonize and to civilize, until no wind can sweep the earth which does not bear the echoes of an English voice" (1:18). As this description suggests, one thing that makes the novel unusual for the period is its interest in "representative men" rather than individuals: characters serve as types, and the novel itself works almost as allegorically as Spenser's *Faerie Queene*, to which it repeatedly refers (Spenser figures as an aid to Sir Walter Raleigh and Elizabethan imperialist ambitions, making clear the connections between epic and empire). As Peck recognizes, this tendency contributes to the book's political effect: *Westward Ho!* appears to resist the trend in realistic Victorian novels of addressing the political by reducing it to the personal.[30] Amyas functions as a model of manliness: "his training had been that of the old Persians, 'to speak the truth and to draw the bow'" – and to believe "it to be the finest thing in the world to be a gentleman" (I:14). His "character" is to be an agent of the plot: a true man of action, "he never thought about thinking, or felt about feeling" (I:15). Asked how Amyas would respond to hearing that a woman was in trouble, a friend clarifies: "Say? He'd do. He isn't one for talking" (II:215).

Amyas's conception of action is essentially forceful. G. A. Lawrence, writing his own Crimean War novel, *Sword and Gown* (1859), invoked him as a model of one version of English manhood (curiously, Lawrence sees George Eliot's Adam Bede as the same type in a realistic mode[31]):

> There is a heavy run just now against the "physical force" doctrine. It seems to me that some of its opponents are somewhat hypocritical . . . It is true that there are some writers, not the weakest, who still cling to the old-fashioned mould. Putting Lancelot and Amyas Leigh out of the question, I think I would have sooner have "stood up" to most heroes of romance than to sturdy Adam Bede . . . It is perfectly true, that to thrash a prize-fighter unnecessarily, is not a virtuous or glorious action; but I contend that the *capability* of doing so is an admirable and enviable attribute. There are grades of physical as well as moral perfection; and, after all, the same Hand created both.[32]

But in *Westward Ho!*, Kingsley makes it quite clear that simple force is not enough: one must be ready to be violent. W. E. Aytoun recorded in *Blackwood's* how "lust for blood and plunder, are expressed in almost every page."[33] Even Frank Leigh (who stands for the scholarly and courtly man in contrast to his brother's physicality) recognizes that "there is nothing more noble and blessed than to fight in behalf of those whom we love" – an abstract statement of morals rendered more substantial by Amyas when he expresses his satisfaction at beheading a Frenchman for his Queen (I:156–57). To be a good leader, one must be willing to kill; one must know "when to hang a man" (II:157). Compare such claims to those of Kingsley's pamphlet "Brave Words to Brave Soldiers and Sailors," written early in 1855 to send to the troops in the East as a counterweight to what he saw as the dispiriting reports about the war being published in *The Times* and elsewhere. There Kingsley argues against too pacific an understanding of Christianity: "For the Lord Jesus Christ is not only the *Prince of Peace*; He is the *Prince of War* too."[34] To Hughes, he attributed the new concerns addressed by *Westward Ho!* to the fact that the war had changed his conception of progress: "if I have held back from the Socialist Movement [the subject of his earlier Condition-of-England novels], it has been because I have seen that the world was not going to be set right in any such rose-pink way, excellent as it is, and that there are heavy arrears of *destruction* to be made up, before *construction* can even begin."[35]

In championing violence-injected manliness, *Westward Ho!* initially marginalizes its female characters. One of its moral arbiters, Sir Richard Grenville, warns Amyas against "that silly fashion of the French and Italians, to be hanging ever at some woman's apron-string, so that no boy shall count himself a man unless he can 'vagghezziare le donne'" (1:211). Herbert Sussman has argued for the importance of a "masculine poetic" in the early Victorian period, one situating "silent heroes" "within a fictional world imagined as wholly male" – often, as in *Westward Ho!*, a world displaced in time, because "an integrated manhood can be achieved only with great difficulty, if at all, within industrial England."[36] War can create such a world. Thus in Kingsley's novel, the original love interest of the story, Rose Salterne, becomes superseded in importance by the homosocial group formed around her, a fellowship known as the "Brotherhood of the Rose," made up of loyal Englishmen (including Amyas and Frank) who have all fallen in love with Rose but refuse to compete over her. As Kingsley declares, "What breeds more close communion between subjects, than allegiance to the same Queen?" (1:285). Free from the need to pursue love, the "Brothers" channel their energies towards different – and the implication is, more nationally useful – goals.

But as elsewhere in the novel, Kingsley's apparently nationalistic intents self-destruct; Peck describes how frequently "rhetoric is undercut by immediate and practical problems"[37] – that is, by plot. Amyas's attempt to find a North-West Passage through Newfoundland fails. Moreover, the effect of the Brotherhood is that Rose is "left alone with her looking-glass," as the final words of volume 1 acknowledge (1:303). Lacking a proper English suitor, Rose elopes with the unscrupulous Spaniard Don Guzman, who whisks her off to his posting in the Americas. And while the Brotherhood embarks for the New World to "rescue" her (what they plan to do when they get her is never quite clear), the narrator calls the result a "fatal venture of mistaken chivalry" (11:315); Frank is captured, and both he and Rose are burned at the stake by the Inquisition.

This failure leaves remaining members of the Brotherhood free to resume imperialist objectives: they attempt to discover the legendary El Dorado. But the effort to escape the feminine faces new challenges when instead of the City of Gold the Brotherhood encounters a tribe of Indians led by an "Amazon" (III:40) – the lovely Ayacanora. The Indian tribe proves a "Siren" (III:97) temptation; its women divert several of Amyas's men from their (the implication is, epic) goal. While Amyas eventually leaves, thinking to resume his "work" in England (III:97), Ayacanora stows away on the galleon he captures for the passage home. Moreover, she appears – during the taking of the vessel – just in time to save Amyas's life (III:162).

Back in England, Amyas's intention to pursue Don Guzman (in a boat christened the *Vengeance*) has to be put off by the news that the Armada has set sail. The defeat of the Armada should be the central military achievement of the tale. The Elizabethans were to have served as models to the men of the present day:

> Well it was for England then, that her Tudor sovereigns had compelled every man (though they kept up no standing army) to be a trained soldier ... Well for England, in a word, that Elizabeth had pursued for thirty years a very different course from that which we have been pursuing for the last thirty, with one exception, namely, the leaving as much as possible to private enterprise.
>
> There we have copied her; would to Heaven that we had in some other matters! It is the fashion now to call her a despot; but unless every monarch is to be branded with that epithet whose power is not as circumscribed as Queen Victoria's is now, we ought rather to call her the most popular sovereign ... confess the Armada fight to have been as great a moral triumph as it was a political one; and (now that our late boasting is a little silenced by Crimean disasters) enquire whether we have not something to learn from those old Tudor times, as to how to choose officials, how to train a people, and how to defend a country. (III:258–59)

But such modeling repeatedly fails. Kingsley's sense of the disjunction between past and present appears in his belief that he must represent the victory over the Armada via quotations from historical sources; modern English, the intimation is, has been too damaged by having to shout above the drone of industry to sing this song: "It is a twelve days' epic, worthy ... not of dull prose, but of the thunder-roll of Homer's verse; but having to tell it, I must do my best, rather using, where I can, the words of contemporary authors than my own" (III:304). This rhetorical method drains the narrative of the English victory of drama. Moreover, past glories have become infiltrated by present "disasters" which, by the time the final sections of the book were written, had already become apparent, as the passage above indicates. Kingsley even goes so far as to use the anticlimax of the Elizabethan military victory to imply an excuse for the Crimean debacle:

> The Armada was defeated, and England saved. But such great undertakings rarely end in one grand melodramatic explosion of fireworks . . . [T]he game was played out, and the end was come, as the end of such matters generally comes, by gradual decay, petty disaster, and mistake; till the snow mountain, instead of being blown tragically and heroically to atoms, melts helplessly and pitilessly away. (III:332)

His description resonates prophetically with the end of the Crimean War, which happened months after the mixed "victory" at Sebastopol, where the English suffered humiliating defeat even as the French dealt the Russians their deathblow. After all, the metaphorical snow mountain more aptly describes the Russian Empire than the Spanish.

And like so much Victorian fiction, the novel ends not with the political (victory over the Spanish), but with the personal (Amyas's quest to seek out and kill Don Guzman): following the Armada's defeat, the *Vengeance* quite literally changes tack. Here, once again, Kingsley's plotting undercuts his rhetoric of militant masculinity. A character seems to predict the disastrousness of this quest by describing it in terms that Kingsley must have known to resonate with the Crimean endeavor: "Eastward-ho never brought us luck," he laments (III:346). While Amyas eventually wreaks revenge on Don Guzman, he does so not through honorable hand-to-hand combat, either on the battlefield or in a duel, but rather by driving the Spaniard's ship of 500 men on to the rocks, so causing all to drown (and this in the wake of English memories of the disastrous hurricane of November 1854 in Balaklava Harbor, in which the *Prince* was lost). Furthermore, his obsessive desire for revenge is portrayed with some ambivalence; as Peck notes, the book is "almost cynical in its understanding of the unbalanced warlike temperament of a character like Amyas."[38] The narrator describes how Amyas "had entered into the darkness in which every man walks who hates his brother" (III:246); Amyas himself acknowledges to his mother, "I am mad at heart . . . There's a fire burning me up, night and day, and nothing but Spanish blood will put it out" (III:272). The naval chase leading to the shipwreck reads like a cross between Frankenstein's final pursuit of his monster and the voyage of the Ancient Mariner. Amyas has been crazed by his emotion: "You are not yourself," one crew-member declares, to which he responds, "Do you believe . . . that men can be possessed by devils?" (III:345). During a lull, he must stand by passively, as he watches his enemy through the fog. When the wind rises again, Amyas announces that his prey is finally "[s]afe as a fox in a trap. Satan himself cannot take him from us." But just as he reaches his goal, a gust sends the Spaniard's vessel crashing against the rocks. Amyas is devastated: "'Shame,' cried

Amyas, hurling his sword far into the sea, 'to lose my right, my right! when it was in my very grasp!' " (III:351). The sword of honor proves useless as a tool of vengeance.

The novel's extraordinary conclusion underscores the unheroic manner of Don Guzman's defeat: struck by the same bolt of lightning that kills his enemy, Amyas incurs a Rochester-like blinding. Like Charlotte Brontë, Kingsley needs this emasculating blow to unite hero and heroine.[39] Although Ayacanora is discovered to be half-English, Amyas had long refused to consider her romantically because of her tainted Spanish blood. Yet after his injury, he can no longer resist, and England's conflict with Spain resolves itself through Amyas's marriage to an Amazonian Spanish-Englishwoman. This mixture actually allows Ayacanora to take over from Amyas as the real model of imperial Britishness. When she learns of her half-English parentage, Ayacanora works to live up to it (and to Amyas), ceasing her wild "bird-song" and instead reading from the "history of the Nine Worthies" (she stumbles over the word "heroical" before it is defined for her as being like Amyas) (III:263–64). But while she successfully translates her "Amazonian" aggression into a domestic register, that domesticity remains surprisingly aggressive: "You cannot escape from me now!" she "triumphantly" announces to Amyas on discovering his injury, "You cannot go to sea! You cannot turn your back upon wretched me! I have you safe now!" For all the adventuresome wandering of Kingsley's hero, Amyas ends up in "a violent flood of tears," trapped in the arms of his bride (III:371–72).

The final lines of the book prove Ayacanora's victory to be complete by the resumption of her "power of song," "bearing with it the peaceful thoughts of the blind giant to the paradise of the West, in the wake of the heroes who from that time forth sailed out to colonise another and a vaster England, to the heaven-prospered cry of Westward Ho!" (III:373). The Amazon has metamorphosed into Britannia, serving (through song) as a figurehead on the prow of imperial progress. But while the novel ends with a gesture towards future British greatness, Kingsley cannot convince us of the peace it claims to have brought to its representative Briton, whom it leaves a "blind giant." And if *Westward Ho!* can be read as a kind of *Eastward Ho!*, it also brings to mind the old proverb, "East or West, Home is best." Kingsley's – and his hero's – epic ambitions have been reduced to novelistic (albeit wide-reaching) hearth-song. Both Amyas's maimed state and Ayacanora's elevated power result from the collision of such ambitions with the hard realities of the Crimean experience. And as gender roles adjust in the aftermath of the clash, genres shift to accommodate those adjustments.

Two Years Ago

Such focus on the home front becomes more pronounced in Charles Kingsley's second attempt at a Crimean tale, *Two Years Ago*; the *British Quarterly*'s review of the novel actually opened by announcing, "Homeward Ho!"[40] If in *Westward Ho!*, Kingsley discovered how hard it was to envision Crimean epic masculinity by looking to the past, in *Two Years Ago*, he attempts to reinvigorate masculinity by relocating the Crimean experience in space. Having failed with epic, Kingsley also shifts his generic focus, returning to his Condition-of-England mode. It is to the resulting novel that the term "muscular Christianity" was first affixed – with some element of sarcasm – in the *Saturday Review*.

> We all know by this time what is the task that Mr. Kingsley has made specially his own – it is that of spreading the knowledge and fostering the love of a muscular Christianity. His ideal is a man who fears God and can walk a thousand miles in a thousand hours – who, in the language which Mr. Kingsley has made popular, breathes God's free air on God's rich earth, and at the same time can hit a woodcock, doctor a horse, and twist a poker round his fingers.[41]

The label and description suggest a manly tale of crusading adventure. But actually, the novel's relationships to both Christianity and muscularity are rather vexed. Once again, this war provides only limited possibilities for masculine heroism to flourish.

While almost contemporary in its setting, *Two Years Ago* – like *Westward Ho!* – wants to define a historical moment through consideration of the heroic. We can see this desire in the title (compare Carlyle's "Two Hundred and Fifty Years Ago" [1850]), but it also appears in the book's opening pages, where Kingsley draws attention to the idea of history. He begins in the present day, with an acknowledgement that the passage of time since the war has been necessary to come to grips with its significance: "Two years ago, while pestilence was hovering over us and ours; while the battle-roar was ringing in our ears; who had time to think, to ask what all that meant; to seek for the deep lesson which we knew must lie beneath . . . But now the storm has lulled once more."[42] Taking its cue from a recital of some lines from "The Lady of Shalott" brought to mind by the landscape before the speakers, the discussion (between the artist Claude Mellot and the dilettantish American Stangrave, hero of a secondary plot-line) then turns to changes in the nature of English heroism:

> There, upon the little island, are the castle ruins, now converted into a useful bone-mill. "And the lady? – is that she?"

It was only the miller's daughter, fresh from a boarding-school, gardening in a broad straw-hat.

"At least," said Claude, "she is tending far prettier flowers than ever the lady saw; while the lady herself, instead of weaving and dreaming, is reading Miss Yonge's novels, and becoming all the wiser thereby, and teaching poor children in Hemmelford National School."

"And where is her fairy knight," asked Stangrave, "whom one half hopes to see riding down from that grand old house which sulks there above among the beech-woods, as if frowning on all the change and civilisation below?"

"You do old Sidricstone injustice. Vieuxbois descends from thence, now-a-days, to lecture at mechanics' institutes, instead of the fairy knight, toiling along in this blazing June weather, sweating in burning metal, like poor Perillus in his own bull."

"Then the fairy knight is extinct in England?" asked Stangrave, smiling.

"No man less; only he . . . has found a wide-awake cooler than an iron kettle, and travels by rail when he is at home: and when he was in the Crimea, rode a shaggy pony, and smoked Cavendish all through the battle of Inkermann."

"He showed himself the old Sir Lancelot there," said Stangrave.

"He did. Wherefore the lady married him when the guards came home; and he will breed prize pigs; and sit at the board of Guardians; and take in the *Times*; clothed, and in his right mind; for the old Berserk spirit is gone out of him; and he is become respectable, in a respectable age, and is nevertheless just as brave a fellow as ever." (1:18–19)

With its many "signs of the times" – including, for that matter, *The Times* newspaper – the passage demonstrates the degree to which the novel situates its conception of heroism historically.

Also among these signs is the mention of the novels of "Miss Yonge," which have converted the lady dreamer of poetry into a useful member of society. The allusion suggests how involved novels were in negotiating the broader cultural interplay between gender and models of heroism. As this passage shows, Kingsley was a professed admirer of Charlotte Yonge's work, which espouses a rather un-muscular type of Christianity, and, indeed, of manliness. Remarkably, *The Heir of Redclyffe* (1853) – Yonge's morality tale about the need for controlling masculine temper – was the most-requested novel among officers in the hospitals in the Crimea. Her *Heartsease* (1855) was the last book read by Lord Raglan before his death.[43] And while *The Young Step-mother* (1861), which Yonge began to write as the war was ending, does send the heroine's troublingly timid and wavering stepson Gilbert to the Crimea, he learns only a false form of courage from his participation in the charge of the Light Brigade (a rite of passage for heroes of the war novels): "Albinia [the heroine of the book's title] understood whence came Gilbert's heroism. He had charged at first, as he had hunted with Maurice, because there was no doing otherwise, and in the critical moment the warm heart had done the rest, and equalled constitutional courage."[44] Real manliness turns out to be spiritual rather than martial and comes to Gilbert only through suffering his final illness at Scutari.

Kingsley's own riff on modern heroism suggests that he would like to think positively about the effects of the war on English manhood. Yet to call his former knight turned pig-breeder "just as brave a fellow as ever" feels forced, to say the least. Nevertheless, *Two Years Ago* seems written to preserve the memory and foster the future of a more active, "muscular" brand of heroics. The chivalric tenor of its opening, typical of the art of the mid-1850s (including *Westward Ho!*, which offers extensive reflection on the chivalry of the Elizabethans), demonstrates the pressure felt during the period to prove that true heroism had not been rendered "extinct" by the long peace (or in this case, by the return to peace).[45] *Two Years Ago* addresses notions of chivalry through Stangrave's plot. A Southerner, Stangrave comes to realize his quest in life (Abolition) through the teachings of the object of his love: Marie, a former slave passing as Italian. Initially, Marie laments Stangrave's dandyish languor in Carlylean terms: "Christ was of old the model and Sir Galahad the hero. Now the one is exchanged for Goethe, and the other for Wilhelm Meister" (1:181). Over the course of the novel, though, Stangrave learns that for life to have worth, one must have a crusade. He discovers his goal during a visit to Ehrenbreitstein, the German castle that bequeathed its name to the influential book *The Broadstone of Honour* (1822), recognized by Mark Girouard as central to the chivalric craze in Victorian England.[46] The Crimean connection appears in the language of Stangrave's conversion to the cause:

Art? What if the most necessary human art, next to the art of agriculture, be, after all, the art of war? It has been so in all ages. What if I have been befooled – what if all the Anglo-Saxon world has been befooled, by forty years of peace? We have forgotten that the history of the world has been as yet written in blood; that the story of the human race is the story of its heroes and its martyrs – the slayers and the slain. Is it not becoming such once more in Europe now? (11:206)

And the realization reaches its climax just as several other characters in the novel are departing for the Crimea.

But for all that Stangrave's account of the art of war suggests the fervor of muscular Christianity, Kingsley's novel is rather harder to pin down;

as in *Westward Ho!*, plot and rhetoric undermine each other. *Two Years Ago* tells a convoluted tale of the war years. Its primary hero, Tom Thurnall, a young, adventurous, and ungodly doctor, is washed ashore on the Cornish coast after a shipwreck.[47] The schoolmistress of the town, Grace Harvey, saves him from the waves. But in the confusion of the shipwreck, Tom loses the moneybelt in which he had carried the rewards of difficult years spent gold-prospecting in Australia. Tom believes that Grace has stolen the belt; this confusion provides the tension in the love affair that must be resolved before hero and heroine can unite. First, though, they fall in love over joint nursing during a cholera epidemic at home – and Grace follows Tom out to the Crimea in order to attempt to return his belt (which she finally extracts from her mother, the real thief).

Compared with Amyas Leigh, Tom seems neither particularly muscular nor particularly Christian. Rather, he is most notable for a surprising desire to dominate others through knowledge:

he was one of those men with whom the possession of power, sought at first from self-interest, has become a passion, a species of sporting, which he must follow for its own sake. To whomsoever he met he must needs apply the moral stethoscope; sound him, lungs, heart, and liver; put his tissues under the microscope, and try conclusions on him to the uttermost. They might be useful hereafter; for knowledge was power. (1:121)

Time and time again, the narrator reminds us of Tom's will to power. As this passage suggests, Kingsley is suspicious of this aspect of his hero's personality, which he sees as an offshoot of his godlessness, implying as it does Tom's desire to assume a godlike perspective. Yet Tom's knowledge saves many, and not just villagers dying of cholera. He practically blackmails several unattractive characters, including the inept local pharmacist and a drunken squire, into reforming themselves (the squire is saved by joining the militia). For all his ability in a fight, Tom represents a "modern man": his power comes from intelligence rather than muscle. But where he and Amyas are alike is in their "restless, alienated energy" (Peck's words for the new kind of aggression to emerge in the period[48]). And Tom's particular form of aggression renders him troublingly unsympathetic. So, for example, just after having saved Grace from an attack by the squire, he himself attempts to embrace her, adding emotional blackmail to the physical assault: "I shall keep you in pawn for my belt. Till that at least is restored, you are in my power, Grace!" (1:319). Amyas Leigh would never have treated a woman thus.

The most interesting version of the blackmailing reform plot in *Two Years Ago* concerns a case of hidden identity and insanity (a motif that will be repeated in *Ravenshoe*). John Briggs began life as the rather bullied (by Tom) apprentice to Tom's father, also a doctor, but decided to run away to pursue a career as a poet under the aristocratic-sounding name of Elsley Vavasour. In this incarnation, he marries a daughter of a noble house, to whom he proves to be an inadequate husband: selfish, jealous, and too much the demon of moods easily brought on by poor reviews or a flagging muse. Elsley is the dreamer to Tom's doer. He writes clearly spasmodic volumes of poetry like *The Soul's Agonies*; Tom, in contrast, believes that feelings are "like chemicals, the more you analyse them, the worse they smell" (1:38). (Although his use of a simile here again shows his distance from Amyas, who would never have reflected at all – much less in metaphor – on his preference for action over feeling: it was stated of him.) But Kingsley does not endorse Tom's opinion; it prevents Tom from recognizing his own feelings for Grace until he has almost lost her. And Elsley's position as blackmailed elicits readerly sympathy. All-in-all the text is far less secure in its message than it tries to be.

Indeed, the novel seems to be inching towards sensation fiction with this subplot. And in a way, to say this is to say that it is inching away from the budding manliness of boys' adventure stories. As I have suggested, sensation fiction can be seen as the female correlative of masculine romance, allowing women an unrealistic access to the arena of action. But in Kingsley's novels (and in his brother's work, too), the circumscribed actors are male rather than female, and their deeds are limited in spite of the backdrop of a war that one might think would have provided an outlet for action. The Kingsleys' novels thus partake both of some of the externalized psychological insight of sensation fiction and of the rather thoughtless muscularity of boys' adventure tales. And this kind of instability cannot be divorced from the weirdness of the Crimean background to the stories.

To put the matter simply, the problem in *Two Years Ago* is that Tom isn't fighting in the war. Nor is he doctoring there. Grace, whom we first encountered in full Nightingale-mode (as a "saint and a heroine" [1:19]) caring for Tom's sick father in the present-day frame narrative of the novel, works as a nurse at Scutari and Balaklava.[49] But Tom's war years are occupied less stereotypically. Rather than participating in the charge of the Light Brigade, Tom goes to the East to serve underground as a spy – thus potentially putting his blackmailing skills to good patriotic use. But the novel undermines even this intellectualized vision of a Crimean heroic: Tom spends much of the war in prison – and not a Russian prison at that; early on, he is mistakenly captured by "a boorish villain of a khan [i.e., an ally], on a drunken suspicion" (II:328). The frustration of such captivity, and not the discovery of honor and glory in war (or, for that matter, of "Grace," although her memory does help), brings him religious conviction. And as the critic of the *Saturday Review* puts it, "we should have preferred his coming into the right path by a more ordinary channel."[50]

Moreover, *Two Years Ago*'s Crimean episodes are reported "offstage" rather than shown. The Crimea stands in the novel as a field of honor for which characters must and do depart in order to prove their worth. Yet we see nothing of what happens there, and the heroism of soldiers is replaced by that of doctors and nurses fighting against the cholera, not in Scutari but on the Cornish coast. So instead of offering an opportunity for manly action, the background of war serves to highlight the difficulties of achieving what Sussman calls an "integrated manhood" in the period. In contrast, the English foreground works to transpose the idea of a heroism that was sadly lacking in the Crimean experience back on to native ground. It is a process that we shall see echoed in another Condition-of-England novel, *North and South*.

Ravenshoe

In Henry Kingsley's *Ravenshoe*, we finally encounter a hero who spends significant time in the Crimea under our eyes. Once again, the war promises to offer an arena of action in which "integrated manhood," threatened by the conditions of modernity, can be achieved. Yet once again, the process fails, as the hero emerges from the war having this time demonstrated his muscle but lost his mind.

Madness characterizes the plot of the novel, too, which models social upheaval through disruptions of patrilineal inheritance. Charles Ravenshoe is the younger son of an ancient Catholic family; he, however, has been raised Protestant to fulfill the deathbed wishes of his Anglican mother. Afraid that Cuthbert, the Catholic and sickly older Ravenshoe brother, will die young (thus leaving the house and name in Charles's Protestant hands), the family priest reveals information gained in the confessional: that the gamekeeper's Irish Catholic wife (the wet-nurse) had in fact exchanged Charles as an infant with her own son; the real scion of the house of Ravenshoe is thus not Charles but his childhood companion and servant, William Horton, the gamekeeper's boy. Devastated by the news, Charles flees and assumes a false identity as the groomsman to a young swell. When this swell departs for the Crimea, Charles enlists as well. Only later is it revealed that the gamekeeper had in fact been grandfather-Ravenshoe's older half-brother, and thus a legitimate son of the family, born under the auspices of an official but secret marriage. So Charles belongs to the elder branch of the Ravenhoes (while both Cuthbert and William belong to the younger branch), making him the true heir to Ravenshoe.

This convoluted plot obviously speaks to the class-consciousness of a period in which aristocratic hold over landed estates was beginning to sway and its hold over the army was being brought into question. In 1924, Michael Sadlier called Henry Kingsley "the prose-laureate of wasted beauty," arguing that "No writer of the mid-Victorian age had so delicate a sympathy for splendour in decay, so sensitive an admiration for the forlorn present of a noble past."[51] Indeed, the novel has rightly been compared to another famous tale of post-war disintegration and nostalgia: Evelyn Waugh's *Brideshead Revisited* (1945). Like *Brideshead*, *Ravenshoe* tells the story of a passing way of life by describing the danger posed to a great Catholic family: the novel threatens to expose that Charles Ravenshoe, heir to a "proud old name" and a "noble old house, the pride of the west country . . . was now just this – a peasant, an impostor" (168–69). While the "imposter" turns out to have been the real thing all along, this revelation does not occur until Charles has come to some unsettling realizations about the shifting nature of class identity. Charles's initial discovery of his false position unbalances him. He laments to the narrator:

I have known what very few men have known, and lived – despair; but perhaps the most terrible agony for a time was the feeling of a *loss of identity* – that I was not myself; that my whole existence from babyhood had been a lie. This at times, at times only, mind you, washed away from me the only spar to which I could cling – the feeling that I was a gentleman. (168)

But even his status as "gentleman" fails to hold him out of the abyss into which he is falling. When, having lost all sense of self, Charles changes his name to Horton and disguises himself as a groomsman, the narrator calls the move a suicide (185).

Enter the war. Battle promises to resurrect Charles by negating the impact of class-consciousness; the chapter in which we first see him in the Crimea is entitled, "In which Charles Comes to Life Again" (ch. LI). War is, after all (through its association with death) a great leveler – especially this war, in which private men were eulogized in an unprecedented fashion even as the glories of the officer class were rendered suspect. Of Charles's early days as an enlisted man, we are told: "In all his troubles this was the happiest time he had, for he had got rid of the feeling that he was a disgraced man. If he must wear a livery, he would wear the Queen's; there was no disgrace in that. He was a soldier, and he would be a hero" (302). And on the battlefield, Charles proves his essentially "gentlemanly" nature. Thus Kingsley seems to imply analogically that the war will cure the general modern ailment and offer a field on which the honor of England will be regained. For example, the account of Charles's ex-master's participation in the charge of the Light Brigade makes him sound a lot like one of Tennyson's famous six hundred:

But everywhere all the day, where the shot screamed loudest, where the shell fell thickest, with his shako gone, with his ambrosial curls tangled with blood, with his splendid gaudy fripperies soiled with dust and sweat, was Hornby, the dandy, the fop, the dicer; doing the work of ten, carrying out the wounded in his arms, encouraging the dying, cheering on the living. (352)

This is just the kind of transformation that the war was meant to enable.

Yet Charles is resurrected not as himself but as someone else, under a third name: he enlists not as Horton but as "Simpson." And if we expect war to provide a panacea for our hero, the medicine proves to be rather ineffective. For one thing, it fails on a narrative level to restore order to the plot. Charles's relatives, who have tracked him to the Crimea in an attempt to bring him back and reinstate him in what has turned out to be his rightful position, cannot find him in the confusions, bureaucratic and otherwise, of the war (they are told he is dead [326]). And all the possible recognition scenes on the battlefield – a place where men of very different social backgrounds are bound to cross paths, especially in novels – do not produce an actual discovery. Back in England, an advertisement in *The Times*, the great public organ of the war years, does not unearth the marriage certificate that would prove Charles's legitimacy. Meanwhile everyone ignores the one person who could have led his friends to Charles – a poor bootblack whom Charles had befriended. The fact that the bootblack appears cut and pasted from a novel by Dickens emphasizes the narrative oddness of all these failures in Dickensian Providential plotting.

More surprisingly, although he never fought in a war, Henry Kingsley seems attuned to some of the stresses of wartime life; the war-cure also has bad side effects. Thus while Charles, too, finds stereotypical glory in the charge of the Light Brigade (355), there are moments when Kingsley focuses rather on the psychological costs of war. The narrator examines Charles's mental state amidst the depression of barracks-life:

Were there no other dreams? No. No dreams but ever-present reality. A dull, aching regret for a past forever gone. A heavy, deadly grief, lost for a time among the woods of Devna, but come back to him now amidst the cold, and the squalor, and the sickness of Balaclava. A brooding over missed opportunities, and the things that might have been. Sometimes a tangled, puzzled train of thought, as to how much of this ghastly misery was his own fault, and how much accident. And above all, a growing desire for death, unknown before. (351)

While narrating the Battle of the Alma, in a lovely detail, Kingsley explains how the mind can respond strangely to the pressures of war:

Charles would have given ten years of his life to know what was going on on the other side of the hill. But no. There they sat, and he had to look at the back of the man before him; and at the time he came to the conclusion that the patch of grease on his right shoulder was the same shape as the map of Sweden . . . [E]ver after, when the Battle of Alma was mentioned before him, Charles at once began thinking of the map of Sweden. (334)

This permanent "patch" on the map of Charles's mind suggests the mental scars that will come home with him after the war, and it suggests how such black spots will disrupt ordinary processes of thought.

Indeed, the war leaves Charles in a state that could be described as "shell-shocked." He returns to England in if anything a worse condition than when he left:

Creeping every day across the park to see the coachman and his son. Every day getting more hopeless. All energy gone. Wit enough left to see that he was living on the charity of the cornet [an aristocrat whose life he had saved in the Crimea]. And there were some splinters in his arm which would not come away, and kept him restless. He never slept now. He hesitated when he was spoken to. Any sudden noise made him start and look wild. I will not go on with the symptoms. Things were much worse with him than we have ever seen them before. He, poor lad, began to wonder whether it would come to him to die in a hospital or –

Those cursed bridges! Why did they build such things? Who built them? The devil. To tempt ruined, desperate men, with ten thousand fiends gnawing and sawing in their deltoid muscles, night and day. Suppose he had to cross one of these by night, would he ever get to the other side? (387–88)

Kingsley's description, with its staccato rhythms and fragmented sentences, shows the fragmented, "splintered" state not only of Charles's "muscles" but also of his mind. In this landscape, both physical and mental, bridges do not connect parts of the self; rather, they endanger the very existence of that self. War has not only failed to integrate manhood, it has contributed to its collapse.

Once again, as in *Westward Ho!* and *Two Years Ago*, the cure must come on the home front, and once again, it does so in the shape of the love of a good woman: the sisterly Mary (who plays a kind of Biddy to Charles's cousin Adelaide's Estella). Yet while the story concludes with marriage to a heroine from the tradition of domestic realism, the resolution of the plot hinges upon a particularly Crimean version of the sensation-novel heroine: Charles's biological sister, Ellen, a fallen woman who had been cleansing herself of her sins by serving as a nurse in an Irish Sisterhood that had gone out to the Crimea. Ellen returns to England to reveal her knowledge of the place of the wedding of Charles's grandparents (so allowing the necessary proof to be obtained from the church register), and the suspense culminates in this declaration: "the words that we had been dying to hear for the last six month," as the narrator puts it, are "At Finchampstead, in Berkshire" (433). Thus the dénouement of this tale of manly adventure in the Crimea is produced by a marriage certificate from the home counties. And it takes two women, two marriages (past and present), and two versions of novelistic form that are associated with the feminine, to resolve the line of masculine family inheritance and the plot of the novel. As in Charles Kingsley's novels, the wartime setting helps to create heroines. But it only endangers the hero.

II FROM EAST AND WEST TO 'NORTH AND SOUTH'

The Kingsley brothers' novels engage with the war directly, even if to ambivalent effect. But one of the best-known novels of the war years deals not so much with questions of East and West as with those of North and South. While overt signs of the war may be absent from Elizabeth Gaskell's work of that title, reading it in a Crimean context demonstrates how the conflict pervaded the atmosphere of the day – and how novelists shaped their work within this medium.

Gaskell was preoccupied with thoughts of the war throughout the writing of *North and South*. Her concern was heightened by the fact that she wrote much of the novel from Lea Hurst, the Nightingale family home. As Jenny Uglow notes, the famous accounts in *The Times* of the desperate conditions at Scutari were published during Gaskell's first days there (in October of 1854); almost immediately, Florence Nightingale began organizing her departure for the East.[52] While the Nightingale family was in London helping Florence prepare, Elizabeth sat in their house, concocting her own story of a young woman's heroism. Her letters are full of references to the war, in particular to the working-class reaction to the war effort. She describes (probably to Dickens) how "Some fine-spinners in a mill at Bolton, earning their 36 shillings a week, threw up their work and enlisted last week, on hearing of the sufferings in the Crimea, for they said they could neither sleep nor eat for thinking how the soldiers there wanted help."[53] And to Parthenope Nightingale (Florence's sister), she writes that

Babies ad libitum are being christened Florence here; poor little factory babies, whose grimed stunted parents brighten up at the name, although you'd think their lives & thoughts were bound up in fluffy mills. But it's the old story "for we have all of us one human heart", & these poor unromantic fellows are made, somehow, of the same stuff as *her* heroes of the East, who turned their faces to the wall, & cried at her illness.[54]

In *North and South*, Gaskell uses the same quotation (from Wordsworth) to suggest the possibility for reconciliation in the war between masters and men.[55] And the conflation of her "unromantic" workers with the "heroes of the East" suggests that the novel can be read as an attempt to add some Crimean romance to a conflict closer to home. A letter from Parthenope to Gaskell, discussing efforts at raising money to support Florence's activities in the Crimea, bolsters this conflation. Parthenope begins by proclaiming that "Truly 'North and South' have mingled their good thoughts in this. I believe much charity to our neighbours and love of God is brought forth by the war." But her words easily lead her down a different path: "By the bye, I must say what a deal of wisdom there seems to me in 'N&S.'"[56]

John Peck argues that *North and South* provides an example of the army in its domestic capacity of maintaining civil order at home. As Peck describes it, "the army is called in [during the strike at Thornton's mill], as at Peterloo, to suppress political unrest." Indeed, he claims more broadly that "in a period when most people all but ignore the army, [Condition-of-England] works actively consider its role."[57] Although earlier novels in the category may have been unusual for their military concerns, it seems odd to claim a general lack of interest in the army during wartime. Nevertheless, while Mrs. Thornton's question, "When can the soldiers be here?" (175), punctuates the riot scene in *North and South*, it turns out that the answer to her demand is not until "five minutes too late to make this vanished mob feel the power of authority and order" (180). Instead, Margaret's act of feminine heroics (albeit accompanied by Thornton's manly reprimand, expressed in a tone inflected with "the traditional qualities of military leadership"[58]) serves to diffuse the anger of the crowd. But to read the "thread of dark-red blood" (179) that trickles down Margaret's face in the climactic riot scene of *North and South* as a replacement for the "thin red line" made famous as a symbol of heroism at Balaklava[59] is to recognize the Crimean War as a part of the condition of England – a recognition that would also be addressed by Kingsley's *Two Years Ago*, as I have argued. The Kingsleys' novels are attuned to war for its impact on masculine heroics. But Gaskell's work reveals Florence Nightingale's impact on the contemporary understanding of female heroism, as I will argue in section III. To show the full force of this impact, though, I must first demonstrate how even a domestic novel (i.e., one focused on a courtship plot and the condition of England itself rather than of Empire) written in wartime can be read as a home-front reflection on war.

While Gaskell's novel contains no obvious mention of the Crimean War, contemporary readers understood it as a product of the war years. As the *Athenaeum* declared, "We imagine that this year of the war will produce few better tales than 'North and South.'"[60] Moreover, Thomas Ballantyne noted in an article in *Blackwood's* on Lancashire strikes (which cites Gaskell's novel as evidence in arguing against unions) that the strike upon which Gaskell bases her story coincided with the onset of the war: "The Preston Strike of 1853 began a few months after Russia had crossed the Pruth." So one might contend that the war had an unspoken effect on the plot of *North and South* by virtue of its effect on trade. As Ballantyne explains, "The period chosen by the Preston operatives for their trial of strength with the masters was very unfortunate" because, in addition to the usual problems following a deficient harvest, "the Eastern question . . . assumed all at once a more complicated and unsatisfactory aspect."[61]

Ballantyne asserts that although the strike "lasted about half a year, the public mind was too much occupied with Vienna negotiations and the impending war to pay much attention to a mere quarrel between a few thousands of work-people and their employers."[62] Recall Clough's letter discussing the predominance of journalism: "Our literature, at present, is the war column in the newspaper."[63] While Gaskell's own letters of the war years contain repeated reference to the newspapers (and in particular to *The Times*),[64] it is possible to read her novel as both redressing and supporting this point. The redress lies in her telling a tale that depends heavily on those supposedly unnoticed stories in the papers about the

Preston strike.[65] But support of Clough's statement can also be seen in how the newspaper stories are transformed by Gaskell – in the signs of *The Times* found in her work. One can in fact think of the novel as an offshoot of journalism.

Since journalism was by far the most prominent literary form of the day, the few novels that portray the Crimean War tend to evince nervousness at having to compete with correspondents' accounts from the East – especially Russell's dispatches for *The Times*. As the narrator of *Ravenshoe* puts it, "I could [describe Sebastopol] capitally by buying a copy of Mr. Russell's 'War' . . . But I think you will agree with me that it is better left alone. One hardly likes to come into the field in that line after Russell" (350). The competition was perhaps particularly strong because Crimean War reportage – and Russell's in particular – is often novelistic in its methodology. I discussed in chapter 1 John Peck's proposition that "What Russell offers" – in contrast to traditional war writing, which is based on epic conventions – "is a largely static plot, where the fighting is almost incidental; what is of interest is what he sees in the details beyond the fighting. And essentially, in the manner of a realistic novelist, what Russell sees is a social problem."[66] It is suggestive to reconsider this comment in the context of a "realistic" novel that contains a non-incidental episode of fighting (and an obscure but relevant epic backdrop: Thornton first employs Mr. Hale to read Homer with him, and the question of the use-value of such reading enters when concern for the strike arises[67]). But if Russell's dispatches are novelistic, then Gaskell's novel is journalistic: in *North and South*, Gaskell melds journalism to the novel by fictionalizing a variety of newspaper and other non-fiction accounts. More specifically, she transforms journalism by participating in the development of a new form: what will come to be called the "human interest" story.

The term "human interest" appears at a crucial juncture in the text, in a scene that generates both the novel's title and one of its central methods of resolution: the idea that class division can be healed through contact between individuals. In this scene, Margaret first comes to feel concern for Milton through her encounter with Higgins. Higgins comments on Margaret's being from Hampshire: "That's beyond London, I reckon? And I come fro' Burnley-ways, and forty miles to th' North. And yet, yo see, North and South has both met and made kind o' friends in this big smoky place" (73). From that day forth, we are told, "Milton became a brighter place to [Margaret]. It was not the long, bleak sunny days of spring, nor yet was it that time was reconciling her to the town of her habitation. It was that in it, she had found a human interest" (74). The earliest usage of the phrase in the *OED* is from 1824 – from Byron, describing his attempt to make angels humanly sympathetic. Actually, a broader search brings up older examples; nevertheless, the phrase's popularity seems to have blossomed in the Romantic period.[68] The second *OED* example, from Dickens in 1860, has attached a commercial element to the expression (it is from *All the Year Round*). Dickens proclaims, "Figuratively speaking, I travel for the house of Human Interest Brothers." But by the twentieth century, all the examples listed by the *OED* are linked explicitly to the journalistic idea of the human interest story, a story melding reportorial fact with Romantic emotion. This evolution of the phrase is already implicit in Gaskell's usage: you can think of the novel *North and South* as a human-interest-story version of the journalistic reports both in the newspapers and in works like Gaskell's friend James Phillip Kay-Shuttleworth's *The Moral and Physical condition of the Working Classes employed in the Cotton Manufacture in Manchester* (1832). And the form owes something to the Crimean background to the tale, to the pull of journalism in the period.

Of course, the kind of journalism of most immediate relevance to *North and South* is found in its method of publication; the novel first appeared serialized in Dickens's *Household Words*. Again, considering this fact can help us to contextualize the novel in terms of the war. Cynthia Dereli has argued that "The editorial policy of *Household Words* . . . under Dickens's editorship, was to concentrate on the issues of concern at home, instead of jumping on the war bandwagon."[69] Actually, Dickens seems to have recognized that it was becoming harder and harder to distinguish between concerns at home and abroad. As consecutive installments of *North and South* appeared in the journal, more and more surrounding articles and poems reflected the political realities of the war in the East. Stories gave sociological insight into the cultures of the combatant nations, such as a piece on "Devil Worshippers" (a sect of peaceful "Mohamedans" who faced forced conscription into the Turkish Army), or an article entitled "At Home with the Russians." There were discussions of military dress ("Mars à la Mode") and of artillery ("Field Service").[70] These articles showed how "telescopic philanthropy" towards the Turks should not blind readers to more proximate problems. Consider "The Home Office," offering "a plain account of the manner in which the government business of this country is transacted" and reflecting the burgeoning concern with the administrative flaws revealed by the war effort.[71] Or "A Home Question," which begins with this declaration:

> In the war that we now wage with Russia, should it be ended in another year or two, we shall scarcely have lost upon all the fields of Alma, and before all the Sebastopols, in all the campaigns, as many of our fellow countrymen as cholera has slain DURING THE PAST FEW WEEKS in London. Even to our troops in the East, Pestilence has proved incomparably more destructive than the redoubts and batteries of any mortal foe.

The article continues by describing the "battle" being waged by working men for their health and by arguing that typhus is "a more deadly enemy than any Czar."[72]

In addition to such articles, the volumes of *Household Words* in which *North and South* came out contained a series of poems about the war that immediately preceded installments of Gaskell's novel in the journal's layout. For example, "The Moral of this Year" (which precedes the tenth portion of *North and South*) also compares the enemy abroad to the enemy at home (disease):

> But white-robed peace droops down and dies, as from a serf-trod shore
> Comes o'er the land, like flash of brand, the gathering din of war;
> Where sword to sword, and hand to hand, in brotherhood advance
> The warriors of England, the chivalry of France!
>
> And whilst with peaceful scythe we cut the poppy-bannered grain;
> Whilst crimson War *his* harvest reaps on the sad battle-plain;
> Comes yet another enemy, with pain, and ruth, and blight,
> To mow another harvest-field – to wage a darker fight!
>
> A Giant-King, a dread disease, with poison in his breath.[73]

Once again, the Condition-of-England question entwines with the Eastern Question. Such thematic overlap is especially understandable given that disease prevailed on the battlefront as well as the home front – an overlap that would be central to the plotting of *Two Years Ago*.[74]

Many of the war poems in *Household Words* were written by Gaskell's acquaintance (and Queen Victoria's favorite poet), Adelaide Anne Procter.[75] Procter's poem "Waiting" tells a typical tale of female patience (the basic premise can be compared to Tennyson's "Mariana" [1830]).[76] A working-class woman explains to a "Lady" why she continues to live by the sea awaiting the return of a beloved sailor instead of retiring inland to a life of "rest and ease." As we shall see, the dangerous temptations of ease in a time of war were registered by Gaskell, also, and would culminate in Margaret's reflections during a seaside holiday. Joseph Bristow points to how a later Procter poem, "The Lesson of the War," describes a seemingly passive female figure, representative of England, actually taking an active stance in calling on her "children" to do their "duty";[77]

Gaskell places Margaret in a comparable position in the riot scene, when she calls on Thornton to go down and face his men (177).

Both Procter poems also express a commonplace theme of the war literature in theorizing how the conflict might unite a nation that had been divided by class distinctions. As an article in *Blackwood's* put it, "War . . . makes us feel we are countrymen, brothers, friends, and neighbours, all of us (not Quakers only), while peace sets us all together by the ears like hounds in an ill-regulated kennel."[78] In "Waiting," the conversation between the speakers promises a form of unity resting largely on a kind of paternalism (or rather, maternalism), as the "Lady" tries to take care of the cottager. But in "The Lesson of the War," concord comes through negotiating more lateral relationships, of both brotherhood in arms, and also, more strikingly, of what could be called a "motherhood in arms" implied in the (albeit, in this poem masculinized) shared home-front experience of the war. As though joining the three classes of *North and South* (represented in Gaskell's novel by London, Helstone, and Milton), Procter records how "The rich man who reposes / In his ancestral shade, / The peasant at his ploughshare, / The worker at his trade" are all the "children" of mother England:

> The rulers of the nation,
>   The poor ones at their gate,
> With the same eager wonder
>   The same great news await!
> The poor man's stay and comfort,
>   The rich man's joy and pride,
> Upon the bleak Crimean shore
>   Are fighting side by side.

Finally, a third Procter poem, "The Two Spirits," again couches a discussion of the war in terms that resonate in Gaskell's novel.[79] Voices representing mothers past and present argue over old and new forms of glory; like *North and South*, the poem debates the values of different eras. Indeed, Procter's poems suggest collectively that the urge to use poetry to create a Nation out of the experience of the war resembles the unifying work of Gaskell's novel, how her conclusion seeks to resolve conflicts between North and South, rich and poor, past and present, and man and woman in an "imagined community" of marriage. *North and South* thus participates in the cultural disputes that had been brought to the fore by the war, a participation that would have been obvious to its original readers in *Household Words*.

Procter's "The Two Spirits" also hints both at the attractions of pacifism and the notion of a just war. The concept of the just war was central to the pro-war faction at the onset of the Crimean War. The term had gained currency with a recent translation (in 1853) by Professor William Whewell of Grotius's treatise on the topic. Clough, for example, somewhat dryly commented to Charles Eliot Norton, "Well, here we are going to war – and really people after their long and dreary commercial period seem quite glad; the feeling of the war being just, of course, is a great thing."[80] Or as Elizabeth Barrett Browning declared, "if we cannot fight righteous and necessary battles, we must leave our place as a nation, and be satisfied with making pins."[81] As these poets suggest, the idea of the just war was often combined with the claim that the forty years' peace or *Pax Britannica* had been no such thing – that it had merely disguised an ongoing civil war in the land, a battle between rich and poor, the blame for which could be laid at least in part at the feet of industrial progress and the uncaring commercial ethos with which it was associated.

Such a "civil war" is the topic of *North and South*; hints permeating the text of the English Civil War underscore the connection.[82] The Crimean context to these overlapping ideas can be seen more clearly, though, in Tennyson's *Maud*, where a state of "Civil war" at home leads the speaker finally to embrace the war abroad.[83] Gaskell's letters suggest (albeit in a comic register) a slightly more alarming version of the connection between civil and foreign wars – the idea that the lack of soldiers on the home front would precipitate an uprising:

I bade farewell to a Capn Campbell, bound for the East, last week – he told me there {was}\would/not [be] a soldier left in Manchester on Saturday last; whereupon somebody observed that we were on the edge of a precipice! I don't know what they meant; but don't be surprised if you hear of a rising of the weavers, headed by a modern Boadicea.[84]

But they also imply that the war can produce an unprecedented feeling of national unity, as in her citation of Wordsworth's claim that "We have all of us one human heart," quoted above.

In *Maud*, Tennyson's speaker rants at the "Quaker" who is unable to see the difference between "lawful and lawless war" (II.330, 332). Gaskell's attitudes toward the Peace Society – the Quaker pacifist group founded in 1816 but coming to prominence at the onset of the Crimean War (against which the Society campaigned) – are rather more complex. Two references to the Society in *North and South* constitute the novel's most obvious nod towards the war in the East. In the first, Edith writes from

Corfu, asking Margaret and her mother to visit. She adds, though, that she does not ask Mr. Hale, "because, I dare say, he disapproves of war, and soldiers, and bands of music; at least, I know that many Dissenters are members of the Peace Society" (235). Later, Mr. Bell comments that Margaret has been changed by her time in the North: "Her residence in Milton has quite corrupted her. She's a democrat, a red republican, a member of the Peace Society, a socialist" (330). Included in the list of Dissenters with involvement in the Peace Society were the Gaskells themselves; Gaskell later told Florence Nightingale that she and her husband lived "in the very midst of what was once called the peace party" in Manchester.[85]

But it would be a mistake to see Gaskell as an unconditional advocate for peace in the novel. Comments about the war in her letters tend to focus on the soldiers' heroism, not on the justice or injustice of their cause. Yet her attitudes towards the workers' violence are sympathetic (even if not condoning), and her discussion of the conflict between a morality of "rights" upheld by the men and one of "duties" that should be the province of the masters shows that issues of justice are central to her conception of class struggle.[86] Moreover, Higgins himself invokes a military parallel when describing his "cause o' justice": "I just look forward to the chance of dying at my post sooner than yield. That's what folk call fine and honourable in a soldier, and why not in a poor weaver-chap?" When Margaret objects that the soldier dies not for himself but for "the cause of the Nation," Higgins retorts that with his family and the families of others dependent upon him, his battle "is just as much in the cause of others as yon soldier" (134). In fact, while she prefers a peaceful outcome to the crisis, Gaskell recognizes that the absence of war does not equal the presence of peace. Late in the novel, as Margaret reflects on her cosseted London life, she becomes aware that "She was getting surfeited of the eventless ease in which no struggle or endeavour was required. She was afraid lest she should even become sleepily deadened into forgetfulness of anything beyond the life which was wrapping her round with luxury. There might be toilers and moilers there in London, but she never saw them" (373). Indeed, the chapter containing these reflections is entitled "Ease not Peace" – a title that would have been translated during the war years as a reference to the ongoing civil war that had until recently been obscured by the *Pax Britannica*.

It would also have come to the attention of Gaskell's readership at a time when "blood-red" war had (as *Maud* puts it) "blossom[ed]" (III.53). Tennyson's macabre phrase conflates the garden imagery of the domestic love-story in his poem with the martial tones of the foreign conflict. But in *North and South*, the transfer of the war to the home front is accompanied by a nostalgic sanitizing (given contemporary events) of military life, which seems to be all ease, and if not peace, certainly not war. Edith's description of her life in Corfu as one of "war, and soldiers, and bands of music" dramatically de-emphasizes the first term in her list. It makes Corfu seem like an island out of a romance (it has been identified as the utopian Skheria, home of the Phaiakians in the *Odyssey*). But in reality, during the war, Captain Lennox's regiment would have been engaged in supplying troops in the Crimea with goods; several regiments in Corfu were even sent to the front. A leader in *The Times* of November 27, 1854 actually suggests Corfu as a possible way-station for holding large numbers of British reserves.[87] Gaskell's novel obscures all such marks of the Crimean conflict.

If Captain Lennox and Corfu provide one version of military life in the novel, Frederick Hale provides another. Andrew Sanders has argued that "Frederick's stand against military oppression, his moral uprightness and his resistance to injustice were ... singularly apposite to readers caught up in the progress of the war in the Crimea."[88] Still, like Captain Lennox, Frederick is described in unrealistic and outmoded terms. In many ways, he serves as Margaret's double. But his rebellion is the stuff of romance (as Gaskell's chapter epigraphs from Byron suggest), whereas Margaret's is implicated in the modern world of the strike. And Catholicism – to which Frederick converts – stands for the ways of the past, just as Margaret's turn to industry represents the future.

In truth, the novel's descriptions of army life owe more to old-fashioned notions of an aristocratic military than to the military as it would come to be perceived during the Crimean War. For many years (ever since the end of the Napoleonic wars), British soldiers had been identified with dandified dress rather than daring deeds; as a character says of the young hero in Thackeray's *The Newcomes*, "I think I should send him into the army, that's the best place for him – there's the least to do, and the handsomest clothes to wear."[89] But as the war progressed and news came home from the front, perceptions of soldiers were changing. Gaskell herself implies the shift in commenting to Nightingale about her involvement in the Peace Society when she adds that before the war, that group "spoke lightly of, if not positively sneered at" the army.[90] After the war, such sneers were no longer possible. And, as I have noted, one of the greatest changes was that from a conception of the military centered upon the aristocratic officer-class to one centered upon the heroism and suffering of the common soldier. As *Punch* would put it (referring to the creation in 1857 of the Victoria Cross, awarded regardless of rank), while "Some talk of ALEXANDER, / And some of HERCULES," if a hero "Of genuine pluck and pith" was wanted, one need look no farther than "To full British PRIVATE SMITH":

> Too long mere food for powder
>   We've deem'd our rank and file,
> Now higher hopes and prouder,
>   Upon the soldier smile.[91]

Gaskell's repeated interest in her letters in showing workers' sympathy for the soldiers in the East supports her recognition of the changing opinions about the military.

It also suggests that in depicting the suffering of the men in her novel – and in using language of them that implicitly compares their suffering to that of the men in the Crimea – she may well have been taking advantage of the shifts in perception occasioned by the war. *North and South* proposes a domestic "hot pot" solution to the conflict between masters and men (that is, the establishment of a dining hall for the workers, which Thornton visits). But a parallel with the war experience appears in Thornton's insistence on leaving the men their independence: "If they had not asked me, I would no more have intruded on them than I'd have gone to the mess at the barracks without invitation" (362). Indeed, Gaskell considers the visits as a kind of peaceful (albeit ludicrously optimistic) substitute for the leveling effects of the battlefield; as Mr. Bell notes, "Nothing like the act of eating for equalising men. Dying is nothing to it" (362). Still, the thrust of Gaskell's military analogy is typically ambivalent. While she uses it to garner support for the suffering of her army of workers, her decision to romanticize military life abroad no doubt also owes much to her desire to emphasize the harsh realities of the war at home.

The cardinal virtue of traditional military life is of course honor. Richard Lovelace's "To Lucasta, Going to the Wars" (1649) describes iconic competing notions of honor, not only martial and romantic but also masculine and feminine. While the nunnery of Lucasta's "chaste breast" holds feminine honor safe, masculine honor must be earned through bravery on the battlefield.[92] During the riot, Margaret calls on Thornton to display something like military bravery: "If you have any courage or noble quality in you, go out and speak to them, man to man" (177). But the question of Thornton's masculine "honor" in this scene is soon supplanted by the issue of Margaret's "truth" in regard to the lie she tells to protect Frederick. The strange emphasis on this lie must ultimately be read as Gaskell's attempt to navigate the rocky terrain of Margaret's sexual desire (the lie acts as decoy, drawing attention away from the more difficult question of Margaret's passion, manifested in the symbolic deflowering of the riot scene). Yet the choice of "truthfulness" as the virtue in question can be read not only in a sexual or military register but also in a commercial one, as Margaret's thoughts about her lie suggest:

Her cheeks burnt as she recollected how proudly she had implied an objection to trade . . . because it too often led to the deceit of passing off inferior for superior goods, in the one branch; of assuming credit for wealth and resources not possessed, in the other. She remembered Mr. Thornton's look of calm disdain, as in few words he gave her to understand that, in the great scheme of commerce, all dishonourable ways of acting were sure to prove injurious in the long run . . . She remembered – she, then strong in her own untempted truth – asking him, if he did not think that buying in the cheapest and selling in the dearest market proved some want of the transparent justice which is so intimately connected with the idea of truth: and she had used the word chivalric – and her father had corrected her with the higher word Christian. (302–03)

North and South often makes its case by shifting between registers, by arguing that, for example, Frederick's mutiny, Mr. Hale's crisis of doubt, and the workers' strike all represent comparable forms of rebellion. Here, something similar seems to be happening to the idea of honor or truth.

Alexander Welsh notes that truth became a vital virtue in the nineteenth century in part because of the strain on religious belief; Mr. Hale's decision to leave the church rests on his unwillingness to tell a lie. But Welsh also points out that "The new sociology confirmed that increased truthfulness was one of the important differences between an 'industrial' and a 'military' society. W. E. H. Lecky ventured that 'industrial veracity' was the *only* positive contribution of the growth of manufactures to morals."[93] This opinion was not held universally: in *Maud* the aristocratic speaker sees commercialism as a threat to truth ("When only the ledger lives, and when only not all men lie" [1.35]). But Gaskell's substitution of commercial for military honor in *North and South* was made easier by the increasingly managerial attitude held towards the ongoing war effort. As early as July 24, 1854, Austen Henry Layard asked the Commons, "Why does not the government allow some great firm to contract for carrying on the war?"[94] In October, *The Times* announced that "War has become an affair of science and machinery, of accumulated capital and skilful combination." By March, 1855, that organ of popular opinion was lamenting how "this great commercial and mechanical country is governed by an official body comparatively ignorant of commerce and the mechanical arts."[95] In such a climate, the idea of honor would naturally comprise both military and industrial senses, allowing the novel's much-contested title of "gentleman" to be expanded from its aristocratic and soldierly definition to include the honorable bourgeois industrialist.[96]

So just as Gaskell's home-front working-class heroes could be elevated by subtle allusions to their brothers in the East, so Thornton's machine-spun honesty gleamed all the brighter for its contrast with the dull light bouncing off the rusty armor on display in the Crimea. A novel about the "condition of England" thus defines that condition by reflecting attitudes to the war abroad. Yet for all its concern for class, the interplay between its portrayals of gender and of heroism demonstrates *North and South*'s most compelling engagement with the war. And here, the figure of Florence Nightingale looms large.

III "HEROIC WOMANHOOD"

Margaret Hale

As in the Kingsleys' fiction, a novel version of heroic manliness emerges from the backdrop of war in *North and South*. Yet while the war helped allow for Thornton's more mercantilized form of honor, the shift from a military to a commercial register still threatens to undermine his masculinity. This threat arises because such masculinity's dependence on market forces renders it fragile; "I may be a man one day and a mouse the next," as one Victorian merchant put it.[97] The danger becomes apparent in the pivotal riot scene, when Margaret demands that Thornton "face" his workers "like a man" (177). Gaskell revealed in a letter that she fretted about Thornton's manliness: "I want to keep his character consistent with itself, and large and strong and tender, and *yet a master*."[98] But an equally difficult problem – one that can similarly be read in the context of shifting gender roles during the war years – arose in negotiating Margaret's womanliness. Part of Gaskell's worry over Thornton came from the fact that she had made her heroine so strong. And Margaret's forceful nature must be considered in the context of Florence Nightingale's remarkable rise as a heroine.

In literary terms, the quality of Margaret's strength can be seen by measuring her against her exact contemporary, Coventry Patmore's "angel in the house," Honoria Vaughan. The war years saw the publication of the first two parts of Patmore's ode to the wife (*The Betrothal* came out in 1854; *The Espousals* followed in 1856), which both reflected and consolidated mid-Victorian opinions about the place of woman in society. For Patmore, the function of woman is to serve man, as he explains in "Womanhood," one of the lyric "Accompaniments" adorning the "Idyls" that comprise the narrative portions of his long poem:

> Be man's hard virtues highly wrought
>   But let my gentle Mistress be,
> In every look, word, deed, and thought,
>   Nothing but sweet and womanly!
> Her virtues please my virtuous mood,
>   But what at all times I admire
> Is not, that she is wise and good,
>   But just the thing which I desire.[99]

"Man's hard virtues" appear distinct from the "sweet and womanly" attributes of the female sex; indeed any shared virtues (such as wisdom and goodness) are proved inessential to feminine perfection by the fact of overlap.

But Patmore's ability to keep the virtues – and spheres – of man and woman so separate depends, I believe at least in part, on his decision to push the war to the side in his poem, in favor of domestic concerns. This move is rendered concrete in the Prologue of *The Espousals*, when the poet's playful children interrupt him even as he is intoning the strangely martial opening lines of the book (dissonant from everything that follows) to his wife:

> 2.
> "The pulse of War, whose bloody heats
>   "Sane purposes insanely work,
> "Now with fraternal frenzy beats,
>   "And binds the Christian to the Turk,
> "And shrieking fifes" –
> 3.
>   But, with a roar,
> In rush'd the Loves [i.e., the children].

And when the poet (Felix by name) repeats these verses in the opening of the body of the poem, they are followed by the observation that it is "Too late" for the kind of "song" that would "Through quiet England, teach our breath / The courage corporate that drags / The coward to heroic death." Rather,

> Who henceforth sings,
> Must fledge his heavenly flight with more
> Song-worthy and heroic things
> Than hasty, home-destroying War.[100]

Note the difference between Patmore's and Gaskell's methodologies: both writers use the war to argue for a focus on domestic concerns. Yet while Gaskell works expansively with the backdrop of war, allowing it to extend and color the reach of her argument, Patmore wishes to deny the relevance of the conflict. One must ask, "Why?"

When the war does reenter *The Espousals* briefly in its concluding sections, it takes the form of a rejected suitor: Honoria's cousin, whose failure to win her (it is suggested) depended on his military occupation. As the commander of a man-of-war (now berthed off the very seaside resort at which the young couple is honeymooning), Frederick was absent in the East while Felix was winning his bride. Significantly, when Patmore quotes Lovelace's "To Lucasta" shortly thereafter, he purges it of the martial meaning for honor. The allusion comes up in reference to Felix's poetic "task," to describe in future volumes the "flames" of married love, of which he has until now only painted the "fumes": "I could not love thee, Muse, so much / Loved I not Honor more!" declares Felix, both invoking his wife's name rather than the concept of glory in war and reversing the hierarchy of loves in the original poem to put domestic love first.[101] Patmore can make these changes safely because male and female honor are so obviously unlike for him; his desire in "Womanhood" to distinguish absolutely between woman's role and man's suggests that her highest "virtues" differ in kind from masculine virtues. But his aggressive avoidance of the available martial context, so often used to create such separate spheres (as in Lovelace's poem), also hints that something about this present war's relationship to gender unsettles rather than supports his worldview.

In contrast, Gaskell's novel works hard through its analogical methods to allow Margaret to participate in the cultural debates of her day. In *North and South*, qualities can be seen to operate simultaneously in martial and marital, male and female registers. In the process, these binaries become blurred. Such blurring appears in the novel's treatment of passion, which (through Margaret's lie) is in turn affiliated with ideas of both sexual and military honor. Gaskell's novel also aligns sexual passion with social conflict, as the "stormy passions" (178) of the mob in the riot scene suggest, beginning with a phallic breaching of the gates of the mill and ending with Margaret's symbolic rape. But passion works on an individual level as well: for example, Frederick's mouth gives his sister "such an idea of latent passion, that it almost made her afraid" (247). And not only Frederick, but also Bessy, Higgins, Thornton, and – above all – Margaret herself (whose fear of Frederick's "latent passion" owes much to her recognition of her similarity to her brother), have to learn the appropriate balance between a life of passion and one of self-control. These two key terms in the text are also key elements of army life, where the passion required to steel oneself to battle must be controlled by an ability to submit to military authority.

Indeed, for all Gaskell's pacifism, *North and South* seems to argue in an almost Kingsleyan fashion that one problem with peace is that it inhibits productive passion. The speaker of *Maud* initially proposes a life of "passionless peace" (1.151) as a substitute for lost happiness but soon discovers his need for both passion and war; Margaret experiences the same discovery in a domestic key. Late in *North and South*, she shows awareness of the benefits of conflict in appreciating Edith's boy's "stormy passions" (note the repetition of the phrase earlier applied to the mob):

Margaret almost liked him better in these manifestations of character than in his good blue-sashed moods. She would carry him off into a room, where they two alone battled it out; she with a firm power which subdued him into peace, while every sudden charm and wile she possessed, was exerted on the side of right, until he would rub his little hot and tear-smeared face all over hers, kissing and caressing until he often fell asleep in her arms. (405)

Language of the war pervades the passage: from the allusion to the blue ribbon of a knight of the garter to the mentions of battle, peace, and right. Of course this encounter stands in for the novel's primary "antagonistic friendship" (239): that between Margaret and Thornton. And if the resolution of the conflict between these two represents in turn the resolution of a larger class conflict and the resolution of North and South and of past and present, it can also be read in terms of what I have shown to be a broader discussion during the war years of the merits of passionate, violent struggle.

While conflict has always been central to romance (think of Beatrice and Benedick or Darcy and Lizzy), this form of struggle struck Gaskell's contemporaries as something new. In her review of the novel for *Blackwood's*, Margaret Oliphant complains of the "desperate, bitter quarrel out of which love is to come." "Shall all our love-stories be squabbles after this?" she protests, "Shall we have nothing but encounters of arms between the knight and the lady – bitter personal altercations, and mutual defiance?" Oliphant traces the trend to the influence of *Jane Eyre* (1847), but she couches it in terms of the current war: "Talk of a balance of power which may be adjusted by taking a Crimea, or fighting a dozen battles – here is a battle which must always be going forward." She describes how the modern heroine, a "new Bellona," "rushes into the field, makes desperate sorties out of her Sebastopol . . . and finally permits herself to be ignominiously captured." Of *North and South* itself she adds, "There is one consolation: Have we not in these favoured realms a Peace Society?"[102] Oliphant's comments suggest again how debates about the relative merits of war and peace are being played out in both military and sexual registers, and with some overlapping effects; in particular, she points to the issue of "a balance of power" between men and women.

This balance is just what sensation fiction disturbs by allowing its female protagonists more active roles. As I have mentioned, Oliphant would recognize the Crimean War as a contributing factor in the development of the new genre in her 1862 article on "Sensation novels" in *Blackwood's*. But the connection appears already in the review from 1855. Oliphant acknowledges the "strange change" that "has passed upon . . . this peace-loving nation. What piece of abstract literature, though its writer were laureated poet or throned philosopher, would not be put aside to-day for the simple letter of some poor soldier private from the fated seat of war?" Once again, we see the importance of the soldiers' letters discussed in chapter 1. But Oliphant also notes how the perpetual need in this climate for what she calls "Something new!" drives Wilkie Collins to produce a "sensation" for his readers.[103] While, like so many sensational heroines, Margaret possesses an important secret, *North and South* hardly qualifies as sensation fiction. But when Oliphant writes of Margaret as allowing herself to be "ignominiously captured," her assessment fails to address the radical aspects of the conclusion of *North and South*: the way Gaskell alters the balance of power by letting Margaret retain the upper hand over her husband in making her his financial savior.

Yet this move also seems reminiscent of the conclusion of *Jane Eyre*, in which Rochester's blinding and maiming enables Jane to take control over her former "master." And in fact, Charlotte Brontë's novel generally serves as literary touchstone for the discussion of female heroism in the mid-1850s. It was immediately recognized as revolutionary for portraying a passionate, active heroine; as Oliphant remarks of Brontë's creation, "suddenly there stole upon the scene . . . a little fierce incendiary, doomed to turn the world of fancy upside down . . . [A]nd the most alarming revolution of modern times has followed the invasion of *Jane Eyre*."[104] But curiously, *Jane Eyre*'s reappearances in the literature of the period often occur in the context of the war.[105] Thus both *North and South* and *Westward Ho!* echo the earlier novel's conclusion. This conjunction can be explained: if Jane's passion held an important position in the public imaginary, Florence Nightingale's authority occupied an adjacent spot. Nightingale's promotion to heroine of the war occurred in part to compensate for a notable absence of male heroes, but it also suggested a new range of possibility for female power.

Appropriately, Nightingale seems to have admired Brontë's heroine: "Now Jane Eyre seems to me to be real life – we know her, we have lived with her, we shall meet her again."[106] Moreover, as Catherine Judd has argued, Jane herself (while often considered through her profession as educator: first governess and later schoolteacher) can be thought of as a nurse, a position she assumes in caring for Mrs. Reed on her deathbed, but which also characterizes her relationship with Rochester from start (when he falls off his horse) to finish. To look at *Jane Eyre* this way is to see Jane as doubled not by Bertha Mason, the madwoman in the attic, but rather by Bertha's nurse, Grace Poole. Jane thus becomes a representative of what Judd has termed the "new-style nurse" – cultured and capable, in the mold that would soon be fixed by Nightingale – in opposition to Poole's "old-style" lower-class drunk, who threatens to turn into another Sairey Gamp (from *Martin Chuzzlewit* [1843]). Crucially, the role of nurse constitutes Jane's authority – in particular, the authority that comes with surveillance over an "incarcerated" (Judd's term, following Foucault) patient.[107] And Ferndean (Jane's Crimea, so to speak: her theater of action) becomes the proper final home for Jane and Rochester precisely because its insalubrious and remote location, divorced from patriarchal associations, promises to allow Jane to maintain the control offered by her role as nurse.

So while Nightingale is not the mother of the debate about heroism at mid-century, she acted as midwife to it. And if comparisons to Jane Eyre can help make sense of Gaskell's creation of a passionate heroine, comparisons to Nightingale help explain Margaret's determination. We can recognize Gaskell herself thinking about the relationship when she responds to Charlotte Brontë's opinion of her novel by contrasting Nightingale's saintliness with her own heroine's more human virtue: "I'm glad she likes 'North and South'. I did not think Margaret *was so over* good. What would Miss B. say to Florence Nightingale? I can't imagine!"[108] Moreover, by making this comparison, we can see Gaskell struggling not only with models of heroism but also with their generic implications.

North and South begins with a rather gentle vision of womanhood in Edith: "If Titania had ever been dressed in white muslin and blue ribbons, and had fallen asleep on a crimson damask sofa in a back drawing-room, Edith might have been taken for her" (5). Yet Gaskell soon supplants Edith's kittenish Titania – woman as fairy queen – with a representative of a different kind of queenliness in Margaret (versions of this label keep reappearing[109]). Margaret's own dress in the opening scene emphasizes that her reign is to be less placid (the novel, set in part in the mills of Lancashire, makes careful use of fabrics); Edith's muslin and ribbon are replaced by the Indian shawl that Margaret models for her aunt, "the garb of a princess" (9), but also a symbol of empire. Significantly, this is how the shawl strikes Thornton at their first meeting, when he takes note of "a large Indian shawl, which hung about her in long heavy folds, and which she wore as an empress wears her drapery." The effect undermines – even unmans – him: "Mr. Thornton was in habits of authority himself, but she seemed to assume some kind of rule over him at once" (62).

Margaret's looks belong to the figure of Britannia (figure 4), not fairy queen but warrior queen (recall Oliphant's Bellona), who would appear often in the cartoons of the day as a representative of the motherland at war: "the short curled upper lip, the round, massive up-turned chin, the manner of carrying her head, her movements, full of a soft feminine defiance, always gave strangers the impression of haughtiness" (62).[110] Contemporary critics may have mocked her description – the repeated mention of the haughtily curved lip and "flexile throat" (63) – but they must have done so in part because of its obviousness; it would be like giving the heroine of a novel written during World War II the polka-dotted headscarf and bulging bicep of Rosie the Riveter.[111] Britannia attained unprecedented iconic significance during the period of the Crimean War because of the conjunction of two influential icons of authoritative womanhood: Queen Victoria and Florence Nightingale. Actually, these two figures were often conflated; Nightingale herself was frequently represented as a queen.[112]

As critics note, both Nightingale and Victoria provided acceptable models of womanhood because of the ambivalence of their roles. Mary Poovey records how the Queen "was compared less frequently to a patriarchal commander than to a loving mother." She also describes the "two faces" of the "mythic" Nightingale, domestic and military:

> One was obviously allied to the normative definition of the middle-class woman . . . it was the image of the English Sister of Charity, the self-denying

Figure 4 "Right Against Wrong," *Punch* 26 (1854), 144

caretaker – a mother, a saint, or even a female Christ . . . The second face of Florence Nightingale bore a greater likeness to a politician or a soldier than a gentle mother; it was the image of the tough-minded administrator who "encountered opposition" but persevered.[113]

Consider, for example, "A Nightingale In the Camp," published in *Punch* in 1855:

> And there is Mercy's Amazon, within whose little breast
> Burns the great spirit that has dared the fever and the pest.
> And she has grappled with grim Death, that maid so bold and meek:
> There is the mark of battle fresh upon her pallid cheek.
>
> That gallant gentle lady the Camp would fain review.[114]

"Mercy's Amazon," a "gallant gentle lady," "bold and meek" – the language is rife with unsuccessful attempts to resolve Nightingale's two faces into one. Similarly, depictions of Britannia in the pages of *Punch* during the war portrayed her alternately as woman-warrior and almost Christ-like mother-figure, as Joseph Bristow has described.[115]

But the coexistence of these two faces not only allowed Nightingale to serve as a publicly acceptable model of female heroism, it also explains what might be called her "generic malleability": the way she functions as both epic and novelistic inspiration for writers. Indeed, to me the most curious thing about the ambiguity of Nightingale's status is how questions of gender and genre overlap in considerations of her role. As Lytton Strachey wrote in his infamous evaluation, "She was heroic . . . Yet her heroism was not of the simple sort so dear to readers of novels and the compilers of hagiologies – the romantic sentimental heroism with which mankind loves to invest its chosen darlings: it was made of sterner stuff . . . It was not by gentle sweetness and womanly self-abnegation that she had brought order out of chaos in the Scutari Hospitals." That "sterner stuff" belongs rather, it is implied, in the manly world of epic. Nightingale's mother spoke of her as a "wild swan" hatched from a family of ducks, suggesting a fairy tale; Strachey corrects the metaphor: she "was an eagle."[116]

Nightingale appears also to have thought of her life in a manner translatable into generic terms. Thus her private notes show both awareness that she moved in a novelistic world and a sense that she belonged in a different medium: she used military language to express her maneuverings in quest of her goal, and she compared herself to Christ and Joan of Arc when describing her mission.[117] The role models she selected for herself in turn influenced the "plot" of her life. In a private journal entry from 1850 (years after receiving her first mystical "call" to nursing in 1847), Nightingale records her options: "I had 3 paths among which to choose. I might have been a married woman, a literary woman, or a Hospital Sister."[118] Her decision not to marry Richard Monkton Milnes (in 1849) indicates that she felt her vocation to be incompatible with the format of the domestic novel:

I have an intellectual nature which requires satisfaction and that would find it in him. I have a passionate nature which requires satisfaction and that would find it in him. I have a moral, an active, nature which requires satisfaction and that would not find it in his life. Sometimes I think I will satisfy my passional nature at all events, because that will at least secure me from the evil of dreaming. But would it? I could be satisfied to spend a life with him in combining our different powers in some great object. I could not satisfy this nature by spending a life with him in making society and arranging domestic things.[119]

These deliberations oddly mimic Jane Eyre's patterns of speech and thought. You can think of them as reversing Jane's arguments against marrying St. John Rivers in order to become his helpmate in India: Jane had chosen to satisfy her "passional nature" with Rochester, perhaps at the expense of her "moral, active nature." But the marriage plot could not allow for the scope of Nightingale's epic ambitions.

Nightingale's *cri de coeur*, *Cassandra*, composed in 1852 (a year before her parents finally permitted her to begin work, as a supervisor of the Institution for the Care of Sick Gentlewomen in Distressed Circumstances, a London nursing home), gives a good indication of the tortured suppression she went through before starting out towards her "great object." The pamphlet describes in passionate strains how conventional forces like family and society "extinguished" the lives of young upper-class women, "rust[ing]" their "noble rising heroisms," leaving them "nothing to do."[120] Curiously, clues suggest that *Cassandra* was planned as a novel; its title reads like that of an eighteenth-century female *Bildungsroman*, and an early version includes a character named Cassandra. Sir Edward Cook, Nightingale's first modern biographer, also records the existence of a manuscript book entitled "Novel" that was destined (like *Cassandra*) to become part of *Suggestions for Thought*.[121] Nightingale might easily have followed a different career path. As Catherine Judd points out, the professions of nurse and novelist actually share an emphasis on observation. She quotes Nightingale's *Notes on Nursing* (1859): "A man who really cares for his patients, will soon learn to ask for and appreciate the information of a nurse, who is at once a careful observer and a clear reporter." Nightingale's invocation of the idea of the "reporter" stands out in the Crimean context given today's use of the word to signify "journalist." While it did not possess quite this resonance in the period, the idea of, say, a "parliamentary" or "court reporter" was already current. Judd also points to the curious fact that for all our memories of her as a nurse, "Nightingale was primarily a writer, her literal manifestation as a nurse spanning only a few years of her sixty-odd-year career."[122]

Yet *Cassandra* – an indictment of the forces of domesticity that lie at the heart of the realist novel – would have had to enter into the realms of romance (or sensation) for its heroine to find success. Indeed, such was Nightingale's conception of the genre:

the first thing in a good novel is to place the persons together in circumstances which naturally call out the high feelings and thoughts of the character . . . romantic events, they are called. The second is that the heroine has *generally* no family ties (almost *invariably* no mother), or, if she has, these do not interfere with her entire independence.[123]

Nightingale's life was heavily encumbered by her extensive and demanding family. As these comments hint, her mother (along with Parthenope) was especially adamant that Florence perform what *Cassandra* refers to (using scare-quotes) as the "claims of social life."[124] And the novelistic world in which Nightingale moved – until her escape to the East, the realm of romance – was notably realist; even in the East, she worked primarily as an administrator, in a manner one might associate with realism. Indeed, Judd suggestively surmises that Florence and her sister Parthenope served as models for Dorothea and Celia Brooke.[125] Realistically, a woman's life was a life of constraint; hence Nightingale's plea, in an imaginary dialogue with her mother, that her sex be ignored: "You must look upon me as your son, your vagabond son, without his money."[126]

In fact, a curious alternative to Nightingale's story that realizes the gender-bending she only imagines here can be found in the history of her fellow veteran of the Crimean War, Dr. James (Miranda) Barry (?1790–1865). Barry, the Deputy Inspector General of Army Hospitals in Corfu during the war (site of Edith's military experience in *North and South*), was "discovered" by the charwoman who laid him out after his death to have been a woman (although there was also conjecture of hermaphroditism). The speculation is that as a very clever girl growing up in progressive circles of the Edinburgh of the day (his probable uncle was the artist James Barry), Barry's sex (whether female or intersexed) was disguised in order to allow entry to the University of Edinburgh, where "he" (as Barry seems to have thought of himself from his university days on) studied literature and medicine, qualifying as a doctor in 1812. From 1813 to 1859, Barry served as "an outstanding Army Surgeon and a physician who practised preventative medicine years ahead of her time,"[127] performing, for example, one of the first Caesarean sections survived by both mother and child.

Still, Barry's rather "Regency" solution to the constraints placed upon him by his sex were less successful by the time Nightingale had risen to prominence. Rachel Holmes describes Barry's adoption of an "effeminate" but male persona: "A noted dandy, Barry combined extravagant dress with a love of entertainment and social ritual. The charismatic, peripatetic and irredeemably flirtatious doctor charmed women and men alike. A child of the dreams of radical democracy and the scientific enlightenment of the eighteenth century, Barry grew up uneasily into the more austere venture of Victorianism."[128] In contrast, Nightingale's negotiations with gender come across as being very (even "eminently") Victorian, both in how she configures the problem and in how she constructs the solution. Yet Barry's predicament does give the impression of emerging out of the pages of the brand of sensation fiction engendered by the war (recall Caroline Volmar's assumption of masculine disguise in order to nurse her estranged husband back to health in G. W. M. Reynolds's *Omar*) and suggested by Nightingale's description of the novel in *Cassandra*: the *Manchester Guardian* published an article a few weeks after Barry's death, entitled "A Strange Story," in which the tale of the discovery of Barry's sex elicits the comment that "I doubt whether even Miss Braddon herself would have ventured to make use of it in fiction."[129] In spite of this warning, Mary Elizabeth Braddon was responsible for abridging Col. Edward Rogers's "three-volume potboiler entitled *The Modern Sphinx* [1881], loosely based on Barry's life."[130]

Nevertheless, while the actual Nightingale struggled like a character in a more realistic novel, Gaskell's letters describe her as a woman who was untroubled by questions about the conflict between private and public duties, whose "clinging to one object" appears to belong to "a creature of another race so high & mighty & angelic, doing things by impulse – or some divine inspiration & not by effort & struggle of will."[131] In contrast, Gaskell portrays Margaret's self-control as a product of heroic effort, and her authority stands as a central issue in the work – ironically, in a manner that calls to mind Nightingale's private records of her frustrations. Thus while Margaret's looks may suggest that she rules over her domain, her experiences highlight the degree to which she is restrained by her position: as daughter, as sister, as middle-class woman. Even after her parents' death and her achievement of financial independence through Mr. Bell's bequest, Gaskell records how Margaret "tried to settle that most difficult problem for women, how much was to be utterly merged in obedience to authority, and how much might be set apart for freedom in working" (416) (again, for all Gaskell's sense of difference, the question might have been pulled from Nightingale's diaries). Gaskell also explicitly contrasts Nightingale's saintliness with her own heroine's less perfect virtue. But Margaret is not "*so over* good" only because she is less icon and more person. We know her from the inside in a way you can never know an icon, which remains resolutely two-dimensional. This is what makes her the heroine of a novel; as Gaskell saw her, Nightingale would have required an epic to contain her.[132]

But if Gaskell flattens Nightingale out into iconic status, she also takes advantage of the ambiguities attendant on that status in order to create Margaret. Cynthia Dereli has suggested that poets and journalists of the war period transformed Nightingale, who would seemingly have been breaking gender barriers, into a symbol of national unity by occluding the "problematic aspects" of her role and bringing to the foreground "the acceptable role of carer," which was "reinforced through religious imagery";[133] while she may have escaped the house, Nightingale remained an angel. Dereli's analysis contrasts, though, with the ways in which Gaskell actually relies on the "problematic aspects" of Nightingale's role to make her argument about Margaret's strengths and ambitions. Poovey astutely observes that the fact that the two models of womanhood she identifies "converged in Florence Nightingale suggests that the military narrative was always at least compatible with – if not implicit in – the domestic narrative"; in female sexuality, "the domestic ideal always contained an aggressive element."[134] Recall Charles Kingsley's Ayacanora, the epitome of the domestic Amazon. To Gaskell, trying to create a figure of female heroism in a novel in which the political Condition-of-England plot and the private courtship plot were so interdependent – if Amyas Leigh was to serve as an allegory of English manhood, Margaret's *Bildung* had to represent that of the nation as a whole – such blurring and overlap would have been particularly welcome.

The compatibility between military and domestic models of womanhood appears forcefully in the riot scene of *North and South*. When Margaret describes the act of throwing her body in front of Thornton to shield him from the mob as "woman's work" (191), she is suggesting that her position was one of what Poovey calls "self-denying caretaker." And her suffering, including her pietà-like position in Thornton's arms after she faints (complete with the stigmata of her wounds), could be seen to turn her into a female Christ, like Nightingale. But even as Gaskell modeled Margaret's stance on what she recognized as Nightingale's Christ-like ability to sacrifice herself to her cause, she also saw Nightingale's soldierliness, comparing her to an archetypal female soldier, Joan of Arc.[135] And this awareness enters her portrayal of Margaret's position in front of the mob, too. (Margaret's attempts to command that mob – albeit with little success – might remind us as well of the Anglo-Saxon warrior queen of Gaskell's letter: "don't be surprized if you hear of a rising of the weavers, headed by a modern Boadicea.") If Gaskell's correspondence describes how the workers see Nightingale as "*their* heroine,"[136] her own heroine seeks to assume, more modestly, a similar role.

Nightingale's appreciation for *North and South* seems to have been rather straightforward (she was already an admirer of Gaskell's work, having approved greatly of *Ruth* [1853], in which a fallen woman redeems herself in part through embarking on a career as a nurse[137]). In a letter from the Crimea, she asks to be sent a "whole Edition" copy of the book, which she had read in *Household Words,* calling it a "good Novel" for the hospital reading room.[138] But Gaskell's admiration for Nightingale is mixed with a degree of suspicion that is related to her perception of both the heroic nurse's gender and what I have been describing as her "generic status." Jenny Uglow argues that Gaskell was simultaneously "intrigued and appalled" by Nightingale's "self-isolation" and her ability to annihilate private feelings for individuals in her broader concerns for the race – her ability, in other words, to do like Aeneas and sacrifice Dido for Rome. She also notes that Nightingale may have stood behind Margaret's musings towards the end of *North and South,* after her visit to a changed Helstone: "If I were a Roman Catholic and could deaden my heart, stun it with some great blow, I might become a nun. But I should pine after my kind; no, not my kind, my love for my species could never fill my heart to the utter exclusion of love for individuals" (400).[139] Gaskell actually implies that there is something "unwomanly" in this attitude when she singles out for objection Nightingale's belief that children are better off in a "well managed crèche" than with their mothers.[140] Ultimately, according to Uglow, Gaskell's suspicions win out: "Although Gaskell described Nightingale's tireless efforts in the Crimea as 'a visible march to heaven' . . . the whole of her own fiction – and especially *North and South* – opposes the route that Florence had chosen, the subordination of relationships to causes and of people to ideas."[141] As Uglow hints, these are not just moral imperatives but novelistic ones. Margaret spends significant portions of the book serving as nurse to her mother and to Bessy, who sees her in a dream as a saintly figure, "drest in shining raiment," with her "hair blown off from [her] brow, and going out like rays round [her] forehead" (149) – an iconography one might associate with Nightingale, the lady with the lamp. But unlike the epic Nightingale, Margaret nurses only those individuals in whom she has a specific "human interest."[142]

Still, in Gaskell's novel individual relationships can both foster and stand in for larger causes; the political effectiveness of the comic ending to the book – its unifying, Nation-building impulse – depends upon its ability to signify a larger bond than that between one man and one woman. And most significantly, her marriage does not turn Margaret into an Edith-like wife and mother. One can imagine her more along the lines of the officers' wives whom Gaskell describes in her letters: "Lady Errol, Mrs Daubeny, & Mrs Galton the 3 officer's [sic] wives who are with the Camp in the Crimea, dress as Viviandieres & wash their husbands' shirts, cook {each other's} \their/dinners &c, & say 'they were never so happy in their lives.'"[143] Like Nightingale, these women have found freedom in the conditions of war – freedom from class constraint and (to some degree) from gender constraint, freedom to work. And while Thornton and Margaret's (and the novel's) final exchange may suggest an essentialist conception of gender distinctions – "That man!" and "That woman!," they declaim of each other – these are the views of the outmoded parts of society, figured in Aunt Shaw and Mrs. Thornton, whose responses they are anticipating. The lovers themselves have assumed roles in which such essentials belong to sex (the realm of passion) rather than gender, and spheres are far more difficult to separate; the independence – both financial and familial – that Margaret has achieved allows her to exert an authority over her husband that is marked by the "gentle violence" with which she takes the Helstone leaves from his hand (436). Thus to recognize in Margaret Hale a home-front counterpart to those officers' wives, if not, indeed, to Florence Nightingale herself – to see her as a kind of "Britannia of the market-place" (to steal and misuse an epithet from Henry James) – is to demonstrate how the war illuminates the issue of "heroic womanhood" in *North and South*. Paradoxically, for all its resistance to epic, this novel delivers a far more successful picture of British heroism than anything produced by the Kingsleys in response to the war. And it does so through its heroine, "That woman!," as one might also exclaim, using yet a different tone, perhaps, from both Thornton and his mother.

Aurora Leigh

Like Jane Eyre, Margaret Hale retains some independence in marriage by making her husband a dependant – in her case, a financial one, as is appropriate to such an industrial battle-queen. Yet the most notorious (if unacknowledged) borrowing of the ending of *Jane Eyre* in the war years occurs at the conclusion of Elizabeth Barrett Browning's *Aurora Leigh* (1856; postdated 1857), in which Romney Leigh's blinding, incurred as a result of the burning down of Leigh Hall, enables the *éclaircissement* with Aurora.[144] While her letters are full of comments about the conflict in the East, Barrett Browning never engaged directly with the events of the war in her poetry – as she did, for example, with the struggle for Italian nationhood. Nevertheless, she was capable of imagining a different scenario. On Wordsworth's death in 1850, H. F. Chorley, the editor of the *Athenaeum*, had recommended Barrett Browning for the Laureateship, arguing that a woman Laureate would be appropriate for a nation headed by a queen. In June of 1854, writing sympathetically to her friend Mary Russell Mitford about a negative review in the *Athenaeum*, Barrett Browning remarked upon her own debt to Chorley: "he has been very good-natured to *me*, and it isn't his fault if I'm not Poet Laureate at this writing, and engaged in cursing the Czar in Pindarics very prettily."[145] Having been preempted from the need to assume such public responsibilities by Tennyson (who accepted the difficult burden, with results that I shall discuss in the next chapter), Barrett Browning was free to pursue the novel-poem on which she was currently working. Not a response to the war so much as a counter-cry of the times, *Aurora Leigh* nevertheless offers another curious antidote to the version of heroism proposed by Amyas Leigh,[146] even as the poem can be read, like *North and South*, as a reflection on the model of female heroics offered by Nightingale.

Like Gaskell's work, Barrett Browning's epic novel-in-verse tackles the interplay of issues of heroinism, genre, and the condition of England during the war years. But its author's opinions of Nightingale were rather different from Gaskell's. They were expressed in a letter to her friend Anna Jameson, the essayist and art critic, who had a few weeks before (on February 14, 1855) delivered a lecture on Sisters of Charity (a term often used synonymously with "nurses" in the war context) that would be published later in the year as *Sisters of Charity, Catholic and Protestant, at Home and Abroad*.[147] Jameson's interest in female heroism was longstanding: she had made her name with a book entitled *Characteristics of Women, Moral, Poetical and Historical* (1832), better known as

Shakespeare's Heroines. Her belief in the possibilities for the new role for women offered by Nightingale encouraged her to write a follow-up lecture, subsequently published as *The Communion of Labor: A Second Lecture on the Social Employments of Women* (1856).

Barrett Browning responds by protesting Nightingale's ascendancy as model heroine. She begins in an apparently complimentary mode: "I know Florence Nightingale slightly. She came to see me when we were in London last; and I remember her face and her graceful manner, and the flowers she sent me afterwards. I honor her from my heart. She is an earnest, noble woman, and has fulfilled her woman's duty where many men have failed." Already, though, one hears in her condescension the root of the poet's mistrust; Nightingale's epic ambitions have been reduced to the fulfillment not of duty writ large, but of "woman's duty." Moreover Barrett Browning seems caught up in her perception of the graces of the lovely society girl who sent flowers. After hinting at the problem, she takes it on more directly:

> At the same time, I confess myself to be at a loss to see any new position for the sex, or the most imperfect solution of the "woman's question," in this step of hers. If a movement at all, it is retrograde, a revival of old virtues! Since the siege of Troy and earlier, we have had princesses binding wounds with their hands; it's strictly the woman's part, and men understand it so, as you will perceive by the general adhesion and approbation on this late occasion of the masculine dignities. Every man is on his knees before ladies carrying lint, calling them "angelic she's," whereas, if they stir an inch as thinkers or artists from the beaten line (involving more good to humanity than is involved in lint), the very same men would curse the impudence of the very same women . . . I can't see on what ground you think you see [in nursing] the least gain to the "woman's question," so called. It's rather *the contrary*, to my mind.[148]

Nurses are still angels, and while they may have escaped the confines of the house, the hospital ward is but an extension of the domestic sickroom, as masculine opinion seems to recognize. Of course, Nightingale was herself no fan of "angelic she's," objecting bitterly to the tendency to feminize nursing by treating it romantically rather than professionally: "popular novelists of recent days have invented ladies disappointed in love or fresh out of the drawing-room turning into the war-hospitals to find their wounded lovers, and when found, forthwith abandoning their sick-ward for their lover, as might be expected."[149] Like Gaskell, Barrett Browning was unfair to Nightingale.

Suggestively, this letter was composed even as the poet was writing *Aurora Leigh*, her own manifesto for the heroine – and for the heroine as artist. Barrett Browning's nervousness about the status of women in the arts comes out both in her argument about the superior good done by art ("involving more good done to humanity than is involved in lint") and in her pleas for sympathy from a fellow artist: "For my own part (and apart from the exceptional miseries of the war), I acknowledge to you that I do not consider the best use to which we can put a gifted and accomplished woman is to *make her a hospital nurse*. If it is, why then woe to us all who are artists!"[150] Margaret Hale's novelistic commitment to individual human interest reflects her creator's dissatisfaction with the moral and personal limitations of Nightingale's epic aspirations. But to Barrett Browning, Nightingale offers too feminine a model of heroism – one might almost say too novelistic a model, for all her mention here of the *Iliad*. And as a response, her own heroine will steel her "womanly" nature with "manly" ambitions, even as her work will build the courtship plot of the traditionally feminine novel upon a scaffolding of traditionally masculine epic verse.[151] It is indeed tempting to draw connections between these writers' views of Nightingale and their generic choices.

While the war plays no part in the poem, like *North and South*, *Aurora Leigh* is full of signs of the times: "It is intensely modern, crammed from the times (not the 'Times' newspaper) as far as my strength will allow," Barrett Browning wrote – indicating once again, in her very defensiveness, the cultural hegemony of the great journalistic voice of the day.[152] Barrett Browning's letter to Jameson demonstrates the degree to which – again, like Gaskell – she thought about the war largely through its effects outside of the Crimea. And while for her some of the most important of these effects concerned the international balance of powers (and especially the cause of Italian unification), the letter also demonstrates that Barrett Browning considered the war in relation to the home front, and in particular, to the "woman's question."[153] So, for example, in October of 1855 (after detailing her response to hearing Tennyson read *Maud*), she agonizes, "War, war! It is terrible certainly. But there are worse plagues, deeper griefs, dreader wounds than the physical. What of the forty thousand wretched women in this city? The silent writhing of them is to me more appalling than the roar of the cannons."[154] While masculine war represents a "physical" wrong, the grief of "wretched women" is (it is implied) a spiritual wrong. And the cure for such a wrong, *Aurora Leigh* will prove, will come not from the real labors of man (Romney), but from the ideal labors of woman (Aurora).

The same oppositions appear in a letter from March of 1855 describing the work-in-progress (note again the emphasis on the poem's contemporaneousness):

An autobiography of a poetess – (not me) . . . opposing the practical & the ideal lifes, & showing how the practical & real (so called) is but the external evolution of the ideal & spiritual – that it is from inner to outer . . . whether in life, morals, or art – A good deal, in this relation, upon the social question, & against the socialists – A good deal, in fact, about everything in the world & beyond . . . taken from the times, "hot and hot." I rather took fright at "Hard Times."[155]

That Barrett Browning sees these issues through the lens of gender, that she indeed considers *Aurora Leigh* to be a poem about a "women's war" (her answer, in a way, to the Laureate's response to his public duties), appears frequently in mentions of the work in the correspondence. Thus she complains of the reaction to her poem,

What has given most offence in the book, more than the story of Marian – far more! – has been the reference to the condition of women in our cities, which a woman oughtn't to refer to . . . Now I have thought deeply otherwise. If a woman ignores these wrongs, then may women as a sex continue to suffer them.[156]

So the georgic argument of *Aurora Leigh* – its claim that even in times of war, when such pressures are particularly strong, poetry is as useful (or, rather, more useful) than physical forms of social work like nursing – cannot be divorced from the poem's discussion of gender (in what lines of work can women excel?). Consider as proof of the conjunction Romney's oft-quoted lines: "When Egypt's slain, I say, let Miriam sing! – / Before .. where's Moses?"[157] Romney's assertion depends not only on his sense that (especially in wartime) action is more useful than art, but also on his sense that female art cannot be epic. Such art is "play at art, as children play at swords" (ii.229), serving merely as an outlet for women to whom "true action [like true poetry] is impossible" (ii.231). The military simile again gestures towards the wartime context for the argument.

Florence Nightingale stands at the crux of these overlapping concerns. This fact appears clearly in the most overt reference to her work in *Aurora Leigh*. It occurs during Romney's first marriage proposal, to which Aurora responds with indignation: "What you love, / Is not a woman, Romney, but a cause" (ii.399–400). He needs a "helpmate," "A wife . . a sister . . shall we speak it out? / A sister of charity" (ii.401, 416–17). He needs a Nightingale. As though repeating the argument of Barrett Browning's letter to Jameson about Nightingale, Aurora insists that her own work – which Romney has just declared "mere woman's work" (ii.234) – does in fact have social value: "I, too, have my vocation, – work to do, / . . . / Most serious work, most necessary work" (ii.454, 458). And once again, Nightingale and *Jane Eyre* (which Barrett Browning echoes here, with

Romney now standing in for St. John Rivers in asking Aurora-Jane to be his helpmate[158]) serve as double filters for the debate about female models of heroism.

Thus Barrett Browning associates Romney with Nightingale's caregiver face: it is he who pushes the Condition-of-England plot-line that was Margaret Hale's domain. The comparison contributes to his somewhat "womanly" characterization (consider how he describes "The whole world tugging at my skirts for help" [VIII.370–71]). But if Romney is feminized, then Aurora is in many respects masculinized. And in fact, her complex gendering is just one of the ways in which the pre-conclusion Aurora actually resembles the real Nightingale: she also shares both Nightingale's epic ambitions and her self-isolation. Like Nightingale, Aurora objects to her aunt's Patmore-like preference for "a woman to be womanly" (I.443).[159] Barrett Browning has Romney voice his argument against the possibilities for female epic greatness. "You generalize / Oh, nothing!," Romney insists (II.183–84),

> – Women as you are,
> Mere women, personal and passionate,
> You give us doating mothers, and chaste wives,
> Sublime Madonnas, and enduring saints!
> We get no Christ from you, – and verily
> We shall not get a poet, in my mind.   (II.220–25)

But Nightingale, as Gaskell had worried, was perfectly capable of generalizing, of thinking of "the human race" rather than "such a child, or such a man" (II.189–90): consider her faith in crêches. Moreover, while Romney argues against this possibility, Nightingale had prophesied in *Cassandra* that "The next Christ will perhaps be a female Christ."[160] Or, rather, Christ offered the perfect blend of male and female; she called a painting by Dürer "my Crucifixion" and described how "the forehead has all the intellect of the God, the Jupiter, & the mouth all the tenderness of the woman. Power & Sympathy [combined]."[161] This mix allowed Nightingale to model her mission to save mankind on that of Christ. Yet Aurora's blend of male power with female sympathy seems similarly motivated. Indeed, modern chivalry is also female, according to Aurora: "The world's male chivalry has perished out, / But women are knights-errant to the last" (VII.224–25). "All men are possible heroes: every age, / Heroic in proportions," Aurora had claimed (V.151–52). But she is far more interested in proving women to be capable of heroism, and she characterizes the epic dimensions of her own age as female: "The full-veined, heaving, double-breasted Age" (V.215).

Ironically, given Barrett Browning's disparagement of her, the terms of attack used against *Aurora Leigh*'s author by critics suspicious of a woman poet's ambitions towards epic – and of the feminization of epic that ensues – resonate with Nightingale's more soldierly persona. So W. E. Aytoun announces that "Mrs Browning takes the field like Britomart or Joan of Arc, and declares that she will not accept courtesy or forbearance from the critics on account of her sex." His "truthful opinion" is that Aurora is insufficiently womanly (the implication is, like her creator): "She is not a genuine woman . . . with all our deference to Mrs Browning, and with ideas of our own perhaps more chivalrous than are commonly promulgated, we must maintain that woman was created to be dependent on the man . . . The extreme independence of Aurora detracts from the feminine charm, and mars the interest."[162] Barrett Browning's lack of sympathy for Nightingale becomes itself more sympathetic, though, when one considers Aytoun's review of her 1860 volume, *Poems Before Congress*. Here Aytoun blasts Barrett Browning's work as a woman poet by relating it to Nightingale's efforts as a nurse, especially in her Crimean manifestation. He begins by eulogizing women as caregivers: "And when we see them engaged in deeds of true charity – in visiting the sick, relieving the distressed, providing food for the hungry and clothing for the naked, or praying at the lonely deathbed, – we acknowledge that it is no vain figure of poetry, no fanciful association of thought, that likens women to the angels!" And he ends the review with a more overtly odious comparison: "To bless and not to curse is woman's function; and if Mrs Browning, in her calmer moments, will but contrast the spirit which has prompted her to such melancholy aberrations with that which animated Florence Nightingale, she can hardly fail to derive a profitable lesson for the future."[163] Barrett Browning's fear of the prominence of Nightingale's caregiver face as a model of female heroics was legitimate.

Still, Nightingale's epic persona could also have raised doubts in Barrett Browning. Gaskell's comments on Nightingale resonate with Aurora's sense of self: "there is just that jar in F. N. to me. She has no friend – and she wants none. She stands perfectly alone, halfway between God and his creatures."[164] Aurora's self-sufficiency ("I laboured on alone" [v.420]) is something both she and her author question as well, and the novelistic resolution of the epic poem stands in marked contrast to Nightingale's continuing to be "single" – not only maritally but also "-minded." When Romney dismisses the young Aurora's talents because he believes women cannot generalize, he bases this claim on their being too firmly rooted in particular human relationships. As he puts it, a woman needs to feel a "personal pang" (II.185) to have sympathy. This orientation might produce lyric, but it won't bring forth epic. But as Gaskell showed in *North and South*, the "personal pang" (or what she there called "human interest") also lies at the heart of the efficacy of the novel. And the conclusion of Barrett Browning's novel-poem, in which Aurora learns to acknowledge a specific human interest in Romney, reenacts some of the conciliatory functions of the conclusion of *North and South*: it represents a plea for the possibility of a poetry that blends the general with the particular, the real with the ideal, the masculine with the feminine, the novelistic (the marriage) with the epic (the vision of the New Jerusalem). It seems an attempt, in a way, to transplant Nightingale's two faces on to a single heroine while leaving intact the "double vision" that Aurora insists a poet should "[e]xert" (v.183). So when Aurora concludes, in that difficult line, that "Art is much, but Love is more" (IX.656), she does so because good art (even good epic) is predicated upon love (the "personal pang"), not opposed to it.

Deidre David (who also notes the correspondence concerning Nightingale) sees Aurora as succumbing at the end of the poem to the role of "angelic she": helpmate to Romney in his attempt to erect a New Jerusalem, "Servant of Patriarchy," as her chapter title would have it: "What I am trying to get at here is [Barrett Browning's] ratification of a deeprooted foundation of Victorian patriarchy – women serve men, and women and men together serve God"[165] – the view Patmore espouses in *The Angel in the House*. While she argues that Barrett Browning thinks of the poet (and especially the female poet) as "a ministering healer to an infected world" in *Aurora Leigh*, thereby aligning Aurora's work with that of the disparaged Nightingale, she implies that Barrett Browning had set out to be a doctor rather than what David calls an "ancillary" nurse.[166] But her claim for the conservatism of Barrett Browning's final message in the poem depends (at least in part) upon her having in effect followed Barrett Browning herself in misreading Nightingale's professional aspirations (Barrett Browning's – and Nightingale's – sense of service to a God who could be deemed patriarchal is hard to contest).

Yet Aurora Leigh is much closer to the real, epic Nightingale than to the Nightingale of Barrett Browning's mistaken conceptions. And for Nightingale, nurses were not "helpmates" to doctors so much as rulers of parallel (rather than ancillary) domains. Indeed, Nightingale's often-commented-upon disparagement of female doctors stemmed not from belief in women's incapacities for the work but from her anger at the implied slight to her own profession, which she saw as superior. Consider her remarks to J. S. Mill (*apropos* the example of Dr. Elizabeth Blackwell): "instead of wishing to see more Doctors made, by women joining what there are, I wish to see as few Doctors, either male or female, as possible."[167] Similarly, her recollections (in a letter to Parthenope) of Dr. James Barry focus on what she perceived to be the doctor's poor treatment of her when they met briefly at Scutari, not on the scandal of his discovered sex:

I never had such a blackguard rating in all my life – I who have had more than any woman – than from this Barry sitting on (her) horse, while I was crossing Hospital Square with only my cap on, in the sun. (He) kept me standing in the midst of quite a crowd of soldiers . . . etc., every one of whom behaved like a gentleman during the scolding I received, while (she) behaved like a brute.
  After (she) was dead I was told (he) was a woman.
  PS I would say (she) was the most hardened creature I ever met.[168]

The fluid alternation between male and female pronouns suggests Nightingale's relative lack of interest in gender here. Nightingale's statements about the women's movement were clearly often disparaging, as were Barrett Browning's (whose views about "weak-minded woman" and whose less-than-decided partisanship of "the Rights-of-Woman-side of the argument" David quotes[169]). But as "strong-minded" women forging new paths in a patriarchal world, some ambivalence about the abilities of their less successful sisters should hardly come as a surprise. *Cassandra* demonstrates the degree to which Nightingale was aware of the cultural constraints faced by her sex. And one can just as easily find Barrett Browning supporting the women's movement – as for example in the letter to Jameson about Nightingale (for all the ambivalence of that "so called"), or as in her comments in a letter about Coventry Patmore: "Mr. Patmore, poet & husband, who expounds infamous doctrines on ['the woman question'] – see 'National Review.'" In the same letter, Barrett Browning describes herself as "militant" and "foam[ing] with rage" – although she also laments that Patmore will "have the best of it as far as I am concerned" as he will be reviewing "my poor 'Aurora Leigh.'"[170]

Patmore recognized in Barrett Browning's epic achievement a threat to his own vision of the angel in the house. To a friend, he wrote of *Aurora Leigh* as "a strange book for a modest sensible little woman like Mrs. Browning to have written"[171] – the phrasing indicates how steadily he held to his construction of womanhood, seeing in Barrett Browning herself a figure not unlike a slightly older version of the woman Barrett Browning saw in Nightingale. Patmore's public review was actually remarkably measured, finding much to admire in the poem. No doubt the conclusion, which he believed preferable to a threatened and threateningly unconventional marriage between Marian Erle and Romney, helped.[172] But in that conclusion, when Aurora and Romney stand arm in arm as she describes to him the colors of the dawn (a stand-in for herself) that he will never again be able to witness without such aid, Aurora has the upper hand – even as she, and her poetry, have the last word. Shakespeare's Romeo reminds us that the sweet song of the lark – not of the nightingale – brings with it the first hint of morning. The question here is whether the promise of Aurora's earlier moment of vocation – "The June was in me, with its multitudes / Of nightingales all singing in the dark, / And rosebuds reddening where the calyx split" (II.10–12) – is replaced or realized by this final dawn of love, what Romney describes as a "human, vital, fructuous rose, / Whose calyx holds the multitude of leaves" (IX.886–87). And I am tempted to read in that "multitude of leaves" not only the variety of loves that Romney goes on to list but also the fulfillment of Aurora's poetic promise in the multitudinous and heterogeneous pages of Barrett Browning's novel-poem.[173]

Cassandra had ended with dawn, too: with a call to women to awaken from their long sleep of subjection. Both these mornings may have still been but flickering signs of things to come, hovering in the Eastern sky. In the same edition of the *North British Review* in which Patmore's response to *Aurora Leigh* appeared, J. W. Kaye wrote a review of recent publications on "the woman's question," including Anna Jameson's *Communion of Labour*. Kaye regards the presence of Nightingale in Jameson's lecture as "inevitable," acknowledging that "Nothing, in these times, is ever written on the subject of the employment of women, without reference to this honoured lady. And in good truth she deserves the honour." Yet he also observes that the services Nightingale had been performing in obscurity before the war were perhaps even more to be admired than those that had "made her a popular heroine." Then he adds:

But although we can see clearly the difference between attendance upon the sick and wounded in military hospitals, during a great national crisis, and such ministrations as alleviate the sufferings and sorrow of less interesting specimens of humanity in uneventful times, we are still hopeful that the example of Florence Nightingale will have an abiding effect upon the women of England, irrespective of the war or the peace.[174]

And while the true dawn of women's rights followed but belatedly on Nightingale's rise to fame, I have argued here for the existence of an overlapping network of responses to the concept of the heroine during the war years that coalesced around her unavoidable figure. The conditions of the Crimean War may have damaged the very muscular form of heroism to which they had initially given birth. Amyas Leigh, a son of the conflict, was also blinded by it. But Aurora Leigh – like Margaret Hale and the other heroines of the war novels – offered a compensatory vision: not only of "heroic womanhood," but of a future "condition of England" in which the separate spheres, of North and South, poor and rich, social worker and poet, novel and epic, and (above all) woman and man, have merged into one.

CHAPTER 3

*"The song that nerves a nation's heart":
the poetry of the Crimean War*

While some of the novels discussed in chapter 2 conclude with unifying rhetoric, the genre itself resists this tendency. In contrast to the dialogism of the novel, though, war poetry – whether epic narrative or lyric song – traditionally works to bring voices together; one of its primary objectives is to ensure that a nation under threat marches in syncopated lockstep.[1] But what happens when the war in question is an unpopular one, in which public awareness of bureaucratic bungling and general "blunder" (Tennyson picks up this word from a *Times* account in "The Charge of the Light Brigade") results in the toppling of a government? In this chapter, I will ask how the Victorians translated their response to such a conflict into verse. While earnestness generally precluded irony in favor of outrage, imaginative reactions to the war show nascent signs of ironic techniques we associate with the poetry of the First World War. Tennyson's "Charge" has been called "probably the last great battle piece that could be written in English";[2] although I will contest the straightforwardness implied by this designation, the Crimean War does represent a watershed moment.

Even before war erupted, mid-century Britain was a poetic battleground. Matthew Arnold's "Preface" to *Poems* (1853) had loudly lamented the absence of "great human action" in the work of modern poets; epic had received its death notice.[3] Arnold and his friend and fellow poet Arthur Hugh Clough debated the proper roles for thought and action in poetry; both felt strongly that poetry had become too subjective, although they disagreed on the form of action required by the times (Arnold favored epic action located in the past, while Clough championed the kind of small-scale and modern action that Carlyle called *work*).[4] Not incidentally, Clough's uneasy resolution to his poetic concerns has a Crimean connection: after the war, he decided to put versifying more-or-less to the side and to spend his time, instead, helping Florence Nightingale, his wife's cousin, as she tried to parlay her new-found Crimean celebrity into improvements in nursing on the home front.

The early 1850s also generated a related uproar about the growth of "spasmodic" poetry, lyrical outpourings that indulged in exploring interior life at the expense of external action – that whined rather than roared. The term gained prominence after Charles Kingsley used it in a review in November of 1853, just as conflict erupted in the East;[5] like muscular Christianity, the spasmodic controversy arose from the same cultural conditions as the war. Kingsley's Elsley Vavasour of *Two Years Ago*, author of *The Soul's Agonies*, would have been recognized by a contemporary readership as a spasmodic poet. And while he avoided branding Tennyson's *Maud* (1855) with the label, Kingsley suggested his friend's poem suffered from the flaws of spasmodism (the ever-sensitive Tennyson seems even to have believed – incorrectly – that he had been used as a model for Vavasour).[6] Others were less gentle, and *Maud* joined the ranks of works by fellow war poets Alexander Smith and Sydney Dobell to be burdened with the classification.[7] In fact the war intensified these debates about poetry, as critics called for the birth of a modern Homer to transform the mess before them into something more exalted.

The increasing influence of the chivalric can be seen as an answer to this call, an attempt (like the war itself) to revive dying models of aristocratic militarism. But the necessary temporal doubleness associated with the chivalric, a mode that tries to bring the past into the present, allows for the opening of a critical space in which we can begin to find something akin to ironic response. Similarly, while the dramatic monologue – the other prominent poetic trend of the war years (Browning's *Men and Women* was published in 1855) – may present us with a single voice, it "presupposes a double awareness on the part of the author, an awareness which is the very essence of historicism. The dramatic monologuist is aware of the relativity, the arbitrariness of any single life or way of looking at the world."[8] Robert Langbaum's seminal study of the form describes how in forcing the reader to balance sympathy with judgement, dramatic monologues encourage ironic awareness.[9] In other words, the two major poetic methods of the day (often used in conjunction) were inherently open to similar instabilities.

To explore the difficult process of converting the experience of the Crimean War into patriotic poetry, I want to turn eventually to Tennyson's "Charge of the Light Brigade" and *Maud*. But before considering the Laureate's efforts, I will give a sense of the poetic landscape within which Tennyson operated by exploring the war poems of less well-known writers: poets such as Adelaide Anne Procter and Arabella and Louisa Shore (whose distinctly female voices of war are notably absent in both poems by Tennyson), and Smith and Dobell (whose sonnets present a veritable cacophony of disjointed voices). Through their work, I will consider the problem of composing armchair poetry in time of war and so present a kind of moral quandary: how does one write without first-hand experience about a war that journalists and soldiers were recording from the thick of the action (see chapter 1)? But while journalism's dominance exerted significant pressures, these came atop a deeper epistemological problem created by the type of war it was: how does one write poetry about what one cannot understand not just for lack of personal experience, but because it does not fit into preconceived categories of experience? I take responses to the charge of the Light Brigade to be paradigmatic here: the bewilderment they express reflects the general confusion manifested by the war poetry (a product in part of those shifts in conceptions of the heroic discussed in chapter 2). Thus my readings of verses about the charge occupy the center of this chapter. The motif of the charge also brings me, inevitably, to Tennyson. Tennyson's two famous poems present remarkably dissimilar solutions to the problem of composing Crimean war verse. "The Charge," in which "All the world wondered" (lines 31, 52) seems to offer the unifying and heroic voice expected of martial and chivalric song.[10] In contrast, *Maud*, for all that it is a "monodrama," gives the reader a jarring experience of multiple voices. Paradoxically, while labeled spasmodic by critics, it was also denounced as warmongering. Yet for all their formal diversity, when considered together these poems reveal notable areas of thematic overlap. In the work of the Poet Laureate, we can see the most complex negotiation of the terrain of patriotic martial verse from the midst of a war that was notoriously marked more by dissonance than by harmony.

I THE POETIC (BATTLE-) FIELD

A poetry of sympathy

Poets of the Crimean War faced an obvious problem that was in essence an issue of sympathy: how to describe something so distant, so unfamiliar? The Romantics had installed the process of sympathy at the heart of poetry (hence the spasmodic tendency to use a first-person voice that thinly veiled – if at all – an autobiographical perspective). But war poetry, with its peculiar documentary demands, also makes peculiar demands of the sympathetic imagination: how dare one pretend to know what it was like? Crucially, the Crimean War poets were not soldiers – unlike the poets of World War I. Nor were they journalists, who were at least witness to the scene and subject to some of the dangers faced by troops in the Crimea.

Critics of the war poetry repeatedly contrasted the heroic virtues of men of arms with the more pacific virtues of men of words; *Punch* laughed at "our patriotic poets" for "shedding a little ink" instead of blood.[11] But they also used the difference to mock poets for their imaginative excesses – or their lack of imagination, which rather oddly came down to the same thing. As E. B. Hamley, a Crimean officer and author (see chapter 1), remarked in a review of the war poetry in *Blackwood's* written from the front:

Scenes of the campaign glow and expand in the pictures of an imaginative "own correspondent" writing up to the requirements of an excited public. The poet, catching the enthusiasm, burns to sing of the war. Fancy and invention he need not call on for aid, as those elements of poetry have already done their utmost in the columns of the newspaper he subscribes to. Nothing is wanted but verse; and his eye, in a fine frenzy rolling, glances from the *Times* to a quire of foolscap, which he presently covers with ballads, sonnets, or some other form of lay, plaintive as the odes of Sappho, or sanguinary as the songs of Tyrtaeus.[12]

Notice how a journalist (William Howard Russell) is the Homer of his age; poetry derives from his sympathetic and "imaginative" labors at the scene of conflict. The poet's "frenzy" is thus simultaneously a mark of excess and of sham; his own artistic labor boils down to mechanical translation of prose into verse.

Such focus on the armchair experience of war dominates responses to the war poetry. Consider Goldwin Smith's review of "The War Passages in *Maud*" in the *Saturday Review*, in which poet and reader are jointly implicated in the perspective:

We do not, like the nations of antiquity to whom Tyrtaeus sung, literally *go* to war. We send our hired soldiers to attack a nation which may not be in need of the same regimen as ourselves. To most of us, the self-sacrifice involved in war with an enemy who cannot get at us consists in paying rather more taxes.[13]

Here, Tyrtaeus stands as indicator of the antique efficacy of war poetry: such song actually made people willing to die for the cause of Nation. But (at least in legend), Tyrtaeus not only sang; he marched and fought along with his fellow Spartans. Smith hints at this contrast by emphasizing economic transactions. Rather than lifting Britain out of its money-grubbing present to restore to it the virtues of a more noble past (a great theme of the pro-war literature), the Crimean war requires of most people – including the poets – only a contemporary economic sense of heroism. And Smith goes on to comment on another poem published alongside *Maud* in the 1855 volume ("To the Reverend F. D. Maurice") as a portrait of a nation at war: Tennyson and his friend chat about events in the East while cozily ensconced at home, glass of wine in hand; the martial poet has – like the epic – been domesticated.

In "The Due of the Dead," William Makepeace Thackeray avoids such accusations of self-serving complacency by directing them toward himself:

> I sit beside my peaceful hearth,
>   With curtains drawn and lamp trimmed bright;
> I watch my children's noisy mirth;
>   I drink in home, and its delight,
>
> I sip my tea, and criticise
>   The war, from flying rumours caught;
> Trace on the map, to curious eyes,
>   How here they marched, and there they fought.
>
> In intervals of household chat,
>   I lay down strategic laws;
> Why this manoeuvre, and why that;
>   Shape the event, or show the cause.
>
> Or, in smooth dinner-table phrase,
>   Twixt soup and fish, discuss the fight;
> Give to each chief his blame or praise;
>   Say who was wrong and who was right.
>
> Meanwhile o'er Alma's bloody plain
>   The scathe of battle has rolled by –
> The wounded writhe and groan – the slain
>   Lie naked staring to the sky.[14]

The force of that "Meanwhile" is too obvious to belabor. And Louisa Shore, who with her sister Arabella wrote a volume of verses on the war, goes so far as to suggest that perhaps the true poets of this war are the soldiers themselves, who write their deeds in acts rather than words:

> The merest soldier is to-day
>   The poet of his art,
> Though he should neither sing nor say
>   The transports of his heart.
> His genius writes in words of steel,
>   And utters them in thunder –

> Whilst we want speech for what we feel,
> Who sit at home and wonder.[15]

Indeed, as both these poems suggest, one solution to the problem of sympathy is to write not of events at the front but of the effects of those events on people "[w]ho sit at home and wonder" – and, *contra* Goldwin Smith, not all effects were economic. Many poems focus on suffering family members left behind rather than on the deeds of soldiers. Perhaps unsurprisingly, women poets especially favored this approach; recall Hamley's dual models for the modern war poem: if one were unable to write poems as "sanguinary as the songs of Tyrtaeus," one might attempt verse as "plaintive as the odes of Sappho." Several "poetesses" picked up on the available motif of a woman's waiting for the return of her beloved, for which Tennyson's "Mariana" provided one familiar example.[16] After all, that is what happens in a war: men fight while women wait at home – the story is as old as that of Hector and Andromache.[17]

In some ways, the war poems of the women poets seem very conventional. As Tricia Lootens has argued, there was a tradition of female patriotic poetry within which they could work. Lootens traces the tradition back to Felicia Hemans, and she explains that this genealogy has consequences: "through Hemans, Victorian patriotic writing . . . came to be intimately linked to longings for home." The idea of home was one that "sought to translate 'natal' loyalties into a larger love of country" – and who better than women, who reigned over the domestic sphere, to attempt this often-complex act of translation?[18] But an even surface, what W. M. Rossetti called (in the preface to his edition of Hemans's poems) "the monotone of mere sex," frequently hid the complexity of the operation.[19] And today, critics still comment upon the simplicity of these works. Joseph Bristow has contrasted the war poems of Adelaide Anne Procter with *Maud*, claiming for the former a levelheadedness against which to view the mood swings of Tennyson's poem: "Procter's poetry is written in a consistently direct style," he remarks.[20] Nevertheless, her very directness can reveal tensions so prevalent in the culture of the time as not to register as unconventional; as Isobel Armstrong has argued (also noting Procter's "boldly simple directness"), "with women writers, the more conventional the didactic lyric, the more accepting of its conventions the writer is, the more it can be used as a way of looking at conformity from within." According to Armstrong, Procter "virtually typifies the woman poet's interests" at mid-century in her ability to write "the poem of the affective moment and its relation to moral convention and religious and cultural constraint."²¹ In Procter's war poems, the relevant "affective moments" – the moments requiring sympathetic identification with the emotional experiences of others – are located in domestic experience that looks afar to think about home.

Thus "Waiting" (which I addressed in relation to *North and South* in chapter 2) tells a characteristic tale of female patience in recording a working-class woman's conversation with a "Lady" as she explains why she dwells at the seashore instead of passing a life of "rest and ease" at the castle: she is waiting for the return of her long-departed sailor-lover.²² In "Waiting," the war remains in the background, something to be inferred.²³ But the inference is supported by a later Procter poem, "The Lesson of the War," in which the nation "waits, and listens / For every Eastern breeze / That bears upon its bloody wings / News from beyond the seas."²⁴ As I argued previously, both these poems attest to the prevalent belief at the time that the war promised to forge class unity out of a divided nation. So the "monotone," if monotone it be, comes from the desire to harmonize a set of previously divergent voices; the poems attempt cultural reconciliation akin to the leveling effects of the battlefield. And they achieve this in part through placing readers into a shared "affective" experience of waiting on the home front.

Curiously, only in a third Procter war poem that strays from this model of sympathy to embrace a more abstract, philosophical mode does the act of cultural reconciliation prove difficult. As its very title suggests, "The Two Spirits" wants to differentiate rather than simply to reconcile – or rather, perhaps, it attempts to reconcile through differentiation. In Procter's lyric dialogue the Spirit of the Past and the Spirit of the Present, represented by mother-figures, debate the claims of their soldier-sons to glory. The poem touches on many themes of the day, hinting at the contest between pacifism and "just war" theory even as it rehearses a dispute between old and new forms of heroism. The voice of the Past is resolute in the conviction of the value of glory; the voice of the Present is more muted, more sorrowful, more desiring of peace – and also more insistent on the cause being one of right:

THE SPIRIT OF THE PAST.
Then, with all valiant precepts
    Woman's soft heart was fraught;
"Death, not dishonour," echoed
    The war-cry she had taught.
Fearless and glad, those mothers,

> At bloody deaths elate,
> Cried out they bore their children
> Only for such a fate!
>
> THE SPIRIT OF THE PRESENT.
> Though such stern laws of honour
> Are faded now away,
> Yet many a mourning mother,
> With nobler grief than they,
> Bows down in sad submission:
> The heroes of the fight
> Learnt at her knee the lesson
> "For God and for the Right!"

But what is perhaps most curious here is how in voicing the distinction between the bloodiness of the old conception of heroism and the more benign face of the new, both mother-figures accept responsibility for the codes of honor that lead their sons to death. The result is a poem of some anguish; Procter tries to assert a difference between the voices, but the very force of the meter – which remains steady throughout the dialogue (a brief first-person dream-vision frame in a less martial and more thoughtful iambic pentameter surrounds the body of the poem) – seems to work against her. And while the Spirit of the Present gets the last word, this word proves particularly disturbing: "Though nursed by such old legends" – as originally recounted by the Spirit of the Past, but as told also, the poem makes clear, by the mothers of the present –

> Our heroes of to-day,
> Go cheerfully to battle
> As children go to play.[25]

The jarring simile reinforces the degree to which those mothers are implicated in their own suffering: it is they who taught their sons to play so. Such women are a part of the culture that has produced the present suffering, for all their ostensible attempt to create a more peaceful, feminized society. Compare Elizabeth Barrett Browning's "Mother and Poet" (published posthumously in 1862), which relates the wartime death of two sons of a nationalist woman caught up in the battles of the *Risorgimento*: "*I* made them indeed / Speak plain the word *country*," "*I* taught them, no doubt, / That a country's a thing men should die for at need."[26] The poems give a new meaning to the link between the idea of a "mother-tongue" and that of the motherland. Procter's verse uses conventional patriotic terms to question, albeit quietly, conventional beliefs.

A related conjoining of natal and national bonds occurs in the much more jingoistic war poetry of the sisters Louisa and Arabella Shore, whose *War Lyrics* appeared in 1855.[27] Once more, most of the poems are written from a home-front perspective. Thus the *we* in Arabella Shore's "The British Soldier" indicates a possession of the war experience based on patriotic and familial bonds rather than direct knowledge: "We know our soldier," the poem begins, "recognise / In him the land whose huts and towers, / Whose social freedom, household ties, / Alone could train such men as ours" (lines 1–4). This poem, too, attempts to reconcile divergent forces: note again the insistence on class union in those "huts and towers." A comparably coalescing force operates on the soldier's body, which merges with the land in which he was born, and appears also in the forced union of "freedom" and constraint ("ties") under the overarching aegis of "social" and domestic spheres that seem more similar than separate. In the poem's second section, the speaker's claim to an understanding that also bridges gender divides is given biological support, even as it is made clear that the poem's collective voice is female:

> Oh British Soldier! 'mid thy feats
> Of wonder, still show what thou art –
> That in thine iron frame yet beats
> Thy mother's and thy sister's heart.   (lines 37–40)

So bonds of blood, soil, and society allow for an imaginative connection between women on the home front and their men at the battlefront.

But while the poems begin on the home front, they do not remain there. Rather, the Shores use their privileged female capacities for sympathy to take their speakers into battle. Arabella Shore's "The Maiden at Home" represents yet another example of a "Mariana"-esque poem of waiting, but here passive waiting shifts into imaginative action. This poem, like Tennyson's *Maud*, begins in an animated and echoing English landscape:

> Fast, fast I pace the long, green walk,
> I wander wide and far;
> The woods are full of phantom talk,
> And all their speech is war.   (lines 1–4)

The Maiden's wandering mimics physically the much more distant travels of her soldier-lover, as she yearns not only for him but also for the breadth of his experience:

> Oh! these dull limits to enlarge,
> This blank with life to fill!

> Oh! to have been in that grand charge
>   Up Alma's deadly hill!   (lines 69–72)

And her marching, enhanced by the metrical march of the verse, facilitates a form of identification:

> See, step by step, how firm and slow
>   Those peerless men march on!
> Through showers of death unmoved they go,
>   And the dreadful heights are won!
>
> Love whirls me with an eager pain
>   Into the battle blast –
> Oh! for an angel's wing to gain
>   And hold my hero fast!
>
> Still must dumb frozen distance prove
>   The blank 'twixt him and me?
> I *will* be with thee, oh! my love,
>   Whate'er thy fate may be.   (lines 73–84)

That "blank" is partly filled by the words on the page, as the poet uses her art (as much as her love) to bridge the gap between her and her beloved.

But perhaps the most interesting of the war poems – other than Tennyson's – are those by the fellow spasmodics Alexander Smith and Sydney Dobell. Their jointly composed *Sonnets on the War* (1855) were followed by Dobell's own collection, *England in Time of War* (1856). As its title suggests, the latter volume is expressly dedicated to recording, through the use of loose dramatic monologue form (the poems are in a first-person non-authorial voice),[28] home-front experiences of the war. Many of the verses are written in a Scots brogue that brings to mind the cockney, working-class voices of Kipling's soldiers; they reflect the new concern for the ordinary private soldier produced by the Crimean War.[29]

Dobell's ventriloquism, however, is far-ranging; he also takes on female roles, as in the effusion "An Evening Dream," in which a soldier's sister gazes at a view of cornfields while imagining the experiences of her brother at the front:

> I love it, soldier brother! at this dim weird hour, for then
> The serried ears are swords and spears, and the fields are fields of men.
> Rank on rank in faultless phalanx stern and still I can discern,
> Phalanx after faultless phalanx in dumb armies still and stern.[30]

There seems to be something enabling to the male poet in taking on for the moment this "maiden's dream of war" (line 31); it saves him from the peculiar guilt of the male noncombatant poet. And, as for Arabella Shore, the landscape itself proves an aid to overcoming distance. In the middle section of the poem, pastoral and martial merge, as the maiden describes a dawn attack on the British camp (the onset, presumably, of the Battle of Inkerman). As the visions take over, relatively measured fourteeners speed up into a much more uneven verse form, accelerated by increasingly frequent internal rhymes, to accommodate the action of the dream:

> A gun! and then a gun! I' the far and early sun
>   Dost thou see by yonder tree a fleeting redness rise,
> As if, one after one, ten poppies red had blown,
>   And shed in a blinking of the eyes?
> They have started from their rest with a bayonet at each breast,
>   Those watchers of the west who shall never watch again!
> 'Tis nought to die, but oh, God's pity on the woe
>   Of dying hearts that know they die in vain!
> Beyond yon backward height that meets their dying sight,
>   A thousand tents are white, and a slumbering army lies.
> "Brown Bess,"[31] the sergeant cries, as he loads her while he dies,
>   "Let this devil's deluge reach them, and the good old cause is lost."
> He dies upon the word, but his signal gun is heard,
>   Yon ambush green is stirred, yon labouring leaves are tost,
> And a sudden sabre waves, and like dead from opened graves,
>   A hundred men stand up to meet a host.
> Dumb as death, with bated breath,
> Calm upstand that fearless band,
>   And the dear old native land, like a dream of sudden sleep,
> Passes by each manly eye that is fixed so stern and dry
>   On the tide of battle rolling up the steep.   (lines 61–81)

Those blown red poppies strike the modern reader as omens of the poetry of the First World War.[32] Here, their color functions as an imagistic bridge to the East. The English scene before the maiden's eyes (to which they presumably belong, given that she has been looking at the cornfields in which they often grow) melds with that of the Crimea, so that it becomes hard to know where exactly "yon" leaves of line 74 are being tossed. When, as this section closes, the maiden – in dreaming of the East – imagines her brother's "manly eye" (among others) dreaming of home ("the dear old native land"), the perspectival reversal initiates the disappearance of the English pastoral from the poem: the dreaming girl has been transported into the world of the soldiers.

And the poem closes entirely in that world, with no reference to the maiden or to the dream-vision frame, as we witness the charge through her eyes:

> Our host moved on to the war,
> While England, England, England, England, England!
> Was blown from line to line near and far,
> And like the morning sea, our bayonets you might see,
> Come beaming, gleaming, streaming,
> Streaming, gleaming, beaming,
> Beaming, gleaming, streaming, to the war.
> Clarion and clarion defying,
> Sounding, resounding, replying,
> Trumpets braying, pipers playing, chargers neighing,
> Near and far
> The to and fro storm of the never-done hurrahing,
> Thro' the bright weather, banner and feather rising and falling, bugle and fife
> Calling, recalling – for death or for life –
> Our long line moved forward to the war.   (lines 159–73)

For all the shared use of repetition, the poem lacks the beautiful and ennobling restraint of Tennyson's "Charge."[33] But it also tries to achieve an "our" – a collective national identity ("England, England, England, England, England!") – that resonates with the conclusions of both "The Charge" and *Maud*. Indeed, "resonates" is an apt word in this context, as the verse attempts to create meaning precisely by allowing sound to resonate – to echo – so that "to and fro," "calling" and "recalling" can meld, even as event (the brother's experience abroad) and memory (the sister's imaginative home-front reenactment) merge. But while the poem performs a feat of sympathetic engagement that is intended to facilitate the creation of a Nation-at-war, a question remains: what role does the breakdown of language, as words follow words through the force of similarity in sound, play in achieving this goal? Why does the poem have to descend from sense to noise in its conclusion?

The poetry of bewilderment: vox populi

We can begin to answer these questions by considering the use of ventriloquism in *Sonnets on the War*, the collection that Dobell and Alexander Smith composed together. While the poems I have considered thus far tend to address the issue of sympathy through focus on a single subject, the *Sonnets* apply a wider lens. They were written separately but published without attribution, and many come in pairs. Collectively, the poems record the war experience by presenting a loose chronological history of the conflict from a range of perspectives. "The Crystal Palace" (symbol of the *Pax Britannica*) appears early, followed by "Murmurs," to indicate the approach to war. Major battles have sonnets dedicated to them, as do representative participants: "The Army Surgeon," "The Wounded," "Worthies," "A Statesman," and, of course, "Miss Nightingale." But while the sonnets function as a collection, they also exhibit collectivity individually: several poems are collages of snippets of speech, both quoted and indirect, from multiple speakers. In a fine treatment of the poems, Natalie Houston has argued that this methodology acknowledges a diversity of viewpoints on the war; indeed, she invokes the term *heteroglossia* and suggests that as a collection, the work "stretch[es] poetic language towards the novel."[34] As a result of this tendency, the *Sonnets* do not display the univocality one generally expects of Victorian war poetry. While the patriotic intent of the authors appears throughout the volume, which was written in part to salvage the poets' reputations from the taint of effeminate spasmodism,[35] the poems nevertheless generate readerly disquietude. The confusion – even bewilderment – stemming from their refractive diversity demonstrates further challenges of interpretation created by the war.

A pair of sonnets entitled "The Wounded" typifies the impact of the collection as a whole:

> "Thou canst not wish to live," the surgeon said.
> He clutched him, as a soul thrust forth from bliss
> Clings to the ledge of Heaven! "Would'st thou keep this
> Poor branchless trunk?" "But she would lean my head
> Upon her breast; oh, let me live!" "Be wise."
> "I could be very happy; both these eyes
> Are left me; I should see her; she would kiss
> My forehead; only let me live." – He dies
> Even in the passionate prayer. "Good Doctor, say
> If thou canst give more than another day
> Of life?" "I think there may be hope." "Pass on.
> I will not buy it with some widow's son!"
> "Help," "help," "help," "help!" "God curse thee!" "Doctor, stay,
> Yon Frenchman went down earlier in the day."
>
> "See to my brother, Doctor; I have lain
> All day against his heart; it is warm there;
> This stiffness is a trance; he lives! I swear, –
> I swear he lives!" "Good doctor, tell my ain

> Auld Mother;" – but his pale lips moved in vain.
> "Doctor, when you were little Master John,
> I left the old place; you will see it again.
> Tell my poor Father, – turn down the wood-lane
> Beyond the home-field – cross the stepping-stone
> To the white cottage, with the garden-gate –
> O God!" – He died. "Doctor, when I am gone
> Send this to England." "Doctor, look upon
> A countryman!" "Devant mon Chef? Ma foi!"
> "Oui, il est blessé beaucoup plus que moi."[36]

While sentimentally patriotic, these two poems are also curiously multi-faceted. This despite their formal unity as (albeit comparatively irregular) sonnets; it is as though the poets wanted to impose order on confusion through the imposition of form. Nevertheless, the sonnets' proliferating voices register the range of the wounded soldiers' responses: from the desperate attempt to cling on, to the brave willingness to sacrifice self for other, to stoic acceptance, to (most surprisingly) downright anger ("God curse thee!"). They also register the diversity of the soldiers themselves, with regard to age, class, and even nationality, as in the Scots of "my ain / Auld Mother" and the French of the second sonnet. Simultaneously, the poems appeal to different home-front contingents: lovers, mothers, and fathers. They remind us of the expanding web of pain inflicted by the war. Unlike in Procter's poems, where the war's unifying power generally secures a positive bottom line in the tally of gains against losses attributable to it, voices here refuse to coalesce. One might compare the ecstatic repetition of "An Evening Dream" – "England, England, England, England, England!" – to the less unanimous call of these sonnets: "'Help,' 'help,' 'help,' 'help!' 'God curse thee!'" We feel for the doctor who must perform his duties in the midst of this cacophony of individual demands. Yet even as he mediates events on the battlefront for the poems' home-front audience, the sonnets' overall emphasis on sympathy also discourages readers from passing judgement.

Thus the divergence of voices in the sonnets emphasizes not so much debate about the merits of war as the poems' concern for the nature of collective experience itself. Such experience lay at the heart of what became known as "the people's war." As I discussed in chapter 1, David Urquhart commented cynically on this designation, devoting particular scrutiny to the concept of "public opinion" and its relationship with "private judgment."[37] During times of war, the contest between public and private ways of thinking tends to come to the fore, and war poetry serves as a major locus of this confrontation. As Tricia Lootens has argued, even blatantly jingoistic poetry tries "openly to unite developing conceptions of subjective identity, at its most intimate, private, and inescapable, with shifting definitions of the powers and duties of public political subjects."[38] But with access to events of the war rendered possible by the documentary efforts of journalists and artists in the Crimea, the junction between private and public perspectives became unusually fraught. As E. B. Hamley remarked in his review of the war poetry, new technologies allowed for the rapid translation of events into publicly accessible cultural commodities:

we receive with tolerable speed and regularity, commentaries from home upon our doings; and not only does the council of chiefs find its deliberations aided by the ever unerring *vox populi*, but the Crimean Achilles reads the inspiriting stanzas which tell of his own deeds in the last battle, before the blood has rusted on his bayonet; while (alas that it should be so often so!) the British Laodamia hears her wail for the lost Protesilaus echoed with bewildering iteration in musical verse.[39]

Note how as a result of the "media culture," Hamley's heroes and heroine (Achilles, Laodamia, Protesilaus) find themselves backed by a chorus: a "*vox populi.*" Like its synonym "public opinion," "*vox populi*" was a slogan of the day. As a letter to *The Times* put it in December of 1854, "For the present attitude of this country is . . . such a *vox populi* as we are almost entitled to call *vox Dei.*"[40] Natalie Houston has argued how Smith and Dobell's sonnets "transform public events into reproducible yet privately held souvenirs" that "explore the intersection of private emotion and public events."[41] But the poets are also interested in what happens when public emotion intersects with private events – that is to say, in the ways in which a group-mentality can take over in response to war, leaving little room for what Urquhart denominates "private judgment."

"Vox Populi" is in fact the title of one of the more curious poems in Smith and Dobell's collection:

> What if the Turk be foul or fair? Is't known
> That the sublime Samaritan of old
> Withheld his hand till the bruised wretch had told
> His creed? Your neighbour's roof is but a shed,
> Yet if he burns shall not the flame enfold
> Your palace? Saving his, you save your own.
> Oh ye who fall that Liberty may stand,
> The light of coming ages shines before
> Upon your graves! Oh ye immortal band,

> Whether ye wrestled with this Satan o'er
> A dead dog, or the very living head
> Of Freedom, every precious drop ye bled
> Is holy. 'Tis not for his broken door
> That the stern goodman shoots the burglar dead. (19)

Here Dobell dispenses with direct dialogue to indicate that the ideas put forth express collective opinions about the war; one is reminded of Browning's strategy in the opening parts of *The Ring and the Book* (1868–69).[42] Dobell's poem can be divided into sections, each presenting an argument about the merits of the conflict. The first three and a half lines claim (with Biblical precedent) that one should help one's neighbor (i.e., Turkey) regardless of his moral standing; the argument is essentially one of principle. But the second section of two and a half lines gives a prudential reason for war – the opposite type of argument (stop the spread of the Russian Empire before it reaches more obvious British interests). As though recognizing the intellectual confusion created by such contrasting styles of justification, the next six and a bit lines avoid the issue altogether by offering a paean to the soldiers, who (everyone can agree) must be honored for their sacrifice, whether the cause be noble or no. Yet as far as the "message" of the poem is concerned, the real question here is how to read the final sentence. Why does the goodman shoot the burglar dead? If not for his broken door – a thing of little worth – it could either be for the principle of the matter (as in lines 1 through 4), or for the valuables that were inside (a prudential argument in the style of lines 4 through 6). So the conflict between modes of argument, which the middle section of the poem intends to dispose of through sympathy with the soldiers, cannot be so easily avoided. In the prudential case, the discovery that you were wrestling over a "dead dog" rather than Freedom renders the shooting (and thus the war) a terrible waste. The effect of this poem is thus not to create a sense of national unity but to create a sense of unsuccessful striving towards such unity.

While the poems on "The Wounded" focus on sympathy, "Vox Populi" is about judgement: was war justified? So when Houston claims that it "takes no stand" on the various positions it presents – that they are merely "set forth as markers of public opinion"[43] – her assessment does not fully acknowledge the poem's bewildering effect. And although sympathy for the wounded may be accepted as given, "public opinion" itself was a contested idea in the period. To Urquhart, "Public Opinion" is something of a misnomer, signifying a consensus that is achieved only at the expense of individual thought:

We say "the public interest," "the public debt," how is it that we cannot employ the definite article in this case also, and say "*the* public opinion." It is that we imply something indefinite; but opinions are many, not indefinite, and opinion taken generally must include the several opinions of which it is the aggregate. The anomaly of the expression is to be found in the incongruity of the process. The opinions are those of parties. There is the opinion of the Whigs, the opinion of the Tories, the opinions of the Radicals, the opinions of the Chartists. Aggregate, indefinite opinion is thus Toryism *plus* Whiggery, *plus* Radicalism, *plus* Chartism. Then it would take the definite article, but these are not *plus* but *minus* each other. The one neutralizes the other, just as by the addition of an alkali to an acid, there remains neither alkali nor acid, but effervescence . . . Public opinion, however, is true as a label, signifying the prostration of the faculties, public and private.[44]

Urquhart's summation of opinions that add up to nothing ("effervescence") seems not altogether unlike the effect of Dobell's sonnet, which is confusing, to say the least. Even the most careful reader can feel some sympathy with E. B. Hamley's response to Smith and Dobell's collection: "Among the jointly-produced sonnets are some which we don't understand, and therefore cannot conscientiously speak of. There are others which we only think we understand, and, therefore, will also leave unnoticed, for fear of going off on a wrong track."[45] And while the confusion of the poems may be unintentional, it appears as a by-product of their multivocal methodology that is itself a by-product of something important – and new – about the experience of this war in particular.

Journalism has again exerted its influence; as Houston observes, newspapers provide a likely source for the opinions expressed in "Vox Populi" (and many other sonnets in the collection).[46] But the role of the press in the war was subject to much debate, as I have argued – not least because of the forms of language it produced. To Carlyle, for example, the war-talk was devoid of poetic potential precisely because it was devoid of meaning: "I am very sad, in thinking of the general matter: a War undertaken to please Able Editors and the windy part of the population . . . a War carried on amid . . . the unmelodious rumour of 'Own Correspondents' at every step."[47] "Unmelodious" wind and rumor have taken over from sensible discourse. Urquhart uses the potentially poetic idea of "voice" to make a related point; he claims that the editorial "We" – especially that of *The Times* – has usurped the individual voices of the British people, effectively silencing them: "The *Times* is no longer an organ of public opinion; it is the organ of England – she sees by it – she hears by it – she speaks by it . . . other nations know England only by its voice."[48] To read the bewildering opinions of "Vox Populi" in the light of such comments is to see the war as productive not so much of national unity but of national nonsense; recall Hamley's reference to "bewildering iteration in musical verse." *Vox populi* becomes the sign not of a working democracy but of a kind of coercion.

"Freedom of mind," Urquhart insists, "resides in private judgment."[49] And curiously, "Vox Populi" is preceded in the collection by a poem entitled "Self," which argues for the primacy of individual experience: "Each man hath his own personal happiness, / . . . / Each hath his separate rack of sore distress" (18). With the unprecedented media coverage that gave everyone access to events directly affecting most Britons only economically, the Crimean War created a new set of conditions for writing patriotic poetry. Smith and Dobell attempted to negotiate this novel terrain by offering a collection that could simultaneously address collective and individual experiences. Yet for all their efforts, a gap persists between what Lootens identifies as "subjective identity, at its most intimate, private, and inescapable" and "the powers and duties of public political subjects." And the poetry manifests this gap in its confusions.

The poetry of bewilderment: "The Charge of the Light Brigade"

The particular interpretive demands created by the conditions of the Crimean War appear most clearly, though, in responses to its best-remembered military engagement: the charge of the Light Cavalry Brigade at Balaklava. There, on the morning of October 25, 1854, over 600 British men rode the wrong way down what *The Times* (and later Tennyson) called a "valley of death," as enemy guns showered them with "murderous fire, not only in front, but on both sides, above, and even in the rear."[50] Fewer than 200 returned to the camps that day. No other event of the war proved as difficult – and as tempting – for poets to translate into verse.[51]

Suggestively, the charge was itself the product of confusion, the result of a series of bungled orders. Earlier in the morning, Lord Raglan had ordered the cavalry division's commander, Lord Lucan, to advance upon some Russians who had stormed the Turkish redoubts above the valley and were now preparing to remove the British cannon they had taken there. But the poorly transcribed order was misunderstood by Lucan; he kept the cavalry at bay. Angered by Lucan's failure to act, Raglan sent a second order: "Lord Raglan wishes the cavalry to advance rapidly to the front – follow the enemy and try to prevent the enemy from carrying away the guns – Troops Horse Artillery may accompany – French cavalry is on yr. left – Immediate." Unfortunately, this message made no sense from Lucan's perspective; where he stood, he could not see the guns in question. So, according to Russell's report in *The Times*, Lucan asked for clarification: "Where are we to advance to?" Here personality got in the way: Captain Nolan, the headstrong cavalry officer who had delivered the message, held Lucan (who had gained the nickname "Lord Look-on" for his supposed cowardice) in contempt. "There are the enemy, and there are the guns, sir, before them; it is your duty to take them," Russell records Nolan (who died in the charge) as responding, with an accompanying gesture: a pointed finger.[52] But the valley indicated (or at least understood by Lucan to be indicated) was not that which Raglan had initially intended. Lucan nevertheless felt obliged to pass the order on to Lord Cardigan, the commander of the Light Brigade and a despised brother-in-law (the feeling was mutual). And Cardigan, motivated by what Kinglake termed "chivalrous obedience," but also, no doubt, by his stubborn anger towards Lucan, led his men into the very mouths of the Russian cannon.[53]

Why has this military blunder become a symbol of the war, and what does our memory of it have to do with poetry? The answers to these questions intersect in the fact of Tennyson's immortal ballad, "The Charge of the Light Brigade," the source of so much of our cultural memory of the war. But Smith and Dobell's poems can also speak to the issue. As Russell's reports make clear – and as several modern critics have noted – the charge has always been considered as an event requiring interpretation. This despite its having been so much the product of witnessing; *The Times*'s leader records how "Two great armies, composed of four nations, saw from the slopes of a vast amphitheatre seven hundred British cavalry proceed at a rapid pace, and in perfect order, to certain destruction."[54] These two facts about the charge – its impenetrability and its visibility – coalesce in the barrage of debate it produced. So, for example, *The Times* begins by announcing the error to have been one of "unusual simplicity": "There was no surprise, not even too short a notice. There was no misconception of the enemy's strength . . . This grand military holocaust was an entirely distinct affair." The language suggests a Cartesian clarity. And yet in the very same paragraph, the leader-writer acknowledges that "How far the order was itself the result of a misconception, or was intended to be executed at discretion, does not appear, and will probably afford the subject of painful but vain recrimination."[55]

And, of course, Tennyson's tag for what the soldiers actually engaged in the charge refused to do – "Their's not to reason why" ("The Charge," line 14) – placed no such prohibition on the British public.[56] Trudi Tate puts it nicely:

What went wrong? Was Raglan's order ambiguous; or was it misunderstood? Was the error caused by topography? Precisely who said what and what it meant has never been fully established. And what the charge itself meant was a matter of dispute, both at the time and since. Were the cavalry heroes, or idiots? Did the charge advance the British cause, or hinder it? Who, if anyone, was to blame? The charge raised questions of knowledge and interpretation that were to trouble both the literature and the politics of the 1850s.[57]

As *The Times* demanded, "What is the meaning of a spectacle so strange, so terrific, so disastrous, and yet so grand?"[58] General Bosquet's famous comment on the charge, "*C'est très magnifique, mais ce n'est pas la guerre*," speaks to the confusion: if not war, what was it?[59] Meaning had to be constructed out of something so apparently meaningless. This was an occurrence that required an act of translation to be understood, even as the event itself came about through a mistranslation: the bungled string of orders.

Appropriately, many visual responses to the event focus on the need for interpretation, for revisiting or reenacting the incidents of the day in order to come to grips with them. Consider John Leech's cartoon (discussed in chapters 1 and 4) "Enthusiasm of Paterfamilias, On Reading the Report of the Grand Charge of the British Cavalry on the 25th" (figure 13).[60] And Ulrich Keller notes two other pictures on the same theme. In "The Heroes of Balaklava Fighting their Battles Over Again," a wood-engraving after a drawing by Captain Henry Hope Crealock, a group of officers and ladies have assembled above the valley where the battle took place.[61] The officers (the "heroes") act as tour-guides, pointing out the scene of their glory – the touristic milieu suggesting perhaps an element of satire. An even more curious take on the subject comes in James Sant's painting, *Lord Cardigan Giving an Account of the Charge of the Light Brigade to the Prince Consort and the Royal Children* (1855), which Cardigan commissioned to hang in his family's country house. The work displays an interior grouping at Windsor palace, with a map laid across a stand on the left of the canvas, Cardigan and Albert in its center, and the clearly entranced children assembled around them (the Queen's absence from the picture is a mystery – she appears to have been present at the actual scene). It offers a private (insofar as it would have been seen only by people of his own circle) self-defense on Cardigan's part, as his role in the charge had come under fire. As Keller argues, it also suggests a shift in representations of the war: "Instead of showing us what Cardigan *did at Balaklava*, Sant lets us know what the general *said at Windsor Castle*. The secondary event overshadows the primary one."[62] The perspective demonstrates the peculiar interpretive demands of the charge.

But poets also had to come to grips with the confusing events of the 25th. Dobell titled his response "The Cavalry Charge" – the lack of specificity registering the occasion's impact on the British consciousness (the Heavy Brigade's successful charge that day received far less attention at the time and has since faded from popular memory):

> Traveller on foreign ground, whoe'er thou art,
> Tell the great tidings! They went down that day
> A Legion, and came back from victory
> Two hundred men and Glory! On the mart
> Is this "*to lose?*" Yet, Stranger, thou shalt say
> These were our common Britons. 'Tis our way
> In England. Aye, ye heavens! I saw them part
> The Death-Sea as an English dog leaps o'er
> The rocks into the ocean. He goes in
> Thick as a lion, and he comes out thin
> As a starved wolf; but lo! he brings to shore
> A life above his own, which when his heart
> Bursts with that final effort, from the stones
> Springs up and builds a temple o'er his bones.   (*Sonnets*, 21)

Yet instead of clarifying the incident, the poem bewilders further. As Patrick Waddington admits, while "evocative and even touching," the sonnet is "strangely diffuse in its basic meaning and message."[63]

Waddington's puzzlement stems partly from the reference to the marketplace: "On the mart / Is this '*to lose?*'" Actually, discussions of the charge commonly enlist economic metaphors to signal the event's resistance to standard methods of evaluation. A clear military loss believed simultaneously to be a great symbol of national superiority, the charge inevitably fostered discussion of competing standards. Thus *The Times*'s leader of the 13th uses confused cost–benefit analysis: "Had there been the smallest use in the movement that has cost us so much," it wonders, right before referring to how the soldiers "sold their lives as dearly as the manifest odds against them would allow." "Causeless as the sacrifice was, it was most glorious," the editorialist concludes. Such paradoxical language (how can we measure such value?) appears also in Alexander Smith's companion sonnet ("Who would not pay that priceless price to feel / The trampling thunder and the blaze of steel – " [*Sonnets*, 22]) and, in a less obvious form, in Tennyson's ballad.[64] Tennyson's friend Henry Lushington sarcastically quotes from "The Charge of the Light Brigade" in "La Nation Boutiquière" (1855) to indicate the lesson that a nation of shopkeepers should have taken (but in his view, didn't take) from the cavalry charge – and his friend's poem (notice that here the reference is not to the charge in particular but to the war in general):

> For her noble thousands
> Dead and yet to die,
> She must have a VALUE,
> Or A REASON WHY.[65]

This demand, Lushington implies, is unreasonable because it uses false numerical methods to measure a kind of value beyond enumeration. Houston claims that Dobell's poem "deliberately acknowledges the fact that the charge was a dreadful loss."[66] And Dobell was indeed capable of recognizing the comfortlessness of glory in the face of death, as "A Hero's Grave" (from *England In Time of War*) shows. In this poem (singled out for praise by George Eliot in her review of the book), he records, in language that movingly negates the kinds of arguments we encounter in responses to the charge, the lament of a father searching for his dead son's grave:

> Thro' echoing lands that ring with victory,
> And answer for the living with the dead,
> And give me marble when I ask for bread,
> And give me glory when I ask for thee –
> It was not glory I nursed on my knee.   (lines 40–44)[67]

But placed in the context of other discussions of the charge, Dobell's sonnet's italics ("*to lose?*") attack the false clarity of economic standards of gain and loss, which fail to account for the intangible added value of "Glory."

Nevertheless, while one can make sense of the poem's use of paradoxical economic language, its description of the glorious cavalry obscures rather than illuminates meaning. The final metaphor of the "English dog" who dies in the rescue of the shipwrecked man is both graphic and arresting, but to have the soldiers compared to dogs – even "English" ones – hardly elevates them. Moreover, does the "starved wolf" into which the originally lion-like dog is transformed allude critically to the condition of the British soldiers in the Crimea following the long hard winter of 1854–55, as well as to the shrunken numbers emerging from the "Valley of Death" during the charge? And consider Dobell's use of the phrase "common Britons": as everyone knew, and as most other poems on the charge make clear, the Light Brigade was unusual in part for being a remarkably aristocratic force. *The Times* emphasized that the glory of the charge was the greater for involving not "soldiers of fortune" but soldiers *with* fortunes: "They were men who risked on that day all the enjoyments that rank, wealth, good social position, and fortunate circumstances can offer to those who are content to stay at home."[68] Is Dobell, as Houston argues, using deliberate irony here to expose the aristocratic military code on which the nationalist sentiment surrounding the charge is based?[69]

Collectively, though, rather than present a coherent ideological perspective, these questions highlight a broader quality to the poem: the way it seems to embrace a confusion that becomes its own ideology. To put the matter so is to note how much the bewilderment generated by Dobell's sonnet on the charge resembles the kind of perplexity that arises in regard to the other sonnets in the collection. For example, once again (although in a less obvious manner than in the multi-voiced "Vox Populi") a puzzle arises from the poem's uncertain point of view. The sonnet offers us not only a narrator but also a Traveller. Yet is the Traveller ("whoe'er thou art") also the Stranger, or is the narrator imagining him to be addressing a stranger? And who is speaking starting in line 6 of the poem, the Traveller or the narrator (there are no quotation marks)? Moreover, is the Traveller British or foreign (Houston calls him foreign,[70] but to make sense of "*our* common Britons" it helps to assume the former)? Either way, he is asked to tell his tale of British honor – encapsulated in a poem written for a British audience – to foreigners; the demand suggests a national identity produced from a shared defensiveness.

Curiously, Dobell's addressee evokes Shelley's "traveller from an antique land" in "Ozymandias." For both poets, the traveler figure works to increase the distance between the poet and the subject of the poem, so underscoring what could be called the "Russian doll" structure of the sonnets. The odd perspective on events reminds readers of Dobell's poem of his distance from the participants in the charge. In fact, because of the geography of the site of the charge, almost all reports register awareness of what it means to witness an event from a distance – a crucial aspect, as we have seen, of the armchair poetry of the war.[71] But included in this awareness is a muted sense of the danger of taking pleasure in the theatricality of it all – a recognition of a failure of sympathy with what the cavalry endured. Thus Dobell's "Traveller" also threatens to turn into a tourist, like one of Clough's tourists in *Amours de Voyage* (composed

1849), who watch the French siege of Rome from atop the Pincian Hill, as though war were one more sight to take in on the Grand Tour:

> So we stand in the sun, but afraid of a probable shower;
> So we stand and stare, and see, to the left of St. Peter's,
> Smoke, from the cannon, white . . .[72]

Recall Bosquet's aesthetic response – "*C'est magnifique*"; *The Times* referred to the charge of the Light Brigade as a "fearful death-parade."[73] Russell described how "Lord Raglan, all his staff and escort, and groups of officers, the Zouaves, French generals and officers, and bodies of French infantry on the height, were spectators of the scene as though they were looking on the stage from the boxes of a theatre."[74] He doesn't mention the tourists (known as TGs, for "Travelling Gentlemen"), but they were there, too.

But while a theatrical analogy (prevalent in almost all accounts of the engagement, even more modern ones[75]) might taint Dobell's various narrators, it could also suggest that the cavalry's charge was "an act" rather than genuine "heroic action." The threat of the inauthentic was perhaps especially dangerous given the identification of the army with dandyism. Indeed, the notoriously vain Lord Cardigan saw his first – and only – real action in the charge; he spent much of the war ensconced in his private yacht (perhaps appropriately, he has given his name to an article of dress). The Earl of Ellesmere's distinctly aristocratic take on the charge makes use of this tension by drawing upon its audience's preconceptions about the cavalry:

> They said we were heroes best fitted to shine
>   In the barrack and ball-room, the ring and parade,
>   . . .
> It was hopeless. All knew it; but onward they bounded
>   With the order and speed of some festival day;
> When with kings to behold them, by gazers surrounded
>   They have mimicked the semblance of battle's array.[76]

Dobell's sonnet plays down the pageantry of the event. But he substitutes a different form of nervousness about witnessing (or should we say not witnessing, given Dobell's distance from the events described?): the almost ancient-mariner-like moral compulsion to retell to which it can give birth.

In fact the echo of Shelley's poem also brings to the fore the concerns of memorializing shared by both sonnets. Critics had been calling on poets to commemorate the charge, and what better form than the sonnet, which since Shakespeare's time ("Not marble, nor the gilded monuments / Of princes shall outlive this powerful rhyme") had been associated with memorial, to perform this task?[77] But "Ozymandias" calls into question the ability of both monuments and empires to resist the passage of history; the allusion hardly presages well, either for the "temple" of Dobell's final line (the poem before us) or for the British effort in the Crimea. And in general, when the idea of the memorial comes up in the *Sonnets*, it is subjected to considerable authorial nervousness. In "Rest," the poet begins by announcing "A victory!" but continues in rather a different vein:

> Thank God this troubled century of noise
> Shall grow as the untrodden desert dumb.
> This England's fame of which we sing and rave,
> Shall seem, years hence, unto the eyes of some,
> Like the effaced inscription on a grave.
> Our many-noised metropolis shall pass,
> And Silence shall grow over it like grass.   (28)

Once more, the ghost of "Ozymandias" seems to hover over the page, and once more, war-song descends into "rav[ing]." The threat of effaced inscription attests to the occasional nature of the poetry, its journalistic impulse. Gerald Massey actually prefaced his collection of poems on the war, *War Waits* (1855), with a disclaimer: "These rough-and-ready war-rhymes can scarcely be looked upon as poetic fruit maturely ripened, but rather as windfalls, shook down in this wild blast of war. I hasten to present them while they may yet be seasonable, lest they should not keep."[78] But Dobell's verse offers thanks for future forgetfulness, as though recognizing the dangers to national pride in lingering over memories of this war.

And yet we do remember the charge – if not through Dobell's sonnet, then through Tennyson's ballad. And this is at least in part, I would argue, because for all that it seems so different – as *The Times* put it, "It is difficult not to regard such a disaster in a light of its own, and to separate it from the general sequence of affairs"[79] – the charge of the Light Brigade can stand in for a more general phenomenon about the war. Thomas Carlyle appears to recognize this fact in arguing for the cultural force of Balaklava in a letter to Massey (acknowledging the receipt of his volume of poems):

To my mind [words missing] fountain of them all is (little as we yet suspect it) precisely excess of "saying" and talking and palavering, – which the English Nation, for a great while past, has grown to consider as the chief function of man, and the substitute for silent hard work in all kinds. I believe the cure of

Balaklava, – and of the *Universal* "Balaklava," which that small *Crimean* one is but a symbol of, – lies far beyond the dominion of *Speech*: at any rate, my sad ominous thoughts upon it are better to be kept silent than spoken, if they were even speakable.[80]

The sound-connection between "palaver" and "Balaklava" reinforces (or perhaps helps create) Carlyle's sense that while the events of the charge are usually seen to embody a certain conception of heroic action, its impact and resonance owe as much to its relationship to speech, to an excess of speech that stands in the way of "silent hard work." (He may have been thinking in part of the "blundered" string of orders that lay behind the fatal charge.) Here again we see the claim that Balaklava registers so forcefully because it instantiates a truth about the Crimean experience more generally (rather than an exception to it), and that, furthermore, the Crimean experience is but a "small" version of something even more general, if not a "*Universal* 'Balaklava,'" an "English" one. But since the disease seems to be linked to speech, the cure cannot come from speech, Carlyle maintains. Or at least not from ordinary speech – or ordinary poetry; the letter is a peculiar one to write to a friend who has sent you his latest book of verses.

Still, Carlyle's claim accords well with the sense one gets from reading Smith and Dobell's volume that – while they were not exactly trying to effect a cure – in their bewildering impact, the *Sonnets* represent a descriptive, even paradigmatic, response to the poetic challenges brought on by the Crimean War. These poets were attempting to create forms that would do justice to a variety of experience – both in the Crimea and on the home front – for which they could find no precedent. They were trying to give voice to what Carlyle alludes to as unspeakable not only because it did not fit in with patriotic proprieties ("better to be kept silent"), but because the language to articulate it did not exist ("far beyond the dominion of *Speech*"). This unspeakable, I shall argue in the second half of this chapter, finds its truest expression in Tennyson's war poems.

II GIVING VOICE TO THE WAR: TENNYSON'S "CHARGE" AND *MAUD*'S BATTLE-SONG

Like Smith and Dobell, Tennyson appears to have felt the need to "do" this war "in different voices": while "The Charge of the Light Brigade" deals impersonally but respectfully with a collective action, an epic deed, in six rapid stanzas, *Maud* wallows spasmodically in an individual's suffering. Perhaps these formal distinctions explain why the poems are so rarely discussed together (as opposed to individually or serially), in spite of the fact that "The Charge" was written even as Tennyson was working on *Maud*.[81] An intimate link between the poems does appear, though, in the crucial place of a martial ballad in the narrative of *Maud*. When the speaker first encounters Maud, she is "Singing of Death, and of Honour that cannot die" (1.177):

> She is singing an air that is known to me,
> A passionate ballad gallant and gay,
> A martial song like a trumpet's call!
> Singing alone in the morning of life,
> In the happy morning of life and of May,
> Singing of men that in battle array,
> Ready in heart and ready in hand,
> March with banner and bugle and fife
> To the death, for their native land.   (1.164–72)

Although this "chivalrous battle-song" (1.383) remains unrecorded – "far beyond the dominion of *Speech*," in Carlyle's terms – it manages to reverberate throughout the pages of the poem that bears its singer's name.

Many critics have been tempted to read Maud's ballad in contrast with the larger work into which it is (albeit silently) embedded. Thus Herbert Tucker has argued that it is "traditional," belonging to an "aristocratic past" at odds with the dismal present of *Maud*.[82] Similarly, Tricia Lootens claims that "What sings itself, through [*Maud*], is the combined folk and chivalric tradition from which the future author of the *Idylls of the King* (1859–85) was to draw his most ambitious attempts to link England's idealized past to its future."[83] Yet the aristocratic nostalgia invoked might belong as much to the poet's current works as to his future ones: it may be that commonly attributed to Tennyson's "Charge," a poem to which he himself referred repeatedly as a "ballad"[84] and which, according to Jerome McGann, also represents an attempt to reinstate the "historically threatened" aristocracy.[85] After all, both *honour* and *death* figure prominently there, too. "Honour" takes over the imperative form in the final stanza of the poem from the otherwise controlling "Charge" of the title, seeming almost to be similarly reified – converted from verb into noun – in the process of being written into the meter (lines 53, 54). And the other end towards which the ballad charges irrevocably is *death* – as in both "valley of" (lines 3, 16) and "jaws of" (lines 24, 46).

In what follows, I shall consider what it means to imagine Maud's battle-song as an air known to the poet as well as to his speaker: as

Tennyson's own "Charge."[86] Why did Tennyson feel the need to silence Maud – in essence, to erase from the longer poem his own recently published ballad?[87] Can we perhaps think of this silence as a presence, as a third "voice" of response to the war? I will begin by looking at how Tennyson's two poems struggle formally to shape history. Then I turn more directly to the verse to see what it might mean imaginatively to embed "The Charge" into *Maud*. Only by considering these poems together can we come to understand the poetic challenge brought about by the Crimean War.

Composing history

At the heart of this challenge lie Tennyson's feelings about the war, feelings that shaped the forms of both his Crimean War poems. Critics of the verses have been fixated by the question of the poet's warmongering. The issue appeared early in reaction to *Maud*, partly because by the time that poem was published (on July 28, 1855), a not-insignificant portion of the public had become disenchanted with the war. Gladstone's initial dislike of *Maud* for its "war-spirit" was symptomatic of the public mood.[88] Goldwin Smith voiced the objection succinctly in the *Saturday Review*: "To the glorification of war as a remedy for the canker of peace, the common sense of the nation, even of the most warlike part of it, has answered, that war, though to be faced, and even to be accepted with enthusiasm, for other ends, is not to be incurred for this."[89]

I say the *question* of Tennyson's warmongering because, as many critics have also pointed out, the poem's formal structure prevents us from equating the speaker's opinion – that "the blood-red blossom of war with a heart of fire" (III.53) would purge Britain of the "canker of peace" (III.50 [1855]) – with that of Tennyson. While Tennyson affixed the subtitle *A Monodrama* to *Maud* only in 1875, the dramatic elements of what he also spoke of as his "little *Hamlet*"[90] were both intended and recognized from the first. R. J. Mann based his defense of the work on this fact; after quoting from a string of accusatory reviews, in which the speaker's failings are attributed to his poet, he insists that "*Maud* is a drama."[91] Thus the speaker should be considered as tragically flawed, not as a paragon to be held up for imitation. While there is some disagreement, most critics today use the term "dramatic monologue" (a label used synonymously with *monodrama* in the period) to describe *Maud*, a designation that allows us to discuss the ways in which the poem's speaker can be responded to with judgement as well as with the sympathy that seems to be demanded by the lyric confessional-first-person mode.[92] This was essentially Tennyson's own take on his work (at least after he had been barraged with accusations of warmongering), as comments made in a letter to Archer Gurney in December of 1855 indicate: "Strictly speaking I do not see how from the poem I could be pronounced with certainty either peace man or war man . . . The whole was intended to be a new form of dramatic composition."[93] While Tennyson may have been using the dramatic argument *ex post facto*, to defend himself from attacks he had not anticipated in writing the poem, *Maud* nevertheless exhibits a degree of ambivalence about its hero that renders it appropriate, as we shall see.

But if Tennyson's use of the dramatic monologue destabilizes his position with regard to the war in *Maud*, "The Charge of the Light Brigade" seems on its surface (indeed, by means of its extraordinarily polished surface) to avoid such ambiguities. It is this quality that has led it to be called "probably the last great battle-piece that could be written in English" – the last great poem, that is, to avoid the ironic awareness that would subsequently plague patriotic writing.[94] "The Charge" gives the impression of upholding the pro-war aristocratic and military code entrenched in the chivalric mode upon which Tennyson is drawing (after all, these are cavaliers he is writing about). McGann's reading suggests how it can be considered as an "attempt to show not merely that the English aristocracy has not lost its leadership qualities, but in what respect this historically threatened class still exercises its leadership."[95] The response exacted by "The Charge" thus appears much simpler than that which *Maud* demands. The judgement required of the reader of the ballad – so much a matter of contention in *Maud* – seems dictated by the repeated imperative of the final lines:

> Honour the charge they made!
> Honour the Light Brigade,
>   Noble six hundred!   (lines 53–55)

If the imperative tells us what to think of the action, the long-delayed epithet *noble* – the only adjective (other than the titular "Light") applied to the Brigade itself in the whole poem – ensures that we know what to make of the actors.[96]

Moreover, if the ballad's final lines dictate judgement, the verses also dismiss any effort at sympathy (the other axis of response to the dramatic monologue) in favor of remote awe – a lack of comprehension for the other, rather than an attempt at comprehension through identification.

This sense of inaccessibility resulted from a deliberate effort on Tennyson's part to avoid accusations of armchair commentary that had plagued the Crimean War poets. In their detailed account of the "creation" of the poem, Edgar Shannon and Christopher Ricks explain how earlier drafts included a witnessing "we" ("We saw their sabres bare / Flash all at once in air") that was removed when the poet realized that it "imperilled" the carefully achieved "respectful distance of the acknowledged non-combatant."[97] Tennyson, who was always acutely aware of the issue of audience, seems to have solved some of the problems he initially faced with writing "The Charge" after deciding that his readership for it was to be the soldiers themselves (with whom the newspaper version had become a great favorite); still, "The Charge" talks to the soldiers only by refusing to claim any understanding of them – *they* being the poem's dominant pronoun[98] – that is, it talks *to* rather than talks *with*.

This distanced perspective creates an astoundingly enclosed piece of poetry – less "well wrought urn" than well wrought sphere – making it a rich mine for formal close reading. Shannon and Ricks have argued convincingly the appropriateness, the significance, of every choice in diction, syntax, and structure made by Tennyson, each question mark and exclamation point, each pronoun, every repetition, and every image. Nevertheless (while they disagree as to the poem's politics) both McGann and Trudi Tate have described how such aesthetic perfection belies the rather messy historical truth that lay behind the work: its occasional nature. Tate in particular shows that the ballad's apparent univocalism masks a much more complicated response to the war. She points out that for all Tennyson's attempts to enclose meaning in the poem, its very subject refuses codified meaning, as I have described. Thus when Tennyson re-invokes a wondering world in the final stanza of the poem, right before the injunction to honor and the designation of nobility attempt to bring to a halt the gallop of the verses and fix their significance, the meaning of *wonder* comes across as lingeringly ambiguous – not just indicating awe, but also suggesting a perplexed and questioning stance. As Tate remarks,

The poem, like the news reports, half-imagines – or wishes – that action might be unambiguous. The physical act of the charge arrests, or prevents, interpretation. At the same time, Tennyson recognizes that action, too, produces contested meanings. Two contradictory impulses drive Tennyson's poem and other writings about the charge: to interpret, endlessly, and to bring to an end interpretation. It must stop; it cannot stop.[99]

In fact, an unintended consequence of all of those repetitions that Shannon and Ricks bring to our attention is the sense that we get when reading the poem, why stop here?

And the poem's genesis is correspondingly troubled. As has often been noted, it was written in response to *The Times*'s reports of the charge, discussed above. But the part of the newspaper editorial that served as its real "germ" is the phrase "some hideous blunder," which provided the dactylic meter for the ballad.[100] The centrality of the concept of *blunder* to Tennyson's poem would seem to undermine the straightforward patriotism often attributed to it. When Thomas Hughes asked Charles Kingsley to write a ballad on the war, Kingsley answered that he could not bring himself "to make fiddle rhyme with diddle about it – or blundered with hundred, like Alfred Tennyson."[101] Poetry about this war (note that Balaklava again symbolizes the war more broadly) appeared almost inevitably to devolve into doggerel once the concept of "blunder" had entered the picture.

Curiously, the idea of blundering also emerges twice in the correspondence between Tennyson and John Forster (friend and editor of the *Examiner*, in which the ballad was first published on December 9), during a discussion about corrections to the proofs of the poem. On the 8th, Tennyson wrote to Forster: "On receiving the *printed* ballad I wished that *my* 'order' (my last) had been 'blundered' and that the first edition had stood – never mind – I have corrected."[102] Forster responded the next day in the same vein:

That you may see how determined I was to carry out your order without a blunder – though I may say I disapproved of its suggestions, which, if you had persisted in them, I would *not* have said – I enclose you the proof which was before me this morning when your letter arrived.

But by a sharp effort there *was* time to try back again – and here you see it is done. I am particularly glad that Mrs. Tennyson thinks with you, with all of us, the original version the best.[103]

At first glance, such light punning about the mistaken orders and stoic obedience brought out during the charge (here rendered unnecessary by a timely revocation of the order) seems almost shockingly irreverent. But the easy translation of the terms into the debate about the composition of the poem suggests how issues brought to the fore by the charge could be understood in literary terms.

It also intimates how Tennyson's attempt to control the meaning of his poem can be seen in part as an attempt to control the significance of the war; to *compose* is to create order out of chaos, and this was what Tennyson was trying to do through the many changes and corrections made to the ballad – including a deletion in the version of the ballad published along with *Maud* in 1855 of the eight lines acknowledging that "Some one had blundered."[104] And notably, while Tennyson was generally keen on revision, the Crimean War poems were both subjected to an unusual amount of editorial work, both pre- and post-publication. If this fact reflects Tennyson's efforts to negotiate his way through the messy politics of the period, it simultaneously suggests problems he might have had in coming to terms with his own feelings and opinions about the war – revision representing a continued effort to refine and fix meaning. So if Tennyson was able to stabilize "The Charge" only after deciding on an audience of the soldiers,[105] the revisions to *Maud* were made in reaction to an increased awareness of the feelings of his audience brought about by the reviews that Tennyson read and to which he referred obsessively.[106] These changes also mark an effort at clarification[107] – and often at toning down the perception of warmongering, in part by emphasizing that the poem's speaker could not be equated with its poet.[108]

But as the disagreements about the politics of both poems suggest, stabilizing the texts failed to fix their meanings. Indeed, critics tend to argue for a stability and self-consciousness to Tennyson's views about the war that misses what I take to be their defining characteristic: an ambivalence that (as in Smith and Dobell's work) registers not as the fixed double-awareness of irony but as a kind of bewilderment. In what follows, I want to look at a few of the ways in which this bewilderment creates areas of thematic overlap – despite their formal difference – between Tennyson's poems. By imagining what it might mean to insert "The Charge" into the narrative of *Maud* in place of Maud's unrecorded battle-song, we can recognize the presence of a set of overlapping concerns: a common confusion as to the relationship between public and private selves, a fascination with suicide, and the expression of a hermeneutics of uncertainty. Finally, I will argue that these themes point to a poet trying to find ways in which he can express the unspeakable.

"The song that nerves a nation's heart"

Like other war poems, Tennyson's Crimean verses attempt a complex negotiation between the demands of society and the individual. But the two poems come at the problem from opposite perspectives. With a long history of ceremonial recital (including, as Tate notes, during World

War I, when it experienced a resurgence in popularity[109]), "The Charge" is part of the public sphere. And the ballad both had its genesis and was first issued in the most public of Victorian media, the newspaper. Curiously, though, some concern about its appropriateness – perhaps because of the centrality of blunder in the poem – can be registered from its appearance there under the poet's initials, "A. T." The fact that a poem so seemingly public, so much what one might expect of a Poet Laureate in his official capacity (Shannon and Ricks make frequent comparisons to Tennyson's "Ode on the Death of the Duke of Wellington," his first work as the nation's poet), was published with some (albeit meager) attempt at privacy suggests both that this war could not call forth the usual patriotic effusions and that the ballad somehow expressed thoughts that Tennyson considered to be private.

In contrast to "The Charge," *Maud* feels like a very private poem. The lyric confessional "I" seems an effort towards not only readerly but also authorial sympathy very different from the distanced "they" of the ballad. Moreover (as Ralph Wilson Rader was the first to set out in detail), Tennyson's monodrama revisits crucial periods of the poet's own life, including intimate aspects of his early love affairs and the family history of mental instability that contributed to his father's death.[110] In the *Edinburgh Review*, Coventry Patmore indicated his sense that *Maud* was not the public work of a Laureate, calling on the poet "to do the duty which England has long expected of him, and to give us a great poem on a great subject."[111] Nevertheless, *Maud* was published with full credentials, "by Alfred Tennyson, D. C. L., Poet Laureate."

But at *Maud*'s center is a claim about the indivisibility of public and private, society and the individual. Herbert Tucker has explored this aspect of the poem most forcefully, and he finds a formal source for the relationship: "[*Maud*] repeatedly represents its solitary central consciousness as instinct with a largely unacknowledged social content. The highly individualistic generic form of monodrama . . . carries [Tennyson's] indictment into the very stronghold of individualism, planting conspicuous social codes within the supposed confessional sincerity of the lyrically speaking, lyrically overheard self."[112] The intersection of public and private is perhaps less surprising if one considers the poem as a dramatic monologue, a form that, as Isobel Armstrong notes, "dramatises the hermeneutic problems in interpretation and communication" and thus "always opens onto cultural problems."[113] Contemporary critics who thought of the poem dramatically also picked up on its propensity for blurring the lines between self and society; George Brimley emphasized how the speaker's "character" connected to the culture out of which it arose, "being related dynamically to the society of the time which serves as the back-ground of the picture."[114] And Tennyson himself voiced a similar link: "I took a man constitutionally diseased and dipt him into the circumstances of the time."[115]

Or as Armstrong puts it, "the war hysteria of *Maud* is a condition of *disease*" – by which she means both of the man and of the circumstances.[116] And in fact, the interpenetration of self and society manifests itself primarily in the disease of madness (at one stage, Tennyson wanted to subtitle *Maud* "The Madness"): Tucker calls the ostensibly private condition of insanity "the poem's most comprehensively public gesture."[117] "I have felt with my native land, I am one with my kind" (III.58), the speaker claims in the conclusion of the poem, thus translating the personal hysteria of madness into the broader cultural hysteria of war fever (like it, experienced somatically: "I have *felt*") and relinquishing the seemingly solipsistic "I" with which *Maud* opens for the collective "We" of the final verse (pronouns are every bit as important here as they are in "The Charge"). As a result of the rule of madness over the poem, *Maud* is peculiarly saturated in its language. As many critics have pointed out, images refuse to stay fixed within the discourse in which the speaker tries to contain them. So, to cite but one example, the floral imagery of *Maud* merges with the martial: the apparently innocent red roses of Maud's garden dissolve into the speaker's heart (which he imagines "blossom[ing] in purple and red" as Maud walks over his grave [1.923]), and finally coalesce into the "blood-red blossom of war with a heart of fire" in the poem's rabid conclusion (III.53).

But for all its apparent control, "The Charge of the Light Brigade" can also be considered as an essay in madness. Indeed one can view the tight shaping of the ballad as a gesture against insanity, an attempt to rein in forces beyond one's control – almost as examples of asylum outsider art (to think of a visual analogue to some of the poem's effects) tend to enclose and organize images in repeated patterns that escape such management in spite of their artists' efforts. Tennyson recalled the general war fervor in "The Charge of the Heavy Brigade" (1885): "O mad for the charge and the battle were we" (line 41). The dual meaning of "mad" – zealously eager and insane – suggests his fundamental ambivalence as to the cultural value of the conflict.

While madness serves as the poems' chief metaphor through which to explore the interpenetration of self and society, within the framework of both works, the disease manifests itself primarily as an omnipresent suicidal urge. The impulse can seem private, as in the opening passages of *Maud* in which the speaker contemplates the location of his father's death even as he fears reenacting it:

> I
> I hate the dreadful hollow behind the little wood,
> Its lips in the field above are dabbled with blood-red heath,
> The red-ribbed ledges drip with a silent horror of blood,
> And Echo there, whatever it asks her, answers "Death."
>
> II
> For there in the ghastly pit long since a body was found,
> His who had given me life – O father! O God! was it well? –
> Mangled, and flattened, and crushed, and dinted into the ground:
> There yet lies the rock that fell with him when he fell. (1.1–8)

On the one hand, we are in the world of individual nightmare here, in a place of sexualized and violent personal memory. But the geography can also be thought of as a grotesque reinterpretation of the stark valley of "The Charge," another hollow in which "death" echoes as the answer to every question posed. Like the witnesses standing on the Heights above the cavalry at Balaklava, the speaker here stands above the scene of horror and can only wonder: "who knows?" (1.9). This perspectival conjunction (and the shared dactylic impulse, both epically and elegiacally inflected) suggests that the two poems are attempting, at least in part, to come to grips with a single phenomenon. For indeed the more licensed public and collective act of (especially non-conscripted) soldiers going to war can be considered suicidal. This fact has led many to argue that the speaker of *Maud* does not overcome his suicidal urges at the end of the poem but has merely managed to translate them into a more socially sanctioned form – just as the "blood-red heath" of the opening lines (which the poet regarded as proof of his speaker's madness[118]) transmutes into the (surely, equally implicating) "blood-red blossom of war" of its penultimate stanza. When the speaker declares himself "at war with myself and a wretched race" (1.364), he is registering the intersection of the private theme of suicide with the more public concerns of the poem – and he is registering the role war plays in the overlap. In this context, the "mangled" corpse of the speaker's father calls to mind the many descriptions of corpses strewn across battlefields in the war literature of the period.[119] He is, after all, a victim of the "Civil war" (1.27) described in the opening sections of *Maud*.

Yet if all war represents a kind of suicide, the charge epitomized the connection. Recall how *The Times*'s leader described it as "splendid self-sacrifice"; Russell wrote somewhat more critically of men "rushing into the arms of death."[120] Tennyson acknowledges the suicidal impulse in the almost casual exchange of one conjunction for another in his ballad:

> Their's not to reason why,
> Their's but to do and die:
> Into the valley of Death
>   Rode the six hundred.   (lines 14–17)

"Do and die," not do *or* die. Shannon and Ricks call this line "one of Tennyson's greatest evocations of duty" – the "unuttered" thought (like Maud's unvoiced ballad) that is the soul of the poem.[121] Surely, though, to "do or die" should be enough. The more common version of the phrase appears in Tennyson's friend Franklin Lushington's poem describing the heroic efforts at the Alma: "Fifty thousand men rise up to do or die."[122] But the substitution of conjunctions marks the difference between bravery and suicide, between "ordinary" battles, such as the Alma, and the extraordinary charge at Balaklava, between what people had thought the Crimean War would represent and what it came to represent. Thus when Emily inadvertently replaced the *and* with an *or* in one version of the manuscript, Tennyson immediately corrected the mistake.[123]

In Tennyson's version of the phrase, the soldier faces not a choice or chance between heroic action and martyrdom but an inevitable conflation of the two. An act that simultaneously expresses the desire to forgo action altogether, the suicidal deed can only very rarely (and with difficulty) be described as epic. Yet the charge of the Light Brigade presented just such a rare occasion, when suicide and what Matthew Arnold had recently called "great human action" coincided. Christopher Ricks sees Tennyson as envious of the "assured simplicity" of the soldiers' response in "The Charge" largely because of the personal attraction to him of the idea of honorable suicide.[124] In a sense, then, this war, with its nationally registered miseries and confusions, allowed Tennyson a way to express publicly his most private desires and terrors by translating them into broadly acceptable patriotic terms. But if nothing else, *Maud*'s thorough exploration of the similarity between dishonorable and honorable suicide demonstrates how keenly alive he was to the ambiguities presented by even so apparently clear-cut an example of heroism as the charge.

Nevertheless, the charge contributed to changing perceptions of the heroic. In *The Heroes, or Greek Fairy Tales for my Children* (1856), Charles Kingsley remarked how "heroes" was the name which the Hellens gave to men who were brave and skilful, and dare do more than other men . . . [A]fter a time it came to mean . . . men who helped their countries . . . And we call such a man a hero in English to this day, and call it a 'heroic' thing to suffer pain and grief.[125]

Suffering has taken over from action as the core quality of heroism. And in "Extracts from a Peace Dictionary," an ongoing satirical commentary in *Punch* on the abuses of language to which war had led, "hero" was defined as "A Fool who dies for his country, when he could stop at home perfectly safe";[126] recall *The Times*'s leader describing the Light Brigade's "fortunate circumstances," had they been "content to stay at home." Indeed the charge – a failure by any normal military standards – came to represent this new, ambiguous (and peculiarly British) form of success. Russell, in his report of the 14th, claimed of the cavalry that "demi-gods could not have done what we had failed to do."[127] While on the one hand, he wanted to defend the failure to take the guns, his words also contain the suggestion that the failed action of the Brigade was more glorious than the successful actions of "demi-gods" would have been. As Tricia Lootens has contended, citing Ruskin, "the idealized Victorian soldier's 'trade' was . . . 'not slaying, but being slain.'" Ruskin posited in "The Roots of Honour" that this willingness for "self-sacrifice" (the phrase repeatedly invoked in discussions of the charge) was the essential distinction between the soldier and the merchant, and thus the source of the respect he was justly accorded.[128] Note how once again these comments imply how the charge was understood as having escaped the seemingly all-embracing social cash-nexus. Appropriately, Ruskin also strongly supported Tennyson's reinstitution of the "blundered" line into the ballad.[129] The British sense of a heroic that is as closely linked to failure as to success has survived: they remain notoriously "good losers." It is, perhaps, a particularly important "value" for a nation of shopkeepers to uphold.

The quest for failure is also the subject of a poem that serves as a bridge between the chivalric austerities of "The Charge" and the grotesque self-revelations of *Maud*: Robert Browning's "Childe Roland to the Dark Tower Came" (published, like *Maud*, in 1855). Isobel Armstrong notes that "Childe Roland" is unusual for Browning: "reaching back to the chivalric world which Tennyson had already laid claim to, it is a symbolic and existential poem of a kind Browning rarely wrote"; Linda Hughes has called Browning's poem a "Tennysonian" manifestation of the dramatic monologue.[130] At its heart is a suicidal journey not unlike the charge of the Light Brigade; thinking of those who had tried and failed before him to reach the Tower, Roland admits that "just to fail as they, seemed best, / And all the doubt was now – should I be fit?"[131] As a gloss on what it means to be "fit" for failure, one could not do better than to consider the charge. And, Armstrong suggests, in their exploration of what they refer to as "the soldier's art" (line 89), Browning's verses can even be thought of as presaging the events of the war:

> This is surely Browning's prophetic Crimean-war poem. It was actually written in 1852. Through the violent terror of the restricted and distorted vision of masculine values it makes its critique indirectly, considering the destructive effect of the coercive ideology of heroism, the black mythos which was to cause such carnage in the Crimean war. The inexplicable caged cats and poisoned toads become less the product of sadistic imaginings than a prescient understanding of the significance and implications of the martial beliefs which sent men into "the valley of Death", as Tennyson called it, in "The Charge of the Light Brigade", written to mark a military blunder two years later.[132]

To take Armstrong's hints a step further, we can think of the poems as "Light" and "Dark" visions of parallel chivalric quests, even as the geography of the Tower of death offers a suggestive contrast to Tennyson's "valley of Death."

But of course Browning's dramatic monologue is much closer to *Maud* in tone, and the aggressively phallic tower finds a better correlative in the bloody labial folds of the hollow in which *Maud* opens. If "Childe Roland" is Browning's most Tennysonian poem, then surely *Maud* is Tennyson's most Browningesque work. Perhaps "Childe Roland" is what "The Charge" would have become had it been directly translated into the world of *Maud*, had it been sung by the speaker rather than by the unrecorded Maud (as I am imagining). The grotesque visions of the poems' two narrators do seem eerily comparable: Roland's sense of trampling on "a suicidal throng" (line 118) as he fords the river and of spearing a water rat that utters "a baby's shriek" (line 126) remind one of the nightmarish ravings of *Maud*'s speaker from the other side of experience in the "mad scene," as he believes himself to be buried in a community of shallow graves (II.239–342).

Crucially, both Browning's and Tennyson's speakers initially find the worlds they inhabit impossible to read. Armstrong's comments on "Childe Roland" apply with equal justice to *Maud*: "The language is crude and violent and heavy with overwrought physical horror and hysteria. Sexual hatred and disgust emerge in a miasma of perceptual uncertainty . . . Language is unreliable."[133] Browning's dramatic monologue opens by voicing such unreliability – "My first thought was, he lied in every word" – but Roland's words could easily be attributed to *Maud*'s hero, who constantly expresses his uncertainty about the truth of his perceptions and others' claims. His core suspicions and hopes concern Maud's truthfulness: "Yet if she were not a cheat, / If Maud were all that she seemed" (1.280–81). And both poems conclude by offering certitude. Even as "Childe Roland" ends with a claim of knowledge ("I saw them and I knew them all" [line 202]), Tennyson's speaker learns to shift his accusations from Maud and her family to the Czar, the "giant liar" (III.45) who becomes the receptacle for any lingering doubts, allowing him finally to "embrace" his jingoistic convictions (III.59). Still, for all their apparent resolution, the poems leave readers with a sense of uncertainty that is linked to their peculiarly grotesque reinterpretations of chivalric quest narrative. Ruskin's third category of the Grotesque in *Modern Painters, Volume III* (1856) suggests a form of bewilderment not unlike what I am ascribing to Tennyson's Crimean War poetry: "C). Art arising from the confusion of the imagination by the presence of truths which it cannot wholly grasp."[134] Browning's poem thus helps us to see the grotesque underpinnings not only of *Maud* but also – less obviously – of "The Charge."

The tonal overlap between the poems leads me to wonder whether we are witnessing something new in how poets were using the chivalric during the period of the war. Chris R. Vanden Bossche has argued in reference to *Maud* that "the modern psyche results from the dissolution of the chivalric social order; for the subject as social entity, the modern world substitutes the isolated, solipsistic individual."[135] The "return to chivalry" thus indicates an attempt to return to "communitarian values," or to provide "a point of vantage from which to criticize" modern individualistic commercial values.[136] But as "Childe Roland" makes clear – even if *Maud* leaves it in some doubt – in poetry of the period chivalric motifs can be used precisely to indicate the existence of the "isolated solipsistic individual." What we have in such instances is not so much a nostalgic use of the chivalric as a modern, grotesque reinterpretation of it. And for all its nostalgic invocation of chivalry, where *Maud* feels most modern is where it also seems most grotesquely, almost existentially, suicidal, as in the closing passages of the poem.

What could be called the chivalric-grotesque arises in other verse of the period, too, such as William Morris's *The Defence of Guinevere and Other Poems* (1858). Armstrong sees these poems as embodying a "traumatic understanding" of the Crimean War through a "grotesque fascination with violence [that] refuses to match the complexities from which it emerges. Violence is the Grotesque's oversimplification of the complexities to which the numbed consciousness cannot respond."[137] Christopher Ricks has suggested that "Tennyson liked the idea of battles because they seemed simple, not difficult";[138] again, violence may offer an escape from the confusions of modern life. Yet as Walter Bagehot argued in a review of *Idylls of the King*, while claims of simplicity may have been true for the battles of the past, they no longer held for modern ones. These, as often as not, devolved into versions of the battle of Epipolie, where (in Arnold's famous words) "ignorant armies clash by night." Hence, Bagehot concluded, "the events of the chivalric legend are better adapted" to poetry than more recent wars, because they "present human actions in a more intelligible shape."[139] Nevertheless, the charge offered a clarity – or at least a visibility – that made it reminiscent of chivalric jousts: the cavalry rushed forward, all 600 men functioning as a unit, and then (what was left of it) rushed back. And the duel at the center of *Maud* replaces the confusions of the "civil war" in which Britain was enmeshed with what seems to be a simple one-on-one confrontation.[140] Still, these instances of violence proved more complex than is suggested by their straightforward appearances; for all their invocations of the chivalric past, Tennyson's Crimean War poems are far from offering clarity.

Childe Roland's quest takes its direction from an ambiguously pointed finger (line 16) – the very gesture that was said to be responsible for the charge at Balaklava, when Captain Nolan, the officer who delivered the fateful order, supposedly pointed the cavalry in the wrong direction. As it happens, Tennyson's two Crimean poems are plagued by issues of a different kind of finger-pointing: of determining responsibility. Shannon and Ricks have argued how "The Charge" attempts to avoid assessing blame by not naming names in its finalized version (the one name included in the version first published in the *Examiner* was Nolan's: "'Take the guns,' Nolan said" [line 6]).[141] But with "blunder" so central to both event and poem, the question "whose?" cannot be so easily dispensed with. If the poem describes a collective act of bravery based upon the revocation of individual will or judgement ("Their's not to reason why"), it also suggests the possibility of a collective responsibility for the charge (a silent "Ours").

In contrast, an unmistakable atmosphere of guilt and blame pervades *Maud*. But the issue of responsibility arises most forcefully in regard to the private duel that results in the death of Maud's brother. Tucker has discussed the odd ambiguities surrounding the start of Part II, "'The fault was mine, the fault was mine' – ," calling this line "both the most naked admission of responsibility in all of *Maud* and the most resistant to personal attribution. 'The fault was mine'; but the words are whose? They repeat what the brother has said, yet obviously they tell the hero's truth too."[142] And as in "The Charge," culpability for death spreads like a disease through the poem, simultaneously implicating everyone and no one in the tragedy. Aggravating the sense of free-floating responsibility, the duel itself happens in the interstices of the poem, in the gap between Parts I and II. By the time events are described, they are already over, giving the impression that nothing could have been done to prevent them. "What is it, that has been done?" (II.7), the speaker wonders, the passive construction indicating the degree to which he is dissociated from his own deed, which becomes not an act of individual will but rather yet another manifestation of a diseased culture.

The speaker's question about the duel also resonates with the broader confusions of "The Charge," which describes an event that (as we have seen) proved just as difficult to account for. At the heart of the ballad, immediately following its "germ" – the acknowledgement that "Some one had blundered" – come the three lines of the poem that speak most directly (even if in the negative) to the issue of hermeneutical uncertainty:

> Their's not to make reply,
> Their's not to reason why,
> Their's but to do and die.   (lines 13–15)

Suggestively, the reply-why-die rhyme is repeated in a curiously parallel passage of *Maud*: the "Courage, poor heart of stone!" lyric:

> Courage, poor heart of stone!
> I will not ask thee why
> Thou canst not understand
> That thou art left for ever alone:
> Courage, poor stupid heart of stone. –
> Or if I ask thee why,
> Care thou not to reply:
> She is but dead, and the time is at hand
> When thou shalt more than die.   (II.132–140)

This lyric occupies a similarly central position in the longer work, following hard upon the memory of the duel, in which issues of responsibility and agency appeared so opaque, and immediately preceding its "germ," "O that 'twere possible" (II. 141–238).

Written in the first two weeks of August 1855, "Courage, poor heart of stone!" marks Tennyson's earliest revision of *Maud* after the poem's publication, and it was added in part to make Maud's death clear.[143] Yet the declaration – "She is but dead" – represents the only point of certainty in the passage (its boldness suffers, too, from the inclusion of that mediating "but"). Indeed, as an effort at clarifying an ambiguous event, the lyric also resonates more broadly with the interpretive agenda of "The Charge." One might even argue that it stands in place of Maud's unvoiced ballad, as an unsuccessful attempt, as it were, to lay that ghostly presence to rest as well. These added words thus express Tennyson's unconscious sense of a connection between his Crimean poems; hence the repeated rhyme sequence. The refusal of interpretation on the part of the cavalry reappears as the tortured self-questioning of the speaker of *Maud*, in which the idea of such refusal is unmasked for the fiction it must be: "Or if I ask thee why" – of course, he must ask. The question cannot be avoided, even if the answer remains unattainable.

The lyric actually toys cruelly with our desire to understand, using its very rhyme scheme to mock us. Structurally, we can think of its first three lines as introduction, each line offering a new end-sound. Line 4 not only adds syllables to the metrical pattern of the first section, it also revisits the end-sound of the first line by giving us the first rhyme of the lyric ("stone"–"alone"). In line 5, this rhyme is repeated to give us a couplet in the "a" rhyme, a pattern that lines 6 and 7 repeat with the "b" rhyme ("why"–"reply"); in both of these couplets, one line ends in a word introduced in the first three lines of the poem. So when we encounter the "–and" rhyme ("c") in "hand" at the end of line 8, it makes perfect sense to expect the pattern to be continued with a couplet in the final two lines of the poem, a couplet in which the word that introduced the "c" sound to us is repeated (as "stone" and "why" have already been repeated). That word would have been "understand." In its place, though, after a promising hint in "than" of the desired sound pattern, Tennyson gives us "die." As Thomas J. Assad puts it in discussing this configuration, "Instead of satisfactorily completing the suggested pattern, the last line turns the reader back, by its meter and rhyme, into the middle of the poem."[144] But it also returns us to the rhyming patterns – and the fatalism – of "The Charge." The closure of understanding gives way to the closure of death.

The change speaks to the issue of directionality in both poems, the way in which repetition works in them. In "The Charge" we go into the valley and we come out of it, and hopefully stay out. But do we? In *Maud*, the parts of the poem also appear structured to take us in and out, down into the morass of madness and up and out into sanity.[145] But do they? In both cases, repetition that should promise the upward circling of dialectic instead threatens to spiral on endlessly without synthesis.[146] Recall Trudi Tate's comments on the ballad: "Two contradictory impulses drive Tennyson's poem and other writings about the charge: to interpret, endlessly, and to bring to an end interpretation. It must stop; it cannot stop." All that the poems leave us with for consolation are their imperatives: "Charge," "Forward," Honour," and, most urgently, "Courage."

Courage was precisely what ballads like Maud's unrecorded song and Tennyson's "Charge" were designed to give. While Maud's song may remain unrecorded, Tennyson's didn't: "The Charge" was chosen to immortalize the poet's voice on to Edison's newly invented wax cylinders in 1890.[147] Although it was made in part to promote the recently formed Light Brigade Relief Fund (to support the remaining survivors of the charge), the choice is unsurprising, given that both Crimean poems have a history of being read aloud – and even of being sung.[148] The incantatory nature of "The Charge" comes out beautifully in Tennyson's recitation for the phonograph, which sounds not unlike the "something between a croak and a song" Virginia Woolf attributes to Mr. Ramsay's rendition of the ballad in *To the Lighthouse* (1927), during his reenactment of the charge on his front lawn.[149] And apparently, the soldiers to whom the poem was originally dedicated also felt song to be the natural way in which to give voice to it. In a letter to Forster, Tennyson quoted the request of a chaplain in the Crimea for copies of "The Charge" (he eventually sent two thousand): "It is the greatest favourite of the soldiers – half are singing it and all want to have on black and white – so as to read – what has so taken them."[150] Although they may have desired texts for the purposes of reading, the soldiers' initial impulse towards song seems appropriate to a poem so perfectly written for recital, with or without music. Indeed, Rudyard Kipling points to this quality in "The Last of the Light Brigade" (1890), written in response to the sad story of the apparently unsuccessful Fund (note the further pun on *charge*, as it is converted into an economic register): "Our children's children are lisping to 'honour the charge they made' – / And we leave to the streets and the workhouse the charge of the Light Brigade!"[151] Even a child can memorize Tennyson's ballad.

While *Maud*'s length precludes such memorization, it is also a poem of the voice. In his investigation of the work as monodrama, Dwight Culler points to the genre's close relationship with performance, and especially musical performance – R. J. Mann is not the only one to comment on *Maud*'s "word-music."[152] And then, of course, there is Tennyson's obsession with reading the poem aloud, an obsession so marked as to have become the subject of Woolf's satire in her play *Freshwater* (written in 1923). As in "The Charge," voiced repetition seems to be a crucial part of the story, of how meaning is generated by the poem. Tennyson's proclivity may have owed something to his desire to prove the critics wrong about his cherished work, but his ability to prove them wrong through recital is also interesting. As Hallam Tennyson remarked, "It is notable that two such appreciative critics as Mr. Gladstone and Dr. Van Dyke wholly misapprehended the meaning of *Maud* until they first heard my father read it, and that they both then publicly recanted their first criticisms [of the poem's violent militarism]."[153] Elizabeth Barrett Browning was also impressed, declaring of the reading of *Maud* at her home on September 27, 1855 (at which Dante Gabriel Rossetti sketched the poet performing): "it *was* wonderful, tender, beautiful, and he read exquisitely in a voice like an organ, rather music than speech."[154]

Linda Hughes has argued of the repeated readings that "Tennyson's eccentricity may suggest that only by hearing *Maud* do we understand it fully."[155] And in fact, the poet himself said as much in a letter to Charles Richard Weld: "I think that properly to appreciate it you ought to hear the author read it."[156] But maybe the readings converted so many listeners precisely because they allowed their contemporary audiences to understand the poem not fully but partially – that is, to close off and fix interpretation in a manner that permitted the work to fit in more easily with Victorian conventions, whether pro- or anti-war. I am reminded of the Romantic understanding of closet drama as a mode that refuses such fixed meaning, especially given that Tennyson called his poem a "little *Hamlet*," thus associating it with a play that was revered by the Romantics for its readerly qualities: all those soliloquies, all that meditative inaction. Charles Lamb described his response to having seen a great performance of a play by Shakespeare in his youth:

It seemed to embody and realize conceptions which had hitherto assumed no distinct shape. But dearly do we pay all our life after for this juvenile pleasure, this sense of distinctness. When the novelty is past, we find to our cost that instead of realizing an idea, we have only materialized and brought down a fine vision to the standard of flesh and blood.[157]

Lamb disliked such fixture, preferring the open possibilities of the reading experience. But when dealing with events as complex and troubling to conventional beliefs as those of the Crimean War, "distinctness" – of any kind – would have been perhaps rather comforting than the reverse. Hallam's recollection of his father's mode of reading – "The passion in the first Canto was given by my father in a sort of rushing recitative through the long sweeping lines of satire and invective" – suggests how interpretation became set in the process.[158] Alternatively, the focus on musicality that characterized so many listeners' responses to the poem could have allowed them to avoid some of its more disquieting aspects by calling forth an emotional rather than a rationally coherent response.

Tennyson's recorded recital of "The Charge" draws a similarly emotional response: it is almost impossible not to feel a surge forward along with the verse. Such declamation brings poetry into the realm of action; as Tennyson puts it in "The Charge of the Heavy Brigade," "The song that nerves a nation's heart, / Is in itself a deed" (Epilogue, lines 79–80), a convenient belief for an armchair poet of war. Woolf draws on this aspect of the poem's effect in *To the Lighthouse* when she imagines Mr. Ramsey being propelled forward by his performance of the poem: it becomes an act, a physical "Charge." Yet if the ballad can "nerve" when recited, reading it somehow unnerves (for all that the poem obscures signs of the kind of unhinged nerves so prevalent in *Maud*). And as Eric Griffiths has argued, "Tennysonian eloquence leads a double life; it invites and repays voicing, it also asks for constant recognition of the quieter life of the words on the page."[159] This quieter life allows us to hear the uncertainties expressed by "The Charge of the Light Brigade," uncertainties that manifest Tennyson's difficulties in responding to this perplexing war.

But nothing is quieter than the silent presence of Maud's ballad. Perhaps the ballad is silent because, as I have suggested, the poem's form could only have allowed us to hear it through the muddying medium of the speaker's unhinged voice. Or perhaps Maud's battle-song can't be written down because, in the wider context – not only of *Maud* but of the Crimean War – to write it down would be to open it up to suspicious readings (like that to which I and others have subjected "The Charge") from which Tennyson wished to preserve it. But maybe its very silence provides the purest expression of the bewildering problems faced by the poets of the Crimean War – and their most perfect solution. Not only a song that can no longer be sung (the pure chivalric values it espouses having passed into history), Maud's ballad can also be thought of as a song that cannot yet be sung, a ghostly precursor to the protest poems of later wars.

CHAPTER 4

Painters of modern life: (re)mediating the Crimean War in the art of John Leech and John Everett Millais

Thomas William Robertson's comedy *Ours* (1866) uses a backdrop of the Crimean War to focus on the battle between the sexes.[1] Robertson had a reputation for writing plays that tackled contemporary problems head-on, as in *Caste* (1867), deemed a "tiny theatrical revolution" by George Bernard Shaw.[2] But he is best known today as the father of Victorian "cup and saucer" realism, and it is in this light that I wish briefly to consider *Ours*.[3] At a crucial point in the play, as the hero is about to leave for the war, hero and heroine offer a naturalized *tableau vivant* of a painting by John Everett Millais. Robertson's stage directions (one revolutionary aspect of his dramatic practice) make the reference explicit:

Bugle without, at distance. Roll on side drum, four beats on big drum, then military band play "Annie Laurie" – the whole to be as if in the distance. **Angus** starts up, and goes to window. **Blanche** springs up and stands before door, L. **Angus** goes to door, embracing **Blanche**. They form **Millais's** picture of the "Black Brunswicker."[4]

Maynard Savin writes of the moment, "The highly artificial is carried to ridiculous lengths."[5] And it seems a fair criticism: why would a realist playwright "quote" a painting here – a painting depicting not a Crimean scene but a German officer's departure from his beloved prior to the Battle of Waterloo?

Such quotation suggests the generic permeability of the art of the period, and it is this permeability – both the need for it and the consequences of it – that leads me to turn to the visual arts, where its cumulative impact can best be registered, in my final chapter. For if Robertson looks to a painting to produce a curiously "staged" form of realism, domestic painters and draughtsmen tackling the subject of the Crimean War – in particular, John Everett Millais and his friend, the illustrator and cartoonist John Leech – also referenced other media to create effects that oddly combined the realistic with the artificial and the contemporary with the ahistorical. The very painting Robertson enacts demonstrates Millais's commitment to realism through a Crimean connection. At a dinner party (thrown, as it happens, by Leech), Millais had presented the subject of *The Black Brunswicker* (1860) to none other than William Howard Russell for approval; he had even enlisted the famous Crimean correspondent's aid: "Russell was quite struck with it . . . Nothing could be kinder than his interest, and he is to set about getting all the [military] information that is required."[6] While Russell serves as one kind of "source" for Millais's painting, *The Black Brunswicker* also quotes another work of art; on the wall behind the embracing couple hangs an engraving of Jacques-Louis David's *Napoleon Crossing the Alps* (c. 1800–01) – an allusion both to the officer's upcoming fate at Waterloo and to current events (Napoleon III's 1859 effort to expel the Austrians from northern Italy). This quotation collapses history instead of isolating the specific moment (as Russell's military expertise presumably helped Millais to do), gesturing simultaneously towards two separate Napoleonic pasts and towards the present. Thus Robertson's reference to Millais's painting, which adds the Crimean War and a new present to the temporal mix, becomes part of a network of allusions that span both time and a variety of media.

Stefan Morawski refers to such interpolated pictures – ones demonstrating "a stimulatory-amplificatory function" – as *paraquotations*. He notes that such quotations "accumulate in art when the boundaries between it and other forms of social consciousness become vague."[7] In the art of the Crimean War, these boundaries seem particularly porous, as I have argued throughout this book. But the vagueness in the case of Millais's and Leech's work owes much to their shared narrative tendencies, which allowed access to a wide variety of discourses about the war. In the third volume of *Modern Painters* (1856), John Ruskin declared that painting was beginning "to take its proper position beside literature" – partly because, like literature, the new paintings told stories.[8] He was thinking about works by the recently dissolved (in 1853) Pre-Raphaelite Brotherhood, of which Millais had been a founding member. If the paintings of the PRB told stories, so did the cartoons of John Leech and his fellow illustrators for *Punch*. Moreover, these two narrative visual modes operated by referencing other media, both verbal media like newspapers and novels and – as I shall show, crucially – each other.

Jay David Bolter and Richard Grusin have termed "the representation of one medium in another" *remediation*, and they have called a tendency to remediation the "defining characteristic of the new digital media."[9] Yet it also helps define narrative painting and drawing of the Crimean

War – no doubt in part because of the unprecedented influence exerted by the newer analog media of the period. In addition to the influential *Times* and the *Illustrated London News* (*ILN*), which published articles and pictures by "Special Correspondents" and "Special Artists" (illustrators at the seat of war), photographers like Roger Fenton were sending back "real" images from the front.[10] In what follows, I show how narrative paintings and drawings offer ambivalent responses to the Crimean War from within this media milieu. They do so by simultaneously suggesting the straightforwardness and modernity of realism and by allowing – through their use of paraquotation and remediation, among other tactics – for a "dense superflux of signification."[11] Kate Flint has identified such "superflux" in Victorian painting as a by-product of nineteenth-century consumer culture; the complex culture of the war produced similar results.

Indeed, if Robertson's *Ours* and Millais's *Black Brunswicker* stand as two examples of visual quotation, a Crimean War painting with a narrative bent offers what might be called a superflux of remediating paraquotation. *A Welcome Arrival* (1857), by Millais's friend and studio-mate during the war, John D'Albiac Luard, was the most significant product of the artist and former military-man's journey east in the winter of 1855–56 (figure 5). It shows three figures in a Crimean hut – the painter and two officers (one of whom is Luard's brother) – gathered around a newly opened crate of goods from England, which had contained the now-visible food and tobacco scattered about it and the small portrait that is delicately cradled by one of the officers. But perhaps the most striking thing about the painting is its background, depicting a wall plastered with scenes from the illustrated magazines of the day.

Many journals and letters indicate that such plastering was common practice; the background thus contributes to the picture's realism. This quality was lauded from the first in a manner recognizing the painting's connection to the work of the Special Artists and photographers; *The Times* called *A Welcome Arrival* "the most life-like picture of the many to which the Crimean campaign has given rise . . . The picture is capitally painted – evidently from actual study on the spot."[12] Indeed, it is easy to see these engravings simply as realistic "background"; their very number renders them resistant to the more symbolic "stimulatory-amplificatory function" that Morawski demands of paraquotation and that can so clearly be applied to the engraving in *The Black Brunswicker*. The illustrations – which would have been shipped over from Britain (*The Times*'s reviewer recognizes them as "pasted cuts from the *Illustrated London News* and *Punch*") – are also notable proof of the interpenetration of home

Figure 5 John D'Albiac Luard, *A Welcome Arrival* (1857)

front and battlefront during the war. Matthew Lalumia argues they represent nostalgia for home, calling them "chaste forerunners to the twentieth-century pin-up."[13] Yet many of the engravings – which while not clearly delineated are distinct enough to offer tantalizing glimpses of their subjects – appear to be sketches not of the home front but rather scenes of the seat of war.

Flint has argued convincingly that Victorian narrative painting, for all that it seems to allow spectators freedom to interpret "stories" pictured according to their own lights, "in fact relied upon certain highly predictable trajectories, 'strong narratives' in prevalent circulation within Victorian culture."[14] As I have shown, though, the Crimean War resisted such codification. This resistance is suggested in the excessive opportunities presented by treating the illustrations in the background of *A Welcome Arrival* as genuine paraquotations. Are these "pin-ups" – whether of home-front pleasures or of battlefront glories – or do they rather serve as pincushions, allowing the officers present (and viewers) a way to express their frustrations? Captain Fred Dallas records in a letter how "We have been amusing ourselves papering the drawing-room with pictures from the *Illustrated News*, & anything else pictorial that we can lay our hands on, and it makes the room very cheerful." But Alexis Soyer reports that his friend Dallas and his companions had in fact cheered themselves partly by desecrating the images of the leaders under whom they fought. He comments on the confusion among some visiting aides-de-camp who, although "much taken with the engravings,"

> could not make out how it was that general Pelissier wore a Russian uniform, and Prince Menschikoff the French military order – that General Canrobert was dressed like the Emperor Alexander II while his Majesty was dressed in the French general's costume. Count Orloff wore the French imperial uniform; and, above all, their general-in-chief, Prince Gortschikoff, appeared attired as a Highlander.[15]

Such mix-and-match hints at both recognition of the war's absurdity and an easy dismissal of authority (albeit foreign authority: no British leaders are mentioned). It also implies a kind of "people's choice" attitude towards the illustrations quite different from the clear legibility identified by Flint – rather closer, in fact, to the public investment in the newspapers I outlined in chapter 1. Indeed, the background illustrations in *A Welcome Arrival* might have given viewers (either of the painting or in the painting, so to speak) the opportunity to escape linear narrative by accessing what now seems akin to hypertext potential: home in on your choice of illustration, and see where the story takes you from there.

As I mentioned, Luard's painting was recognized primarily for its journalistic realism, generated by the portrayal of plastered journal illustrations that the painter had seen on his visit to the Crimea. But the realism of the distant experience (to a domestic audience) presented by *A Welcome Arrival* is also remediated through home-front viewers' first-hand knowledge of that familiar journalism, posted on the wall of the otherwise defamiliarized domestic space of the hut (not to mention through the wide gap between such public and reproduced art and the singular, private, and – to the viewer – inaccessible portrait so carefully clasped by the seated officer). For their own Crimean War art, John Leech (who may well have been responsible for some of those illustrations) and John Everett Millais (who painted not at the front but in a London studio he shared with Luard) could not claim experience of the seat of war. Nevertheless, the presence of reportorial art dominated the backgrounds of their responses to the war almost as strikingly (if not always as literally) as the pictures in *A Welcome Arrival* dominate that canvas. For that reason, I want to begin by considering how the ascendancy of foreign correspondence in the war shaped not just Leech's and Millais's subjects but also the kinds of art they made and their sense of themselves as artists. I then show how these two artists took advantage of the media culture to produce their own forms of ambiguity.

I "NOTHING LIKE KNOWING THE COUNTRY"

Realism lies at the heart of Millais's and Leech's self-conceptions. Tim Barringer has identified the two key features of the paintings of the Pre-Raphaelite Brotherhood as "revivalism and realism": a "yearning for the past" that combined, paradoxically, with a very up-to-date "creed of 'truth to nature'" depending upon direct observation.[16] After the dissolution of the Brotherhood in 1853 – on the very eve of the war – many of its former affiliates (including Millais) set aside some of the body's revivalist instincts to embrace modern subjects. But while members of the PRB may have demanded direct observation even before the Crimean War, the significance of the tenet changed in its context. The need to have seen what you described was ever more pressing in a culture saturated by the first-hand reports coming from the front. This pressure was felt regardless of medium: as Ulrich Keller has argued, "direct eyewitness observation gained an ascendancy over interpretive historical accounts on the visual level no less than the verbal."[17]

Charles Kingsley's novels show how such forces intersect with the beliefs of the PRB. When Kingsley wanted to explain his difficulty in writing directly about the Crimea, he did so by reference to the Brotherhood: "I am essentially a Pre-Raphaelite in poetry, and can only imagine what I have seen."[18] In what sense he had "seen" the Elizabethan world described in *Westward Ho!* (1855) – the novel he went on to write in lieu of a more overtly Crimean tale – is hard to say, although the book's revivalist impulse does gesture towards the other major tenet of the Pre-Raphaelites. But if the need for direct observation forced Kingsley into the past in *Westward Ho!*, by the time he wrote *Two Years Ago* (1857), he had (like Millais) accepted the present – and realized that one way for the domestic artist to describe war authentically is to focus on home-front experiences. Suggestively, *Two Years Ago* makes a subplot of shifts in the art world. Like many other Crimean War novels, it features an artist. Yet while Claude Mellot begins in a recognizably Pre-Raphaelite mode, by the end of the book, he has become a photographer: "I am tired of painting nature

Figure 6 [Constantin Guys], "Turks Conveying the Sick to Balaclava," *Illustrated London News*, March 17, 1855, 260

clumsily, and then seeing a sun picture out-do all my efforts – so I have turned photographer."[19]

Pre-Raphaelites worked in a high-art (historical) manner that ostensibly defined itself in opposition to journalistic (of the day) impulses. In contrast, illustrators for *Punch* were invested in capturing the moment even before the war. But while comic license to some degree freed them from the burdens of realism, their cartoons were in even clearer competition with the pictures arriving from the East. One can see how these two modes related by comparing an illustration by Constantin Guys, one of the foremost Special Artists for the *ILN* and Baudelaire's original "painter of modern life," to a cartoon by Leech – himself an equally suitable candidate for Baudelaire's epithet.[20] Both works show Turkish soldiers acting as "beasts of burden," but their impacts differ vastly. Guys's illustration, "Turks Conveying the Sick to Balaclava" (figure 6), focuses on the suffering of war – its endless train of wounded receding into the background gives a visually affecting sense of the extent of the misery.[21] While the accompanying written description distinguished between the Turks and their British allies, it pointed to a distinction in degree rather than in kind. Indeed, this picture of Turkish soldiers carrying their

Painters of modern life

wounded followed on two previously published illustrations in which horses and carts convey the British sick and injured – "Carrying the Wounded to Balaclava" and "Carrying the Frost-bitten to Balaclava."[22] Thus the inadequacy of the British ambulance-conveyance had also been a topic of indignant news reports; for example, the carted wounded in "Carrying the Wounded" are pushed forward by fellow soldiers rather than pulled by animals. So rather than appearing as subhuman, the Turkish bearers stand in for their Western allies, serving as reminders of comparable if not equivalent British bureaucratic inefficiency. And if the Turks' dark moustaches and hooked noses suggest a certain amount of racialism, their gaunt, hooded figures also bear a resemblance to those of the wounded British in the earlier illustrations.[23] In fact, their humanity is stressed, both by the presence of the exhausted Turkish infantryman in the lower left of the picture and by the compositional similarity between the river of pain depicted here and those composed of British troops shown the previous week.

Now consider Leech's rather heartless joke, "How Jack Makes the Turk Useful at Balaclava" (figure 7), which depicts a British "tar" seated astride

Figure 7 [John Leech], "How Jack Makes the Turk Useful at Balaclava," *Punch* 28 (1855), 4

one staggering Turkish soldier and leading a spare "mount" behind.[24] As the overburdened horse of the officer on the left of the sketch demonstrates, Leech is gesturing towards the same problem that Guys would illustrate: the failure to prepare in advance for the foreseeable transport needs of the British Army. But Leech's cartoon ignores suffering, instead offering an example of "native British ingenuity" at work. It also suggests an absolute distinction between the British and their Eastern allies: both appear as caricatures, and the fact that the picture shows a British sailor rather than a soldier works further to discourage any perception of "brotherhood" between carried and carrier. Yet significantly, the capacity for humor depends on the lack of realism, of pretense of the artist's "having been there": no one would believe in the reportorial "truth" of this image. And *Punch* seems to have served as byword for such inaccuracy, as Roger Fenton's criticism of a rival artist's work indicates: "Have you seen that picture in the 'Illustrated London News' of Sebastopol from the sea?" he asked his wife in a letter, "It has caused a great deal of astonishment and amusement here, as it is a regular 'Punch' sketch."[25] Nevertheless, the publication was not entirely immune from the pressures for authenticity faced by other journals chronicling the war. Thus an earlier sketch showing the ludicrous amount of baggage with which British officers were encumbered, "Servant and Baggage of the British Officer in the East" (27:63), was published with the parenthetical subtitle, "From an authentic Sketch in the possession of Mr. Punch."

And in fact, Leech often seems uneasy in the Crimean setting; he appears more at home picturing the false combat of the hunt in the many sporting sketches that made him famous. A cartoon from early 1854 even plays upon the assumed contiguity of the activities. Two mounted men exchange words, presumably before a hunt. The caption reads:

Huntsman (To officer going abroad). "Please be so good, sir, as to give my respects to Master Harry."
Officer. "Oh! but my Brother is in the West Indies, and I am going to the East."
Huntsman. "Mayhap you'll meet at t'Cover Side all the same, Sir!"
(26:164)

But Leech would have agreed with the sentiments of the sketch's title: there is "Nothing Like Knowing the Country." Leech jokes quite happily about the discomforts of camp life in the series of sketches he made of the extensive and much-publicized military exercises at Chobham that had taken place just prior to the onset of war. Many of these weirdly prefigure

ONE OF THE HORRORS OF THE CHOBHAM WAR.

Figure 8 [John Leech], "One of the Horrors of the Chobham War," *Punch* 25 (1853), 24

the effects of the disastrous weather in the Crimea.[26] Thus in "Another Night Surprise at Chobham," a tent collapses during a storm, arousing the soldiers within who peer with dismay from among its folds (25:20). But in several cartoons, Leech acknowledges the affair as romance. In "One of the Horrors of the Chobham War" an officer presides over a picnic among the tents, surrounded by a group of lovely lady camp-followers (25:24; figure 8). The artifice of the "war" enables the artifice of the artist, who can access the experience through familiar social tropes. A similar scene set in the Crimea, after the war has begun ("A Little Dinner at the Crimea Club" [27:200]; figure 9), replaces the ladies with cannonballs and reverses the joke to render innocuous what was indeed horrific. On such foreign ground, Leech must again turn to what he knows to make sense of events, depicting them through the lens of the London club world. But in this picture of real war, the romance rings a false note, especially when considered in the context of illustrations like Guys's.

In fact Leech's most "realistic" sketch set in the Crimea is also his most successful. He produces a realistic effect by accessing the foreign through yet another familiar topic: that of dress. Leech's comic takes on male and female costume among the London bourgeoisie and their servants were

A LITTLE DINNER AT THE CRIMEA CLUB.

Figure 9 [John Leech], "A Little Dinner at the Crimea Club," *Punch* 27 (1854), 200

staples for *Punch*; in the Crimean setting – and in January of 1855, at the heart of the public uproar over the mismanagement of the war – the subject takes on a somber note. A picture of two gaunt and rag-clad soldiers in front of tents (looking remarkably like the tents in the Chobham sketches; realism doesn't come from the setting) surrounded by snow, a dead horse lying beside them, has the following caption:

"Well Jack! Here's good news from Home. We're to have a Medal."
"That's very kind. Maybe one of these days we'll have a Coat to stick it on?" (28:64; figure 10)

The absence of the usual title contributes to the starkness of the impact; here the soldiers are allowed to speak for themselves. The editorial silence stands as a respectful acknowledgement of the distance between battle-front and home-front experience.

We can see the influence of journalism operating simultaneously on painters and illustrators by considering a series of cartoons published in *Punch* in the 1850s. The sketches in question humorously evoke the difficulties associated with painting from nature. While the jokes are divided roughly between those aimed at the cartoonists for *Punch* and those aimed at members of the PRB, these two categories often prove indistinguishable. The overlap also appears in the friendship between Leech and Millais, out of which the cartoons can be said to have developed. The artists had met in 1853; in the fall of that year, when

Figure 10 [John Leech], Untitled, *Punch* 28 (1855), 64

Millais went to Scotland with the Ruskins, he wrote to his new friend of his admiration for his work: "We have Punch sent to us, and I cannot resist telling you how good I think your illustrations have been since I left town." A couple of weeks later, Millais indicated that he had sent Leech a sketch that had actually been published in the magazine. He is thrilled, although also slightly nervous of being connected with the lower art-form:

If I ever find myself failing with the brush, I shall appeal to you for your influence on behalf of a place in that paper. I send you other drawings of *facts*. Remember, I do these for yourself, and with no hope that they might appear in Punch, although I shall always be proud to see them there . . . I am glad you do not mention my name which would never go with the serious position I occupy in regard to Art.[27]

The worry was understandable: from its inception, critics had lampooned the PRB by associating it with *Punch*. Paul Barlow notes that in 1851 "*The Times* attacked Millais and Hunt on the familiar ground that their works were 'to genuine art what the designs in *Punch* are to Giotto.'"[28]

One comic drawing Millais sends Leech is titled "Pre-Raphaelite Sketching: inconvenience in windy weather," and he attributes his inspiration to a Chobham image by Leech (25:14): "The sketches of the unfortunate officer clinging to his tent post, and beseeching assistance in the recovery of his bedroom, suggested the accompanying drawing of a disaster equally fearful in its consequences." As Simon Houfe records, this sketch "was not used, but another 'Awful protection against midges' showing artists sketching from Nature was in November 1853."[29] The picture was eventually called "Ingenious Protection Against Midges – A Valuable Hint to Sketchers from Nature" (25:198). It shows two artists (Michael Halliday and Millais[30]) drawing companionably, their heads entirely hooded in ghost-like sacks, with cutouts for eyes and mouth, as a frightened family looks on in the distance. The title of Millais's unpublished "Pre-Raphaelite Sketching" admits its roots in the PRB; the title of the published sketch offers a wider frame of reference. In a series of "Our Artist" cartoons appearing in *Punch* in the first half of 1854, the acknowledged focus has shifted to the "Special Artists" for the magazine itself (as indicated by the possessive pronoun), as they face the trials and tribulations of their craft. But the connection between the two schools of art remains: in "Our Artist 'Goes to Nature'" a "Special Artist" is pictured in the snow with a gigantic tube of floor white as he follows the famous maxim of Ruskin and the PRB (26:33; January, 1854).

Yet Millais's idea of a comic drawing as a "*fact*" implies a desire to report the reality of experience that alters its tenor as a real war in the East supplants the pretend war at Chobham. Thus the humor of the series changes subtly when it reaches the subject of the Crimea. A cartoon from the spring of 1854 makes fun of the inaccuracies of domestic military painting, again using the "Our Artist" designation that was becoming more resonant of the front-line correspondents recently arrived in the East. Under the heading "A Friend in Need," the following caption appears, addressed to a rather corpulent and surprised-looking man:

Our Artist. "OH! MY DEAR OLD BOY! I'M SO GLAD TO SEE YOU! MY MODEL HASN'T COME, AND I'M IN A REGULAR FIX; SO P'RAPS YOU WOULDN'T MIND BEING MY DEAD ARTILLERYMAN FOR AN HOUR OR SO." (26:213)

While funny, the callous attitude towards the war dead also jars in a culture just beginning to feel the distinction between such staged attempts at realism and the real. The joke can be compared to the magazine's handling of the military spectaculars that flourished on the home front in 1855; repeatedly, these work by emphasizing the distinction between real and false war. An illustration of "One of the Gallant 93rd, as he appears at Astley's [the famed circus]" shows an uncomfortable skinny man in a kilt, as unlikely a soldier as the fat "Old Boy" (27:204). In another piece, *Punch*

Figure 11 "Our Artist in the Crimea," *Punch* 28 (1855), 12

sends a "correspondent" to witness "The Battle of the Alma, as fought at Astley's." He pretends to be present at the actual battle, thus drawing attention to the public's desire to participate in the war through make-believe but also suggesting the distance between his own activity and that of the genuine war correspondents (27:185).[31]

A sketch called "Our Artist in the Crimea" (28:12; figure 11), appearing in early 1855, at the height of British outrage over the mismanagement of the war effort, provides a curious culmination to the series. It shows an artist swathed in winter gear (hands so bundled as to make the idea of his actually painting with them laughable, for all that he grips awkwardly on to his paint-box), knee deep in the Crimean slush and mud. An "Obliging Aide-de-Camp," who has led him there, points out the view and declares: "*There now, What's your name, you can't have a Better Spot than this for a*

Sketch, you see you have the entire range of the Town and Forts." That "what's your name" suggests the dismissive attitude of the military to the artists and journalists in the East, and the cartoon illustrates a cruel joke on the part of the "obliging" ADC. But it also places "our artist" in the same dangers (mark that "range") as the increasingly celebrated war correspondents, approximating the tenor of William Howard Russell's self-description as everyman hero in his columns (he had made his sufferings at the hands of uncooperative military authorities an ongoing theme of the letters). Moreover, the cartoon's depiction of the artist is not itself particularly comic: he looks bewildered, but not silly. Of course, the actual illustrator of this sketch was probably not in the Crimea. Yet at the same time, the picture figures the hardships faced by Crimean correspondents in the same terms as those faced by artists at home, both Pre-Raphaelites and cartoonists. In a letter from the Crimea, Luard recognized the contiguity between these practices, noting that the "cold and rain are not favorable to P. R. B.-ing" as he recorded his on-the-spot experience of sketching the sights and fortifications familiar from journalists' reports ("one of the Redan, two of the town," and so on).[32]

So the artists' commitment to realism becomes the basis not only for comedy but also for their claims to artistic manliness. Herbert Sussman has argued that both Millais and William Holman Hunt negotiated their post-PRB careers by creating masculine personae for themselves that were consonant with their profession as artists. Millais's version of this persona was bound to the British countryside. He became a "gentleman-painter," one whose paintbrush and palette could easily be replaced by gun or rod; as *Punch* had made clear, outdoorsmen and artists faced the same discomforts. And Millais's "professionalism" (the other aspect of his bourgeois manhood identified by Sussman) was formed by his willingness to work hard (in good Carlylean fashion) and to endure the trials of "eyewitness" – that is, outdoor – reporting, as those sketches had also suggested.[33]

But William Holman Hunt illustrates how the Crimean context also offered more exotic opportunities for the establishment of artistic manliness through rigorous commitment to realism. Hunt first embarked for the Holy Land in 1854, in the company of "some newspaper correspondents going to the seat of the threatened war."[34] He visited the Crimea on his way back to England, just prior to the Armistice; on his return journey, he records being accompanied by homeward-bound officers.[35] His letters show his excitement over the war: "Nothing is more strongly in my mind than a wish that I had nothing but ordinary impediments to my joining the army," he wrote in February of 1855.[36] In his memoirs, his descriptions of on-site painting in Palestine describe a quasi-soldierly heroism; a paragraph beginning with his "deepest concern" over the war slides easily into an account of the "personal danger" he faced while away from his own "headquarters" – a term with definite military connotations – in Jerusalem.[37] Sussman notes that Hunt's "account of the act of painting might have stepped out of any Victorian narrative of manly imperial questing";[38] indeed, his manliness seems more secure than that of the heroes of the war novels I described in chapter 2. Hunt describes how one day, while he was at work on *The Scapegoat* (1856), he was interrupted by a party of heavily armed natives: "I continued placidly conveying my paint from palette to canvas, steadying my touch by resting the hand on my double-barrelled gun. I knew that my whole chance depended upon the exhibition of utter unconcern, and I continued as steadily as if in my studio at home."[39] Of course, the whole point is that he wasn't in his studio at home, that – while he may not have been a soldier – like the correspondents and the Special Artists for the newspapers, he was in the midst of the action.

Thus while Hunt and Luard escaped their studios to report from the East, Millais and Leech had to discover ways in which they could uphold their shared credo of "truth to Nature" – a credo that the rise of foreign correspondence, both verbal and visual, had made all the more vital – while yet engaging with the momentous events abroad that were so much a part of "modern life." As I shall show, to answer this dilemma, they embraced as subject the very media culture threatening their artistic significance. But in embracing the media, they also opened their paintings and drawings of the war to ever-expanding networks of interpretive possibility.

II PLAYING AT WAR

Hunt plays at being a soldier even as he works at his art in the East; still, the real danger he faces on foreign ground helps constitute his artistic authenticity. Realist artists who played at war on the home front faced other kinds of danger, more aesthetic than bodily. As I argued in chapter 3, the charge of the Light Brigade served as a locus for questions of authenticity during the Crimean War. George Du Maurier's *Trilby* (1894), set in Paris soon after the Peace, includes among its characters a Crimean officer who has since become an artist:

For three years he had borne Her majesty's commission, and had been through the Crimean campaign, without a scratch. He would have been one of the famous six hundred in the famous charge at Balaklava but for a sprained ankle (caught playing leap-frog in the trenches), which kept him in hospital on that momentous day. So he lost his chance of glory or the grave, and this humiliating misadventure had sickened him of soldiering for life, and he never quite got over it. Then, feeling within himself an irresistible vocation for art, he had sold out; and here he was in Paris, hard at work, as we see.[40]

Taffy (as he is called) turns from his disappointment at not finding glory in war to look for glory in art. But although the childish "play" in the trenches that caused him to miss out on military glory must be opposed to the "hard . . . work" at art that follows (as if to purge the earlier sin), the authenticity of both vocations seems compromised by his ignoble experience at Balaklava. Du Maurier, who started illustrating for *Punch* in 1860, took over as the magazine's social cartoonist on Leech's death in 1864. Leech had also recognized the imaginative possibilities offered by the subject of Balaklava. He saw that among the greatest dangers to a domestic illustrator of war was the taint of inauthenticity that accompanies not having been there, the hazard of being accused of just playing at war. Yet if Taffy's "play" prevented him from engaging in the work of soldiering at Balaklava, the only way that Leech could experience the charge was through imaginative investment that always threatened to devolve into play.

Leech contributed two cartoons about the charge to *Punch*, appearing in consecutive issues (November 18 and 25, 1854). The contrast, both in style and content, between them suggests some of the problems faced by home-front illustrators of the war – and some of the solutions they developed to these problems. The first to appear was a half-page sketch that Ulrich Keller has described as "rare" (for the satiric journal) in its "laudatory" stance vis-à-vis the conflict; as Keller sees it, *Punch* was jumping on a bandwagon of patriotic "worship of aristocratic generals" in early depictions of the war (before the winter troubles set in).[41] In Leech's cartoon, titled "A Trump Card(igan)," Lord Cardigan is shown in perfect profile, sword in hand, astride his horse, charging head-on into Tennyson's "valley of death" (27:209; figure 12). Indeed, while the cannon on the right side of the image is presumably closer to the fore than the figure, the flatness of the sketch – because the central figure appears in profile, it produces little sensation of three-dimensional depth – increases the viewer's feeling that Cardigan is aimed directly for the mouth of the gun. Notably, Cardigan is the only well-defined cavalryman in the picture; while two Russian gunners fill its right margin, the row of cavalry behind Cardigan retreats into ever-greater abstraction, until only a line

![A Trump Card(igan)]

Figure 12 [John Leech], "A Trump Card(igan)," *Punch* 27 (1854), 209

(designating a sword) and a dot (a horse's eye) remain. And while a pair of ghostly riders joins Cardigan in front of the row, the overwhelming effect of the image is to suggest the dominant heroism of one man and the leadership he exerts over that unwavering line. Aiding this effect is the fact that Cardigan himself is not only legible but recognizable, even without the caption: his generous moustache and aquiline nose would have rendered him immediately identifiable to a Victorian readership inundated with portraits of the heroic earl in the weeks after the news of the charge broke. The cartoon seems an homage to the aristocratic military code.

Nevertheless, there is something vaguely disquieting about the image – something that has to do with its relationship to authenticity. Leech's drawing itself is perfectly adequate: the horse in particular is predictably well rendered. The uneasiness can be ascribed instead to Leech's point of view. His chosen perspective closely resembles that which Keller has identified as most commonly used in depictions of the charge: to show the cavalry – or just Cardigan – jumping out at the viewer, as though we ourselves were standing in the Russian battery. Keller notes the "egregious disregard for reportorial accuracy" implied by this perspective. As discussed earlier, Russell's reports used standpoint to emphasize the "staged" effect of the charge, describing the "spectators of the scene," including Raglan and his staff, "as though they were looking on the stage from the boxes of a theatre."[42] Yet if Russell's theatrical metaphor suggested the bizarre unreality of the charge, it simultaneously demonstrated that he was "really" there, witnessing the events along with the generals. Keller posits, though, that "commercial publishers" interested in generating a visceral response "preferred breathtaking, totally fictive viewpoints close to the action" to such "static" images.[43] They wanted to let us fantasize not only about being on the spot but about taking part in the battle. Leech's imagined view of the charge appears motivated by such fantasy.

But while the point of view Leech assumes is so close as to render it obviously fictive, his decision to show Cardigan in profile rather than turned – even if only slightly – towards the viewer (like all of the images Keller discusses in detail) has the effect of making the sketch surprisingly "static": of discouraging rather than encouraging somatic responses based on imaginative investment. Perhaps in a nod to the pun of its title, the perspective highlights rather the playing-card flatness of the image – the cartoon might even be said to be remediated through such cards.[44] By emphasizing artifice, the two-dimensionality also undermines Cardigan's heroism. Everything about the sketch feels fake: it is playing at war, much as the headline's joke would suggest. (Although the pun also attests to the recklessness of the charge as a kind of roll of the dice, to switch gaming metaphors.) And it is worth stating how very un-Leech-like the lack of realism renders the image.[45]

In stark contrast, Leech's other cartoon about the charge – a "big cut" entitled "Enthusiasm of Paterfamilias, On Reading the Report of the Grand Charge of British Cavalry on the 25th" – is in the gentle domestic realist mode for which Leech was justly famous (27:213; figure 13). It shows a British middle-class family in their drawing room, gathered around a table set for tea and in front of a hearth that occupies the right margin of the sketch. The "Paterfamilias" of the cartoon's title stands squarely upon a disheveled hearth-rug, brandishing a poker, as he reads aloud what one assumes to be Russell's famous account of the charge from a *Times* newspaper that he holds in his other hand (placing remediation at the heart of the image). His cheering children surround him. A young son (on a chair) and elder daughter stand directly behind Pater, peering over his shoulder to read along with him. A boy on the left of the image seems ready to charge forward himself, as he steps up from chair to table, sword (butter knife) and shield (broken plate) in hand. Another girl,

Painters of modern life

Figure 13 [John Leech], "Enthusiasm of Paterfamilias," *Punch* 27 (1854), 213

standing beside him, waves her handkerchief (or perhaps a napkin) aloft in her excitement, while her older sister looks on with an expression that is harder to read. Even the baby watches, although he appears as interested in the slice of bread he holds to his mouth as he is in the antics of his father.

Only two figures (or three, if one counts the just-visible daughter in the background who seems to have "turned her face to the wall") can resist the imaginative pull of the father's "enthusiasm." In the foreground, a mother sits lamenting, holding a handkerchief to her bowed head – whether to ease the ache brought on by the disturbance or from concern over the brutality of war, it is impossible to say. But it is her eldest daughter, occupying the very center of the picture, who really anchors the composition. In contrast with the whirlwind around her, she stands completely still, a point emphasized both by the full-frontal angle from which we see her and by her resolutely (or defensively?) crossed arms. Her head is framed in place by the map – presumably of the Crimea – that hangs above the sideboard behind her. And the diagonal movement of the composition – from her brother's bent knee, to her sister's forward-leaning back, and through to the "sword" in her father's hand – also points to her centrality. All these factors combine to highlight the expression on her face: her uplifted eyes, furrowed brow, and especially the clearly defined tear on her cheek.

The effect of this composition is worth considering. In a wonderful discussion of the sketch (in the context of her reading of Tennyson's "Charge of the Light Brigade"), Trudi Tate points out that "The cartoon suggests, characteristically, that men and women occupy completely different imaginative realms. What delights father is painful to mother" (although she also notes that the younger daughter hints at the possibility of "a new generation of spirited women").[46] Still, such female sorrow need not signify an anti-military stance; it is consistent with the most patriotic and propagandistic of messages. Thus David's *The Oath of the Horatii* (1784) – the painting that Simon Schama has called "a clarion call to arms" and the first of David's efforts at propagandistic revolutionary art "for something called 'The Nation'" – also divides male response from female: in the visually dominant left of the canvas, "the father, gripping the naked blades in his hand, swears his sons to fight or die for the *patria*," while on the right, women and children sit lamenting the fates of their menfolk.[47] But three things are different in Leech's take on what Tate calls "the *fantasy* investment in war."[48] First, Leech has reversed David's visual hierarchy: here the crying girl centers the composition, as I have argued. Second, this composition has also done away with clear-cut male and female realms; even if the response is largely divided by gender, it takes a little longer to read this fact from the sketch. The distinction matters, because it works against the idea of separate spheres coming together to form an "imagined community" – whether of family or of Nation. Leech's picture suggests a household whose divisions result in disorder rather than order.[49] Third – and most obviously – this father is not going off to fight. He is playing at war. And he is not a child.

Pictures of children playing at war were staples of Victorian painting and had been used before to pacifist ends. In William Mulready's *The Convalescent from Waterloo* (1822), a wounded soldier sits listlessly on the shore next to his beleaguered wife and a younger child and looks on as his two boys fight before him.[50] But the Crimean War produced a new crop of such works. Most striking of these is a painting by James Collinson (another former member of the PRB, although he had resigned in 1850) that offers an antidote to the enthusiastic Paterfamilias. *Home Again* (1856) depicts a blinded Guardsman (as identified in the quotation originally exhibited beside it) being greeted by his family on his return from the war (figure 14). As in Leech's cartoon, we get the interior details of his home, but here the space appears to be a rural working-class cottage. Unlike Leech, though, Collinson has divided the canvas: by age rather than gender. On the dominant right, a group of adults, male and female, gather around a table. The soldier's wife has just risen to greet her returned husband, but the mood appears solemn rather than jubilant, and the group – which includes a uniformed sailor and an older Guardsman – seems conscious of the costs as well as the glories of war. A blind man will find it difficult to support his family; the painting demonstrates the new concern for working soldiers (as opposed to officers) engendered by the war.

On the left of the canvas, however, the mood is very different. Children fight: a boy standing atop a mangle holds aloft the Royal Standard and uses it to defend his spot from another boy, who attempts to climb up. Behind him, a print on the wall shows a scene from the war in which a Russian falls before a British bayonet that echoes the line of the boy's flag. Below the fighting boys another child sits nursing a wounded knee injured earlier in the "battle." He leans against a barrel in which float a pair of toy warships. The wounded child, made perceptive by experience, is the only boy to notice his father's entrance. An earlier version of this grouping, entitled "Siege of Sebastopol: by an eye witness" (and probably re-exhibited under the title "Children at Play"[51]), labeled the print in the background "ALMA" and incorporated a sign reading "MANGLING DONE HERE," thus rendering in words the obvious message of the larger painting: war is a serious and violent business, not child's play. Yet Collinson's "eyewitness" account of such play avoids implicating him in the boys' fantasy only by joining in it (if they wish they could be fighting at Sebastopol, he wishes he could be painting there).

The links between boyish play and soldiering have appeared in every variety of response to the war with which I have concerned myself in this book. I have argued that the schoolboy novel was in part produced by the culture of masculinity that came out of the war. In the pages of *The Times*, rival public schools actually contested the number of their war dead and injured.[52] And Adelaide Anne Procter's poem, "The Two Spirits" (discussed in chapter 3), concluded by comparing play and battle: "Our heroes of to-day, / Go cheerfully to battle / As children go to play."[53] But if Procter's poem applauds the heroes, it also hints that these "children" will soon find their fantasy world shattered. One might contrast Henry Newbolt's "Vitaï Lampada" (1897), which sets the standard for describing

Figure 14 James Collinson, *Home Again* (1856)

how wars abroad can be perceived to have been "won on the playing fields of Eton":

> The sand of the desert is sodden red, –
> Red with the wreck of a square that broke; –
> The Gatling's jammed and the Colonel dead,
> And the regiment blind with dust and smoke.
> The river of death has brimmed his banks,
> And England's far, and Honour a name,
> But the voice of the schoolboy rallies the ranks:
> "Play up! play up! and play the game!"[54]

A significant gap separates how artists of the Crimean War portray the "game" of war and how it would be portrayed later in the century by people like Newbolt. Procter acknowledges the connection between play and war to be both naïve and tragic, rather than largely enabling, as it is for Newbolt.

In Procter's poem, soldier-sons learn lessons of glory as they are "nursed" by "old legends" on their mothers' knees. In both Leech's cartoon and Collinson's painting, though, those legends are replaced by something more up-to-date. The prominent place of the print in Collinson's work demonstrates the malleability of the idea of the "eyewitness" in a culture saturated by the spectacle of war, as the title of the preparatory painting notes with irony.[55] And like Leech's cartoon, Collinson's painting also remediates its message through journalism: what appears to be an illustrated magazine (probably the *ILN*) is held open by the elder Guardsman, who seems to have been reading aloud about events in the Crimea mere moments before the harsh reality of war intrudes. Perhaps this journal, read by the older grouping, is meant to represent the newer, more realistic response to the war, in contrast with the militaristic print that provides fodder for the children's fantasy. Of course, that print might also have been torn from its pages. But in either case, Collinson simultaneously acknowledges the degree to which the media evoke fantasies of war and uses his own "realistic" medium to ironize such evocation.

Yet what, exactly, did Leech make of the charge? Collinson's paintings are relatively easy to "read" as documents of the terrible costs of war. Leech's reaction is far subtler, in part because he seems invested in the wider domestic Nation-building effects of the war I discussed in chapter 3 (to which he after all had eyewitness access) rather than in the effects of the war on participants in it. The only written record I have found of Leech's feelings about Balaklava occurs in a letter to Millais, composed in June of 1855, in the aftermath of the country's winter of discontent. He describes a fishing trip he makes with an officer who had participated in the "ever-memorable Balaclava Charge," as he terms it: "He gave me a vivid description of the dreadful business. Altogether I have rarely had a more pleasant day."[56] Whether the pleasantness stems from the fishing (which he goes on to describe in far more detail) or his own enthusiasm at hearing an eyewitness account of the charge – or some combination of the two – is hard to say; nevertheless, both "dreadful" and "business" imply a level of ambivalence, if not outright criticism. And in the cartoon, the Pater, not the viewer, is in the position of fantasizing: we ourselves can look smugly on his excitement, if not as tearfully as the central daughter.

Still, the medium in which this excitement appears (the journal readers hold in their hands, much as the enthusiastic father holds *The Times*) offers analogous fantasizing opportunities. And one feels in Leech a measure of sympathy for his "Paterfamilias": while the handsome and athletic artist may have been a far cry from the balding and round father depicted, Leech was fond of using the epithet of himself in describing his own child-rearing tribulations.[57] Tate describes how the "childish enthusiasm" of the Paterfamilias shows him "thinking beyond the claustrophobic atmosphere of the drawing-room";[58] indeed, the map on the wall, in yet another remediating gesture, operates (and looks) almost like a window offering escape from the cluttered and crowded space of Victorian domesticity, a window that the crying daughter – symbol of a realistic (rather than fantasizing) attitude towards war – seems to guard determinedly, as her defensive posture suggests. This room was also the space of Leech's home-front realism; he, too, may have fantasized about escape. But if in his first sketch about Balaklava, Leech charged after the kinds of popular military art that encouraged fantasy investment in war only to collide against their two-dimensional artifice, in his second, like Collinson, he discovered how remediation could open his art up to an exploration of fantasy-investment itself.[59]

III 'PEACE CONCLUDED'?

Like Leech's "Enthusiasm," John Everett Millais's *Peace Concluded, 1856* depicts a man in the bosom of his family, holding up a copy of *The Times* (figure 15). In this case, though, the newspaper announces peace (the headline, "Conclusion of Peace," is easily legible) rather than the glory of battle, and the man is an officer who has seen duty in the Crimea, as the three clasps on the medal (awarded for participation in individual battles) held by one of his young daughters indicate. Once again, there is a hint of

Figure 15 John Everett Millais, *Peace Concluded, 1856* (1856)

war as play; the officer's other girl holds up a toy dove with an olive branch, while her mother's lap contains a lion, bear, turkey, and cock, national symbols of the combatant states in the Crimea. These have all been taken from a "Noah's Ark" toy-box (a staple of nurseries of the day) at the bottom left corner of the canvas that houses many more animals, "as though there were other overseas lands remaining to be played with," as Kate Flint has put it.[60] The fact that Millais has chosen to surround his handsome officer with daughters rather than with sons suggests, however, a desire to avoid the particular resonances generated by the excited boys of Leech's sketch and Collinson's paintings. Nevertheless, the suspicions aroused by Leech's *Paterfamilias* are nothing to those provoked by Millais's officer. Curiously, the uncertainties surrounding *Peace Concluded* owe something to its relationship to Leech's cartoons – and to a series of other intertextual references that the canvas encodes. More than any other work I can think of, Millais's painting demonstrates how the public response to the war was remediated, and how such remediation allowed for ambiguity to be expressed.

From the start, Millais's painting has been associated with two different titles, indicating alternative and incommensurable readings of the work. The title under which the painting was exhibited at the Academy in 1856 suggests a noble tale of a war well ended: a heroic officer, injured honorably at the front, enjoys a well-earned convalescence in the arms of his loving family; his own peaceful homecoming stands for that of the nation at large, as the reference to the great events of the day in the newspaper indicates. But there is a long history of a contrary reading in a very different vein. Its best-known expression occurs in Hunt's 1905 memoir, *Pre-Raphaelitism and the Pre-Raphaelite Brotherhood*:

During the war it had become a scandal that several officers with family influence had managed to get leave to return on 'urgent private affairs'. Millais had felt with others the gracelessness of this practice when such liberty could not be accorded to the simple soldier, and he undertook a picture to illustrate the luxurious nature of these 'private affairs'. A young officer was being caressed by his wife, and their infant children were themselves the substitutes of the laurels which he ought to be gathering. When the painting was nearly finished the announcement of Peace arrived. What was to be done? The call for satire on carpet heroes was out of date; the painter adroitly adapted his work to the changing circumstances, and put *The Times* in the hands of the officer, who has read the news which they were all patriotically rejoicing over; he with a sling supporting a wounded arm to represent that he had nobly done his part towards securing the peace.[61]

Hunt's memories are demonstrably unreliable, as the reference to the sling (nowhere to be seen in the painting) indicates. Still, Ford Madox Brown's contemporary diary offers the same story; remarking on the sale of the work, he rather snidely comments: "I hear from Lowes [Dickinson, a painter friend and neighbor of Millais's in London] that it was originally intended to be called 'Absent on urgent private affairs' this accounts for the made up look of the thing."⁶² And at least one review also mentioned the mixed genealogy of the painting: "The gentleman on the sofa reminds us of one of Leech's languid swells . . . We are told that the picture was originally intended to be entitled 'Urgent Private Affairs,' and, if intended as a satire upon military imbecility, there may have been more point in the original conception than appears in the work as now finished."⁶³

Thus those viewers who read the painting as "satire" do so in part because they are looking at it through the lens of Leech's satiric cartoons. The review's reference to "one of Leech's languid swells" could be to any number of his pictures of military life, both prior to and in the early months of the war. Consider a cartoon called "The Plunger in Turkey," in which just such a "swell" reclines on pillows in front of his tent, cigar in hand and wine glass beside him, as he drawlingly asks an absurdly mounted fellow officer, "I SAY, OLD FELLAH! – DO YOU THINK IT PWOBABLE THE INFANTWY WILL ACCOMPANY US TO SEBASTOPOL?" (27:126). The pun on "military imbeciles" (as opposed to "invalids" – what Millais's officer needed to be to excuse his return home) also resonates; a *Punch* cartoon from the spring of 1855 shows "The Queen Visiting the Imbeciles of the Crimea" (28:145): a straw man "medical department," a pig dressed as a general and labeled "routine," and a commissariat with a turnip head and a tin of "green coffee" for a body.⁶⁴ Most forcefully, the supposed original title of the work could allude to *Punch*'s satiric campaign against the practice Hunt describes of officers' leaving the scene of danger on trumped-up personal grounds called "Urgent Private Affairs." The label would have immediately suggested to a contemporary audience both the distasteful privileges of class and the concomitant sufferings of ordinary soldiers. Thus in "A New Order – Military and Domestic," *Punch* quips that "A new Military order is about to be instituted for home-sick officers, so many of them having returned. It is to be called – The Order of the Hearth-Rug" (28:27). The language evokes the comforts of Millais's luxurious interior (including its carefully detailed rug) and the disordered hearth-rug of Leech's take on imagined domestic bravery in "Enthusiasm." Leech himself tackled the theme visually in a "big cut" entitled "The New Game of Follow My Leader'" (29:209), in which a diminutive "private" is shown asking James Simpson (temporary and unwilling Commander-in-Chief after Raglan's death), "Please, General, may me and these other chaps have leave to go home on urgent *private* affairs?"⁶⁵

To prove the painting had not been quickly altered "to suit the day," as Hunt and the others claim, Michael Hancher notes the existence of an early preparatory sketch that already incorporates a copy of the *The Times* and the marginal note "Times newspaper Peace."[66] His detailed and conscientious explanation leads him to the following conclusion: "The likelihood is that at some point Millais *had* planned to paint a satire on 'carpet heroes', and had mentioned those plans to friends, but had changed his mind and radically 'revised' the painting *before* he ever set brush to canvas, or pencil to paper."[67] But while Hancher's reasoning suggests that the final painting should be unambiguous, it was not read so even in the day, as he himself admits. The lingering uncertainty – the openness of *Peace Concluded* to radically different readings, ranging from the heroic to the burlesque – is at least as interesting as the question of what the painter "meant" by his work. Indeed, I am far less certain than Hancher seems to be that Millais ever really decided what he meant to say in this painting. Hancher argues that the presence of the newspaper in the early sketch demonstrates general consistency of intention even in the earliest stages of composition. But what was that intention? As Leech's "Enthusiasm of Paterfamilias" shows, the incorporation of the newspaper need not have signified the Peace only; it could also have signified the distinction between reading about war and really being there.

For all Hunt's misremembering, most viewers find it is precisely the absence of visible sign of injury, such as might have been provided by a sling, that first destabilizes the heroic reading of the painting. Thus the *Art-Journal* declares, "it is not shown whether he has returned to his home sick or wounded or on leave"; only one contemporary review cites injury, calling the officer "wounded but convalescent."[68] According to Hancher, the combination of the medal with its clasps indicative of action and the dressing gown worn by the officer – a sign of his convalescent status – should have been enough to dispel doubts on the part of careful "readers." Yet the final composition chosen for the painting seems conspicuously to underplay the officer's invalidism. John Guille Millais's memoir of his father includes a drawing designated as "First sketch for 'Peace Concluded.' 1855." It is almost certainly mislabeled; rather, this sketch appears to be preparatory work for Millais's illustration for the Moxon Tennyson entitled *Dream of fair women (Queen Eleanor of Castile)*, on which the artist was working at the same time as *Peace Concluded*. Nevertheless, the drawing John Guille mistakenly identifies with *Peace Concluded* shows a far less ambiguous conception – even absent a sling – of an injured warrior at home than we find in the finished painting.[69] While in *Peace Concluded*, the wife (who is modeled by Millais's wife, Effie) "towers above and sustains her weaker mate,"[70] in the mislabeled sketch the central figure reclines while his wife kneels beside him, lamenting his illness. He holds her head supportively – even protectively – in his lap, maintaining compositional male dominance in spite of obvious sickness. What appears to be a child stands to the side of the reclining figure (in the finished illustration, a page kneels there), lifting up a bowl as sign of the need of medical care. John Guille's error attests to the force of what might be called the culturally normative reading of *Peace Concluded* as a painting of a returned hero, but this is not the painting his father produced. Millais's ambiguous depiction of heroism suggests once again the difficulties the Victorians faced in portraying this war.

One thing that makes *Peace Concluded* so hard to "read" is the degree to which it is an "intertextual" painting. While the oblique and perhaps even unintended references to Leech and the cartoons of *Punch* contribute to this effect, so does the painting's "quotation" not only of visual but also of verbal texts. In addition to *The Times*, it pictures the latest serial part of *The Newcomes*, a novel featuring both military and painter-protagonists. (It was written by Leech's friend Thackeray – who had just left *Punch* – and illustrated by another friend, Richard Doyle, who had produced art for the magazine until 1850.) Moreover, directly behind the newspaper, in the back right of the canvas, is a barely distinguishable military engraving; Hancher has identified it to be of John Singleton Copley's *Death of Major Peirson* (1784), called by Lalumia "the finest painting with a military subject in British art."[71] All these reflections on war and soldiering dramatically mediate the response to *Peace Concluded*. Like the many prints behind Luard's *A Welcome Arrival*, they open up the horizon of interpretive opportunity to such a degree that the viewer can be left feeling rather like she is floating in space.

Consider the possibilities offered by the Copley engraving, which shows Major Peirson leading his troops in repelling the French invasion of Jersey in 1781. The British were victorious, although Peirson lost his life in the effort, as Copley's title indicates. Both Hancher and Paul Barlow (who devotes considerable attention to *Peace Concluded* in his monograph on Millais) discuss the print, and both notice how Millais presents it obscurely, by rendering it in a hazy grisaille format and by cropping it with the arch of his frame and hiding it behind the plant that grows in the background of the painting (one can compare the highly legible use of *Napoleon Crossing the Alps* in *The Black Brunswicker*). But they come to almost opposite conclusions about its significance. Hancher describes the effect of the paraquotation as essentially supportive: "Copley shows a mother and two children in horrified flight from the scene . . . Millais substitutes for them the Victorian family in his own picture, who must cope with heroic wounds less final than death."[72] In contrast, Barlow sees the engraving as subtly undermining rather than validating Millais's officer's stance. Instead of highlighting what he has given up for Queen and country, the comparison emphasizes his comfortable domesticity: "Peirson's sacrifice, like the news from the Crimea, is pushed towards the background. Both exist only in black and white prints, while the officer's body twists away towards the warm colour and renewed life in the family, just as the plant grows out to cover the obscure image of battle."[73] Barlow suggests that in some deep sense, Peirson's heroism – and the kind of military painting it produced – is "old news": it barely registers within the framework of the painting. That obscuring plant – a myrtle not a laurel, symbol of love rather than of valor (as both Hancher and Barlow point out) – covers the print almost as though it were a ruined edifice (or even a gravestone) overrun by creepers, a connection enhanced by the engraving's stone-like coloration, which makes it look more like *bas-relief* sculpture than a work on paper. Yet unlike Barlow, I would want to distinguish further between the newspaper and the print: the visual centrality of the former should be read in opposition to the peripheral position of the latter, as its up-to-dateness contrasts with the outmodedness of Copley's vision.

If Copley's painting is marginalized, then so is Thackeray's novel; it, too, has been pushed to the edge of the canvas, and it, too, appears a dullish color when compared with the brilliant white of the newspaper. In this case, the position cannot be based on its status as a relic: *The Newcomes*'s serialized release (October 1853 through August 1855) coincided closely with the duration of the major fighting phase of the war. Still, the disregard for the novel could owe something to the marginalized position of fiction during a war in which public taste ran so strongly towards journalism (as I argued in chapter 2); it may have suffered a certain obsolescence as soon as it appeared. But the presence of the novel also suggests interesting divisions between public and private ways of responding to the conflict. In his analysis of the effects of "*lectoral art*" – painting that figures scenes of reading or that includes texts that might be read by people in the scene – Garrett Stewart asks why a painter would "doom the canvas to such recurrent frustration" as develops when a viewer is forced to engage with the necessarily private relationship between a reader and a text. He points out that such scenes can "recruit narrative energy while removing it from view," generating the "silent manufacture of textual meaning." Yet what is curious in *Peace*

Concluded is how it offers two contrasting forms of textuality, as though to emphasize the distinction not only between "fact and fiction," as Stewart notes in his discussion of this painting, but also between publicly and privately formed meaning.[74]

Thus the newspaper's legible headline, which the officer seems to hold up for our benefit rather than his own, creates the effect of communal, or perhaps national, understanding, while the novel contains its significance within its pages, almost like a private secret – even as its barely discernible title is pictured above a more-or-less indiscernible, if tantalizing, cover image (it seems to be a family portrait not unlike that of *Peace Concluded* itself). Only knowing (that is, reading) viewers of the painting would be able to generate a more private relationship to the work by remediating it through Thackeray's novel. And Millais's choice of novel was dictated by more than a desire to plug the work of two such knowing viewers: the friends who wrote and illustrated the book (its position in the composition might even have come as an unpleasant reminder of public disinterest to Thackeray, for all that his novel had garnered positive reviews). Stewart points to an illustration in Thackeray's original text in which characters suspend their own book-reading to pick up newspapers, newspapers containing gossip that does "double duty as the extension of Thackeray's own plot."[75] Such free flow of meaning across media might offer a model for how the significance of Thackeray's novel can flow into Millais's painting – under the right conditions of viewership.

Indeed, many themes connect the works. Hancher suggests a similarity between Thackeray's and Millais's central figures: "The novel's hero, Colonel Newcome, is an extraordinarily virtuous military man who in the end faces personal deprivation with noble dignity, not unlike the officer in [*Peace Concluded*]."[76] Yet Colonel Newcome bears little relation to the handsome young officer of Millais's painting. In spite of his name, he belongs to the past; by the time the novel opens, he has already retired from his military career, and he dies before its conclusion. If anything, Millais's officer resembles the Colonel's son, Clive. While Clive may have made a perfectly decent dandy-soldier in a different era ("I think I should send him into the army," announces an old friend of the Colonel's on meeting the young man, "that's the best place for him – there's the least to do and the handsomest clothes to wear"), in his modern incarnation – and against a real-life backdrop of war that rendered this model of the soldier defunct – he instead becomes a gentleman artist. Rather than fight wars, he paints pictures; as he puts it: "I say a painter is as good as a lawyer, or a doctor, or even a soldier." Clive comes to believe that the hero-artist need not even portray warrior heroes: "What have I been doing," he asks himself, "spending six months over a picture of Sepoys and Dragoons cutting each other's throats? Art ought not to be a fever. It ought to be a calm." It is with him, rather than the Colonel, that Millais, the gentleman painter, would have sympathized. And if Clive's dilettantism somewhat undermines his status as heroic artist, Clive's more professional friend Ridley proves to be a perfect Carlylean Hero as Man of Art: "The palette on [Ridley's] arm was a great shield painted of many colours: he carried his maul-stick and his brushes along with it, the weapons of his glorious but harmless war." The narrator announces Ridley's motto with admiration: "Art is truth: and truth is religion; and its study and practice a daily work of pious duty."[77] So the presence of the novel in the painting does little to add to the luster of its officer-subject (other than through a broad endorsement of the kind of novelistic bourgeois domesticity in which he appears to be so happily ensconced), but it does suggest a defense of Millais's role as home-front artist in a time of war – a defense that would have been especially accessible to the painter's circle of literary and artistic friends.

If the visual and verbal texts within the painting itself destabilize its meaning, then so, too, does *Peace Concluded*'s interaction with the other canvases Millais submitted for the 1856 Exhibition. For example, the tendency to view *Peace Concluded* through the lens of Leech's works would have been enhanced by the presence of Millais's *Portrait of a Gentleman*. This painting depicts an aristocratic child seated on a carpet with a copy of Leech's *Mr Briggs' Sporting Tour* hanging over his legs; it is (as Barlow notes) a pastiche of Velazquez's *Don Diego de Acedo*, in which a middle-age dwarf holds a weighty and presumably scholarly volume open on his lap. Yet Millais's use of remediation resonates with the supposedly more serious work he exhibited alongside it: "here the painterly depiction of the rich clothing against the black and white illustrations of the chaotic slapstick in [the book of cartoons] provides a comic counterpoint to *Peace Concluded*'s use of *The Times* and *Major Peirson*."[78] In fact, one aspect of Millais's populism – a characteristic most obviously manifested in the way *Bubbles* (1886) became the iconic advertising image for Pear's soap – is to reduce the distinction between low and high art, between newspapers and novels, between Leech's cartoons and his own paintings. This leveling instinct was in tune with the leveling mood of the war; Barlow sees an increasing "interest in accessibility" that developed out of Millais's 1856 paintings. While the idea of accessibility might appear to be in conflict with the complex ambiguities of *Peace Concluded*, those ambiguities

Figure 16 John Everett Millais, *L'Enfant du Régiment* (1854–55)

reflected popular ambivalence in a manner that allowed Millais "to explore the possibilities for communal pleasures and common understanding," as Barlow puts it,[79] in spite of a war experience that had divided as well as unified the nation.

Hunt's mistaken impression about the presence of a sling in *Peace Concluded* has been ascribed to his confusion of the work with an earlier painting by Millais incorporating both a military subject and a titled date: *The Order of Release, 1746* (1853) shows an injured Highlander being released from prison by his wife. Like the woman in *Peace Concluded*, this wife was modeled by Effie Millais, and Michael Hancher notes that both paintings are remarkable for portraying dominant females[80] – even within military contexts that should have bolstered their male subjects' authority. But the sling memory might also have been produced by the resemblance of *Peace Concluded* to another painting with which it was originally exhibited: *L'Enfant du Regiment* (figure 16). This resemblance goes still further towards infantilizing the officer portrayed. *L'Enfant* illustrates an imagined moment from the childhood of the heroine of Donizetti's opera, *La Fille du Régiment*. A little girl lies in a church, upon a medieval knight's tomb, her right arm (which has been shot) bandaged conspicuously. A soldier's coat partially covers her sleeping figure. Barlow implies a connection between the paintings when he compares the pose of the officer in *Peace Concluded*, which he notes to be "a pastiche of the traditional effigy of the Christian knight – lying with a dog (for Fidelity) at his feet," to that of "the tomb of Gervaise Alard depicted in *L'Enfant*."[81] The question arises, of course, whether the officer's pose should be read as straightforward "pastiche" or as satire; does it emphasize his heroic martyrdom, or does it turn "what was once romantic to burlesque," to steal a phrase from Byron?

Links between Millais's two works accentuate the suggestion of satire. The hard, gothic architectural setting of *L'Enfant* – detailed in full Ruskinian glory – offers a strange contrast to the soft opulence surrounding the officer, even as the slight figure of the wounded girl, covered by a grenadier's jacket, seems a further indictment not only of "the violating results of masculine 'heroism,'" as Barlow would have it,[82] but also of the dressing-gown-clad officer's apparent health. Moreover, in *L'Enfant*, actual soldiers fighting a battle (the episode would have occurred in the middle of the Napoleonic wars) occupy the top left corner of the composition, as though in place of the simulacrum of war (the engraving after Copley) just visible in the opposite corner of *Peace Concluded*. Color underscores this relationship: the faint red and blue of the soldiers' coats stand out against the surrounding stone of *L'Enfant* much in the manner that the engraving's greys register in contrast with the lushly colored setting of *Peace Concluded*. And while the architectural details of *L'Enfant* might seem a gesture towards the revivalist instincts of the PRB, and its operatic source might suggest romance rather than reality, the painting would have been recognized as relevant at the time. Donizetti's 1840 work was put on in London in the summer of 1856 in a Crimea-inflected revival, taking advantage of the topicality of its *vivandière*-heroine by dressing the lead (who was pictured in costume in *The Illustrated Times* on July 12, 1856) to look exactly like Fenton's recently exhibited photograph of a *Cantinière* in the Crimea.[83]

Paul Barlow actually compares the combined effect of Millais's 1856 paintings to the impact of a novel: "all the exhibits of 1856 cross-reference themes in a way that indicates the remarkable integration and variety of his art at this time . . . It is reminiscent of Dickens's novels in its range of social reference and shifts between comedy and pathos."[84] This effect seems to coalesce in *Peace Concluded* – as the inclusion of Thackeray's novel in the painting perhaps hints. Indeed, a certain stylistic affinity connects the written to the painted work, and not just because Thackeray's satiric bent resonates with a satiric reading of *Peace Concluded*. Hancher suggestively compares the novelist's understanding of realism to that of Millais: "Thackeray's dictatorial power matches Millais's own command of the illusions of realism."[85] If Thackeray periodically pulls back the curtain to reveal his puppet-master manipulating the strings, Millais is the prop-master extraordinaire, coolly combining an obsessive "truth to nature" with a willingness to load his stages with an outrageous number of symbolically laden objects.

The heavy symbolism of the painting further exaggerates the confusion created by its intertextuality. Chris Brooks describes the bewildering visual impact of Pre-Raphaelite painting:

Insistent linearity, isolation of the individual form, the forcing of random detail to the frontal plane, the de-structuring of the visual field, overlapping and awkwardness are all aspects of the same intention: to challenge our conventions of perceptual organisation and, by extension, the existential and metaphysical structuring we derive from that organization. The visual world of Pre-Raphaelitism constantly escapes the spectator's control, for the demands upon visual comprehension have deliberately been pushed too far . . . Pre-Raphaelite painting seems to argue that visual hierarchy and organization are only habits by means of which man ignores or dismisses so much of the real.[86]

One need only consider the awkward pose of *Peace Concluded*'s officer, his body broken in two by his wife's curiously elongated seated form, or the great reddish black-hole of her lap, against which the toys appear with gem-like specificity, to recognize the aptness of Brooks's description. And while the trends he notes concern painterly techniques of brushwork and composition, the peculiar habits of focus he identifies stem in part from the Pre-Raphaelites' desire to allow even minor details of their paintings to resonate symbolically. In *Peace Concluded*, the deep ambivalence of Pre-Raphaelite vision finds its perfect subject in a war that generated the most ambivalent of feelings; style and substance merge to bewildering effect.

Kate Flint has contrasted *Peace Concluded* with a fourth painting Millais exhibited in 1856, *The Blind Girl* (a picture of a blind girl and her sister sitting in a field, surrounded by a prospect laden with biblical typological symbolism), to argue that Millais was experimenting with two different symbolic orders in the period:

Peace Concluded draws on symbols which derive their force through a system of signification which has been produced through political and nationalistic associations, whilst to some extent, *The Blind Girl* relies on a far older tradition, the idea that the world is an intelligible text, the "book of nature." The slippage between the two – the shift from reading the world to "looking at it as an observable but meaningless object," to use Martin Jay's terms, and using its contents as a means towards one's own conceptual concretization – may be read as the shift which Foucault and others have discerned between the old and the modern epistemological orders.[87]

Peace Concluded is undoubtedly invested in modernity: one might note, for example, how a large proportion of the readable symbolic objects in the painting would have been bought. They represent a very up-to-date process of self-fashioned meaning. But one of the work's peculiarities is the way in which it combines the older and newer symbolic orders in a manner that destabilizes not just the significance of the objects in question, but also the "epistemological" status of the painting as a whole. Thus if Flint sees in the Blind Girl's headdress and "expression of rapt attention to an inner vision" a visual shadow of "a multitude of representations of the Virgin Mary," Barlow notes how "the traditional effigy of the Christian knight" lies behind the officer's pose in *Peace Concluded*, and Alison Smith has suggested that this pose is also reminiscent of a *pietà*, with Effie's crown of hair "form[ing] a halo-like circle around her head [that] lends her a timeless and a spiritual quality."[88]

In fact, for all its modernity, *Peace Concluded* incorporates a fair amount of Christian symbolism. The toys Flint reads – correctly – in a political and imperial context also have obvious biblical resonance not that different from the symbolic resonance of the double rainbow in the sky of *The Blind Girl*. Nevertheless, like the dog at the officer's feet (modeled by Millais's dog, Roswell), they register both symbolically and naturalistically. At least one contemporary critic was caught between these two ways of seeing them, complaining that the "allusions" to the combatant nations in the toys "could not be understood by children of such tender years – hence this passage of the composition becomes caricature."[89] But the intense specificity with which the toys are depicted – their quasi-photographic realism – appears to have struck contemporary viewers nonetheless. Ruskin, in a footnote to his *Academy Notes*, wrote that other painters should take to heart "the hint for bringing more of nature into our common work, in the admirable modeling of the polar bear and lion, though merely children's toys."[90] I am reminded of Dante Gabriel Rossetti's brilliant poem, "The Woodspurge" (composed in 1856), in which the poet describes an experience of the three-cupped flower that replaces religious intensity (generated by symbolism) with pure aesthetic appreciation.[91] There is something about how Millais has painted those

Painters of modern life

toys that allows one momentarily to concentrate perception in consciousness of the objects *qua* object, before they slide back into symbols.

Given the saturated significance of the toys, the mock war that takes place in the blood-red space of the wife's velvet-clad lap even suggests a hint of sexual symbolism. Hancher quotes the "obtuse allegorizing" to which Millais's fellow Pre-Raphaelite Frederick Stephens subjected the painting:

"Peace concluded, 1856," was a large picture of a matrimonial reconciliation: – the husband lies upon a sofa, with *The Times* in his hand, while reclining against his chest sits his wife, caressing him; her face shows that preliminaries have been exchanged and that the troubled waters are fast subsiding, while round the mouth a few poutings linger, as the last waves dash upon the shore after a storm. Two children, who stand by, are puzzled by the tempest, which one evidently resents upon its father, upon whom it gazes earnestly.[92]

Note the suggestion of biblical Deluge in those "fast subsiding" waters: Stephens, too, has picked up on the allusion. Actually, his reading responds to both the novelistic domesticity evoked by the painting (thus novels like *The Newcomes* and Trollope's *The Warden* [1855] would use the language of the war during which they were written to describe wars between the sexes) and to the rather enigmatic expression on the wife's face, her almost defiant manner of looking out from the canvas at the viewer.[93] The painting incorporates sufficient "signs of the times" (including, of course, the newspaper itself) to render obvious the limitations of ahistorical reading. But Hancher finds himself drawn to it nonetheless. As he concludes, in spite of its apparently "public" subject, the painting also offers a psychological tableau. And if it "is indeed one of several obscure variations by Millais on the anxious theme of male dependency, there is some justification for its 'scandalous' misnomer 'Urgent Private Affairs.'"[94] Yet if one considers the disturbance to gender relations caused by a war in which heroic warriors were supplanted in the public imaginary by the heroic nurses who took care of them, even the private domestic reading becomes public and historical.

Still, Ruskin's notion that the toys represent a "truth to nature" seems laughable; in place of nature "red in tooth and claw," of not only real bears and real lions but – more importantly – real war, Millais shows us meticulously painted playthings snuggled in those plush red velvet skirts. Millais's ludicrous use of the toys actually calls to mind an 1855 cartoon in *Punch* mocking the Pre-Raphaelites, an offshoot of the series of such cartoons I discussed earlier (29:130; figure 17).[95] Above the title "Sketching

SKETCHING FROM NATURE.
Miss Raphael makes a study for her grand Picture, "The Day after the Deluge."

Figure 17 [Henry R. Howard], "Sketching from Nature," *Punch* 29 (1855), 130

from Nature," a spinsterish-looking woman sits outdoors on a collapsible artists' stool (of the sort used by the *plein air* school), sketchpad and pen in hand. Before her lie the carefully arranged components of a Noah's ark toy-set like that depicted by Millais; the ark itself rests atop an upturned flowerpot representing Mount Ararat. Under the title, a caption reading *"Miss Raphael makes a study for her grand Picture, 'The Day After the Deluge'"* indicates the lady's artistic affiliations. The "Sketching from Nature" cartoon makes fun of the limitations placed on the Pre-Raphaelites by their credo of "truth to nature" – especially given their desire to paint scenes from the past. Millais circumvents his own geographical rather than temporal version of Miss Raphael's dilemma of eyewitness observation by allowing the toys in his painting to be – on one level at least – just toys in a Victorian parlor. Nevertheless, his use of them hints that he, too, has attempted a modern "grand Picture" worthy of the title "The Day after the Deluge." And *Peace Concluded* makes those toys – in conjunction with the dated newspaper, Copley's engraving, Thackeray's novel, and references to both Leech's cartoons and Millais's own paintings – capture on its canvas surface the deluge of meanings that the Crimean War had poured forth.

A smaller Crimean painting by Millais exhibited the following year takes a very different perspective on war.[96] It shows a Highlander at the front reading a letter – the titular *News from Home* – with his gun securely held in the crook of his arm. Behind him, two more soldiers can be vaguely seen: a seated man seems to be eating; a standing one peers cautiously over the top of the trench that protects them all. Curiously, though, in spite of belonging to a scene from within "the deluge" – that is, set during the war and in the Crimea – Millais's soldier-subject remains miraculously "dry" (this is especially surprising given that the trench would have been particularly vulnerable to flooding, both metaphorical and literal). The painting demonstrates genuine effort towards realism in the carefully detailed trench-setting (no doubt copied from photographs, William Simpson's popular lithographs, and *ILN* illustrations) and uniform of the Highlander. But while the presence of the remediating letter seems promising, it does not remedy the broader documentary failure of the work. Ruskin wondered – legitimately – whether "Highlanders at the Crimea ... always put on new uniforms to read letters from home in?"[97] The doubt brings to mind yet another *Punch* joke, a cartoon from January of 1856 showing side-by-side portraits of Highlanders: one, "Highland Officer in the Crimea, according to the Romantic Ideas of Sentimental Young Ladies" (in kilt and regalia); two, "Ditto, according to the Actual Fact" (fully wrapped up in furs and trousers with beard and cigar) (30:20); it's not a comparison the manly Millais would have wished to elicit. All-in-all, while it tries to reproduce the effects of the Special Artists in the East, *News from Home* feels much more staged than *Peace Concluded*, much less real.[98] In some ways, its peculiarly un-Millaisian effect can be compared to Leech's efforts in the "Trump Card(igan)" cartoon: in both cases, the artists felt like they had to abandon their usual observational methods in response to the war, and in both cases, the resulting works are disturbingly flat. In contrast, Millais's and Leech's apparently more "closeted" domestic pieces are able to use remediation, paraquotation, and symbolism to open themselves up to much wider terrain while preserving a certain "truth to nature" based on the artists' eyewitness experience of scenes like those they are depicting.

These two Crimean paintings also demonstrate the tug-of-war Millais was undergoing between what might be called "history painting" and journalism, between high and low art, between exclusivity and populism. *News from Home* provides a nice counterpoint to *Peace Concluded*'s use of *The Times*: here a soldier reads the private letter – also designated as "News" – while in a very public theater of war, whereas in the earlier painting the public newspaper was read in the private sphere of the home. (The works in conjunction offer proof once more of the interpenetration of home front and battlefront and of private and public space during the war.) But the fact that it is a letter rather than a newspaper simultaneously gives the less ambitious painting a timeless quality that *Peace Concluded, 1856*, with its precise date, could never achieve: this form of "news" never grows stale. Remember Hunt's comments on the brief shelf-life of Millais's original theme for *Peace Concluded*: "The call for satire on carpet heroes was out of date."[99] One might also recall, though, that *Peace Concluded* is the third installment in Millais's "virtual triptych" (Hancher's term) of dated works: *The Proscribed Royalist, 1651* (1853), *The Order of Release, 1746* (1853), and *Peace Concluded, 1856* (1856). These paintings share more than the historical format of their titles: all three have military themes, and all three are images of "love and duty."[100] But something extraordinary has happened between the second and third paintings in the series, marked in the unprecedented repetition in *Peace Concluded* between the titular and compositional dates: *1856* (1856).

In this case, the date reminds me of another famous date in a work of Victorian art: *Wuthering Heights* (1847) opens with a number – 1801 – that sets up some of the great questions of interpretation in the novel. Emily Brontë uses a threshold year to symbolize the upheavals of the revolutionary era of the novel's publication. But the date also introduces the ambiguities of the novel's mode: is it a public record of a moment in history, or is it a private document of a personal story that represents eternal and essential truths about the human condition? On the one hand, "1801" suggests the specificity one might associate with, say, the byline of a newspaper. No "once upon a times" here – we know exactly when – and we will soon know exactly where – we are. In fictional terms, this is the world of the realist novel, an idea that will soon be supported by the multitude of clues Brontë provides concerning the times and places of her narrative. But the date also seems like what one would find at the start of a diary entry. And this mode is further evoked, if one reads on, by the first-person voice one encounters.

Similarly, the date in *Peace Concluded, 1856*, registers the painting's ambivalent negotiation of the relationship between private and public spheres in a time of social and political turmoil. We must decide whether to "read" it as journalism (through the newspaper), as history (through the Copley engraving), or as something more personal and inaccessible (through the novel). We must decide whether the toys are playthings of children, symbols of a specific contemporary war, or abstract symbols of a kind of apocalyptic imagination. We must decide whether Millais's officer is a medieval saintly knight or a Leechian languid swell. Or must we decide? For while it is there in all three paintings of Millais's "love and duty" series, the implication of the date has special resonance for the third image: the attempt at marking an era has also become a journalistic impulse, history and the now have collided in an unprecedented fashion. I said that something extraordinary had happened between the last two installments of Millais's triptych. That something was the Crimean War.

Afterword

Elizabeth Thompson, Lady Butler, The Roll Call, *and the afterlife of the Crimean War*

On May 4, 1874, opening day of the Royal Academy Exhibition, Elizabeth Thompson (later Lady Butler) echoed Byron in her diary: "I may say that I awoke this morning and found myself famous."[1] Her sudden fame was the result of her entry for the Exhibition, *Calling the Roll after an Engagement, Crimea* (figure 18), which shows a group of soldiers standing exhaustedly to muster after a harsh winter battle as a mounted officer inspects the ranks.[2] The twenty-seven-year-old painter did not exaggerate; the response to her painting was immediate and sensational. *The Roll Call* (as it became known) was the artist's second work to be shown at the Academy, but whereas her first entry (a scene from the recent Franco-Prussian War) had been "skied," this one was hung on the line. It was the third exhibit ever to require protection by railing from the eager crowds. Thompson became the toast of the town – and of the Prince of Wales, who singled out her canvas at the Academy dinner.[3] Queen Victoria purchased *The Roll Call* (allowing an engraving to be made so her citizens could own it, too); a bed-ridden Nightingale was accorded a private showing. After the exhibition closed, the painting "toured the country to overwhelming public acclaim," as Paul Usherwood and Jenny Spencer-Smith have documented:

In Newcastle-upon-Tyne, it was advertised by men with sandwich-boards which simply read "*The Roll Call* is Coming!" Such was its reputation that no further information was needed. In Liverpool, 20,000 people saw the picture in three weeks, an immense number at that time. A quarter of a million carte-de-visite photographs of the artist, now referred to by the press as "Roll Call Thompson" ... were sold by J Dickinson & Co.[4]

In "Punch's Essence of Parliament" for 1874, Edward Lindley Sambourne's visual summary of the London season, Thompson sits like Britannia atop the composition, beside a cherub who holds her painting

Figure 18 Elizabeth Thompson, Lady Butler, *Calling the Roll after an Engagement, Crimea* (1874)

and blasts a trumpet announcing her reign, while the other figures of the day cascade outwards from her centrifugal presence.[5]

What caused such a response? And what does the response – and Lady Butler's subsequent career as a military painter – reveal about the legacy of the Crimean War? I turn to *The Roll Call* to ask these questions because one of the curiosities of this war is how slight a cultural footprint it appeared to have left behind, even a mere ten years after its end. The review of Thompson's painting in the *Morning Post* begins with precisely this point:

> It is singular that so prolific in incident and so picturesque in detail as was the Crimean war, it has been so little utilised by authors and painters. It is true that the Poet Laureate has made a portion of it the subject for one of his most vigorous lays [presumably "The Charge of the Light Brigade"], Mr. Kinglake has written of it in his most graphic manner, the late T. W. Robertson made it an especial incident in his comedy of "Ours," and the late J. D. Luard painted an excellent picture of the interior of an officer's hut in the Crimea about fifteen years ago. Save and except these few instances, the indefatigible [*sic*] special correspondents, and the artists of the illustrated papers, the subject so brimming with every class of suggestive matter has been well-nigh let alone. It is, therefore, with considerable satisfaction that we find an artist of Miss Thompson's power has taken an excellent incident in the Crimean war as the subject for her picture.[6]

In the preceding chapters, I have argued that the influence of the war on the literature and art of the day was broader than has been recognized – extending to such works as Elizabeth Gaskell's *North and South*, for example – and that the relative paucity of more straightforward responses to the conflict may have owed something to the difficulty in embodying its "incidents" and "details" in a suitably patriotic fashion, not to mention a "picturesque" one. But a decade after the Crimean War began, the public appetite for both Thompson's painting and for Thompson herself suggests a broader acceptance of shifts in understanding initially brought forth by the war.

To explain what these shifts are, one might begin by noting that the term "excellent incident" seems woefully unsuited to describing the subject of *The Roll Call*. The phrase suggests a focus on action, as in Wordsworth's description of the unhealthy "craving" for a literature full of "incident" in the wake of the gothic events of the French Revolution.[7] But Thompson's paradigmatic conception of the Crimean War shows a scene of suffering in the aftermath of battle rather than of fighting during battle. While some movement is implied by the mounted officer's trajectory, even this is an action of review, oriented towards the past rather than the present. And the only other object to break the compositional line of the painting is its most static feature: the collapsed body of an exhausted (dead?) guardsman, towards which a comrade reaches an arm in sympathy and enquiry. To make up for the lack of action, Thompson focuses instead on character. Her subjects – while representative – are also painted with remarkable specificity; she used ex-soldiers (including Crimean veterans) as models and found inspiration in their personal reminiscences. The resulting portraits were much admired for their realism; as *The Times*'s critic remarked: "All those heads, without a grimace or exaggeration, have well-distinguished character and expression, and one reads them with interest."[8] And in his appreciation of his sister-in-law's career, Wilfred Meynell would later write that "Lady Butler has done for the soldier in Art what Mr Rudyard Kipling has done for him in Literature – she has taken the individual, separated him, seen him close, and let the world so see him."[9]

Significantly, as Meynell's reference to Kipling suggests, Thompson's "dark battalion" (as she called it [106]) is composed not of glorious officers or generals (the standard focus of military painting) but of ordinary men. Its fundamentally "'democratic' design" appears in its substitution of a horizontal composition for the "pyramidal format that once had been the norm for battle paintings."[10] Ulrich Keller has argued for the redefinition "of what constituted military Spectacle" that *The Roll Call* implied and pointed out that this redefinition included an aspect of class role-reversal: "In the academy exhibition of 1874, [Thompson's] guardsmen stood in a physically and morally elevated position, immovably gazing at the pushing and shoving crowds below . . . [T]he exhibition visitors found themselves challenged to pass muster and to ask themselves whether they measured up to the painted heroes."[11] As Matthew Lalumia has explained, such concern for her lower-class subjects came in response not only to memories of the Crimean War but also to the more recent legislative debates – themselves a product of the lessons learned during the war – that led to the Cardwell Reforms (named after Gladstone's war minister, Edward Cardwell), which were passed in 1870 and 1871. The reforms of 1870 improved the lot of common soldiers by reducing the enlistment period from twenty-one to twelve years. The 1871 legislative measures ended the purchase system that had resulted in such inexperienced military leadership in the Crimea (often invoked in the debates). In place of purchase, a merit-based system of promotions and commissions was instituted, thus opening up military advancement to all.[12]

If *The Roll Call*'s success owed much to its sensitivity to shifts in perceptions of class brought about in part by the war, the success of its creator should be considered in relation to the conception of heroinism that I discussed in chapter 2. Thus while the painting depicts Thompson's male subjects and the events of war without sensationalism, the painter herself became the sensation. The Nightingale connection, apparent in the decision to allow the great heroine of the war a private viewing, can also be seen in the common assumption at the time that *The Roll Call*'s much-vaunted realism could only be explained by its painter's experiences as a wartime nurse (in some versions of this story, the youthful Thompson had even served in the Crimea).[13] Reviews of the painting universally considered the work's merit in terms of its creator's sex, and usually, the attempt to do so produced a curiously gender-bending descriptive language. The *Spectator* described *The Roll Call*'s "thoroughly manly point of view"; the *Daily Telegraph* announced of Thompson, "we hail her appearance with this honest, manly Crimean picture, as full of genius as it is full of industry"; and in *The Times,* Tom Taylor called the work "a picture of the battlefield, neither ridiculous, nor offensive, nor improbable, nor exaggerated, in which there is neither swagger, nor sentimentalism, but plain, manly, pathetic, heroic truth, and this is the work of a young woman."[14]

Taylor's negatives show his difficulty in coming to grips with the painting's relationship to its painter: not only was this "manly" painting the work of a woman, but of a young woman, and a beautiful and unmarried one at that. "There is no sign of woman's weakness," he added, again resorting to definition through negation.[15] But if not the work of woman, then what was Thompson? Ruskin, on viewing her next painting (a Napoleonic scene entitled *The 28th Regiment at Quatre Bras* [1875]), was forced to consider the same logical dilemma, and ended up resorting to familiar labels: "I have always said that no woman could paint . . . But it is amazon's work this; no doubt about it";[16] the Amazon, the heroic nurse: stock figures of the war novels keep reappearing in assessments of Elizabeth Thompson. Yet while Ruskin's about-face was significant, it had its limits. Although Thompson was seriously considered for a place in the Academy (with Millais among her champions), she fell two short of the necessary number when it came to a vote.[17] Moreover, Thompson's work was lauded in part because – like the work of nurses – it could be aligned with some more conventional beliefs about woman's proper role. Thus when George Augustus Sala, writing for the *Daily Telegraph*, announced that in the excellence of *The Roll Call,* "we see a manacle knocked off a woman's wrist and a shackle hacked off her ankle," he could do so because of the woman artist's ability to operate from within the domestic sphere: "We see her endowed with a vocation which can be cultivated within her own home, and in the very utmost privacy." She becomes, in Anthea Callen's terms, an "angel" – perhaps even an Amazon – "in the studio," but in a studio that exists as an extension of her own house.[18]

If, however, the Crimean War produced a female painter of heroic proportions and a battle painting that radically revised conceptions of military heroism, the conditions that propelled Thompson to fame were soon to give way to the militaristic mood that accompanied the imperialist agenda of the 1880s and 1890s. Thompson's next two Crimean canvases, *Balaclava* (1876) and *The Return From Inkerman* (1877), followed in the vein of *The Roll Call* by depicting the aftermath of battle and focusing on suffering soldiers (a particularly noteworthy treatment of Balaklava, where aristocratic inflections were the norm). But in 1881 – while the First Boer War was providing fodder for an explosion of British jingoism – Lady Butler (as she had become in 1877) produced her most sensational painting, *Scotland for Ever!*, the stance of which is captured by an exclamation point that recalls the patriotic effusiveness of *Westward Ho!*. The work shows the charge of the Scots Greys at Waterloo, horses and riders portrayed in full frontal view as they lunge out of the canvas. If the effect of *The Roll Call* on viewers is to emphasize the thoughtful act of review, the effect of *Scotland for Ever!* is to urge them to get out of the way; its fundamental impact is somatic.[19] Yet while the painting – the most familiar of Butler's images – is magnificent, it is hardly typical of its painter's work. The *Athenaeum* remarked on Butler's uncharacteristic lack of attention to the individual personalities of the horsemen; here the focus is on action.[20]

Nevertheless, if *Scotland For Ever!* seems reactionary in its ostentatious militarism, it is so as a by-product of a specifically painterly vein of conservatism; Butler records how the idea for the work came from her "annoy[ance]" while touring an exhibition of paintings by "'Aesthetes' of the period, whose sometimes unwholesome productions preceded those of our modern 'Impressionists'" (186). The canvas was thus intended not so much as a political comment as an artistic one. Indeed, most of Butler's later works continued to portray war with some ambivalence; as she noted, "I never painted for the glory of war, but to portray its pathos and heroism."[21] No doubt this fact contributed to her waning popularity; Usherwood and Spencer-Smith tell how "By the early 1880s, her particular type of sombre, intimate battle scene had already been supplanted in public esteem by the more triumphal work of her followers and rivals, such as Richard Caton Woodville, Charles Edwin Fripp, and Godfrey Douglas Charles."[22]

Perhaps reflecting the pressures exerted by a market with such tastes, Butler's final large Crimean painting, *The Colours: Advance of the Scots Guards at the Alma* (1899), was not only by far her most overtly patriotic image of this war, but one of the more militaristic images in her broader oeuvre. Significantly, *The Colours* looks back to the first major battle of the Crimean War – the battle that preceded the general uproar about mismanagement that was to stamp the conflict on the British imagination as a failure. The work's subject and style both suggest that by the time Butler returned to the topic at the end of the century, the Crimean War had shifted its place in the public mind. Her only Crimean painting to depict the action of battle, *The Colours* is also Butler's only Crimean "history painting" – complete with the traditional triangular compositional form. It thus seems to portray a distant past. As the catalogue entry for the 1898 Academy exhibition remarked of the Alma (quoting General Earle): "It was the last battle of the old order. We went into action in all our finery, with colours flying and bands playing."[23] Once more aesthetics rather than politics fuel Butler's nostalgia; it is the pageantry – alluded to in the painting's title – that she misses and tries to recapture on canvas (the *Autobiography* remarks that this was "the last time British troops wore [full parade dress] in action" [271]). Yet the Crimean War could function aesthetically rather than politically in *The Colours* in part because more recent events could now stand in for it; it would soon be supplanted in popular consciousness by a new model of military debacle: the Second Boer War (1899–1902), which would produce its own form of anti-war protest art in works like Thomas Hardy's "Drummer Hodge."[24] Painted on the very cusp of that conflict (against which Butler's husband, who was Commander of British troops in South Africa, protested in vain – to the point of resigning[25]), *The Colours* signals the end of the modernity of the Crimean War; it could now be accorded almost the same nostalgic treatment as Napoleonic-era battles.

Still, Butler's career also suggests that the ambiguous response first generated by the Crimean War would linger, reemerging periodically – perhaps most forcefully during World War I. Thus Butler's obituary in *The Times* makes note of an enactment of *The Roll Call* at Aldershot in 1915. While the obituary sees the event as a "tribute" that helped to "recapture for [Butler] some of the glamour of her earlier days," it seems likely that the painting resurfaced at this moment because its ethos of

Afterword 217

suffering and sympathy for the ordinary soldier coincided with public opinion about the current war.[26] But the Crimean influence could also be considered more obliquely, as a primal source for Butler's ambivalent feelings about war throughout her career. Butler's *Autobiography* (1922), written in the shadow of the Great War (about which her sister, Alice Meynell, composed poems[27]), finishes on Armistice Day. Yet its final two pages include references to the Crimean and Boer Wars: that is, to wars that had become symbols of military blunder. In both cases, these references work by ostensibly differentiating past failures from present triumphs. Balaklava provides a standard against which to measure the less ambiguous glory of a contemporary charge: that "of the Warwick and Worcester Yeomanry at Huj, near Jerusalem, which charge outshone the old Balaclava one we love to remember, and which differed from the Crimean exploit in that we not only captured all the enemy guns, but *held* them" (331). And the celebrations of Armistice Day are described by contrast with the uproar during the Second Boer War: "The streets were thronged with the *true* happiness in the people's eyes, and there was no "*maffiking*" [a term alluding to the unruly revels that followed the relief of the British garrison besieged at Mafeking], no horseplay, but such *fun*" (332).

A POST-CARD, FOUND ON A GERMAN PRISONER, WITH "SCOTLAND FOR EVER" TURNED INTO PRUSSIAN CAVALRY, TYPIFYING THE VICTORIOUS ON-RUSH OF THE GERMAN ARMY IN THE NEW YEAR, 1915.

Figure 19 Elizabeth Butler, *An Autobiography* (1922), tailpiece engraving

Nevertheless, in presenting these contrasts, Butler also reminds us of the past: of the disastrous charge to which her painting could do justice only by showing its aftermath of suffering; of the rowdy jingoism that represented the ugliest face of a Nation at war. And the *Autobiography* concludes on a truly bizarre note, implying that such historical awareness necessarily undermines any simple message of militaristic glory: the last page shows a German New Year's greeting card for 1915 that reproduced *Scotland for Ever!* but replaced the Scots uniforms with Prussian ones and added an inset picture of a waiting mother and children (figure 19). The caption for the image (the only commentary provided on it, Butler's text itself being silent) tells us that it was discovered on a German prisoner, and that it "typif[ied] the victorious on-rush of the German Army" in 1915. Thus Butler ends by documenting the reach of her fame, but also by implicitly questioning her own most blatantly patriotic message. In the context both of her book and of her career, the German reinscription appears not so much as desecration of her art that must be reappropriated by its original creator – even as the British have taken back the category of the victorious from the Germans – but as a salutary reinterpretation: one must remember that even the enemy fights with glory, and one must remember that their women and children also pray for what the card calls the soldiers' "*baldige Heimkehr*" – their speedy homecoming. It is an image much closer to the ethos of Butler's wider oeuvre, learned from the lessons of the Crimean War, than the original painting had been – closer to what she calls her "own reading of war": "that it calls forth the noblest and the basest impulses of human nature" (46–47).

Notes

INTRODUCTION

1. Matthew Arnold, "Stanzas from the Grand Chartreuse," lines 84–85, in *Matthew Arnold: Selected Poems and Prose*, ed. Miriam Allott (London: J. M. Dent, 1993), p. 89.
2. Leader, *The Times*, December 29, 1854, 6.
3. Karl Marx, "War Debate in Parliament," in *Dispatches for the New York Tribune: Selected Journalism of Karl Marx*, ed. James Ledbetter (London: Penguin, 2007), p. 134. The article was first published on April 17, 1854. Christopher Hitchens notes that Marx here echoes his famous witticism, inspired by Hegel, that tragic history repeats itself as farce. See "The Grub Street Years," *Saturday Guardian* (London), June 16, 2007, Review, 6.
4. [E. B. Hamley], "Poetry of the War: Reviewed Before Sebastopol," *Blackwood's Edinburgh Magazine* 77 (May, 1855), 531.
5. Ulrich Keller discusses these examples of the phenomenon of interpenetration in *The Ultimate Spectacle: A Visual History of the Crimean War* (Amsterdam: Overseas Publishers Association, 2001), pp. 174, 177.
6. Jay David Bolter and Richard Grusin explore how this process, whereby "media refashion themselves to answer the challenges of new media," operates in the age of virtual media (*Remediation: Understanding New Media* [Cambridge, MA: MIT Press, 1999], p. 15).
7. Florence Nightingale, *Cassandra*, intro. Myra Stark, epilogue Cynthia Macdonald (New York: The Feminist Press, 1979), p. 36.
8. Henry Wadsworth Longfellow, "Santa Filomena," line 40, in *Poetical Works*, 6 vols. (Boston: Houghton Mifflin and Co., 1889–92), III:54.
9. Explorations of versions of this process and the century's ambivalent response to epic include my own book, *The Crisis of Action in Nineteenth-Century English Literature* (Columbus, OH: The Ohio State University Press, 2006); Nancy Armstrong, *Desire and Domestic Fiction: A Political History of the Novel* (New York: Oxford University Press, 1987); Herbert Tucker, *Britain's Heroic Muse: 1790–1910* (New York: Oxford University Press, 2008); and Simon Dentith, *Epic and Empire in Nineteenth-Century Britain* (Cambridge: Cambridge University Press, 2006).

10. Quoted in Paul Fussell, *The Great War and Modern Memory*, 25th anniversary edn. (Oxford: Oxford University Press, 2000), p. 234.
11. See Linda Colley, *Britons: Forging the Nation, 1707–1837*, 2nd edn. (New Haven: Yale University Press, 2005).
12. Richard Helgerson, *Forms of Nationhood: The Elizabethan Writing of England* (Chicago: University of Chicago Press, 1992), p. 15.
13. M. Van Wyk Smith, *Drummer Hodge: The Poetry of the Anglo-Boer War (1899–1902)* (Oxford: The Clarendon Press, 1978), p. 12.
14. James Chandler, *England in 1819: The Politics of Literary Culture and the Case of Romantic Historicism* (Chicago; University of Chicago Press, 1998), p. xiii. In its focus as an imaginative translation of the experience of war through a variety of media, this book also shares an agenda with Samuel Hynes's wonderful *A War Imagined: The First World War and English Culture* (London: The Bodley Head, 1990).
15. Hitchens, "Grub Street Years," 6. Hitchens refers to the ongoing struggle over the stewardship of Jerusalem, but I would argue for a wider regional frame of comparison. As this book goes to press, the Crimea itself also threatens (in the wake of disputes over Georgia) once again to become the scene of Great Powers conflict.
16. See, for example, Gautam Chakravorty, *The Indian Mutiny and the British Imagination* (Cambridge: Cambridge University Press, 2005); M. Van Wyk Smith, *Drummer Hodge*; and Paula M. Krebs, *Gender, Race, and the Writing of Empire: Public Discourse and the Boer War* (Cambridge: Cambridge University Press, 1999).
17. The relationship of the Crimean War to the rise of imperialism during the Victorian period will not be a significant concern of this book. But as Patrick Brantlinger has argued, the 1850s are a crucial stage in the development of the British Empire: "The Australian gold rush, the search for the Nile's sources, the Crimean War, and the Mutiny made that decade a turning point for imperialist ideology." Brantlinger remains almost altogether silent about the Crimea. But William Holman Hunt suggests a connection between the Crimean War and later imperialism that resonates with my discussion of the war as a formative experience of failure when he posits that "The Persian War, the Chinese War, and the Indian Mutiny came as the price of [British] loss of prestige" in the Crimea. Patrick Brantlinger, *Rule of Darkness: British Literature and Imperialism 1830–1914* (Ithaca: Cornell University Press, 1988), p. 14; William Holman Hunt, *Pre-Raphaelitism and the Pre-Raphaelite Brotherhood*, 2 vols. (London: Macmillan, 1905), II:78.
18. Brian Friel, *Translations* (London: Faber and Faber, 1981), p. 66.
19. W. C. Sellar and R. J. Yeatman, *1066 and All That: A Memorable History of England* (Stroud, Gloucestershire: Sutton Publishing, 1993), pp. xv, 111. The Crimean War is the subject of ch. 53, pp. 111–12. Further quotations are taken from these pages. Most of this book first appeared in *Punch*, a journal to which I will turn frequently for contemporary images of the Crimean War.

20. See Winfried Weingart, *The Crimean War, 1853–1856* (London: Arnold, 1999), p. 4. Weingart's book offers a clear and comprehensive history of the war; chapters 8 and 12 are particularly relevant to my concerns. Several recent historians of the war have argued against what Andrew Lambert (in *The Crimean War: British Grand Strategy, 1853–56* [Manchester: Manchester University Press, 1990]) calls the mistaken (if popular) "Crimeocentric" (p. 346) take on its events, suggesting instead that it be more properly seen as possessing "the germs of a world war" (Weingart, *Crimean War*, p. 10). If what follows is indeed Crimeocentric, this is because I am interested in popular perceptions of the war in Britain, both past and present.
21. Quoted in Trevor Royle, *Crimea: The Great Crimean War, 1854–1856* (New York: Palgrave Macmillan, 2004), p. 74.
22. Lambert has argued that the importance of naval efforts in the Baltic Sea has been vastly underappreciated by historians – a fault his own military history attempts to rectify.
23. While the modern spelling is "Inkerman," the Victorians tended to use a final double "n"; hence the discrepancies in spelling thoughout this book. I favor a "k" for Balaklava and will use "c" only if quoting from a source with that spelling.
24. Arnold, "Dover Beach," line 37, in *Matthew Arnold: Selected Poems and Prose*, p. 77.
25. James Morris, *Pax Britannica, The Climax of an Empire* (London: Faber, 1973), p. 337. Morris comes up with this term when describing the art of Elizabeth Thompson, Lady Butler, whose career began with her paintings of the Crimean War, as I discuss in my Afterword.
26. Royle, *Crimea*, p. 502; Weingart puts the figure at 20 percent (*Crimean War*, pp. 215–16).
27. See J. B. Connacher, *Britain and the Crimea: 1855–56: Problems of War and Peace* (Basingstoke, Hampshire: Macmillan, 1987), pp. 21–22; and Olive Anderson, *A Liberal State at War: English Politics and Economics during the Crimean War* (London: Macmillan, 1967), p. 114. Anderson's excellent account of the political war on the home front has been particularly helpful to me.
28. Royle, *Crimea*, p. 412.
29. Quoted in Weingart, *Crimean War*, p. 163.
30. Royle, *Crimea*, p. 482. Briefly stated, the "Four Points" of the peace treaty effected (1) the establishment of the degree and extent of Russian control in Bessarabia; (2) the free navigation of the Danube; (3) neutralization of the Black Sea; and (4) determination of the treatment of non-Muslim subjects of the Sultan (the Sultan promised equality; the Powers agreed not to interfere). See Connacher, *Britain and the Crimea*, pp. 204–05; and Weingart, *Crimean War*, pp. 17–18 and ch. 17. Other historians have been more positive than Royle in their evaluation of the Treaty of Paris. Thus Philip Warner argues that it was successful in containing Russian expansion (*The Crimean War: A Reappraisal* [London: Arthur Baker, 1972], p. 221).
31. Anderson, *Liberal State*, p. 23.

I RUSHING INTO PRINT: JOURNALISM AND THE CRIMEAN WAR

1. George Frederick Dallas, letter to his family, January 14, 1855, in *Eyewitness in the Crimea: The Crimean War Letters (1854–1856) of Lieutenant Colonel George Frederick Dallas*, ed. Michael Hargreave Mawson (London: Greenhill Books, 2001), p. 71.
2. Dallas, letters to his family, December 6, 1854, April 20, 1855, *ibid.*, pp. 54, 113.
3. Dallas, letter to his family, January 14, 1855, *ibid.*, p. 70.
4. Dallas, letter to his family, January 6, 1855, *ibid.*, p. 66.
5. As Phillip Knightley records, the epitaph on Russell's memorial at St. Paul's Cathedral calls him "the first and greatest" war correspondent – and although Knightley disputes both parts of the claim, he begins his own history of the war correspondent with Russell. See *The First Casualty: The War Correspondent as Hero and Myth-maker from the Crimea to Iraq* (Baltimore: The Johns Hopkins University Press, 2004), p. 2.
6. Henry Kingsley, *Ravenshoe*, ed. William H. Scheuerle (Lincoln: University of Nebraska Press, 1967), p. 350.
7. Dallas, letter to his family, February 25, 1855, in *Eyewitness*, p. 91.
8. Mary Seacole, *Wonderful Adventures of Mrs. Seacole in Foreign Lands* (Oxford: Oxford University Press, 1988), p. 162.
9. Jürgen Habermas, *The Structural Transformation of the Public Sphere: An Enquiry into a Category of Bourgeois Society*, trans. Thomas Burger with Frederick Lawrence (Cambridge, MA: MIT Press, 1991), pp. 171, 169.
10. For the paper's use of the phrase, see, for example, the leader of May 5, 1854, which begins, "The present war is a people's war, and the people will not object to pay for it" (6). The phrase was also used frequently in World War II. See Angus Calder, *The People's War* (London: Pimlico, 1992), p. 138.
11. [W. R. Greg], "The Newspaper Press," *Edinburgh Review* 101 (October, 1855), 470.
12. Matthew Paul Lalumia, *Realism and Politics in the Art of the Crimean War* (Ann Arbor: UMI Research Press, 1984), p. 104. I will discuss Millais's painting in detail in chapter 4.
13. See O. Anderson, *Liberal State*, p. 82.
14. [Greg], "Newspaper Press," 474–75.
15. The *DNB* records that Crabb Robinson's "claim to the title of first modern war correspondent is enhanced by his dispatches," based on eyewitness experience, "from Corunna between 9 August 1808 and 26 January 1809 during his assignment in the Peninsula at the rear of Sir John Moore's army." Vincent Newey, "Robinson, Henry Crabb (1775–1867)," in the *Oxford Dictionary of National Biography*, ed. H. C. G. Matthew and Brian Harrison (Oxford: Oxford University Press, 2004), www.oxforddnb.com/view/article/23842. But Elizabeth Grey disagrees: "[Crabb Robinson] was not an energetic reporter; he based his dispatches on translations from local papers rather than personal observation," failing, for example, to report Moore's

death. Elizabeth Grey, *The Noise of Drums and Trumpets: W. H. Russell Reports from the Crimea* (London: Longman, 1971), p. 15.
16. Mobray Morris, letter to Chenery, July 13, 1854, quoted in *The Tradition Established (1841–84)*, vol. II of *The History of The Times*, 3 vols. (London: 1939), p. 135. The appeal of a journal of a siege has roots that reach back to Homer's portrayal of the siege of Troy in the *Iliad*.
17. Quoted in *ibid.*, p. 135. Russell also had some previous experience as a war reporter, having covered the conflict over Schleswig-Holstein for *The Times* in 1850. See Alan Hankinson, *Man of Wars: William Howard Russell of The Times* (London: Heinemann, 1982), pp. 38–39.
18. These increases in speed had been achieved at great cost and effort on the part of newspapers of the day, as the company history of *The Times* discusses at length. See "Speeding Up the News," in *The Tradition Established*, pp. 54–72, esp. pp. 71–72.
19. The telegraph lines reached the Crimea in April of 1855. See Royle, *Crimea*, pp. 179, 350.
20. While newspapers were not allowed access to the Eastern telegraph lines that had been laid to allow for official dispatches, readers of the papers could see tantalizingly into a future where the almost immediate transmission of long stories like Russell's was possible. A letter to the editor of *The Times* recounts an experiment performed in Paris demonstrating how "20,000 words, using round numbers, would be transmitted in an hour; six columns of such correspondence as you publish would be transmitted *in two hours.*" Dion. Lardner., letter to the editor, *The Times*, September 26, 1855, 6.
21. [Russell], "The Fall of Sebastopol," *The Times*, September 26, 1855, 6.
22. Leader, *The Times*, November 6, 1854, 6.
23. A. Aspinall, *Politics and the Press, c. 1780–1850* (London: Home & Van Thal, Ltd., 1949), p. 33.
24. *Ibid.*, p. 34 (note).
25. O. Anderson, *Liberal State*, p. 73.
26. Habermas, *Structural Transformation*, p. 89.
27. "Vates," letter to the editor, *The Times*, November 22, 1854, 7.
28. Leader, *The Times*, December 7, 1854, 6.
29. Dallas, letter to his family, July 23, 1855, in *Eyewitness*, p. 162.
30. Knightley, *First Casualty*, p. 15. The order was issued on February 25, 1856.
31. See *The Tradition Established*, p. 133.
32. O. Anderson, *Liberal State*, pp. 71–72; she is quoting from *The Tradition Established*, pp. 191–92.
33. [Greg], "Newspaper Press," 494.
34. The closest rival in terms of circulation appears to have been the *Morning Advertiser*, with a daily print run of about 6,000. See O. Anderson, *Liberal State*, pp. 71, 84. To give some sense of the recent growth of the circulation of *The Times*, in 1845 it had stood at just 23,000.
35. Leader, *The Times*, October 13, 1854, 6.
36. O. Anderson, *Liberal State*, p. 75.

37. Leader, *The Times*, December 23, 1854, 9.
38. Leader, *The Times*, October 9, 1854, 6.
39. "A West Country Gentleman," letter to the editor, *Morning Chronicle*, November 7, 1854, 7.
40. [Greg], "Newspaper Press," 492–93.
41. David Urquhart, *The Effect of the Misuse of Familiar Words on the Character of Men and the Fate of Nations* (London: Trübner & Co., 1856), p. 282. I quote from this volume, but a version of much of the book appeared in 1855, and parts of that version were so popular as to be reissued in shorter form as *Public Opinion and its Organs*. Urquhart, a career diplomat and Russophobe, had long pointed to various failures of government that the war effort was now exposing; his ideas influenced Karl Marx. For more on Urquhart, see O. Anderson, *Liberal State*, p. 139 ff. As its title suggests, Urquhart's book also dissects many of the other tag-phrases of the war, such as *national*, *patriotic*, and *public opinion*, arguing – in an almost proto-Habermasian fashion – that these phrases had been used to curtail real political thought. I discuss his treatment of *public opinion* in more detail in chapter 3.
42. "B. B.," letter to the editor, *The Times*, February 8, 1855, 9.
43. Urquhart, *Misuse of Familiar Words*, p. 279.
44. See my reading in chapter three and the wonderful account in Edgar Shannon and Christopher Ricks's "'The Charge of the Light Brigade': The Creation of a Poem," *Studies in Bibliography* 38 (1985), 1–44.
45. Leader, *The Times*, October 12, 1854, 6. "Citizens of London" strikes a slightly off note, as the paper had a significant provincial readership. In fact, an earlier leader emphasized that the metropolis and the nation were at one in their concern for the war: "It is no mere mob that leads the metropolis, nor does the metropolis lead the nation against its will. It is the whole nation that speaks this way, and it is the whole nation that in heart and spirit goes with every regiment chosen for service from its barracks to the ocean steamer and thence to the seat of war." Quoted in Royle, *Crimea*, p. 122. Royle cites a leader in *The Times* of February 27, 1854; I could not locate the passage.
46. Leader, *The Times*, October 12, 1854, 6.
47. See *The Tradition Established (1841–84)*, p. 141.
48. Russell's frequent willingness thus to correct himself contributed to his public reputation for reliability.
49. [Russell], "The Fall of Sebastopol: The Final Bombardment," *The Times*, September 21, 1855, 7.
50. These features reappear during the war years in the fiction of muscular Christianity, discussed in chapter 2.
51. John Peck, *War, the Army and Victorian Literature* (New York: St. Martin's, 1998), p. 30.
52. See Hankinson, *Man of Wars*, pp. 56–57.
53. [Blakeley], "The Battle of the Alma, [from our own Special Correspondent]," *Morning Chronicle*, October 10, 1854, 5.

Notes to pages 28–35

54. Leader, *Morning Chronicle*, October 10, 1854, 4.
55. See Fussell, *The Great War*, ch. 7 ("Arcadian Resources"), esp. pp. 235–39, 245–46. Byron takes advantage of the same pun in *Don Juan*, VIII.98.
56. See Peck, *War, the Army*, p. 30; and Hankinson, *Man of Wars*, p. 68. At one point, for example, Russell attributes to Raglan just such a crucial decision as Peck sees as being characteristic of "traditional war writing": "It was the crisis of the day . . . Lord Raglan saw the difficulties of the situation . . . [His] act relieved our infantry of a deadly incubus, and they continued their magnificent and fearful progress up the hill." [Russell], "The Battle of the Alma," *The Times*, October 10, 1854, 7.
57. W. H. Russell, *The British Expedition to the Crimea: A Revised Edition, with Numerous Emendations and Additions, Illustrated with Plans, Woodcuts, &c.* (London: G. Routledge and Co., 1858), pp. 139–40. As the full title suggests, this book frequently incorporates new materials in its attempts to translate journalism into history. Russell remarks on the translation in his note to the reader:

> In correcting and condensing the present edition of the History of the British Expedition during the War of 1854–56, I could not but feel that I was in some measure sacrificing whatever merit the original letters may have possessed, as descriptive of contemporaneous events, by changing the present to the past tense, and by other alterations necessarily introduced for the purpose of shaping those separate letters into a continuous narrative . . . I can only commend this work to the reader as a condensed narrative of the principal events of the Crimean war, of which I was an eye-witness, corrected by the results of personal knowledge and investigation, the value of which is increased by the addition of official despatches, and of tables, maps, plans, and returns, calculated to confer on it a permanent character as a book of reference. (iii)

58. [Russell], "The Battle of the Alma," *The Times*, October 10, 1854, 7.
59. [Russell], "The British Expedition," *The Times*, August 29, 1854, 7.
60. [Russell], "The British Expedition," *The Times*, May 23, 1854, 10.
61. See Grey, *Noise of Drums*, p. 46.
62. [Russell], "The British Expedition," *The Times*, October 20, 1854, 7.
63. See "An officer who was on the spot," letter to the editor, *The Times*, February 13, 1855, 7.
64. Peck, *War, the Army*, p. 32.
65. [Russell], "The British Expedition," *The Times*, May 10, 1854, 9.
66. Kinglake's monumental history, *The Invasion of the Crimea*, was published in eight volumes between 1863 and 1887, and is thus far less immediate than the journalistic responses I consider here. As Peck notes, *The Invasion* subscribes to the conventions of epic literature (*War, the Army*, p. 27). Significantly, it ends not with the conclusion of the war but rather (like the *Iliad*) with the death of the man singled out as the great (and tragic) hero of the conflict: Lord Raglan. It was begun at Lady Raglan's request in 1856, and while Kinglake did visit the Crimea for a month in September and October of 1854, *The Invasion* was based not on personal observation but on

research – including into Raglan's papers, to which Lady Raglan had given access. A sense of the tone of the history can be gleaned from the following excerpt:

> In the moment when Lord Raglan determined to treat the instructions of the Government as imperative, and to put them in course for execution, he came to another determination (a determination which is not so mere a corollary from the first as men unversed in business may think): he resolved to carry the enterprise through. He knew that, though work of an accustomed sort can be ably done by official persons acting under a bare sense of duty, yet that the engine for conquering obstacles of a kind not known beforehand, when they are many and big and unforeseen, must be nothing less than the strong, passionate will of a man. If every one were to perform his mere duty, there would be no invasion of the Crimea, for a rank growth of hindrances, springing up in the way of the undertaking, would be sure to gather fast round it, and bring it in time to a stop.

Alexander William Kinglake, *The Invasion of the Crimea*, 8 vols. (London: William Blackwood and Sons, 1863–87), ch. 4, "The Alma Campaign," II:129.

While Russell's *British Expedition* provides one alternative model of the history of the war, another appears in E. H. Nolan's *Illustrated History of the War against Russia*, published in 1856 (London: Virtue and Co.) in affordable one-shilling parts and six-shilling cloth and gilt "divisions" and in 1857 in 2 volumes. Nolan's *History* is an amalgam of available documentary sources, connected by brief commentary. The historian in this instance is neither eyewitness (Russell) nor researcher (Kinglake) but collector: this "history" is a kind of scrapbook of the war, the sort of thing that any particularly avid reader of journals, newspapers, and parliamentary records and reports could have assembled.

67. See [Margaret Oliphant], "Modern Light Literature: Travellers' Tales," *Blackwood's Edinburgh Magazine* 78 (November, 1855), 590.
68. Peck, *War, the Army*, pp. 28–29. The passage of description is from [Russell], "The British Expedition," *The Times*, April 26, 1854, 9.
69. Thackeray took advantage of the vogue for letters "from our Own Correspondent" that the war was creating in a mock-correspondence entitled "Important from the Seat of War! Letters from the East by Our Own Bashi-Bozouk" [*sic*], written for *Punch* in 1854 (the first letter is dated May 28). The influence of *The Times*'s man is again apparent. Thackeray begins by having his alter-ego attack Russell's credibility:

> I took, but half an hour since, from the shako of a poor Russian friend, whom I have just killed in action, two or three copies of the *Times* newspaper, in which the editors seemed greatly to vaunt the skill of their correspondent in this quarter. Before I ever thought of putting pen to paper myself, I met this young man at Malta, and Gallipoli afterwards; gave him every information in my power, and supplied him with many of the facts, which I need not say he ludicrously distorted and exaggerated in his journal.

Thackeray's Bashi-Bozouk then goes on to retell some of Russell's stories of adventure (such as the journalist's harried landing at Gallipoli) as they

"really" happened, making himself into the hero. The comprehension of the joke thus depends on the reader's familiarity with Russell's columns. See *Punch* 26 (1854), 257.
70. See Hankinson, *Man of Wars*, p. 48; and Roger T. Stearn, "Russell, Sir William Howard (1820–1907)," in the *DNB*, online edn., ed. Lawrence Goldman (Oxford: Oxford University Press, 2006), www.oxforddnb.com/view/article/35889.
71. J. Paul Hunter, *Before Novels: The Cultural Contexts of Eighteenth-Century English Fiction* (New York: W. W. Norton & Co., 1990), p. 194. The fact that Russell's reports subscribe to both epistolary and journal conventions also suggests parallels to eighteenth-century novels, although (as I have intimated), I think they actually have more of the feel of Victorian serialization.
72. See Peck, *War, the Army*, p. 31; and Charles Dickens, *Little Dorrit*, ed. John Holloway (London: Penguin, 1985), p. 145 (ch. 10, "Containing the whole Science of Government").
73. Charles Dickens, letter to Russell, January 3, 1864. Quoted in Hankinson, *Man of Wars*, p. 83.
74. Russell, *British Expedition*, p. 257. The original report was much shorter: "Admiral Boxer has arrived, and will assume the command of the harbour of Balaklava. The harbour and town are much better than they have been." [Russell], "The British Expedition," *The Times*, February 17, 1855, 7.
75. Dallas, letter to his family, July 23, 1855, in *Eyewitness*, pp. 164–66. For Dickens's use of the phrase, see *Hard Times*, ch. 11, "No Way Out."
76. Seacole, *Wonderful Adventures*, pp. 77–78.
77. See Hankinson, *Man of Wars*, p. 137.
78. William Howard Russell, *The Adventures of Doctor Brady*, 3 vols. (London: Tinsley Brothers, 1868), 1:5. Further references internally documented. The novel originally appeared as the first item in the new *Tinsley's Magazine* in August 1867.
79. Even the kind review of the novel in *The Times* opens by acknowledging the author's excessive plotting: "To novel-readers who study with curiosity the construction of plots, this work will seem to be an example of . . . prodigality." Unsigned review of *The Adventures of Dr. Brady*, *The Times*, April 8, 1868, 5.
80. Wilkie Collins, *The Moonstone*, ed. John Sutherland (Oxford: Oxford University Press, 1999), p. 33.
81. John Sutherland, *The Longman Companion to Victorian Fiction* (Harlow: Longman Group, 1988), p. 548.
82. Unsigned review of *The Adventures of Dr. Brady*, *The Times*, April 8, 1868, 5.
83. Rose is almost abandoned by the secret husband she had nursed back to health in Scutari, who initially denies his marriage in order to free himself to wed an heiress (the object of Terence's own secret love). While Russell does not concentrate on Rose, as a heroine the Crimea offers her possibilities unavailable on British soil, as I shall argue in chapter 2.

84. Russell had also covered the "Mutiny," although he had arrived in India after the worst carnage was over.
85. [Russell], "The Battle of Inkermann: further particulars," *The Times*, December 4, 1854, 7.
86. [Russell], "The Battle of Inkermann," *The Times*, November 23, 1854, 6.
87. Leader, *The Times*, December 30, 1854, 6.
88. Dallas, letter to his family, March 2, 1855, in *Eyewitness*, p. 93.
89. Dallas, letter to his family, February 16, 1855, *ibid.*, p. 84.
90. [Fanny Taylor], "A Lady Volunteer," *Eastern Hospitals and English Nurses; the Narrative of Twelve Months' Experience in the Hospitals of Kouali and Scutari*, 3rd edn. (London: Hurst and Blackett, 1857), pp. 123–24.
91. *Punch* repeatedly demonstrated an awareness of the irony in the rank's name. Consider the definition of "PRIVATE" "For the Next Military Dictionary": "Noun Substantive. A Common Soldier. 1st derivation. *Privatio* (Lat.), from the abominable hardships and want of necessaries he endures. – *Newcastle*. 2nd derivation. *Privatus* (Lat.), from the secrecy in which his gallant deeds are kept, while those of his officers are proclaimed in dispatches. – *Raglan*." *Punch* 28 (1855), 70.
92. Tricia Lootens, "Victorian Poetry and Patriotism," in *The Cambridge Companion to Victorian Poetry*, ed. Joseph Bristow (Cambridge: Cambridge University Press, 2000), p. 276.
93. Dallas, letter to his family, November 1, 1855, in *Eyewitness*, p. 197.
94. The importance of letters also appears in pictures of the war. Many genre pieces show families at home reading letters from the front or soldiers in the East receiving mail from home. Millais's second "Crimean War painting" falls into the latter category: *News From Home* (1857) depicts a guardsman in the trenches reading a letter. It can be thought of as a companion piece to the newspaper-reading officer in the earlier *Peace Concluded*. In this context, the idea of *news* (like the corresponding concept of the *novel*) demonstrates its generic malleability.
95. "Letters from the Crimea," *The Times*, November 28, 1854, 8.
96. "Letters from the Crimea," *Morning Chronicle*, November 20, 1854, 3.
97. "Letters from the Crimea," *The Times*, November 28, 1854, 8.
98. Hunter, *Before Novels*, p. 201.
99. Habermas, *Structural Transformation*, p. 172.
100. Hunter opens his discussion of the roots of the novel by looking at a periodical called the *Athenian Mercury* (founded in 1691) that "entertained questions from readers and answered them in print" (*Before Novels*, p. 12).
101. Leader, *The Times*, November 5, 1855, 6.
102. "F. Flyers," letter to the editor, *The Times*, May 26, 1854, 10.
103. "An Old and Sincere Friend of Captain Maude's," letter to the editor, *The Times*, October 21, 1854, 9.
104. R. J. Stratton, Major 77th Regiment, letter to the editor, *The Times*, January 16, 1855, 12.

105. Edward Bruce Hamley, Captain, R. A., letter to the editor, *The Times*, January 16, 1855, 12.
106. [E. B. Hamley], "The Story of the Campaign," *Blackwood's Edinburgh Magazine*, 76 (December, 1854), 41; 77 (January, 1855), 112; 77 (April, 1855), 492.
107. "One Who has a Relative in the Crimea," letter to the editor, *The Times*, February 8, 1855, 9.
108. "J. B. D.," letter to the editor, *The Times*, October 11, 1854, 8.
109. "One Who has Been in the Crimea in Winter," letter to the editor, *The Times*, November 24, 1854, 5.
110. W. H. Sykes, letter to the editor, *The Times*, November 28, 1854, 7.
111. "Spectator," letter to the editor, *The Times*, December 1, 1854, 8.
112. "A Meteorologist," letter to the editor, *The Times*, December 6, 1854, 8.
113. Leader, *The Times*, December 14, 1854, 8.
114. Edward Pearce, letter to the editor, *The Times*, January 24, 1855, 10.
115. David Walkinshaw, "Lord Raglan and the Weather," *The Times*, April 4, 1855, 10.
116. See, for example, "Experte Credo," letter to the editor, *The Times*, November 28, 1854, 7.
117. "A Practical Farmer," letter to the editor, *The Times*, February 8, 1855, 9.
118. "W.," letter to the editor, *The Times*, December 4, 1854, 7.
119. [A. Soyer], letter to the editor, *The Times*, January 20, 1855, 9.
120. A. Soyer, letter to the editor, *The Times*, December 27, 1855, 9.
121. See Alexis Soyer, *A Culinary Campaign*, intro. Michael Barthorp and Elizabeth Ray (Lewes: Southover Press, 1995).
122. See Seacole's *Wonderful Adventures* and Elizabeth Davis, *The Autobiography of Elizabeth Davis*, ed. Jane Williams, 2 vols. (London: Hurst & Blackett, 1857). For more on these two memoirs, see Peck, *War, the Army*, pp. 34–40.
123. Mary A. Favret considers the effects of war correspondence during the Napoleonic wars. She argues persuasively that "the presence of [Napoleonic] war correspondence keeps war itself at a distance: while appealing to domestic and national bonds, letters mark a *différance* – a deferral both physical and temporal – from the violence of war." Favret focuses both on unpublished letters and the published correspondence of officers. But the distance she describes begins to break down when the reading public also becomes a writing public and when cold and disease, products of bad governance rather than warfare itself, become the letters' primary concern ("War Correspondence: Reading Romantic War," *Prose Studies* 19.2 [August, 1996], 175).
124. See for example "Acastus," "T. S.," and "Penseroso," letters to the editor, *The Times*, December 26 and 30, 1805 and January 2, 1806 (respectively), all p. 3.
125. "A Sufferer by the Present War?," letter to the editor, *The Times*, October 14, 1854, 7.
126. "A Yorkshirewoman," letter "To the Women of England," *The Times*, December 5, 1854, 7.

127. Nightingale herself never wrote publicly about her war efforts. Her private correspondence during the war has been collected in *Florence Nightingale: Letters from the Crimea*, ed. Sue M. Goldie (Manchester: Mandolin, 1997). I will discuss Nightingale's writings in chapter 2. While Seacole and Davis wrote as women, perhaps the memoirist who made the strongest attempt to give a specifically female perspective on events was Frances Isabella Duberly. Duberly, wife of the paymaster of the 8th Hussars, accompanied her husband to the Crimea. Her *Journal Kept During The Russian War* (London: Longman, Brown, Green, and Longmans, 1855) caused a stir when it appeared in December of 1855. In it, Duberly purports to be a voice for women: "I wonder if, among the annals of a war, the sickening anxieties of mother, wife, and sister ever find a place," she asks (p. 83). Her untraditional response also comes out in her refusal to treat the conflict in the usual heroic mold: her focus is rather on her own efforts to stay by her husband's side – and on her faithful horse, Bob (Fred Dallas called the book "more a history of a dismal old horse she used to ride about on, than anything else"). But Duberly's presence in the East was seen as unwomanly, and Dallas's horror at what he deemed her masculine desire to witness war (she was called "the Vulture") appears to have been shared by many (there were also rumors, probably unfounded, of an improper association with Lord Cardigan). Still, her impact attests to the public sense of women's unprecedented role in this war. See Dallas, *Eyewitness*, pp. 235, 78.
128. Edmund Venables, "Blakesley, Joseph Williams (1808–1885)," rev. Ellie Clewlow, in the *Oxford Dictionary of National Biography*, ed. H. C. G. Matthew and Brian Harrison (Oxford: Oxford University Press, 2004), www.oxforddnb.com/view/article/2592.
129. See *The Tradition Established*, p. 378 (note).
130. "A Hertfordshire Incumbent," letter to the editor, *The Times*, November 30, 1854, 8.
131. "A. T.," letter to the editor, *The Times*, September 28, 1855, 9.
132. "A Hertfordshire Incumbent," letter to the editor, *The Times*, February 13, 1855, 10.
133. "A Hertfordshire Incumbent," letter to the editor, *The Times*, June 16, 1855, 10.
134. "G. D. N.," letter to the editor, *The Times*, April 12, 1855, 9.
135. "A Hertfordshire Incumbent," letter to the editor, *The Times*, April 16, 1855, 9. And the debate continued.
136. "A Hertfordshire Incumbent," letter to the editor, *The Times*, May 11, 1855, 9.
137. See Henry Williams, E. Napier, "J. A.," and Henry Williams, letters to the editor, *The Times*, May 12, 14, 16, and 17, 1855, pp. 12, 12, 12, and 10 (respectively).
138. Benedict Anderson, *Imagined Communities: Reflections on the Origins and Spread of Nationalism* (New York: Verso, 1991), p. 35.
139. The cartoons can be attributed to Leech by the initials in their lower left-hand corners.

Notes to pages 59–63 231

140. [John Leech], "Crimean Correspondence," *Punch* 28 (1855), 10.
141. [John Leech], "Enthusiasm of Paterfamilias," *Punch* 27 (1854), 213.
142. Trudi Tate, "On Not Knowing Why: Memorializing the Light Brigade," in *Literature, Science, Psychoanalysis, 1830–1970: Essays in Honour of Gillian Beer*, ed. Helen Small and Trudi Tate (Oxford: Oxford University Press, 2003), p. 165.
143. George Eliot, *The Mill on the Floss*, ed. Gordon Haight (Oxford: Oxford University Press, 1996), p. 176.
144. See Anderson's *Imagined Communities* for a similar argument about a moment of national identification that comes out of reading a novel in which the hero reads a newspaper (p. 32). In *Nineteenth-Century American Art* (New York: Oxford University Press, 2000), Barbara Groseclose distinguishes a related subgenre of paintings of "Jacksonian readers" in which usually rural working-class newspaper-readers come together to offer a picture of nationhood (pp. 71–74).
145. Marx, *Dispatches*, p. 150. The article, written by Marx from his Stateside perch as correspondent for the *Tribune*, was published on February 17, 1855.
146. Habermas, *Structural Transformation*, pp. 170–71.
147. "Iraq Uploaded" aired on MTV on July 21, 2006. Matthew Currier Burden's *The Blog of War: Front-Line Dispatches from Soldiers in Iraq and Afghanistan* (New York: Simon and Schuster, 2006) performs a similar function for soldiers' blogs from Iraq.
148. [Russell], "Late Special Correspondent in the Crimea," letter to the editor, *The Times*, July 29, 1856, 9.
149. H. P. Wright, letter to the editor, *The Times*, August 30, 1855, 5. John Leech also found comedy in the subject, in a cartoon entitled "*No! Don't.*" It shows an author sitting in his armchair, holding on to a copy of the newspaper, next to a pile of books and a prominently placed wastebasket. The caption reads: "So they are sending out books to amuse the poor fellows at Scutari – and very proper. I will send five-and-twenty copies of my last five-act tragedy of 'The Roman Grandmother.'" [John Leech], "*No! Don't!*," *Punch* 28 (1855), 18.
150. Florence Nightingale, letter to Mr. and Mrs. Bracebridge, August 7, 1855, in *Letters from the Crimea*, ed. Goldie, p. 144.
151. See Tennyson's letter to Forster of August 6, 1854, mentioning and quoting from Benedict Lawrence Chapman's letter to the poet of August 3, 1854. Quoted in Shannon and Ricks, "Creation of a Poem," 8.
152. [Hamley], "Poetry of the War," 531.

2 FROM AMYAS LEIGH TO AURORA LEIGH: GENDER AND HEROISM IN THE NOVELS OF THE CRIMEAN WAR

1. Quoted in Alan Palmer, *The Banner of Battle: The Story of the Crimean War* (London: Weidenfeld and Nicolson, 1987), p. 172.

2. For a relatively complete list of novels explicitly about the Crimean War, see Anna Belle Laughbaum, *Some English Novels (1855–1917) That Deal with the Crimean War: An Abstract of a Thesis* (Urbana: University of Illinois, 1948). Three useful treatments of *Little Dorrit* in the Crimean context are Trey Philpotts's "Trevelyan, Treasury, and Circumlocution" (*Dickens Studies Annual* [1993], 283–301); Michael Cotsell's "Politics and Peeling Frescoes: Layard of Ninevah and *Little Dorrit*" (*Dickens Studies Annual* [1986], 181–200); and Grace Moore's "Red Tape and Circumlocution: The Crimean War" (ch. 4 of *Dickens and Empire: Discourses of Class, Race and Colonialism in the Works of Charles Dickens* [Aldershot: Ashgate, 2004], pp. 75–90).
3. Clough, letter to F. J. Child, January 31, 1855, in *Correspondence of Arthur Hugh Clough*, ed. F. L. Mulhauser, 2 vols. (Oxford: The Clarendon Press, 1957), II:497.
4. Kate Flint, "The Victorian Novel and its Readers," in *The Cambridge Companion to the Victorian Novel*, ed. Deirdre David (Cambridge: Cambridge University Press, 2001), p. 21.
5. Barrett Browning, letter to Miss Mitford, December 11, 1854, in *The Letters of Elizabeth Barrett Browning*, ed. Frederick G. Kenyon, 2 vols. (New York: Macmillan, 1910), II:183.
6. Thackeray, letter to Lady Stanley, December 4, 1854. Quoted in Hankinson, *Man of Wars*, p. 83.
7. I will cite this work internally by chapter, volume, and page number. *Reynolds's Miscellany* appealed to a lower class of reader than *Household Words*, and the novels published in it tended to be rather less "respectable." But it was immensely popular with its readership of "servant-girls," and in 1855 it boasted a circulation of 200,000. *Omar* was followed immediately by another tale with an Oriental theme: *Leila: Or, The Star of Mingrelia*. For more on the *Miscellany*, see Ian Haywood, *The Revolution in Popular Literature: Print, Politics and the People, 1790–1860* (Cambridge: Cambridge University Press, 2004), and Patricia Anderson, *The Printed Image and the Transformation of Popular Culture, 1790–1860* (Oxford: The Clarendon Press, 1994).
8. George Whyte-Melville, *The Interpreter: A Tale of the War*, new edn. (London: Longman's, Green, and Co, n. d.), pp. 125, 144. Further references internally documented.
9. G. F. Dallas, letter to his family, January 30, 1855, in *Eyewitness*, p. 78.
10. Ernest A. Baker, *The History of the English Novel: Volume VIII, From the Brontës to Meredith: Romanticism in the English Novel* (New York: Barnes and Noble, Inc., 1936 [reprinted 1966]), p. 172.
11. Thomas Carlyle, Lecture I, "The Hero as Divinity," in *Carlyle's Lectures on Heroes, Hero-Worship and the Heroic in History*, ed. P. C. Parr (Oxford: The Clarendon Press, 1920), p. 12.
12. [Margaret Oliphant], "Sensation Novels," *Blackwood's Edinburgh Magazine* 91 (May, 1862), 564–84.

13. E. S. Dallas, *The Gay Science*, 2 vols. (London: Chapman and Hall, 1866 [reprinted by Johnson Reprint Corporation]), II:296–97.
14. Nightingale, *Cassandra*, p. 38.
15. *Ibid.*, p. 36.
16. Quoted in E. Baker, *English Novel*, p. 172.
17. "Florence Nightingale," *Punch* 29 (1855), 225.
18. Charles Kingsley, *Westward Ho!*, 2nd edn., 3 vols. (Cambridge: Macmillan and Co., 1855), 1:3. Hereafter internally documented by volume and page number.
19. [Charles Kingsley], review of Matthew Arnold's *Poems* (1853), *Fraser's Magazine* 49 (February, 1854), 140.
20. See, for example, the claim that "Ireland was then further from Westminster than is the Black Sea now" (II:98). For an example of the phrase "eastward ho!" see Seacole, *Wonderful Adventures*, p. 82.
21. C. Kingsley, letter to F. D. Maurice, October 19, 1854, in *Charles Kingsley: His Letters and Memories of His Life, Edited by His Wife* [Frances Kingsley], 2 vols. (London: Henry S. King and Co., 1877), 1:433.
22. The anti-Catholic bent of the book owes something to Kingsley's altercations with Pusey (Pusey had called *Hypatia* immoral) and his belief that Pusey's lack of support for the war was due to his sympathies with the Russian Orthodox Church. See Brenda Colloms, *Charles Kingsley: The Lion of Eversley* (London: Constable, 1975), p. 183. The term "jingoist" owes its birth to a later war with Russia over Turkey: the fight for Constantinople in 1878. See Royle, *Crimea*, p. 488.
23. See Peck, *War, the Army*, pp. 41–47.
24. C. Kingsley, letter to Maurice, October 19, 1854, in *Letters and Memories*, 1:433.
25. Charles Kingsley, *Westward Ho!* (London: Ward, Lock and Co, n.d.). The scene illustrated is in ch. 1.
26. H. Kingsley, *Ravenshoe*, p. 178. Hereafter internally referenced. Fred Dallas actually records a cricket match in the Crimea between Etonians and Harrovians (letter to his family, August 10, 1855, in *Eyewitness*, p. 169), and Old Boys from the rival schools forged a newspaper campaign, writing letters to *The Times* arguing over which school had sacrificed more lives to the war effort.
27. Thomas Hughes, *Tom Brown's Schooldays* (London: The Epworth Press, n.d.), p. 278; pt. II, ch. 5, "The Fight." A bastard offspring of Hughes's novel actually takes place in the Crimea: George Macdonald Fraser's *Flashman at the Charge* (1973) represents a modern take on a grown-up boys' adventure tale by ironizing the idea of heroism. Flashman, the bully of the *Schooldays*, is lauded as a hero, but readers can see the cowardly motivation behind each "heroic" act.
28. Quoted in Margaret Farrand Thorp, *Charles Kingsley, 1819–1875* (Princeton: Princeton University Press, 1937), p. 118.
29. Charles Kingsley, *The Heroes; or, Greek Fairy Tales for my Children* (Cambridge: Macmillan and Co., 1856), p. 58.

30. See Peck, *War, the Army*, p. 43. He properly cites Nancy Armstrong's *Desire and Domestic Fiction* for the argument.
31. John Reed argues that *Adam Bede* (1859) shows the influence of the Crimean War in its portrayal of both Adam and Arthur Donnithorn: Arthur possesses the "phony" masculinity of the upper-class soldier, reflecting the negative assessment of the aristocratic military in the war, while Adam becomes the symbol of the new masculinity, province of both the common worker and the common soldier. See "Soldier Boy: Masculinity in *Adam Bede*," *Studies in the Novel* 33.3 (2001), 268–84.
32. G. A. Lawrence, *Sword and Gown* (Boston: Ticknor and Fields, 1859), pp. 165–67. The novel narrates the love between Cecil Tresilyan and the fierce and reckless Royston Keene, who turns out to be married. Cecil becomes Keene's "lover," but only in spirit. Just before she is to elope with him, she is "rescued." Royston goes to the Crimea and is fatally injured in the charge of the Light Brigade; he dies after being nursed by Cecil, who has gone to Scutari as a Sister of Charity. Lawrence, the father of "muscular blackguardism," emphasizes "muscularity" over "Christianity." See David Rosen, "The Volcano and the Cathedral: Muscular Christianity and the Origins of Primal Manliness," in *Muscular Christianity: Embodying the Victorian Age*, ed. Donald E. Hall (Cambridge: Cambridge University Press, 1994), p. 18. Lawrence's novel belongs to a tradition of military writing that also includes Ouida's Crimean War novel, *Held in Bondage* (1863) (first published in 1860 with the title *Granville de Vigne*, it was also her first work of fiction). These books attempt to preserve (or, rather, reinvigorate) an outmoded sense of the army as the province of dashing, dandyish aristocrats.
33. [W. E. Aytoun], "The Reverend Charles Kingsley," *Blackwood's Edinburgh Magazine* 77 (June, 1855), 639.
34. Charles Kingsley, *True Words for Brave Men* (London: Kegan Paul, Tench & Co., 1878), p. 200. The title was changed slightly for this 1878 reprint. Quoted in William J. Baker, "Charles Kingsley on the Crimean War: A Study in Chauvinism," *Southern Humanities Review* 4.3 (1970), 251. In spite of Kingsley's claims here, *The Manliness of Christ* – to cite the title of Thomas Hughes's book on the subject (London: Macmillan, 1879) – was a real problem for the Victorians, as Florence Nightingale's use of Christ as a model for herself (discussed below) also indicates.
35. C. Kingsley, letter to Tom Hughes, undated (early 1855), *Letters and Memories*, 1:439.
36. Herbert Sussman, *Victorian Masculinities: Manhood and Masculine Poetics in Early Victorian Literature and Art* (Cambridge: Cambridge University Press, 1995), pp. 44–45.
37. Peck, *War, the Army*, p. 44.
38. *Ibid.*, p. 45.
39. George Eliot makes the comparison in her review of the novel. See [George Eliot], "Belles Lettres," *Westminster Review* 64 (July, 1855), 288–94.

40. Unsigned review of *Two Years Ago*, *British Quarterly Review* 25 (April 1, 1857), 399.
41. Unsigned review of *Two Years Ago*, *Saturday Review* 3 (21 February, 1857), 176. Kingsley himself disliked the tag, preferring to speak of the "manful": "We have heard much of late about 'Muscular Christianity.' A clever expression . . . For myself, I do not know what it means . . . Its first and better meaning may be simply a healthful and manful Christianity; one which does not exalt the feminine virtues to the exclusion of the masculine." From the Cambridge Christmas sermon, 1864. Quoted in Robert Bernard Martin, *The Dust of Combat: A Life of Charles Kingsley* (London: Faber and Faber, 1959), p. 220.
42. Charles Kingsley, *Two Years Ago*, 2 vols., vols. XIII–XIV of *The Life and Works of Charles Kingsley*, 19 vols. (London: Macmillan and Co., 1902), I:1. Hereafter, internally referenced.
43. Althea Hayter, *Charlotte Yonge* (Plymouth: Northcote House, 1996), p. 1.
44. Charlotte Yonge, *The Young Step-mother*, 2 vols. (Leipzig: Bernard Tauchniz, 1861), II:144.
45. The role of the war in reanimating the ideal of chivalry after its deflation following the disastrous Eglinton tournament (1839) has been understated. Chivalry abounds in the poems, prose, and paintings of the war years; as my examples intimate, the war novels almost invariably work within chivalric frameworks. Frederick Watts's first chivalric paintings were from sketches done in a war-crazed Paris in the winter of 1855–56, and Tennyson began his *Idylls* in 1855 (although he had of course used chivalric motifs earlier, as in "The Lady of Shalott" [1832] and the "Morte d'Arthur" [1842]).
46. Kingsley's vol. I, ch. 22 is entitled "The Broad Stone of Honour." See Mark Girouard, *The Return to Camelot: Chivalry and the English Gentleman* (New Haven: Yale University Press, 1981).
47. Tom is an early example of the doctor-as-hero in the English novel. The new mode of hero reflects the attention to medical matters to which the Crimean experience had contributed. The protagonist of Dinah Craik's *A Life for a Life* (1859) makes up for a murder committed in a youthful moment of passion by working as an army surgeon in the Crimea; recall also the doctor-hero of William Howard Russell's *The Adventures of Doctor Brady*.
48. Peck, *War, the Army*, p. 47.
49. The novel has a second nursing heroine. The aristocratic and frivolous Valentia St. Just learns moral seriousness under the influence of the war: "I have envied the nuns their convents. I have envied Selkirk his desert island . . . [A]nything to escape and be in earnest, anything for some one to teach me to be of use! Yes, this cholera – and this war . . . they have wakened me – to a new life" (II:153). Valentia's new life begins when she goes to the Crimea to nurse her brother.
50. Unsigned review of *Two Years Ago*, *Saturday Review*, 177.
51. Quoted in Scheuerle's introduction to *Ravenshoe*, p. xix.

52. See Jenny Uglow, *Elizabeth Gaskell: A Habit of Stories* (London: Faber and Faber, 1993), pp. 363–64.
53. Elizabeth Gaskell, letter to ? Charles Dickens, ? December 17, 1854, in *The Letters of Mrs. Gaskell*, ed. J. A. V. Chapple and Arthur Pollard (Manchester: Mandolin, 1997), p. 324.
54. Elizabeth Gaskell, letter to Parthenope Nightingale, July 21, 1855, *ibid.*, p. 359. Florence had been taken ill with Crimean fever.
55. "Once brought face to face, man to man, with an individual of the masses around him, and (take notice) out of the character of master and workman, in the first instance, they [Thornton and Higgins] had each begun to recognize that 'we have all of us one human heart.'" Elizabeth Gaskell, *North and South*, ed. Angus Easson, intro. Sally Shuttleworth (Oxford: Oxford University Press, 1998), p. 419. Hereafter, internally referenced.
56. Quoted in Elizabeth Haldane, *Mrs. Gaskell and Her Friends* (London: Hodder & Stoughton, 1931), p. 105. Andrew Sanders also discusses the passage in "A Crisis of Liberalism in *North and South*," *Gaskell Society Journal* 10 (1996), 48.
57. Peck, *War, the Army*, p. 94.
58. *Ibid.*, p. 97.
59. William Howard Russell used the term "thin red streak" (later transformed into the famous "thin red line") to designate the 93rd Highlanders as they charged into battle. [Russell], "The Operations of the Siege," *The Times*, November 14, 1854, 7. *Thread* is a particularly appropriate synonym for *line* and *streak* given Milton's industrial context.
60. [H. F. Chorley], review of *North and South*, *Athenaeum*, April 7, 1855, 403.
61. [Thomas Ballantyne], "Lancashire Strikes," *Blackwood's Edinburgh Magazine* 79 (January, 1856), 52.
62. *Ibid.* Writing from America, Karl Marx also recognized the opposing interests (although he believed the workers would prevail): "The eyes of the working classes are now fully opened: they begin to cry: 'Our St. Petersburg is at Preston!'" (August 1, 1854). In Marx, *Dispatches*, p. 144.
63. Clough, *Correspondence*, II:497. Clough was known to both Gaskell and the Nightingales (he accompanied Florence, his wife's cousin, to Calais on her way out to the East and worked for her after the war) and – as a well-known "doubter" whose unwillingness to subscribe to the Thirty-nine Articles dramatically changed his life – perhaps an influence on Gaskell's portrait of Mr. Hale.
64. See Gaskell, *Letters*, pp. 302, 321, 324, 326.
65. See H. I. Dutton and J. E. King, *"Ten Per Cent and No Surrender": The Preston Strike, 1853–1854* (Cambridge: Cambridge University Press, 1981), esp. pp. 198–201.
66. Peck, *War, the Army*, p. 30.
67. See pp. 113 and 334, for example.
68. A *Literature Online with MLA* search generated examples in works by Wordsworth, Coleridge, Shelley, Helen Maria Williams, and in a review

by Charles Kingsley discussing Keats's poetry, among others. The romantic roots of the genre are nicely caught in a poem by Samuel Hoffenstein, "Mr. William Wordsworth Covers a Human Interest Story for a Tabloid Newspaper" (a parody of "We are Seven") (from a collection entitled *A Treasury of Humorous Verse* [1946]).

69. Cynthia Dereli, "Gender Issues and the Crimean War: Creating Roles for Women?," in *Gender Roles and Sexuality in Victorian Literature*, ed. Christopher Parker (Aldershot: Scolar Press, 1995), p. 74.
70. See "Devil Worshippers," *Household Words* 10 (1854), 57–61; "At Home with the Russians," *Household Words* 10 (1855), 533–38; "Mars à la Mode," *Household Words* 10 (1854), 193–96; and "Field Service," *Household Words* 10 (1854), 339–44.
71. "The Home Office," *Household Words* 10 (1854), 270.
72. "A Home Question," *Household Words* 10 (1854), 292, 294.
73. "The Moral of this Year," *Household Words* 10 (1854), 276.
74. Gaskell called Kingsley her "*hero.*" Elizabeth Gaskell, letter to Eliza Fox, November 26, 1849, in *Letters*, p. 90.
75. Procter had stayed with the Gaskells in 1851 (see Uglow, *Elizabeth Gaskell*, p. 369). I will discuss her poems further in chapter 3.
76. [Adelaide Anne Procter], "Waiting," *Household Words* 10 (1854), 204–05.
77. [Adelaide Anne Procter], "The Lesson of the War," *Household Words* 11 (1855), 12. See Joseph Bristow, "Nation, Class, and Gender: Tennyson's *Maud* and War," *Genders* 9 (November, 1990), 107.
78. [G. C. Swayne], "Peace and War: A Dialogue," *Blackwood's Edinburgh Magazine* 76 (1854), 595. For a discussion of this article in the context of *Maud*, see Bristow, "Nation, Class," 97. Consider also *The Times*'s leader of July 25, 1854, which opens by observing that "It is no small set-off against the evils of a war such as that in which we are engaged that it becomes a new bond of unity and a common source of generous feelings in a people otherwise divided by factions, and too little disposed to rise above material considerations" (p. 9).
79. [Adelaide Anne Procter], "The Two Spirits," *Household Words* 10 (1855), 516.
80. Clough, letter to C. E. Norton, February 20, 1854, in *Correspondence*, II:476.
81. Elizabeth Barrett Browning, letter to Anna Jameson, February 24, 1855, in *Letters of EBB*, II:190. Barrett Browning's "pins" originate in Bentham's infamous assertion that the utility of "pushpin" is equivalent to that of "poetry" and Adam Smith's pin-maker in *The Wealth of Nations* (bk. 1, ch. 1).
82. See for example "down with the Rump" (45); also Thornton's comment that "Cromwell would have made a capital mill-owner, Miss Hale" (123). For a brief discussion of the role of the Civil War in the novel, see Robin Gilmour, *The Victorian Period: The Intellectual and Cultural Context of English Literature, 1830–1890* (London: Longman, 1993), p. 52. Ballantyne's article on strikes also refers to "the civil war between labour and capital" ("Lancashire Strikes," 367).

83. Alfred Tennyson, *Maud: A Monodrama*, Part 1, line 27, in *The Poems of Tennyson*, ed. Christopher Ricks, 2nd edn., 3 vols. (Harlow, Essex: Longman, 1987), II:513–84. All further references to Tennyson's poems will be to this edition and will be internally documented by part number (where relevant) and line. I will discuss *Maud* in more detail in the following chapter. As Bristow argues, the poem posits that "a war abroad should rightly make for peace at home" ("Nation, Class," 96). For more on the idea of civil war in the period and in *Maud*, see Chris R. Vanden Bossche, "Realism versus Romance: The War of Cultural Codes in Tennyson's *Maud*," *Victorian Poetry* 24.1 (1986), 74.

84. Elizabeth Gaskell, letter to ? Eliza Fox, ? Summer 1854, in *Letters*, p. 302. Gaskell continues by reverting to an external threat: "I am thinking of fastening Will's scythe to *one* of the wheels of the poney carriage and defending my country if the Russians do land at Liverpool."

85. Elizabeth Gaskell, unpublished letter to Florence Nightingale, December 31, 1858 (Brotherton Library, University of Leeds). Quoted in Sanders, "Crisis of Liberalism," 47.

86. See pp. 117–18 and Shuttleworth's introduction, p. xix.

87. Leader, *The Times*, November 27, 1854, 6.

88. Sanders, "Crisis of Liberalism," 47.

89. William Makepeace Thackeray, *The Newcomes*, ed. D. J. Taylor (London: J. M. Dent, 1994), p. 87. While this comment reveals the general conception of military men in the period leading up to the war, it is said with some irony, to a military man (Colonel Newcome) who represents the moral heart of the novel. Newcome, however, as an "Indian Officer," stands for a different, more experienced and less aristocratic breed of soldier from the standard Crimean officer. In fact, as Cecil Woodham-Smith explains, there was significant prejudice against Indian officers within the Crimean campaign. See *The Reason Why: The Story of the Fatal Charge of the Light Brigade* (London: Penguin, 1958), esp. p. 60 ff.

90. Gaskell, unpublished letter to Nightingale, December 31, 1858. Quoted in Sanders, "Crisis of Liberalism," 47.

91. "The Order of Valour," *Punch* 30 (1857), 79. Edward M. Spiers discusses the shift in attitudes in *The Army and Society 1815–1914* (London: Longman, 1980). Matthew Paul Lalumia shows how changes manifested themselves in visual art in *Realism and Politics in Victorian Art of the Crimean War* (Ann Arbor, MI: UMI Research Press, 1984). For a reading of the shift in terms of a novel, see Reed, "Soldier Boy."

92. Richard Lovelace, "To Lucasta, Going to the Wars," in *The Oxford Book of War Poetry*, ed. John Stallworthy (Oxford: Oxford University Press, 2003), p. 50.

93. Alexander Welsh, *The City of Dickens* (Cambridge, MA: Harvard University Press, 1986), p. 167. The quotation comes from *The History of European Morals* (1869). Welsh also sees a connection between the emphasis on truthfulness and the prominence of chivalric motifs in the period, as in the aforequoted passage.

94. See Cotsell, "Politics and Peeling Frescoes," 188.
95. Leaders, *The Times*, October 31, 1854, 6; March 1, 1855, 8.
96. See for example, ch. 20, "Men and Gentlemen."
97. Sussman quotes this passage (*Victorian Masculinities*, p. 82) from Leonore Davidoff and Catherine Hall's *Family Fortunes: Men and Women of the English Middle Class, 1780–1850* (Chicago: University of Chicago Press, 1987). He also briefly discusses Thornton's manliness (pp. 64–66) in a chapter entitled "The Condition of Manliness Problem: Thomas Carlyle and Industrial Manhood."
98. Gaskell, letter to Emily Shaen, October 27, 1854, in *Letters*, p. 320.
99. Coventry Patmore, *The Angel in the House: The Espousals* (Boston: Ticknor and Fields, 1856), p. 169.
100. *Ibid.*, pp. 17, 21–22.
101. *Ibid.*, p. 203. Compare Lovelace's "I could not love thee, dear, so much, / Loved I not Honour more."
102. [Margaret Oliphant], "Modern Novelists – Great and Small," *Blackwood's Edinburgh Magazine* 77 (May, 1855), 558–60.
103. *Ibid.*, 566.
104. *Ibid.*, 557.
105. Jasper Fforde's *The Eyre Affair* (Penguin, 2002) also brings together many of the ideas about heroism and literature discussed here. The novel (first in a series to star Thursday Next) is set in the mid 1980s against the backdrop of a Crimean War that has never ended, continuing to replay Victorian "blunders" in modern form – including a new version of the charge of the Light Brigade in which Thursday's twin brother is killed while she distinguishes herself admirably. After returning home, Thursday (who is a kind of female action-hero) is sent to rescue the text of *Jane Eyre* from mutilation, allowing Fforde suggestively to link his own heroine to her Victorian precursor.
106. Nightingale, letter to Julia Ward Howe, July 28, 1848, in *Florence Nightingale on Society and Politics, Philosophy, Science, Education, and Literature*, ed. Lynn McDonald, vol. v of *The Collected Works of Florence Nightingale*, 16 vols. (Waterloo, Ontario: Wilfred Laurier University Press, 2003), p. 774.
107. See Catherine Judd, "A 'Scrutinising and Conscious Eye': Nursing and the Carceral in *Jane Eyre* (1847)," ch. 3 of *Bedside Seductions: Nursing and the Victorian Imagination, 1830–1880* (New York: St. Martin's, 1998). In considering Nightingale's public construction, Mary Poovey also notes "the anxieties . . . raised by a woman's assuming even temporary superiority over an infantilized male patient." Mary Poovey, "A Housewifely Woman: The Social Construction of Florence Nightingale," in *Uneven Developments: The Ideological Work of Gender in Mid-Victorian England* (Chicago: University of Chicago Press, 1988), p. 171.
108. Elizabeth Gaskell, letter to Catherine Winkworth, January 1, 1855, in *Letters*, p. 327.
109. See pp. 23, 77, 123.

110. For illustrations of Britannia see "Britannia Taking Care of the Soldiers' Children," *Punch* 26 (1854), 85); "Right against Wrong," *Punch* 26 (1854), 144 (figure 4); "England's War Vigil," *Punch* 26 (1854), 185; and "Britannia takes the Widows and Orphans of the Brave under her Protection," *Punch* 27 (1854), 162. See also Bristow, "Nation, Class," 100, 101.

111. See, for example, the unsigned review of *North and South* in the *Examiner* (April 21, 1855): "We fancy her now and then a little too 'superb' in the description. We have too much of her 'curled upper lip,' of the 'lovely haughty curve' of her face, and of her 'round white flexile throat'" (244–45). Of course, these descriptions (and the critics' responses to them) also alert readers to Margaret's sensuality; Oliphant's objections respond mainly to this feature, making Margaret seem too like a Pre-Raphaelite beauty: "Margaret has glorious black hair, in which the pomegranate blossoms glow like a flame; she has exquisite full lips . . . she is altogether a splendid and princely personage" ("Modern Novelists," 559–60).

112. See Poovey, *Uneven Developments*, p. 171. Ulrich Keller has demonstrated that the Queen made a point of having herself portrayed in the process of reviewing or visiting returned Crimean invalids. As a result, images of Victoria can be remarkably like those of Nightingale: both tended to be depicted inspecting wounded soldiers. See Keller, *Ultimate Spectacle*, esp. pp. 180–92. The conflation appears in Jerry Barrett's *Queen Victoria's First Visit to Her Wounded Soldiers* (1856) and *The Mission of Mercy* (1857), his painting of Nightingale at Scutari. The two works were displayed together in 1858 at Leggatt's Establishment.

113. Poovey, *Uneven Developments*, pp. 171, 168.

114. "A Nightingale In the Camp," *Punch* 28 (1855), 229.

115. See Bristow, "Nation, Class," 99–102.

116. Lytton Strachey, *Eminent Victorians* (New York: The Modern Library, 1918), pp. 151, 137.

117. For examples of military language, see Florence Nightingale, *Ever Yours, Florence Nightingale: Selected Letters*, ed. Martha Vicinus and Bea Nergaard (London: Virago, 1989), pp. 75, 95, 135, 155, 164. For examples of how she considered her mission in relation to Christ's, see *ibid.*, pp. 42, 114. For a comparison to Joan of Arc, see *ibid.*, p. 153.

118. Nightingale, journal entry, July 9, 1850, in *ibid.*, pp. 42–43. These three options also display the choices of the three women, fictional and real, on whom I concentrate in this section: Margaret Hale (married), Aurora Leigh (literary), and Nightingale herself (hospital sister) – although of course the women tested the exclusivity of their roles.

119. Quoted in Cecil Woodham-Smith, *Florence Nightingale, 1820–1910* (London: McGraw-Hill, 1951), p. 77.

120. Nightingale, *Cassandra*, p. 36. The text was finally printed in 1860 as part of *Suggestions for Thought*, which was distributed privately to six prominent men of letters. But it had a healthy public afterlife: among the men was John Stuart Mill, and Virginia Woolf was also influenced by the essay. See the

Introduction to *Suggestions for Thought by Florence Nightingale: Selections and Commentaries*, ed. Michael D. Calabria and Janet A. Macrea (Philadelphia: University of Pennsylvania Press, 1994), pp. xix–xx.
121. See Stark's introduction to *Cassandra* (p. 14) and Sir Edward Cook, *The Life of Florence Nightingale*, 2 vols. (London: Macmillan and Co., 1913), 1:119.
122. Judd, *Bedside Seductions*, pp. 75, 130. Florence Nightingale, *Notes on Nursing: What It Is, and What It Is Not* (New York: Dover, 1969), p. 123.
123. Nightingale, *Cassandra*, p. 28.
124. *Ibid.*, p. 35.
125. The speculation comes in a footnote. Judd discusses Nightingale's fight with George Eliot over her portrayal of the fate of Dorothea Brooke (as heroine of a "home epic" rather than a national epic) in *Middlemarch* (1871–72). In an 1873 article in *Fraser's*, Nightingale argued that "it is past telling the mischief that is done in thus putting down youthful ideals. There are few indeed to end with – even without such a gratuitous impulse as this [that is, Eliot's portrait of Dorothea] to end them." As Judd puts it, to Nightingale, "nursing seems a conspicuous solution to the heroic crisis that faces Dorothea." But, Judd adds, "Eliot's chosen genre, the realist novel, necessarily excludes the celebration of heroic idealism – even if this heroism is based on historical fact" (127). See Judd, *Bedside Seductions*, n. 7, pp. 179–82, and pp. 124–27.
126. Nightingale, private note, December 7, 1851, in *Ever Yours*, p. 55.
127. June Rose, *The Perfect Gentleman: The Remarkable Life of Dr. James Miranda Barry* (London: Hutchinson, 1977), p. 16. Rose's reference to Barry as "she" reflects her interest in the feminist implications of the case and the publication date of her book; more recent commentators tend to favor "he" on the assumption that Barry would today have been thought of as transgendered and would have preferred the designation.
128. Rachel Holmes, *Scanty Particulars: The Life of Dr. James Barry* (London: Viking, 2002), p. 4.
129. Quoted *ibid.*, p. 265.
130. *Ibid.*, p. 2.
131. Elizabeth Gaskell, letter to Catherine Winkworth, October 11 to 14, 1854, in *Letters*, p. 307. For Nightingale's struggles, see Woodham-Smith, *Florence Nightingale*, esp. pp. 23–73.
132. When Gaskell's daughter Meta expressed her desire for a career in nursing, the novelist indicated her belief that the profession required a single-mindedness rare in young women: "I doubt if she has purpose enough to do all this; but I have taken great care not to damp her – and if she has purpose, I will help her, as I propose, to lead such a life; tho' it is not everyone who can be Miss N[ightingale]." Elizabeth Gaskell, letter to Emily Shaen, October 27, 1854, in *Letters*, pp. 320–21.
133. Dereli, "Gender Issues," p. 75.
134. Poovey, *Uneven Developments*, pp. 169, 170.
135. Elizabeth Gaskell, letter to Catherine Winkworth, October 11 to 14, 1854, in *Letters*, p. 307. One might also recall Charles Kingsley's contemporary

argument for a warrior Christ: like Nightingale's, Christ's iconic significance was contested.

136. Elizabeth Gaskell, letter to Parthenope Nightingale, January 18, 1856, in *Letters*, p. 382.

137. A cousin records Nightingale as calling *Ruth* "a beautiful novel" and rereading it in 1859. This rereading of *Ruth* by a largely bed-ridden Nightingale brought on a request for a new copy of *North and South*. Incidentally, Nightingale also read Kingsley's *Two Years Ago* soon after its publication, and her annotations indicate that she identified with its nursing heroine, Grace Harvey. See *Florence Nightingale on Society*, ed. McDonald, pp. 785, 778–79.

138. Florence Nightingale, letter to Mr. and Mrs. Bracebridge, August 7, 1855, in *Letters from the Crimea*, p. 144.

139. Uglow, *Elizabeth Gaskell*, p. 364. Uglow attributes the connection to Nightingale's earlier attractions to Catholicism, but because of the importance of the French Sisters of Mercy in the war, nuns and nursing were often conflated in the popular imagination.

140. Elizabeth Gaskell, letter to Emily Shaen, October 27, 1854, in *Letters*, p. 320.

141. Uglow, *Elizabeth Gaskell*, p. 365.

142. Similarly, when Higgins defends the justice of his cause, he argues that unlike a soldier who fights for the abstract cause of nation, he is fighting to keep those he knows and loves alive (134).

143. Elizabeth Gaskell, letter to Marianne Gaskell, ? October 13, 1854, in *Letters*, p. 311.

144. While Barrett Browning denied an intentional allusion to Brontë's novel, the similarities have always struck readers – including Anna Jameson, to whom Browning made her denial. Barrett Browning, letter to Anna Jameson, December 26, 1856, in *Letters of EBB*, II:245.

145. Barrett Browning, letter to Miss Mitford, June 6, 1854, in *Letters of EBB*, II:171. The idea of her having to "curs[e] . . . prettily" suggests the problems Barrett Browning might have faced as a female laureate. See also in this regard Aytoun's comments on her *Poems Before Congress*, quoted below.

146. While the idea of the novel-poem stems from the mid 1840s, Browning began to work in earnest on *Aurora Leigh* early in 1853. Curiously, the name "Leigh" was not chosen for Aurora until July of 1856 (in manuscript, it had tended to be "Vane"). See Margaret Reynolds, "Editorial Introduction," in Elizabeth Barrett Browning, *Aurora Leigh*, ed. Margaret Reynolds (Athens: Ohio University Press, 1992), pp. 79, 82. Although there is no indication that Barrett Browning was thinking about Amyas Leigh when making her choice, she was familiar with both Kingsley and his works. The connection is intriguing.

147. Nightingale's Crimean mission resulted from the outraged question asked by "A Sufferer by the Present War?" in a letter to *The Times* (discussed in chapter 1): "Why have we no [English] Sisters of Charity?" (*The Times*, October 14, 1854, 7).

148. Letter to Anna Jameson, February 24, 1855, in *Letters of EBB*, II:188–89. Ironically, Nightingale also objected to Jameson's essays on nursing, considering them full of "cant about Women's Rights. If women will but shew what their duties are first, public opinion will acknowledge these fast enough. I dislike almost all that has been *written* [original emphasis] on the subject, Mrs. Jameson especially." Nightingale, letter to Lady Charlotte Canning, November 23, 1856, in *Ever Yours*, p. 166. For all the passionate awareness of the "woman's question" exhibited in *Cassandra*, the post-Crimean Nightingale seems to have felt that the issue of women's rights was a distraction from her real mission: the professionalization of nursing and the improvement of sanitary conditions. But note that her objection is to what is "*written*," not what is *done*.
149. Nightingale, *Notes on Nursing*, p. 134. The force of this narrative can be seen in Grace Harvey's story and in Catherine Volmar's role in *Omar*.
150. *Letters of EBB*, II:188–89.
151. Many critics have discussed the relationship between gender and genre in *Aurora Leigh*. See, for example, Dorothy Mermin, "Genre and Gender in *Aurora Leigh*," *The Victorian Newsletter*, 69 (1986), 7–11; Susan Friedman, "Gender and Genre Anxiety: Elizabeth Browning and H. D. as Epic Poets," *Tulsa Studies in Women's Literature* 5 (1986), 203–28; and Marjorie Stone, "Genre Subversion and Gender Inversion: *The Princess* and *Aurora Leigh*," *Victorian Poetry* 25 (1987), 101–27.
152. Barrett Browning, letter to Anna Jameson, April 12, 1853, in *Letters of EBB*, II:112.
153. The Brownings were in Italy for most of the war (although they spent the summers of 1855 and 1856 in London to see Browning's *Men and Women* [1855] and *Aurora Leigh* through the press). But they kept up with affairs in the Crimea and the state of British feelings at home. Nevertheless, Barrett Browning's attitude towards the war is far more cosmopolitan than that of the other English writers I consider. One sees this in her championing of Louis Napoleon and her hopes that affairs in the Crimea prove beneficial to the cause of Italian unification (because of Sardinia's membership in the Alliance). She also felt that England's humiliation was constructive; her comments on Nightingale are followed by these reflections: "Oh, the Crimea! How dismal, how full of despair and horror! The results will, however, be good if we are induced to come down from the English pedestal in Europe of incessant self-glorification, and learn that our close, stifling, corrupt system gives no air nor scope for healthy and effective organisation anywhere" (*Letters of EBB*, II:189–90). Helen Cooper compares the cosmopolitanism Barrett Browning describes in her heroine (and possessed herself) to that developed by Mrs. Seacole. See Helen Cooper, "England: The Imagined Community of Aurora Leigh and Mrs. Seacole," *Studies in Browning and His Circle* 20 (1993), 123–31.
154. Barrett Browning, letter to Mrs. Martin, October 1855, in *Letters of EBB*, II:213.

155. She had read a review of *Hard Times*, which had run in *Household Words* immediately prior to *North and South*, and feared overlap. Barrett Browning, unpublished letter of March 1855, quoted in the "Editorial Introduction" to *Aurora Leigh*, ed. Reynolds, pp. 85–86.
156. Barrett Browning, letter to Mrs. Martin, February 1857, in *Letters of EBB*, II:254.
157. Elizabeth Barrett Browning, *Aurora Leigh*, lines 171–72, in *Aurora Leigh and Other Poems*, ed. John Robert Glorney Bolton and Julia Bolton Holloway (London: Penguin, 1995). Hereafter internally referenced by book and line number.
158. As Deidre David notes, "Some reviewers accused Barrett Browning of melodramatic borrowings from Brontë's novel, of making Romney both St John Rivers and Rochester." Deidre David, *Intellectual Women and Victorian Patriarchy: Harriet Martineau, Elizabeth Barrett Browning, George Eliot* (Ithaca: Cornell University Press, 1987), p. 120.
159. Paul Turner suggests that Patmore's "Angel" stands behind Barrett Browning's diatribe against "books on womanhood" in which this phrase appears (1.427–46). See "Aurora versus the Angel," *Review of English Studies* 24 (July, 1948), 227–35.
160. Nightingale, *Cassandra*, p. 53.
161. Nightingale, letter to Fanny Nightingale, July 16, 1851, in *Ever Yours*, p. 52.
162. [William Edmonstoune Aytoun], "Mrs. Barrett Browning – Aurora Leigh," *Blackwood's Edinburgh Magazine* 81 (January, 1857), 25, 32. This article includes a more general attack on the "spasmodic school" of poetry, to which he believed Barrett Browning's poem belonged. I will return to the phenomenon of spasmodism in chapter 3.
163. [W. E. Aytoun], "Poetic Aberrations" [review of Barrett Browning's *Poems Before Congress* (1860)], *Blackwood's Edinburgh Magazine* 87 (April, 1860), 490, 494.
164. Gaskell, letter to Emily Shaen, October 27, 1854, in *Letters*, p. 320.
165. David, *Intellectual Women*, p. 151.
166. *Ibid.*, pp. 117–18.
167. Nightingale, letter to John Stuart Mill, September 12, 1860, in *Ever Yours*, p. 210.
168. Nightingale, letter to Frances Nightingale, late 1865. Quoted in Holmes, *Scanty Particulars*, p. 271. The parentheses around the pronouns appear in the extant (Claydon) copy of the letter and seem to have been added for emphasis.
169. David, *Intellectual Women*, p. 146.
170. Barrett Browning, letter to Isa Blagden, n.d. [October 20, 1856], Fitzwilliam Museum. Quoted in *Aurora Leigh*, ed. Reynolds, p. 18.
171. Quoted *ibid.*, p. 7.
172. See [Coventry Patmore], "Mrs. Browning's Poem," *North British Review* 26.2 (February, 1857), 443–62, esp. 462.
173. Romney often quotes Aurora's words back to her (as she does his), but note that here he alludes not to a moment of spoken dialogue but to a moment of

narrative poetry describing Aurora's feelings before his appearance on the scene – almost as though he were a reader of *Aurora Leigh* as well as a character in it.
174. [J. W. Kaye], "The Employment of Women," *North British Review* 26 (February, 1857), 295–96.

3 "THE SONG THAT NERVES A NATION'S HEART": THE POETRY OF THE CRIMEAN WAR

1. See Benedict Anderson's discussion of how poetry and national anthems create "unisonality," "the echoed physical realization of the imagined community" (*Imagined Communities*, p. 145).
2. Van Wyk Smith, *Drummer Hodge*, p. 12.
3. Arnold, Preface to the first edition of *Poems* (1853), in *Matthew Arnold: Selected Poems and Prose*, p. 118. For Arnold's feelings about the war, see D. S. Neff, "*The Times*, the Crimean War, and 'Stanzas from the Grande Chartreuse,'" *Papers on Language and Literature* 33.2 (1997), 174. Neff reads "Stanzas" as a response to the war, arguing that Achilles can be seen as a stand-in for Raglan.
4. For more on the debate, see my chapter on Clough in *The Crisis of Action*.
5. See [Charles Kingsley], "Thoughts on Shelley and Byron," *Fraser's Magazine* 48 (November, 1853), 568–76.
6. See John C. Hawley, "Charles Kingsley and Literary Theory of the 1850s," *Victorian Literature and Culture* 19 (1991), 171; and Brenda Colloms, *Charles Kingsley: The Lion of Eversley*, p. 222. See also [Charles Kingsley], review of *Maud*, *Fraser's Magazine* 52 (1855), 264–73.
7. For the influence of Dobell and Smith on *Maud*, see Joseph J. Collins, "Tennyson and the Spasmodics," *The Victorian Newsletter* 43 (1973), 24–28.
8. J. Hillis Miller, *The Disappearance of God: Five Nineteenth-Century Writers* (Cambridge, MA: Harvard University Press, 1977), p. 108.
9. See Robert Langbaum, *The Poetry of Experience: The Dramatic Monologue in Modern Literary Tradition* (New York: W. W. Norton and Co., 1963), esp. ch. 2.
10. All references to Tennyson's verse are from *The Poems of Tennyson*, ed. Ricks, and will be internally documented by part (where relevant) and line number.
11. "Our Patriotic Poets," *Punch* 26 (1854), 110.
12. [Hamley], "Poetry of the War," 531.
13. [Goldwin Smith], "The War Passages in *Maud*," *Saturday Review* 1 (November 3, 1855), 14–15. In its argument for cultural relativism ("a nation which may not be in need of the same regimen as ourselves"), this passage presents an unusual level of protest against the Crimean War: it protests not only *how* the war was fought but *that* it was fought.
14. [W. M. Thackeray], "The Due of the Dead," *Punch* 27 (1854), 173. Compare this poem to *The Times*'s leader of October 12, 1854 discussed in chapter 1.

15. "War Music," lines 1–8, in A. and L. [Arabella and Louisa] Shore, *War Lyrics* (London: Saunders and Otley, 1855), p. 26. Further references to poems in this edition will be internally cited by line number.
16. Painters also favored this subject during the war. Consider Ford Madox Brown's *Waiting: An English Fireside of 1854–5* (1855). Originally intended as a domestic idyll of a woman sewing while her baby sleeps on her lap, the "subject was modified in 1854 . . . and reworked . . . to represent 'an officer's wife thinking of him at Sevastopol'" (a bundle of letters and a miniature portrait of the husband were added). Tim Barringer, *Reading the Pre-Raphaelites* (New Haven: Yale University Press, 1999), pp. 91–92.
17. Florence Nightingale provides the exception to this rule, and almost every Crimean War poet wrote about her. These poems form a distinct sub-category within the war poetry – poets writing about Nightingale may have struggled with the implications of her work for gender-roles (as my discussion in chapter 2 suggests), but they did not question her heroism or value. For an extensive list of poems about Nightingale, see Dereli, "Gender Issues," pp. 78–79, n. 26.
18. Lootens, "Patriotism," pp. 259, 256.
19. Quoted in Isobel Armstrong, *Victorian Poetry: Poetry, Poetics and Politics* (London: Routledge, 1993), p. 320.
20. Bristow, "Nation, Class," 106.
21. Armstrong, *Victorian Poetry*, pp. 336, 333.
22. [Adelaide Anne Procter], "Waiting," *Household Words* 10 (1854), 204–05.
23. For "Waiting" as a war poem, see Dereli, "Gender Issues," 74.
24. [A. A. Procter], "The Lesson of the War," *Household Words* 11 (1855), 12.
25. [A. A. Procter], "The Two Spirits," *Household Words* 10 (1855), 516–17.
26. Elizabeth Barrett Browning, *Last Poems* (London: Chapman and Hall, 1862). Lootens discusses this poem ("Patriotism," p. 261).
27. The volume's tone can be deduced from the fact that the sisters omitted all but three of their Crimean poems in their *Collected Poems* (1897), explaining, "we have learned to regard the Crimean war, in spite of the heroism of our soldiers, not as a just cause and a glorious achievement so much as a deplorable blunder." Arabella and Louisa Shore, *Poems by A. and L.* (London: Grant Richards, 1897), p. 335. Quoted in Lootens, "Patriotism," p. 268. Note the mention of Tennysonian "blunder."
28. Linda Hughes calls Alan Sinfield (author of *Dramatic Monologue* [London: Methuen, 1977]) "the foremost spokesman" for this "inclusive" understanding of the dramatic monologue, which should be contrasted with Langbaum's "ironic framework." Linda K. Hughes, *The Manyfacèd Glass: Tennyson's Dramatic Monologues* (Athens: Ohio University Press, 1987), p. 7. Generally speaking, the stricter definition is associated with Browning's monologues while the looser seems more descriptive of Tennyson's (see *Manyfacèd Glass*, esp. ch. 1).

29. Lootens notes, citing Van Wyk Smith, that after the Crimean War, "much of the patriotic poetry of war would be spoken through, if not always by, soldiers" ("Patriotism," p. 268).
30. Sydney Dobell, "An Evening Dream," lines 15–18, in *England In Time of War* (London: Smith, Elder & Co., 1856), p. 64. Further references to poems in this edition internally cited by line number.
31. The name for a type of musket used in the war, a heavier gun than the modern Minié rifle.
32. See Paul Fussell's moving account in *The Great War and Modern Memory* (pp. 243–54). "The Moral of this Year" (discussed in the previous chapter) also compares "poppy-bannered grain" to "crimson War" (*Household Words* 10 [1854], 276). The poppy as symbol of doomed youth had of course appeared as early as the *Aeneid*, when Virgil memorably describes the dying Euryalus (bk. 9).
33. Dobell admired "The Charge," immediately recognizing its authorship; he wrote to Tennyson, "no man living but yourself could have written the first verse and the 'cannon' verse." Sydney Dobell, letter to Tennyson, February 7, 1855, quoted in *The Letters of Alfred Lord Tennyson*, ed. Cecil Y. Lang and Edgar F. Shannon, Jr., 2 vols. (Cambridge, MA: Harvard University Press, 1987), II:104 (note). Tennyson also had a kind word for Dobell's war poems; Dobell's *Life and Letters* mentions "a sweet natured note from Tennyson" about the collection of sonnets and the Laureate's "special approval" of "Grass from the Battlefield" (a remarkable effusion in which a dying soldier fixates on the blades of grass in front of his eyes as he fades from consciousness) in the later volume. *Life and Letters of Sydney Dobell*, ed. Emily Jolly, 2 vols. (London, 1876), I:401, II:25. Quoted in Martha Westwater, *The Spasmodic Career of Sydney Dobell* (Lanham, MD: University Press of America, 1992), pp. 106, 107.
34. Natalie Houston, "Reading the Victorian Souvenir: Sonnets and Photographs of the Crimean War," *Yale Journal of Criticism* 14.2 (2001), 362. This claim has also been made of *Maud*.
35. Martha Westwater describes how the poets decided to "leave their heroes in their towers and consider the heroes on the battlefields" (*Spasmodic Career*, p. 102). Kingsley's *Two Years Ago* also suggests war poetry as a cure for spasmodism, although there the cure depends on the poet's actually going to war. As Tom Thurnall proposes to the ailing Elsley Vavasour: "Why don't you become our war poet? . . . There will be a dozen Cockneys writing battle songs, I'll warrant, who never saw a man shot in their lives, not even a hare. Come and give us the real genuine grit of it." To which Elsley responds enthusiastically – "It is a grand thought! The true war poets, after all, have been warriors themselves" – before succumbing once again to an opium stupor (II:230).
36. Alexander Smith and the Author of *Balder* and *The Roman* [Sydney Dobell], *Sonnets on the War* (London: David Bogue, 1855), pp. 15–16. Future references to the *Sonnets* will be to page numbers in this edition. Both sonnets

can be attributed to Dobell by their inclusion in his *Poetical Works* of 1875; further attributions have the same source.
37. Urquhart, *Misuse of Familiar Words*; see especially the chapters "Public Opinion and Private Judgment" and "Organs of Public Opinion."
38. Lootens, "Patriotism," p. 276.
39. [Hamley], "Poetry of the War," 531.
40. "Vigil," letter to the editor, *The Times*, December 7, 1854, 8.
41. Houston, "Victorian Souvenir," 377.
42. Isobel Armstrong calls Browning's novel-in-verse "an exhaustive reading of the implications of *vox populi* " (*Victorian Poetry*, p. 317).
43. Houston, "Victorian Souvenir," 377.
44. Urquhart, *Misuse of Familiar Words*, pp. 219–20.
45. [Hamley], "Poetry of the War," 533.
46. See Houston, "Victorian Souvenir," 377.
47. Thomas Carlyle, letter to Lady Ashburton, October 20, 1854, in *The Collected Letters of Thomas and Jane Welsh Carlyle*, ed. Kenneth J. Fielding (Durham, NC: Duke University Press, 2001), XXIX:175.
48. Urquhart, *Misuse of Familiar Words*, p. 225.
49. *Ibid.*
50. Leader, *The Times*, November 13, 1854, 6.
51. Patrick Waddington has collected an entire volume of poems about the charge: *"Theirs But To Do and Die": The Poetry of the Charge of the Light Brigade at Balaklava, 25 October 1854* (Nottingham: Astra Press, 1995).
52. [Russell], "The Operations of the Siege," *The Times*, November 14, 1854, 7.
53. Kinglake, *Invasion of the Crimea*, v:364. For a wonderful account of the events of the day, see Woodham-Smith, *The Reason Why*, especially chs. 11 and 12.
54. Leader, *The Times*, November 13, 1854, 6.
55. *Ibid.*
56. The phrase "the reason why" became common in contemporary accounts of the war. See, for example, the illustration in *Punch* 28 (1855), 85, "Mr. Bull wants to know 'The Reason Why.'"
57. Tate, "On Not Knowing Why," p. 169. See also Houston, "Victorian Souvenir," 356; and Keller, *Ultimate Spectacle*, pp. 11, 242–43.
58. Leader, *The Times*, November 14, 1854, 6.
59. Leader, *The Times*, November 13, 1854, 6.
60. See also Tate, "On Not Knowing Why," pp. 165–66.
61. *Illustrated Times*, June 9, 1855; see Keller, *Ultimate Spectacle*, p. 11.
62. Keller, *Ultimate Spectacle*, pp. 242–43. For an example of interpretive confusion in novelistic accounts of the charge, see my reading of George Whyte-Melville's *The Interpreter* in chapter 2.
63. Waddington, *"Theirs But To Do and Die"*, p. 75.
64. Leader, *The Times*, November 13, 1854, 6. See also Tate, who discusses in detail the newspaper reports' awareness of the "disparity between the deed and the outcome" and the "anti-utilitarian" aspect of the charge in the

context of her reading of Tennyson's poem ("On Not Knowing Why," pp. 169, 175).
65. Henry Lushington, *La Nation Boutiquière and other Poems, Chiefly Political* (Cambridge: Macmillan & Co., 1855), p. 11.
66. Houston, "Victorian Souvenir," 360.
67. Sydney Dobell, "A Hero's Grave," in *England In Time of War*, p. 92. See [George Eliot], "Contemporary Literature," *Westminster Review* 65 o.s., 9 n.s. (October, 1856), 566–70. Yet even this poem ends on a much more martial note. Another voice enters to teach the old man a lesson in appropriate mourning: "Pity thee? / A son is lost to thine infirmity; / Poor fool, what then? A son thou hast resigned / To give a father to the virtues of mankind" (lines 153–56). Still, the use of repetition, the doubt regarding the value of glory, the resistance to the idea of monuments (marble), and the mode of questioning and answering, followed by the starkness of the father's final line – all these aspects of the poem offer arguments against the majority of verses written about the charge, not only Dobell's but also Tennyson's.
68. Leader, *The Times*, November 13, 1854, 6.
69. See Houston, "Victorian Souvenir," 361; Houston contrasts this anti-aristocratic sensibility with Tennyson's perspective in "The Charge," a poem that she reads as upholding the aristocratic military code. Actually, as I note above, Dobell admired Tennyson's ballad.
70. *Ibid.*, 360.
71. One exception to this general rule comes in Westland Marston's *The Death-Ride: A Tale of the Light Brigade* (London: C. Mitchell, 1855), which is written from the perspective of a cavalry-member. This poem is discussed by Tate ("On Not Knowing Why," pp. 177–78) and Waddington (*"Theirs But To Do and Die"*, pp. 37–39).
72. Clough, *Amours de Voyage*, II.v.115–17, in *Clough's Selected Poems*, ed. J. P. Phelan (London: Longman, 1995).
73. Leader, *The Times*, November 13, 1854, 6.
74. [Russell], "The Operations of the Siege," *The Times*, November 14, 1854, 7.
75. See, for example, Woodham-Smith, *The Reason Why*, p. 216.
76. The Earl of Ellesmere, "Balaklava," in Waddington, *"Theirs But To Do and Die"*, pp. 34–35. Tennyson had also emphasized the charge's pageantry, both with his focus on the visual – the flashing sabers etc. that cause Jerome McGann to compare the poem to French military painting – and with his central and repeated invocation, "All the world wondered" (lines 31, 52). See Jerome McGann, "Tennyson and the Histories of Criticism," in *The Beauty of Inflections: Literary Investigations in Historical Method and Theory* (Oxford: The Clarendon Press, 1985), p. 197.
77. Charles Kingsley wrote in *Fraser's* that the "transcendental and inexhaustible" subject of the charge deserved a "monument worthy of [the participants'] deed." Review of Tennyson's *Maud*, 273.
78. Gerald Massey, "Author's Note," *War Waits*, 2nd edn. (London: David Bogue, 1855). Houston invokes the ideas of souvenirs and scrapbooks in

relation to Smith and Dobell's sonnets, suggesting that the "recognition of the eventual effacement of the experience of history is the impulse behind the collecting of the souvenir. To know that what seems currently affecting and immediate will not seem so in the future, and to believe that it is worth documenting, is the impulse underlying this collection of sonnets" ("Victorian Souvenir," 376–77).

79. Leader, *The Times*, November 13, 1854, 6.
80. Carlyle, letter to Gerald Massey, March 23, 1855, in *The Collected Letters*, XXIX:276.
81. According to Susan Shatto, most of *Maud* had been drafted by the time "The Charge" was written in December of 1854. See "The History of Composition," Part 1 of the Introduction to *Tennyson's Maud: A Definitive Edition*, ed. Susan Shatto (London: The Athlone Press, 1986), pp. 1–33.
82. Herbert F. Tucker, "*Maud* and the Doom of Culture," in *Critical Essays on Alfred Lord Tennyson*, ed. Herbert F. Tucker (New York: G. K. Hall and Co., 1993), p. 181.
83. Lootens, "Patriotism," p. 264.
84. Many of these references to the poem as ballad occur in the correspondence between the Tennysons (Emily often wrote the letters) and John Forster, the editor of the *Examiner*, about the publication of the poem. See the Tennysons' letters of December 7, 1854, December 9, 1854, and August 6, 1855, in *Letters*, II:102, II:117.
85. McGann, *Beauty of Inflections*, p. 195. For a later, nostalgic treatment of Balaklava, see George Meredith's *Beauchamp's Career* (1876), where the eponymous hero's participation in the charge of the Light Brigade serves as a symbol of innocent action, uncorrupted by the cautiousness and political realities that will hamper his future deeds. That is, the *charge* offers an opposing model of action to the failed *career*, its very failure representing a kind of success that the conditions of modern life have rendered impossible. For a purely ironic response, we can look to Beryl Bainbridge's magnificent *Master Georgie* (Gerald Duckworth & Co., 1998), in which the charge is noticed only for the influx of riderless horses it provided to those in the camps.
86. Of course, within the narrative of the poem, historical timing would have precluded both Maud and the speaker from knowing Tennyson's ballad: "The Charge" was published months after the Baltic force that the narrator joins in the conclusion of the poem leaves British shores.
87. The elision was not complete in that a version of "The Charge" was republished in the same volume as *Maud*. But as my discussion will indicate, this version of the ballad was significantly bowdlerized through its erasure of the concept of "blunder."
88. [William Gladstone], "Tennyson's Poems," *Quarterly Review* 106 (October, 1859), 461–64. He later changed his views (see his *Gleanings of Past Years* [London: John Murray, 1879], II:146–47).
89. [G. Smith], "The War Passages in *Maud*," 14–15. While Smith seems to be blaming Tennyson for designating the long peace a "canker," the

metaphor – from *1 Henry IV*, iv.ii.29 ("The cankers of a calm world and a long peace") – was actually more generally current during the period. The quotation "the canker of a long peace" comes up in leaders in *The Times* of October 9, 1854 and February 14, 1855 (both p. 6). As James Bennet has shown, though, far more early reviewers approved of the poem's pro-war expressions than disapproved of them. See James Bennett, "The Historical Abuse of Literature: Tennyson's *Maud: A Monodrama* and the Crimean War," *English Studies* 62 (1981), 34. See also Michael C. C. Addams's argument that in the context of the war, many of the opinions expressed in the poem in favor of war were commonplace ("Tennyson's Crimean War Poetry: a Cross-Cultural Approach," *Journal of the History of Ideas* 40.3 [1979], 405–22).

90. See Tennyson's letter to Robert James Mann of September, 1855 (in *Letters* II:127) and Hallam Tennyson's record of his father's comments quoted in Ricks's head-note to the poem in *Poems of Tennyson*, II:517–18.

91. Robert James Mann, selections from *Tennyson's "Maud" Vindicated: An Explanatory Essay* (1856), in *Tennyson: The Critical Heritage*, ed. John D. Jump (London: Routledge and Kegan Paul, 1967), p. 198. See also George Brimley, selections from "Alfred Tennyson's Poems," in *Cambridge Essays* (1855), pp. 226–81 (in *The Critical Heritage*, ed. Jump, p. 196).

92. For the use of *monodrama* as a synonym for *dramatic monologue*, see Ricks's head-note in *Poems of Tennyson*, II:515. In his much-cited essay "Monodrama and the Dramatic Monologue" (*PMLA* 90.3 [May, 1975], 366–85), Dwight Culler argues for the monodrama as a distinct form, with its own historical origins (crucially, in music), and discusses *Maud* as an example (378–82). Herbert Tucker also prefers to call the poem a monodrama: "In dramatic monologues we require to know more firmly whether and when speakers know what they are talking about; *Maud* very often leaves this question wide open" ("Doom of Culture," p. 177). But critics differ on the point. According to James Bennet, "*Maud* possesses, I believe, all the major signals of a dramatic monologue" ("The Historical Abuse of Literature," 41). Linda Hughes also disagrees with Culler, seeing *Maud* as an expanded monologue in the loose sense of the term: first-person effusions in a voice not the poet's own (*Manyfacèd Glass*, p. 165).

93. Tennyson, letter to Archer Thompson Gurney, December 6, 1855, in *Letters*, II:137–38.

94. Van Wyk Smith, *Drummer Hodge*, p. 12.

95. McGann, *Beauty of Inflections*, p. 195. Notably, Maud's song is almost immediately recognized as arousing similar nostalgia for heroic leadership: "I wish I could hear again / The chivalrous battle-song / That she warbled alone in her joy! / I might persuade myself then / She would not do herself this great wrong, / To take a wanton dissolute boy / For a man and a leader of men." (1.382–88; added in second edition, 1856). But such "simple" nostalgia is complicated by its context in the larger work.

96. See Shannon and Ricks, "Creation of a Poem," 31. McGann sees a reverential pun in *Light*, rendering it adjectival (*Beauty of Inflections*, p. 201).

97. Shannon and Ricks, "Creation of a Poem," 18.
98. See *ibid.*, 17.
99. Tate, "On Not Knowing Why," p. 179.
100. Leader, *The Times*, November 13, 1854, 6. See Hallam, Lord Tennyson, *Alfred, Lord Tennyson: A Memoir by his Son*, 2 vols. (London: Macmillan and Co., 1897), which recalls the phrase as Tennyson's own "some one had blundered" (1:381).
101. Kingsley adds a partial defense of Tennyson: "He is no Tyrtaeus, though he has a glimpse of what Tyrtaeus ought to be." C. Kingsley, letter to Thomas Hughes, December 18, 1854, in *Letters and Memories*, 1:434.
102. Tennyson, letter to John Forster, December 8 (misdated 9), 1854, in *Letters*, II:102.
103. John Forster, letter to Tennyson, December 9, 1854, in Tennyson's *Letters*, II:102.
104. See Shannon and Ricks for the reasons for the changes ("Creation of a Poem," 6–7). Tennyson soon recognized his mistake; the entire meaning of the poem depended upon its genesis in error. For all his work, though, something in Tennyson's ballad resists authorial control. So, for example, in Virginia Woolf's version of it in *To the Lighthouse* (1927), Mr. Ramsay misquotes the line "Boldly they rode and well" as "boldly we rode and well" during his reenactment of the charge on the front lawn of his house. In the process, he nearly upsets Lily Briscoe's easel – and her own efforts at a perfect composition, efforts that stand in for those of her creator, and, by extension, of Tennyson as well. Virginia Woolf, *To the Lighthouse* (New York: Harcourt Brace Jovanovich, 1989), p. 17. Tate discusses this mis-remembering ("On Not Knowing Why," pp. 160–61); Lootens also mentions the episode ("Patriotism," p. 255).
105. So, as Shannon and Ricks suggest ("Creation of a Poem," 32), making the dissemination of feeling about the war much simpler, since the soldiers, unproblematically admirable in themselves, presented him with a uniform set of expectations and responses to the poem.
106. See D. G. Rossetti's comments after a reading of the poem at the Brownings' on September 27, 1855: "I was never more amused in my life than by Tennyson's groanings and horrors over the reviews of *Maud*, which poem he read through to us, spouting also several sections to be introduced in a new edition." Rossetti, letter to William Allingham, November 25, 1855, quoted in Tennyson's *Letters*, II:128.
107. Sometimes, the attempt is to clarify plot, as in the addition of the "Courage, poor heart of Stone!" verse, discussed below, which was to make Maud's death more obvious. See Shatto's edition of *Maud*, p. 203.
108. Consider the changes to the end of Part III, including the removal of the offending phrase, "the long, long canker of peace," its replacement with "the peace that I deem'd no peace," and the addition of a new final stanza of the poem, so as to avoid ending on the note of a "blood-red blossom of war with a heart of fire." See Shatto's edition of *Maud*, pp. 221–22, and

Edgar F. Shannon, Jr., "The Critical Reception of Tennyson's *Maud*," *PMLA* 68 (June, 1953), 410.
109. See Tate, "On Not Knowing Why," p. 160.
110. See Ralph Wilson Rader, *Tennyson's "Maud": The Biographical Genesis* (Berkeley and Los Angeles: The University of California Press, 1963); Shatto's edition of *Maud*, p. 37; and Hughes, *Manyfacèd Glass*, p. 172.
111. [Coventry Patmore], review of *In Memoriam* and *Maud, and Other Poems*, *Edinburgh Review* 102 (October, 1855), 498–519; quoted in Shannon, "Critical Reception," 413.
112. Tucker, "Doom of Culture," pp. 176–77.
113. Armstrong, *Victorian Poetry*, p. 288.
114. Brimley, "Alfred Tennyson's Poems," in *The Critical Heritage*, ed. Jump, p. 196.
115. Tennyson, letter to Archer Thompson Gurney, December 6, 1855, in *Letters*, II:138.
116. Armstrong, *Victorian Poetry*, p. 271.
117. Tucker, "Doom of Culture," p. 190. See also Matthew Allen, *Essay on the Classification of the Insane* (1837): "One part of society, as well as one part of the mind, is at war with another" (quoted in Shatto's edition of *Maud*, p. 168). This book was in Tennyson's possession.
118. See his comments to Henry Van Dyke, quoted in Shatto's edition of *Maud*, pp. 163–64.
119. See, for example, Smith and Dobell's "The Army Surgeon," lines 5–6: "The fearful moorland where the myriads lay / Moved as a moving field of mangled worms" (*Sonnets*, p. 14); or Fred Dallas's account of Mrs. Duberly's (to his mind) horrific and un-"womanly" pleasure at being a tourist of war, watching the "poor mangled wretches" being carried out of the trenches (letter to his family, January 30, 1855, in *Eyewitness*, p. 78).
120. [Russell], "The Operations of the Siege," *The Times*, November 14, 1854, 7.
121. Shannon and Ricks, "Creation of a Poem," 30.
122. Franklin Lushington, "Alma," line 4. In *Points of War*, p. 84.
123. See Shannon and Ricks, "Creation of a Poem," p. 44 (note 50).
124. Christopher Ricks, *Tennyson*, 2nd edn. (Houndmills, Basingstoke, Hampshire: Macmillan, 1989), p. 231.
125. Kingsley, *The Heroes*, p. xvii.
126. "Extracts from a Peace Dictionary," *Punch* 30 (1857), 3.
127. [Russell], "The Operations of the Siege," *The Times*, November 14, 1854, 7.
128. Lootens, "Patriotism," p. 267; Ruskin, "The Roots of Honour," in *Unto This Last*, vol. XVII of the *Library Edition of the Complete Works of John Ruskin*, ed. E. T. Cook and Alexander Wedderburn (London: George Allen, 1905), 36–37 (first printed in the *Cornhill Magazine* [August, 1860]).
129. See H. Tennyson, *Memoir*, I:411; Ruskin, letter to Tennyson, November 12, 1855, quoted in Shannon and Ricks, "Creation of a Poem," 10. Ruskin called it "the most tragical line in the poem."
130. Armstrong, *Victorian Poetry*, p. 314; Hughes, *Manyfacèd Glass*, p. 13.

131. Robert Browning, "Childe Roland to the Dark Tower Came," lines 41–42, in *Robert Browning: The Poems*, ed. John Pettigrew, supplemented and completed Thomas J. Collins, 2 vols. (London: Penguin, 1993), 1:585–92. Hereafter, internally referenced.
132. Armstrong, *Victorian Poetry*, p. 316. The poem was published in *Men and Women*.
133. Armstrong, *Victorian Poetry*, p. 314.
134. John Ruskin, *Modern Painters, Volume III* (London: Smith, Elder and Co., 1856), p. 97 (ch. 8). Armstrong also reads "Childe Roland" in light of Ruskin's Grotesque.
135. Vanden Bossche, "Realism versus Romance," 79–80.
136. *Ibid.*, 80, 82.
137. Armstrong, *Victorian Poetry*, pp. 244–45.
138. Ricks, *Tennyson*, p. 231.
139. [Walter Bagehot], review of Tennyson's *Idylls of the King, National Review* 9 (October, 1859), 378.
140. See my discussion in chapter 2 of the "civil war" between rich and poor that had been obscured by the *Pax Britannica* and that – it was hoped – the Crimean War would help to end.
141. Shannon and Ricks, "Creation of a Poem," 11–12.
142. Tucker, "Doom of Culture," p. 180.
143. See Shatto's edition of *Maud*, p. 203.
144. Thomas J. Assad, "Tennyson's 'Courage, Poor Heart of Stone,'" *Tulane Studies in English* 18 (1970), 76.
145. The poem was divided into two parts in 1859 and into three parts in 1865 – largely, it seems, in response to critics' complaints about its impenetrability. See Shatto's edition of *Maud*, p. 28.
146. According to McGann, Tennyson's poetry always attempts to achieve synthesis, even if it fails to do so because "it remains subject to those (self-generated and unapparent) limitations which bring into focus the social and psychological conflicts which the poetry struggles with, and is itself a part of" (*Beauty of Inflections*, p. 182).
147. This fact seems to belie the commonly made claim that Tennyson disliked the poem. Actually, the much-quoted remark by him – "not a poem on which I pique myself" (H. Tennyson, *Memoir*, 1:409–10) – was made in the context of his mangling of the poem (by removing the "blundered" stanza that had offended some readers) for publication along with *Maud* in 1855. There is no reason to think that Tennyson disliked what he came to call "the soldier's version" after hearing of their great enthusiasm. See Ricks's head-note to the poem in *The Poems of Tennyson* (II:511) and Shannon and Ricks ("Creation of a Poem," 6–7).
148. For details of this recording and its connection to the Fund, see Bennett Maxwell, "The Steytler Recordings of Alfred, Lord Tennyson: A History," *Tennyson Research Bulletin* 3.4 (1980), 150–57. A very brief recording of parts of "Come into the Garden, Maud" (*Maud*, 1.850-921) was also made.

Notes to pages 165–168

149. Woolf, *To the Lighthouse*, p. 16.
150. Tennyson, letter to John Forster, August 6, 1855, in *Letters*, II:117. Tennyson also records giving permission to Mrs. W. H. Owen to publish music set for the ballad (in a letter to William Johnson Fox, October 25, 1855, in *Letters*, II:134).
151. Rudyard Kipling, "The Last of the Light Brigade," in Waddington, *"Theirs But To Do and Die"*, p. 170.
152. See Culler, "Monodrama," throughout; Mann, selections from *Tennyson's "Maud" Vindicated*, in *Tennyson: The Critical Heritage*, ed. Jump, p. 199.
153. H. Tennyson, *Memoir*, II:336.
154. Barrett Browning, letter to Mrs. Martin, October, 1855, in *Letters of EBB*, II:213.
155. Hughes, *Manyfacèd Glass*, p. 168.
156. Tennyson, letter to Charles Richard Weld, November 21, 1855, in *Letters*, II:135.
157. Charles Lamb, "On the Tragedies of Shakspeare Considered with Reference to their Fitness for Stage Representation," in *The Collected Works of Charles Lamb*, ed. E. V. Lucas, 8 vols. (London: Methuen, 1912), I:114–15.
158. H. Tennyson, *Memoir*, I:396. It would, however, only have been fixed for the day, the next reading offering a new version of what Tucker calls the "rhapsode's work-in-progress" ("Doom of Culture," p. 192).
159. Eric Griffiths, "Tennyson's Breath," in *Critical Essays*, ed. Tucker, p. 35.

4 PAINTERS OF MODERN LIFE: (RE)MEDIATING THE CRIMEAN WAR IN THE ART OF JOHN LEECH AND JOHN EVERETT MILLAIS

1. The play describes the romantic entanglements of officers belonging to a regiment ("Ours") that is sent out to the Crimea at the end of Act I; in Act II, the women follow their men to the battlefront. *Ours* thus resonates with my discussion of heroinism in chapter 2. Its title also recalls both the difficulties Tennyson faced in juggling pronouns in his Crimean War poems and the designation of "our own correspondent." For more on Crimean War drama, see J. S. Bratton, "Theatre of War: The Crimea on the London Stage 1854–5," in *Performance and Politics in Popular Drama*, ed. David Bradby *et al.* (Cambridge: Cambridge University Press, 1980), pp. 119–37. Bratton's fascinating account focuses on popular dramas staged even as the war was taking place (with special attention to the spectaculars at Astley's) and does not consider the later *Ours*. She concludes that "Reciprocity between the press, the stage and the public mood resulted in the creation of a myth of the war which, while it dealt with new kinds of information from the scene of war, much of it shocking and profoundly anti-heroic, nevertheless cast it into forms consonant with the old heroic models" (p. 135).

2. See George Bernard Shaw, *Dramatic Opinions and Essays*, II:281–85, quoted in Maynard Savin, *Thomas William Robertson: His Plays and Stagecraft* (Providence: Brown University Press, 1950), p. 84.
3. As Pinero's Tom Wench (based on Robertson) puts it, "I strive to make my people talk and behave like live people" (1.i.266). In Arthur Wing Pinero, *Trelawny of the "Wells" and Other Plays*, ed. J. S. Bratton (Oxford: Oxford University Press, 1995), p. 223.
4. Thomas William Robertson, *Ours*, in *The Principal Dramatic Works of Thomas William Robertson: With Memoir by his Son*, 2 vols. (New York: Samuel French & Son, 1889), II:456.
5. Savin, *Thomas William Robertson*, p. 76.
6. Millais, letter to Effie, November 18, 1859, in John Guille Millais, *Life and letters of Sir John Everett Millais President of the Royal Academy: By his son John Guille Millais With 319 illustrations including nine photogravures*, 2 vols. (London: Methuen and Co, 1899), 1:353.
7. Stefan Morawski, *Inquiries into the Fundamentals of Aesthetics* (Cambridge, MA: MIT Press, 1974), p. 359.
8. Ruskin, *Modern Painters, Vol. III*, p. 94 (ch. 7). He cites William Holman Hunt's *The Awakening Conscience* (1853) and Millais's *A Huguenot on St. Bartholomew's Day* (1852) as examples of the trend.
9. Bolter and Grusin, *Remediation*, p. 45.
10. The *ILN* boasted a readership of a million Britons during the war (Keller, *Ultimate Spectacle*, p. 77). Realism in Crimean War art is most often identified with photography; many Victorians believed cameras could capture truth. Given the Crimean War's status as the first major European conflict to be photographed, it is perhaps unsurprising that Roger Fenton's pictures of the war have garnered more critical attention than its other cultural fruits. John Leech also admired them greatly, as a letter to Millais indicates: "You should come to town, if only to see a collection of photographs taken in the Crimea. They are surprisingly good; I don't think anything ever affected me more. You hardly miss the colour, the truth in other respects is so wonderful" (Leech, letter to Millais, October 23, 1855, in J. G. Millais, *Life and letters*, 1:270–71). But as Lalumia (*Realism and Politics*, p. 121) and Keller (*Ultimate Spectacle*, p. 125) have argued, Fenton's photographs are not as invested in portraying the real experience of war as the work of the "Special Artists" for the illustrated magazines and the watercolors of William Simpson (collected in a popular lithograph set entitled *Seat of the War in the East* [1855–56]). Both critics note, however, that the less famous photographs by James Robertson (and Felice Beato, according to Keller's joint attribution) caught the real feel of a place at war (Lalumia, *Realism and Politics*, pp. 123–24; Keller, *Ultimate Spectacle*, pp. 164–67). See also Helen Groth, "Technological Mediations and the Public Sphere: Roger Fenton's Crimea Exhibition and 'The Charge of the Light Brigade,'" *Victorian Literature and Culture* 30.2 (2002), 553–70. Groth argues that "like Tennyson, Fenton is far more preoccupied with the artistic status of his

Notes to pages 170–179

work and questions of formal experimentation than with the political implications of . . . historic events" (557).

11. Kate Flint, *The Victorians and the Visual Imagination* (Cambridge: Cambridge University Press, 2000), p. 216.
12. "Exhibition of the Royal Academy," *The Times*, May 18, 1857, 9.
13. Lalumia, *Realism and Politics*, p. 102.
14. Flint, *Visual Imagination*, pp. 223–24.
15. G. F. Dallas, letter to his family, December 21, 1855, in *Eyewitness*, p. 213 and note; the episode is recalled in Soyers's *A Culinary Campaign* (p. 277). Frances Duberly also records tampering with the illustrations, albeit more benignly, by coloring them in (*Journal*, p. 296).
16. Barringer, *Reading the Pre-Raphaelites*, pp. 18, 8.
17. Keller, *Ultimate Spectacle*, p. 29.
18. Kingsley, letter to William Cox Bennet, quoted in Arthur Pollard, *The Victorians*, vol. VI of *The History of Literature in the English Language*, 9 vols. (London: Barrie and Jenkins, 1970), p. 214.
19. Kingsley, *Two Years Ago*, II:5.
20. "I have studied [Guys's] archives of the Eastern War – battlefields, littered with the debris of death, baggage-trains, shipments of cattle and horses," Baudelaire wrote, "they are *tableaux vivants* of an astonishing vitality, traced from life itself, uniquely picturesque fragments which many a renowned painter would in the same circumstances have stupidly overlooked." *Charles Baudelaire, The Painter of Modern Life and Other Essays*, trans. and ed. Jonathan Mayne (London: Phaidon Press, 1964), pp. 18, 6. The essay first appeared in December, 1863. Simon Houfe also notes the appropriateness of Baudelaire's designation to Leech, but not its Crimean connection. See *John Leech and the Victorian Scene* (Woodbridge, Suffolk: Antique Collectors' Club, 1984), p. 83.
21. *ILN*, March 17, 1855, 260.
22. Both *ILN*, March 3, 1855, 213. Keller attributes the *ILN* illustrations to Guys (*Ultimate Spectacle*, p. 105).
23. The war, which started during the era of what *Punch* called the "Moustache Movement," also led to a vogue for full beards that had its roots in the inconvenience of shaving at the front.
24. *Punch* 28 (1855), 4. Further references in this chapter to illustrations and articles in *Punch* will be internally documented by volume and page number.
25. Fenton, letter to his wife, May 5, 1855, in *Roger Fenton: Photographer of the Crimean War, His Photographs and his Letters from The Crimea*, ed. and intro. Helmut and Alison Gersheim (New York: Arno Press, 1973), p. 71.
26. Keller notes how the spectacle of the camp at Chobham allowed illustrations of the war to slide easily between the false and the real – the acting of exercises and the action of battle – at its beginning (*Ultimate Spectacle*, pp. 5–6).
27. I believe the published sketch to be a spirited cartoon entitled "This is the Protection a Plaid Affords to Those Who do not Know the Way to Carry It"

(25:162), depicting a man pushing his way blindly through a storm with his head entirely submersed in the said plaid; J. G. Millais records a sketch done the evening of his father's plaid-clad adventures through a storm (*Life and letters*, 1:198). The correspondence between Millais and Leech is quoted in Houfe, *John Leech*, pp. 128–29.

28. Paul Barlow, *Time Present and Time Past: The Art of John Everett Millais* (Aldershot, Hants: Ashgate, 2005), p. 31.
29. Houfe, *John Leech*, p. 129.
30. See Jason Rosenfeld and Alison Smith (with contributions by Heather Birchall), *Millais* (catalogue to the 2007–08 Tate exhibition of Millais's work) (London: Tate Publishing, 2007), p. 82.
31. The Astley's spectacular was also used to point out the inadequacies of the government's war effort: a piece in *Punch* entitled "The Military Authorities at Astley's" declares that "We fear that some of the official managers of our war have been conducting it on Astleian ideas, without recollecting that we have not Astleian fortresses to attack" (28:50).
32. December 11, 1855; quoted in Lalumia, *Realism and Politics*, p. 101.
33. See Sussman, *Victorian Masculinities*, p. 156. Sussman shows that Carlyle positions the "Man of Letters" as a hero in part by identifying him with the work ethic of his "Captains of Industry." He also points out that Samuel Smiles sees "workers in art" as persevering through "indefatiguable industry" to be self-made men – again, the artist is situated among the industrialists (p. 117). *Self-Help* was written before the war, but Smiles was able to find a publisher for the book only after the war had made the idea of class mobility more generally appealing, as Olive Anderson has argued (*Liberal State*, p. 109). Many novels of the war period indicate the changing view of the artist by including artist-figures who use their profession to rise in the world. Consider Gowan in *Little Dorrit* or Clive Newcome in *The Newcomes* for examples of this trend.
34. Hunt, *Pre-Raphaelitism*, 1:368.
35. *Ibid.*, 11:83.
36. Quoted in Lalumia, *Realism and Politics*, p. 92.
37. Hunt, *Pre-Raphaelitism*, 1:498.
38. Sussman, *Victorian Masculinities*, p. 161.
39. Hunt, *Pre-Raphaelitism*, 1:490–91.
40. George Du Maurier, *Trilby*, intro. Elaine Showalter, notes Dennis Denisoff (Oxford: Oxford University Press, 1998), pp. 4–5.
41. Keller mentions the Leech cartoon (without attribution) in a footnote (*Ultimate Spectacle*, p. 264, n. 136). He discusses popular depictions of the charge on p. 50.
42. *Ibid.*, p. 50; [Russell], "The Operations of the Siege," *The Times*, November 14, 1854, 7.
43. Keller, *Ultimate Spectacle*, p. 50.
44. Cardigan's charge was actually emblazoned on playing cards. See Detlef Hoffman and Margit Dietrich, *Geschichte auf Spielkarten 1789–1871. Von*

der Französischen Revolution bis zur Reichsgründung (Stuttgart: Württembergisches Landesmuseum, 1987), pp. 137, 296. Keller cites this source.
45. Indeed, when I first saw it linked to him (by a website dedicated to his cartoons), I doubted the accuracy of the attribution, which can be made securely on the basis of the initials that appear in the bottom left-hand corner. See www.john-leech-archive.org.uk.
46. Tate, "On Not Knowing Why," pp. 165–66.
47. Simon Schama, *Simon Schama's Power of Art* (London: BBC Books, 2006), pp. 196, 193.
48. Tate, "On Not Knowing Why," p. 165.
49. For more on the Nation-building function of the cartoon, see my reading of it in chapter 1.
50. For this painting's antiwar stance, see Marcia Pointon, "Pictorial Narrative in the Art of William Mulready," *The Burlington Magazine* 122 (April, 1980), 229–37. Paul Barlow writes that Mulready's work "was probably Millais's model" for *Peace Concluded, 1856*, discussed below (*Time Present*, p. 65).
51. For my account of Collinson's paintings, I am indebted to *The Tate Gallery 1984–86: Illustrated Catalogue of Acquisitions Including Supplement to Catalogue of Acquisitions 1982–84* (London: Tate Gallery, 1988), pp. 12–17.
52. See "A Briton," "Eton and the War," letter to the editor, *The Times*, December 2, 1854, 10; and "An Old Rugbeian," "Rugby and the War," letter to the editor, *The Times*, December 5, 1854, 6.
53. [Procter], "The Two Spirits," *Household Words* 10 (1855), 516.
54. Henry Newbolt, "Vitaï Lampada," in *War Poetry*, ed. Stallworthy, p. 146.
55. Keller emphasizes the place of spectacle in the home-front experience of the Crimean War, noting in particular the role of spectaculars (like those at Astley's and Cremorne Gardens) and panoramas (Burford's) (see *Ultimate Spectacle*, esp. pp. 59–60).
56. Leech, letter to Millais, June 14, 1855, in J. G. Millais, *Life and letters*, 1:270.
57. See, for example, Leech, letter to Millais, October 23, 1855, in J. G. Millais, *Life and letters*, 1:272.
58. Tate, "On Not Knowing Why," p. 165.
59. Leech's most famous Crimean War cartoon – a "big cut" titled "'General Février' Turned Traitor" – operates on yet another level (March 10, 1855, 28:95). It shows the recently deceased Czar Nicholas succumbing to the same wintry spirit (the titular "General," whose skeletal figure, encased in Russian uniform, reaches a bony hand out to touch the sleeping emperor) that had saved the Russians against Napoleon's invading forces. Fundamentally allegorical, the cartoon (for all its timeliness) has the timeless effect of all political satire directed towards the mortality of kings and rulers.
60. Flint, *Visual Imagination*, p. 76.
61. Hunt, *Pre-Raphaelitism*, 11:105.
62. Ford Madox Brown, *Diary of Ford Madox Brown*, ed. Virginia Surtees (New Haven: Yale University Press for the Paul Mellon Center, 1981), p. 169; entry for April 11, 1856.

63. *The Critic, London Literary Journal* 15 (May 15, 1856), 252. I am indebted to both Lalumia's book (*Realism and Politics*) and Michael Hancher's article, "'Urgent private affairs': Millais's 'Peace concluded, 1856,'" *The Burlington Magazine* 133 (August, 1991), 499–506, for references to the critical reviews and other artists' responses to Millais's painting.
64. Pictures of the Queen inspecting her injured soldiers were common, as Keller has demonstrated (*Ultimate Spectacle*, pp. 180–89). Soldiers had complained that the Commissariat's coffee was unroasted, thus rendering it useless at the front.
65. For other mentions of this cartoon in relation to Millais's painting, see Lalumia, *Realism and Politics*, p. 95; and *The Tate Gallery 1984–86*, pp. 12–17.
66. Hancher, "'Urgent private affairs,'" 501.
67. *Ibid.*, 503.
68. "The Royal Academy," *Art-Journal* n.s. 2 (June 1, 1856), 165; *Morning Chronicle*, May 5, 1856, 7. See also Hancher, "'Urgent private affairs,'" 502.
69. J. G. Millais, *Life and letters*, 1:310. See Tennyson, *Poems* (London: Moxon, 1857), p. 161; and Hancher, "'Urgent private affairs,'" 506. Hancher, who notes the illustration but not the mislabeled sketch, focuses on the fact that this picture also shows a male patient; I am more struck by how King Edward's continued dominance distinguishes him from the officer of *Peace Concluded*. Perhaps the distinction owes something to historical setting; it suggests the gulf between medieval and bourgeois manhood.
70. Hancher, "'Urgent private affairs,'" 499.
71. See *ibid.*, 504–05; he gives Jenny Spencer-Smith credit for the identification. Lalumia, *Realism and Politics*, p. 18.
72. Hancher, "'Urgent private affairs,'" 505.
73. Barlow, *Time Present*, p. 67.
74. Garrett Stewart, *The Look of Reading: Book, Painting, Text* (Chicago: University of Chicago Press, 2006), pp. 7, 3, 24. Stewart attributes the term "lectoral art" to James Heffernan.
75. *Ibid.*, p. 24. See Thackeray, *The Newcomes*, pp. 144–45, for the scene.
76. Hancher, "'Urgent private affairs,'" 504.
77. Thackeray, *The Newcomes*, pp. 87, 128, 208, 655.
78. Barlow, *Time Present*, p. 74.
79. *Ibid.*, p. 60.
80. See Hancher, "'Urgent private affairs,'" 499.
81. Barlow, *Time Present*, p. 66. This connection can be made even more convincing by comparing the composition of *Peace Concluded* to that of the illustration to Tennyson mentioned earlier, which uses the basic pose of the officer in a medieval setting.
82. *Ibid.*, p. 61.
83. Keller notes the production and the Fenton connection but not Millais's painting (*Ultimate Spectacle*, p. 174).
84. Barlow, *Time Present*, p. 74.
85. Hancher, "'Urgent private affairs,'" 504.

86. Chris Brooks, *Signs for the Times: Symbolic Realism in the Mid-Victorian World* (Boston: Allen and Unwin, 1984), p. 127.
87. Flint, *Visual Imagination*, p. 76. She quotes from Martin Jay's *Downcast Eyes: The Denigration of Vision in Twentieth-Century French Thought* (1993). Millais's 1856 exhibit was rounded off (or perhaps topped) by the magisterial *Autumn Leaves*, today probably the most admired and most discussed of his paintings of that year – and (not coincidentally) the least topical. It is also less like a Pre-Raphaelite painting than the works I have considered, having little narrative content. Indeed, its elegiac effect is impressionistic, even proto-modernist.
88. Flint, *Visual Imagination*, p. 75; Barlow, *Time Present*, p. 66; Rosenfeld and Smith, *Millais*, p. 108.
89. "Royal Academy," *Art-Journal* n.s. 2 (June 1, 1856), 166.
90. John Ruskin, *Academy Notes, Notes on Prout and Hunt, and Other Art Criticism, 1855–1888*, vol. XIV of the *Library Edition of the Complete Works of John Ruskin*, ed. E. T. Cook and Alexander Wedderburn (London: George Allen, 1904), p. 57.
91. For more on this poem and aesthetic vision, see Sussman, *Victorian Masculinities*, p. 119. One might also compare the intensity of such visual experience, which (as Sussman notes) Pater terms "the insanity of realism" in his essay on Rossetti, to the peculiar visual perceptiveness kindled by the pressures of war. See Henry Kingsley's description of the latter phenomenon in *Ravenshoe* (p. 334).
92. *Crayon* III (1856), p. 104. See Hancher, "'Urgent private affairs,'" 501. Hancher also notes that the review in the *Morning Post* (May 3, 1856, p. 5) may have suggested this reading of the painting.
93. The pose bears some resemblance to that of the central daughter in Leech's "Enthusiasm" cartoon, although her expression is far more difficult to read.
94. Hancher, "'Urgent private affairs,'" 506. The paintings to which he refers include the *The Proscribed Royalist, 1651* and *The Order of Release, 1746* (mentioned below) and the Tennyson illustration, *Dream of Fair Women* (discussed above). Millais's *The Rescue* (1855) depicts the reverse situation: a firefighter carries two children down the stairs of a burning house, while their mother, who kneels below, reaches up gratefully towards them. Of course this heroic working-class intruder into a bourgeois domestic space that has been ruptured by crisis offers a stark contrast to the gentleman-officer of *Peace Concluded* in more ways than one.
95. This cartoon can be attributed to Captain Henry R. Howard (identified by his trident mark). Howard was known for his fantastical animal illustrations, creatures half-man half-beast. Even when tackling topical subjects, his tendency was towards fantasy rather than realism, as in his depiction of Florence Nightingale as a nightingale (27:215). See M. H. Spielmann, *The History of Punch* (London: Cassell, 1895), p. 476.
96. According to J. G. Millais it was painted in the spring of 1856 – that is, at roughly the same time as *Peace Concluded* (*Life and letters*, 1:291). Gordon

H. Fleming (*John Everett Millais: A Biography* [London: Constable, 1998], ch. 15.), however, attributes the composition to a later date, claiming it was painted to capitalize on the success of *Peace Concluded*.

97. Ruskin, *Academy Notes*, p. 95.
98. For all its critical failure, *News from Home* was a commercial success, selling for more than any previous painting by Millais. Its noble soldier subject and sentimental reminder of the role of letters in the war experience no doubt appealed to popular tastes at the time. See Fleming, *John Everett Millais*, ch. 15.
99. Compare Walter Benjamin's concept of "the outmoded." Benjamin considers the Surrealists' interest in the decaying structures of modernity to represent an attack on bourgeois capitalism's tendency to privilege all that is new – a tendency manifested in *Peace Concluded*. See Walter Benjamin, "Surrealism: The Last Snapshot of the European Intelligentsia," in *One-Way Street and Other Writings*, trans. Edmund Jephcott and Kingsley Shorter (London: New Left Review, 1979), pp. 225–39.
100. Barlow, *Time Present*, p. 48. *The Proscribed Royalist, 1651* shows a Puritan woman protecting a royalist who has hidden in the hollowed-out trunk of a tree in the aftermath of the Battle of Worcester. For a brief description of *The Order of Release, 1746*, see above.

AFTERWORD: ELIZABETH THOMPSON, LADY BUTLER, 'THE ROLL CALL,' AND THE AFTERLIFE OF THE CRIMEAN WAR

1. Elizabeth Butler, *An Autobiography* (London: Constable and Co., 1922), p. 110. Hereafter, internally referenced by page number unless otherwise noted.
2. For all its snowy setting, the painting has often been associated with the Battle of Inkerman, probably (as Paul Usherwood and Jenny Spencer-Smith argue) because its focus on the rank-and-file soldiers accords with Inkerman's designation as "the soldier's battle." See Paul Usherwood and Jenny Spencer-Smith, *Lady Butler, Battle Artist, 1846–1933* (London: Alan Sutton/ National Army Museum, 1987), p. 35. The following account of Butler's career and of critical responses to her work is greatly indebted to Usherwood and Spencer-Smith's superb catalogue.
3. See "The Royal Academy, Second Notice," *Morning Post*, May 7, 1874, 2.
4. Usherwood and Spencer-Smith, *Lady Butler*, p. 31.
5. [Edward Lindley Sambourne], "Punch's Essence of Parliament," *Punch* 67 (1874), 55.
6. "The Royal Academy, Second Notice," *Morning Post*, May 7, 1874, 2.
7. Wordsworth, Preface to *Lyrical Ballads* (1800), in *The Prose Works of William Wordsworth*, ed. W. J. B. Owen and Jane Worthington Smyser, 3 vols. (Oxford: The Clarendon Press, 1974), 1:128.
8. [Tom Taylor], "Exhibition of the Royal Academy," *The Times*, May 2, 1874, 12. For more on the relationship between action and character in the period, see my book, *The Crisis of Action*.

9. Wilfred Meynell, "The Life and Work of Lady Butler," *Art Annual* (1898), 31.
10. Lalumia, *Realism and Politics*, pp. 140–41.
11. Keller, *Ultimate Spectacle*, pp. 246–47. Compare Leech's cartoon, "Grand Military Spectacle: The Heroes of the Crimea Inspecting the Field Marshalls" (*Punch* 29 [1855], 179), in which standing injured privates scathingly "inspect" their clownishly portrayed seated superiors.
12. See Lalumia, *Realism and Politics*, pp. 132–35. Lalumia elsewhere notes that non-military paintings of the period were showing an increased interest in the suffering of the lower classes. See "Lady Elizabeth Thompson Butler in the 1870s," *Woman's Art Journal* 4 (1983), 9–14, esp. 12–13, where he discusses the relationship of Butler's work to the art of the British Social Realists.
13. See *Autobiography*, p. 47; *Saturday Review*, May 16, 1874; and Thompson's father's clarifying letter in *The Times*, May 11, 1874: "May I, once and for all... beg to assure all who are placed to take an interest in my daughter that ... she is not, and never has been, never could be a hospital nurse."
14. *Spectator*, May 9, 1874; [George Augustus Sala], "Exhibition of the Royal Academy," *Daily Telegraph*, May 2, 1874, 5; [Tom Taylor], "Exhibition of the Royal Academy," *The Times*, May 2, 1874, 12.
15. [Taylor], "Exhibition of the Royal Academy," 12.
16. Ruskin, "Academy Notes, 1875," in *Academy Notes*, p. 308. He continues by claiming for *The Roll Call* the distinction of being "the first fine Pre-Raphaelite picture of battle we have had," suggesting (as the previous chapter has posited) the connection between versions of realism to come out of the Crimean War and the Pre-Raphaelite movement that was technically ending as the war began. Butler "was very pleased to see [her]self in the character of an Amazon" (*Autobiography*, p. 146).
17. For more on the election, see Usherwood and Spencer-Smith, *Lady Butler*, pp. 37–40.
18. Sala, "Exhibition of the Royal Academy," 5. See Anthea Callen, *The Angel in the Studio: Women Artists of the Arts and Crafts Movement, 1870–1914* (New York: Pantheon, 1979).
19. See my discussion of Leech's "Trump Card(igan)" cartoon in chapter 4.
20. See "Fine-Art Gossip," *Athenaeum*, April 16, 1881, 534; quoted in Usherwood and Spencer-Smith, *Lady Butler*, p. 83.
21. Quoted in "Lady Butler, A Famous Military Painter," Obituary, *The Times*, October 3, 1933, 7.
22. Usherwood and Spencer-Smith, *Lady Butler*, p. 15.
23. Quoted *ibid.*, p. 112.
24. For the literary response to this war, see M. Van Wyk Smith (*Drummer Hodge*) and Paula M. Krebs (*Gender, Race, Empire*). The First Boer War of 1881–82 had also offered a model of military failure.
25. Indeed, Butler notes that she was in South Africa when the painting was exhibited (*Autobiography*, p. 271).
26. Such an enactment, captured on a postcard photograph, was done at Aldershot in 1909 (see Usherwood and Spencer-Smith, *Lady Butler*,

p. 35), and it is possible that *The Times* got its dates wrong. But a later misremembering would itself be suggestive of what the Crimean War had come to mean.

27. Sharon Smulders considers the tensions in Meynell's war poetry in "Feminism, Pacifism, and the Ethics of War: The Politics and Poetics of Alice Meynell's War Verse," *English Literature in Transition* 36 (1993), 159–77. Meynell's "militant" poem "A Father of Women," which uses First World War losses to put forth an argument for female enfranchisement, is dedicated to Butler (172). Her earlier (Boer) war poetry had connected feminism and pacifism.

Bibliography

Full references to articles, poems, and illustrations from the following sources are given in the notes:

Daily Telegraph
Dictionary of National Biography (DNB)
Household Words
Illustrated London News (ILN)
Morning Chronicle
Morning Post
Oxford English Dictionary (OED)
Punch
The Times

Attributions to unsigned articles and poems are from the *Wellesley Index to Victorian Periodicals, 1824–1900*, unless otherwise stated in the notes. Unattributed reviews are collected alphabetically by title of work reviewed under "Unsigned."

Addams, Michael C. C., "Tennyson's Crimean War Poetry: a Cross-Cultural Approach," *Journal of the History of Ideas* 40.3 (1979), 405–22.
Anderson, Benedict, *Imagined Communities: Reflections on the Origins and Spread of Nationalism*, New York: Verso, 1991.
Anderson, Olive, *A Liberal State at War: English Politics and Economics during the Crimean War*, London: Macmillan, 1967.
Anderson, Patricia, *The Printed Image and the Transformation of Popular Culture, 1790–1860*, Oxford: The Clarendon Press, 1994.
Armstrong, Isobel, *Victorian Poetry: Poetry, Poetics and Politics*, London: Routledge, 1993.
Armstrong, Nancy, *Desire and Domestic Fiction: A Political History of the Novel*, New York: Oxford University Press, 1987.
Arnold, Matthew, *Matthew Arnold: Selected Poems and Prose*, ed. Miriam Allott, London: J. M. Dent, 1993.

Aspinall, Arthur, *Politics and the Press, c. 1780–1850*, London: Home & Van Thal, Ltd., 1949.
Assad, Thomas J., "Tennyson's 'Courage, Poor Heart of Stone,'" *Tulane Studies in English* 18 (1970), 73–80.
[Aytoun, William Edmonstoune], "Mrs Barrett Browning – Aurora Leigh," *Blackwood's Edinburgh Magazine* 81 (January, 1857), 23–41.
  "Poetic Aberrations" [review of Barrett Browning's *Poems Before Congress* (1860)], *Blackwood's Edinburgh Magazine* 87 (April, 1860), 490–94.
  "The Reverend Charles Kingsley," *Blackwood's Edinburgh Magazine* 77 (June, 1855), 625–43.
[Bagehot, Walter], review of Tennyson's *Idylls of the King*, *National Review* 9 (October, 1859), 368–94.
Baker, Ernest A., *The History of the English Novel: Volume VIII, From the Brontës to Meredith: Romanticism in the English Novel*, New York: Barnes and Noble, Inc., 1936, reprinted 1966.
Baker, William J., "Charles Kingsley on the Crimean War: A Study in Chauvinism," *Southern Humanities Review* 4.3 (1970), 247–56.
[Ballantyne, Thomas], "Lancashire Strikes," *Blackwood's Edinburgh Magazine* 79 (January, 1856), 52–60.
Barlow, Paul, *Time Present and Time Past: The Art of John Everett Millais*, Aldershot, Hants: Ashgate, 2005.
Barringer, Tim, *Reading the Pre-Raphaelites*, New Haven: Yale University Press, 1999.
Baudelaire, Charles, *Charles Baudelaire, The Painter of Modern Life and Other Essays*, trans. and ed. Jonathan Mayne, London: Phaidon Press, 1964.
Benjamin, Walter, *One-Way Street and Other Writings*, trans. Edmund Jephcott and Kingsley Shorter, London: New Left Review, 1979.
Bennett, James, "The Historical Abuse of Literature: Tennyson's *Maud: A Monodrama* and the Crimean War," *English Studies* 62 (1981), 34–45.
Bolter, Jay David and Richard Grusin, *Remediation: Understanding New Media*, Cambridge, MA: MIT Press, 1999.
Brantlinger, Patrick, *Rule of Darkness: British Literature and Imperialism 1830–1914*, Ithaca: Cornell University Press, 1988.
Bratton, J. S., "Theatre of War: The Crimea on the London Stage 1854–5," in *Performance and Politics in Popular Drama*, ed. David Bradby, Louis James, and Bernard Sharratt, Cambridge: Cambridge University Press, 1980, pp. 119–37.
Bristow, Joseph, "Nation, Class, and Gender: Tennyson's *Maud* and War," *Genders* 9 (November, 1990), 92–114.
Brooks, Chris, *Signs for the Times: Symbolic Realism in the Mid-Victorian World*, Boston: Allen and Unwin, 1984.
Brown, Ford Madox, *Diary of Ford Madox Brown*, ed. Virginia Surtees, New Haven: Yale University Press for the Paul Mellon Center, 1981.
Browning, Elizabeth Barrett, *Aurora Leigh*, ed. and intro. Margaret Reynolds, Athens: Ohio University Press, 1992.

Aurora Leigh and Other Poems, ed. John Robert Glorney Bolton and Julia Bolton Holloway, London: Penguin, 1995.
Last Poems, London: Chapman and Hall, 1862.
The Letters of Elizabeth Barrett Browning, ed. with biographical additions Frederick G. Kenyon, 2 vols., New York: Macmillan, 1910.
Browning, Robert, *Robert Browning: The Poems*, ed. John Pettigrew, supplemented and completed Thomas J. Collins, 2 vols., London: Penguin, 1993.
Butler, Elizabeth, *An Autobiography*, London: Constable and Co., 1922.
Calder, Angus, *The People's War*, London: Pimlico, 1992.
Callen, Anthea, *The Angel in the Studio: Women Artists of the Arts and Crafts Movement, 1870–1914*, New York: Pantheon, 1979.
Carlyle, Thomas and Jane Welsh, *Carlyle's Lectures on Heroes, Hero-Worship and the Heroic in History*, ed. P. C. Parr, Oxford: The Clarendon Press, 1920.
The Collected Letters of Thomas and Jane Welsh Carlyle, ed. Kenneth J. Fielding, Durham, NC: Duke University Press, 2001.
Chakravarty, Gautam, *The Indian Mutiny and the British Imagination*, Cambridge: Cambridge University Press, 2005.
Chandler, James, *England in 1819: The Politics of Literary Culture and the Case of Romantic Historicism*, Chicago: University of Chicago Press, 1998.
[Chorley, Henry Fothergill], review of *North and South*, *Athenaeum*, April 7, 1855, 403.
Clough, Arthur Hugh, *Clough's Selected Poems*, ed. J. P. Phelan, London: Longman, 1995.
Correspondence of Arthur Hugh Clough, ed. F. L. Mulhauser, 2 vols., Oxford: The Clarendon Press, 1957.
Colley, Linda, *Britons: Forging the Nation, 1707–1837*, 2nd edn., New Haven: Yale University Press, 2005.
Collins, Joseph J., "Tennyson and the Spasmodics," *The Victorian Newsletter* 43 (1973), 24–28.
Collins, Wilkie, *The Moonstone*, ed. John Sutherland, Oxford: Oxford University Press, 1999.
Colloms, Brenda, *Charles Kingsley: The Lion of Eversley*, London: Constable, 1975.
Connacher, J. B., *Britain and the Crimea: 1855–56: Problems of War and Peace*, Basingstoke, Hampshire: Macmillan, 1987.
Cook, Sir Edward, *The Life of Florence Nightingale*, 2 vols., London: Macmillan and Co., 1913.
Cooper, Helen, "England: The Imagined Community of Aurora Leigh and Mrs. Seacole," *Studies in Browning and His Circle* 20 (1993), 123–31.
Cotsell, Michael, "Politics and Peeling Frescoes: Layard of Ninevah and *Little Dorrit*," *Dickens Studies Annual* (1986), 181–200.
Culler, Dwight, "Monodrama and the Dramatic Monologue," *PMLA* 90.3 (May, 1975), 366–85.
Dallas, E. S., *The Gay Science*, 2 vols., London: Chapman and Hall, 1866, reprinted by Johnson Reprint Corporation.

Dallas, George Frederick, *Eyewitness in the Crimea: The Crimean War Letters (1854–1856) of Lieutenant Colonel George Frederick Dallas*, ed. Michael Hargreave Mawson, London: Greenhill Books, 2001.
David, Deidre, *Intellectual Women and Victorian Patriarchy: Harriet Martineau, Elizabeth Barrett Browning, George Eliot*, Ithaca: Cornell University Press, 1987.
Davis, Elizabeth, *The Autobiography of Elizabeth Davis*, ed. Jane Williams, 2 vols., London: Hurst & Blackett, 1857.
Dentith, Simon, *Epic and Empire in Nineteenth-Century Britain*, Cambridge: Cambridge University Press, 2006.
Dereli, Cynthia, "Gender Issues and the Crimean War: Creating Roles for Women?," in *Gender Roles and Sexuality in Victorian Literature*, ed. Christopher Parker, Aldershot: Scolar Press, 1995, pp. 57–82.
Dickens, Charles, *Little Dorrit*, ed. John Holloway, London: Penguin, 1985.
Dobell, Sydney, *England In Time of War*, London: Smith, Elder & Co., 1856.
Life and Letters of Sydney Dobell, ed. Emily Jolly, 2 vols., London: 1876.
Dobell, Sydney and Alexander Smith, *Sonnets on the War*, London: David Bogue, 1855.
Duberly, Mrs. Henry [Frances Isabella], *Journal Kept During The Russian War*, London: Longman, Brown, Green, and Longmans, 1855.
Du Maurier, George, *Trilby*, intro. Elaine Showalter, notes Dennis Denisoff, Oxford: Oxford University Press, 1998.
Dutton, H. I. and J. E. King, *"Ten Per Cent and No Surrender": The Preston Strike, 1853–1854*, Cambridge: Cambridge University Press, 1981.
[Eliot, George], "Contemporary Literature," *Westminster Review* 65 o.s., 9 n.s. (October, 1856), 566–70.
The Mill on the Floss, ed. Gordon Haight, intro. Dinah Birch, Oxford: Oxford University Press, 1996.
Favret, Mary A., "War Correspondence: Reading Romantic War," *Prose Studies* 19.2 (August, 1996), 173–85.
Fenton, Roger, *Roger Fenton: Photographer of the Crimean War, His Photographs and his Letters from The Crimea*, ed. and intro. Helmut and Alison Gersheim, New York: Arno Press, 1973.
Fleming, Gordon H., *John Everett Millais: A Biography*, London: Constable, 1998.
Flint, Kate, "The Victorian Novel and its Readers," in *The Cambridge Companion to the Victorian Novel*, ed. Deirdre David, Cambridge: Cambridge University Press, 2001, pp. 17–36.
The Victorians and the Visual Imagination, Cambridge: Cambridge University Press, 2000.
Friedman, Susan, "Gender and Genre Anxiety: Elizabeth Browning and H. D. as Epic Poets," *Tulsa Studies in Women's Literature* 5 (1986), 203–28.
Fussell, Paul, *The Great War and Modern Memory*, 25th anniversary edn., Oxford: Oxford University Press, 2000.
Gaskell, Elizabeth, *The Letters of Mrs. Gaskell*, ed. J. A. V. Chapple and Arthur Pollard, Manchester: Mandolin, 1997.

North and South, ed. Angus Easson, intro. Sally Shuttleworth, Oxford: Oxford University Press, 1998.
Gilmour, Robin, *The Victorian Period: The Intellectual and Cultural Context of English Literature, 1830–1890*, London: Longman, 1993.
Girouard, Mark, *The Return to Camelot: Chivalry and the English Gentleman*, New Haven: Yale University Press, 1981.
[Gladstone, William], "Tennyson's Poems," *Quarterly Review* 106 (October, 1859): 461–64.
[Greg, W. R.], "The Newspaper Press," *Edinburgh Review* 101 (October, 1855), 470–98.
Grey, Elizabeth, *The Noise of Drums and Trumpets: W. H. Russell Reports from the Crimea*, London: Longman, 1971.
Griffiths, Eric, "Tennyson's Breath," in *Critical Essays on Alfred Lord Tennyson*, ed. Herbert F. Tucker, New York: G. K. Hall and Co., 1993, pp. 28–47.
Groth, Helen, "Technological Mediations and the Public Sphere: Roger Fenton's Crimea Exhibition and 'The Charge of the Light Brigade,'" *Victorian Literature and Culture* 30.2 (2002), 553–70.
Habermas, Jürgen, *The Structural Transformation of the Public Sphere: An Enquiry into a Category of Bourgeois Society*, trans. Thomas Burger with Frederick Lawrence, Cambridge, MA: MIT Press, 1991.
Haldane, Elizabeth, *Mrs Gaskell and Her Friends*, London: Hodder & Stoughton, 1931.
[Hamley, Edward Bruce], "Poetry of the War: Reviewed Before Sebastopol," *Blackwood's Edinburgh Magazine* 77 (May, 1855), 531–35.
The Story of the Campaign, *Blackwood's Edinburgh Magazine* 76–77 (1854–55).
Hancher, Michael, "'Urgent private affairs': Millais's 'Peace concluded, 1856,'" *The Burlington Magazine* 133 (August, 1991), 499–506.
Hankinson, Alan, *Man of Wars: William Howard Russell of The Times*, London: Heinemann, 1982.
Hawley, John C., "Charles Kingsley and Literary Theory of the 1850s," *Victorian Literature and Culture* 19 (1991), 167–88.
Hayter, Althea, *Charlotte Yonge*, Plymouth: Northcote House, 1996.
Haywood, Ian, *The Revolution in Popular Literature: Print, Politics and the People, 1790–1860*, Cambridge: Cambridge University Press, 2004.
Helgerson, Richard, *Forms of Nationhood: The Elizabethan Writing of England*, Chicago: University of Chicago Press, 1992.
Hitchens, Christopher, "The Grub Street Years," review of *Dispatches for the New York Tribune: Selected Journalism of Karl Marx*, *Saturday Guardian* (London), June 16, 2007, Review, 4–6.
Holmes, Rachel, *Scanty Particulars: The Life of Dr James Barry*, London: Viking, 2002.
Houfe, Simon, *John Leech and the Victorian Scene*, Woodbridge, Suffolk: Antique Collectors' Club, 1984.

Houston, Natalie, "Reading the Victorian Souvenir: Sonnets and Photographs of the Crimean War," *Yale Journal of Criticism* 14.2 (2001), 353–83.
Hughes, Linda K., *The Manyfacèd Glass: Tennyson's Dramatic Monologues*, Athens: Ohio University Press, 1987.
Hughes, Thomas, *The Manliness of Christ*, London: Macmillan, 1879.
  Tom Brown's Schooldays, London: The Epworth Press, n.d.
Hunt, William Holman, *Pre-Raphaelitism and the Pre-Raphaelite Brotherhood*, 2 vols., London: Macmillan, 1905.
Hunter, J. Paul, *Before Novels: The Cultural Contexts of Eighteenth-Century English Fiction*, New York: W. W. Norton & Co., 1990.
Hynes, Samuel, *A War Imagined: The First World War and English Culture*, London: The Bodley Head, 1990.
Judd, Catherine, *Bedside Seductions: Nursing and the Victorian Imagination, 1830–1880*, New York: St. Martin's, 1998.
Jump, John D. (ed.), *Tennyson: The Critical Heritage*, London: Routledge and Kegan Paul, 1967.
[Kaye, J. W.], "The Employment of Women," *North British Review* 26 (February, 1857), 291–338.
Keller, Ulrich, *The Ultimate Spectacle: A Visual History of the Crimean War*, Amsterdam: Overseas Publishers Association, 2001.
Kincaid, James R., *Tennyson's Major Poems: The Comic and Ironic Patterns*, New Haven: Yale University Press, 1975.
Kinglake, Alexander William, *The Invasion of the Crimea*, 8 vols., London: William Blackwood and Sons, 1863–87.
Kingsley, Charles, *Charles Kingsley: His Letters and Memories of His Life, Edited by His Wife* [Frances Kingsley], 2 vols., London: Henry S. King and Co., 1877.
  The Heroes; or Greek Fairy Tales for my Children, Cambridge: Macmillan and Co., 1856.
  review of Matthew Arnold's *Poems* (1853), *Fraser's Magazine* 49 (February, 1854), 140–49.
  review of *Maud*, *Fraser's Magazine* 52 (1855), 264–73.
  "Thoughts on Shelley and Byron," *Fraser's Magazine* 48 (November, 1853), 568–76.
  True Words for Brave Men, London: Kegan Paul, Tench & Co., 1878.
  Two Years Ago, 2 vols., vols. XIII–XIV of *The Life and Works of Charles Kingsley*, 19 vols., London: Macmillan and Co., 1902.
  Westward Ho!, or, The Voyages and Adventures of Sir Amyas Leigh, Knight, Of Burrough, in the County of Devon, in the Reign of Her Most Glorious Majesty, Queen Elizabeth, Rendered into Modern English By Charles Kingsley, 2nd edn., 3 vols., Cambridge: Macmillan and Co., 1855.
Kingsley, Henry, *Ravenshoe*, ed. and intro. William H. Scheuerle, Lincoln: University of Nebraska Press, 1967.
Knightley, Phillip, *The First Casualty: The War Correspondent as Hero and Myth-maker from the Crimea to Iraq*, Baltimore: The Johns Hopkins University Press, 2004.

Krebs, Paula M., *Gender, Race, and the Writing of Empire: Public Discourse and the Boer War*, Cambridge: Cambridge University Press, 1999.
Lalumia, Matthew Paul, "Lady Elizabeth Thompson Butler in the 1870s," *Woman's Art Journal* 4 (1983), 9–14.
  Realism and Politics in Victorian Art of the Crimean War, Ann Arbor, MI: UMI Research Press, 1984.
Lamb, Charles, "On the Tragedies of Shakspeare Considered with Reference to their Fitness for Stage Representation," in vol. 1 of *The Collected Works of Charles Lamb*, ed. E. V. Lucas, 8 vols., London: Methuen, 1912.
Lambert, Andrew, *The Crimean War: British Grand Strategy, 1853–56*, Manchester: Manchester University Press, 1990.
Langbaum, Robert, *The Poetry of Experience: The Dramatic Monologue in Modern Literary Tradition*, New York: W. W. Norton and Co., 1963.
Laughbaum, Anna Belle, *Some English Novels (1855–1917) That Deal with the Crimean War: An Abstract of a Thesis*, Urbana: University of Illinois, 1948.
Lawrence, G[eorge] A[lfred], *Sword and Gown*, Boston: Ticknor and Fields, 1859.
Longfellow, Henry Wadsworth, *Poetical Works*, 6 vols., Boston: Houghton Mifflin and Co., 1889–92.
Lootens, Tricia, "Victorian Poetry and Patriotism," in *The Cambridge Companion to Victorian Poetry*, ed. Joseph Bristow, Cambridge: Cambridge University Press, 2000, pp. 255–79.
Lushington, Henry and Franklin, *La Nation Boutiquière and other Poems, Chiefly Political, and Points of War*, Cambridge: Macmillan & Co., 1855.
Markovits, Stefanie, *The Crisis of Action in Nineteenth-Century English Literature*, Columbus, OH: The Ohio State University Press, 2006.
Marston, Westland, *The Death-Ride: A Tale of the Light Brigade*, London: C. Mitchell, 1855.
Martin, Robert Bernard, *The Dust of Combat: A Life of Charles Kingsley*, London: Faber and Faber, 1959.
Marx, Karl, *Dispatches for the New York Tribune: Selected Journalism of Karl Marx*, sel. and intro. James Ledbetter, foreword Francis Wheen, London: Penguin, 2007.
Massey, Gerald, *War Waits*, 2nd edn., London: David Bogue, 1855.
Maxwell, Bennett, "The Steytler Recordings of Alfred, Lord Tennyson: A History," *Tennyson Research Bulletin* 3.4 (1980), 150–57.
McGann, Jerome, *The Beauty of Inflections: Literary Investigations in Historical Method and Theory*, Oxford: The Clarendon Press, 1985.
Mermin, Dorothy, "Genre and Gender in *Aurora Leigh*," *The Victorian Newsletter* 69 (1986), 7–11.
Meynell, Wilfred, "The Life and Work of Lady Butler," *Art Annual* (1898), 1–31.
Millais, John Guille, *Life and letters of Sir John Everett Millais President of the Royal Academy: By his son John Guille Millais With 319 illustrations including nine photogravures*, 2 vols., London: Methuen and Co, 1899.
Miller, J. Hillis, *The Disappearance of God: Five Nineteenth-Century Writers*, Cambridge, MA: Harvard University Press, 1977.

Moore, Grace, *Dickens and Empire: Discourses of Class, Race and Colonialism in the Works of Charles Dickens*, Aldershot: Ashgate, 2004.
Morawski, Stefan, *Inquiries into the Fundamentals of Aesthetics*, Cambridge, MA: MIT Press, 1974.
Morris, James, *Pax Britannica, The Climax of an Empire*, London: Faber, 1973.
Neff, D. S., "*The Times*, the Crimean War, and 'Stanzas from the Grande Chartreuse,'" *Papers on Language and Literature* 33.2 (1997), 169–81.
Nightingale, Florence, *Cassandra*, intro. Myra Stark, epilogue Cynthia Macdonald, New York: The Feminist Press, 1979.
  Ever Yours, Florence Nightingale: Selected Letters, ed. Martha Vicinus and Bea Nergaard, London: Virago, 1989.
  Florence Nightingale: Letters from the Crimea, ed. Sue M. Goldie, Manchester: Mandolin, 1997.
  Florence Nightingale on Society and Politics, Philosophy, Science, Education, and Literature, ed. Lynn McDonald, vol. v of *The Collected Works of Florence Nightingale*, 16 vols., Waterloo, Ontario: Wilfred Laurier University Press, 2003.
  Notes on Nursing: What It Is, and What It Is Not, New York: Dover, 1969.
  Suggestions for Thought by Florence Nightingale: Selections and Commentaries, ed. Michael D. Calabria and Janet A. Macrea, Philadelphia: University of Pennsylvania Press, 1994.
Nolan, E. H., *Illustrated History of the War against Russia*, London: Virtue and Co., 1856.
[Oliphant, Margaret], "Modern Light Literature: Travellers' Tales," *Blackwood's Edinburgh Magazine* 78 (November, 1855), 586–99.
  "Modern Novelists – Great and Small," *Blackwood's Edinburgh Magazine* 77 (May, 1855), 554–68.
  "Sensation Novels," *Blackwood's Edinburgh Magazine* 91 (May, 1862), 564–84.
Palmer, Alan, *The Banner of Battle: The Story of the Crimean War*, London: Weidenfeld and Nicolson, 1987.
Patmore, Coventry, *The Angel in the House: The Espousals*, Boston: Ticknor and Fields, 1856.
  "Mrs. Browning's Poem," *North British Review* 26.2 (February, 1857), 443–62.
  review of *In Memoriam* and *Maud, and Other Poems*, *Edinburgh Review* 102 (October, 1855), 498–519.
Peck, John, *War, the Army and Victorian Literature*, New York: St. Martin's, 1998.
Philpotts, Trey, "Trevelyan, Treasury, and Circumlocution," *Dickens Studies Annual* (1993), 283–301.
Pinero, Arthur Wing, *Trelawny of the "Wells" and Other Plays*, ed. J. S. Bratton, Oxford: Oxford University Press, 1995.
Pointon, Marcia, "Pictorial Narrative in the Art of William Mulready," *The Burlington Magazine* 122 (April, 1980), 229–37.

Pollard, Arthur, *The Victorians*, vol. VI of *The History of Literature in the English Language*, 9 vols., London: Barrie and Jenkins, 1970.
Poovey, Mary, *Uneven Developments: The Ideological Work of Gender in Mid-Victorian England*, Chicago: University of Chicago Press, 1988.
Rader, Ralph Wilson, *Tennyson's "Maud": The Biographical Genesis*, Berkeley and Los Angeles: The University of California Press, 1963.
Reed, John R., "Soldier Boy: Masculinity in *Adam Bede*," *Studies in the Novel* 33.3 (2001), 268–84.
Reynolds, George W. M., *Omar: A Tale of the War*, *Reynolds's Miscellany* 13–15 (January, 1855–January, 1856).
Ricks, Christopher, *Tennyson*, 2nd edn., Houndmills, Basingstoke, Hampshire: Macmillan, 1989.
Ricks, Christopher and Edgar Shannon, "'The Charge of the Light Brigade': The Creation of a Poem," *Studies in Bibliography* 38 (1985), 1–44.
Robertson, Thomas William, *Ours*, in *The Principal Dramatic Works of Thomas William Robertson: With Memoir by his Son*, 2 vols., New York: Samuel French & Son, 1889.
Rose, June, *The Perfect Gentleman: The Remarkable Life of Dr James Miranda Barry*, London: Hutchinson, 1977.
Rosen, David, "The Volcano and the Cathedral: Muscular Christianity and the Origins of Primal Manliness," in *Muscular Christianity: Embodying the Victorian Age*, ed. Donald E. Hall, Cambridge: Cambridge University Press, 1994, pp. 17–44.
Rosenfeld, Jason and Alison Smith (contributions by Heather Birchall), *Millais*, London: Tate Publishing, 2007.
Royle, Trevor, *Crimea: The Great Crimean War, 1854–1856*, New York: Palgrave Macmillan, 2004.
Ruskin, John, *Academy Notes, Notes on Prout and Hunt, and Other Art Criticism, 1855–1888*, vol. XIV of the *Library Edition of the Complete Works of John Ruskin*, ed. E. T. Cook and Alexander Wedderburn, London: George Allen, 1904.
 Modern Painters, Vol. III, London: Smith, Elder and Co., 1856.
 Unto This Last, Munera Pulveris, Time and Tide, with other writings on political economy, 1860–1873, vol. XVII of the *Library Edition of the Complete Works of John Ruskin*, ed. E. T. Cook and Alexander Wedderburn, London: George Allen, 1905.
Russell, William Howard, *The Adventures of Doctor Brady*, 3 vols., London: Tinsley Brothers, 1868.
 The British Expedition to the Crimea: A Revised Edition, with Numerous Emendations and Additions, Illustrated with Plans, Woodcuts, &c., London: G. Routledge and Co., 1858.
Sanders, Andrew, "A Crisis of Liberalism in *North and South*," *Gaskell Society Journal* 10 (1996), 42–52.
Savin, Maynard, *Thomas William Robertson: His Plays and Stagecraft*, Providence: Brown University Press, 1950.

Schama, Simon, *Simon Schama's Power of Art*, London: BBC Books, 2006.
Seacole, Mary, *Wonderful Adventures of Mrs. Seacole in Foreign Lands*, Oxford: Oxford University Press, 1988.
Sellar, W. C. and R. J. Yeatman, *1066 and All That: A Memorable History of England*, intro. Frank Muir, illus. John Reynolds, Stroud, Gloucestershire: Sutton Publishing, 1993.
Shannon, Jr., Edgar F., "The Critical Reception of Tennyson's *Maud*," *PMLA* 68.3 (June, 1953), 397–417.
Shannon, Edgar and Christopher Ricks, "'The Charge of the Light Brigade': The Creation of a Poem," *Studies in Bibliography* 38 (1985), 1–44.
[Shore, Arabella and Louisa], *Poems by A. and L.*, London: Grant Richards, 1897. *War Lyrics*, London: Saunders and Otley, 1855.
Smith, Alexander and the Author of *Balder* and *The Roman* [Sydney Dobell], *Sonnets on the War*, London: David Bogue, 1855.
[Smith, Goldwin], "The War Passages in *Maud*," *Saturday Review* 1 (November 3, 1855), 14–15.
Smith, M. Van Wyk, *Drummer Hodge: The Poetry of the Anglo-Boer War (1899–1902)*, Oxford: The Clarendon Press, 1978.
Smulders, Sharon, "Feminism, Pacifism, and the Ethics of War: The Politics and Poetics of Alice Meynell's War Verse," *English Literature in Transition* 36 (1993), 159–77.
Soyer, Alexis, *A Culinary Campaign*, intro. Michael Barthorp and Elizabeth Ray, Lewes: Southover Press, 1995.
Spielmann, M. H., *The History of Punch*, London: Cassell, 1895.
Spiers, Edward M., *The Army and Society 1815–1914*, London: Longman, 1980.
Stallworthy, Jon (ed.), *The Oxford Book of War Poetry*, Oxford: Oxford University Press, 2003.
Stewart, Garrett, *The Look of Reading: Book, Painting, Text*, Chicago: University of Chicago Press, 2006.
Stone, Marjorie, "Genre Subversion and Gender Inversion: *The Princess* and *Aurora Leigh*," *Victorian Poetry* 25 (1987), 101–27.
Strachey, Lytton, *Eminent Victorians*, New York: The Modern Library, 1918.
Sussman, Herbert, *Victorian Masculinities: Manhood and Masculine Poetics in Early Victorian Literature and Art*, Cambridge: Cambridge University Press, 1995.
Sutherland, John, *The Longman Companion to Victorian Fiction*, Harlow: Longman Group, 1988.
[Swayne, G. C.], "Peace and War: A Dialogue," *Blackwood's Edinburgh Magazine* 76 (1854), 589–98.
Tate, Trudi, "On Not Knowing Why: Memorializing the Light Brigade," in *Literature, Science, Psychoanalysis, 1830–1970: Essays in Honour of Gillian Beer*, ed. Helen Small and Trudi Tate, Oxford: Oxford University Press, 2003, pp. 160–80.
The Tate Gallery 1984–86: Illustrated Catalogue of Acquisitions Including Supplement to Catalogue of Acquisitions 1982–84, London: Tate Gallery, 1988.

[Taylor, Fanny], *Eastern Hospitals and English Nurses; the Narrative of Twelve Months' Experience in the Hospitals of Kouali and Scutari*, 3rd edn., London: Hurst and Blackett, 1857.
Tennyson, Alfred, Lord, *The Letters of Alfred Lord Tennyson*, ed. Cecil Y. Lang and Edgar F. Shannon, Jr., 2 vols., Cambridge, MA: Harvard University Press, 1987.
  The Poems of Tennyson, ed. Christopher Ricks, 2nd edn., 3 vols., Harlow, Essex: Longman, 1987.
  Tennyson's Maud: A Definitive Edition, ed. Susan Shatto, London: The Athlone Press, 1986.
Tennyson, Hallam, Lord, *Alfred, Lord Tennyson: A Memoir by his Son*, 2 vols., London: Macmillan and Co., 1897.
Thackeray, William Makepeace, *The Newcomes*, ed. D. J. Taylor, London: J. M. Dent, 1994.
Thorp, Margaret Farrand, *Charles Kingsley, 1819–1875*, Princeton: Princeton University Press, 1937.
The Tradition Established (1841–84), Vol. II of The History of The Times, 3 vols., London: 1939.
Tucker, Herbert F., *Britain's Heroic Muse: 1790–1910*. New York: Oxford University Press, 2008.
  "*Maud* and the Doom of Culture," in *Critical Essays on Alfred Lord Tennyson*, ed. Herbert F. Tucker, New York: G. K. Hall and Co., 1993, pp. 174–94.
Turner, Paul, "Aurora versus the Angel," *Review of English Studies* 24 (July, 1948), 227–35.
Uglow, Jenny, *Elizabeth Gaskell: A Habit of Stories*, London: Faber and Faber, 1993.
Unsigned review of *Maud*, *Court Journal* (August 11, 1855), 539.
Unsigned review of *Maud, and Other Poems*, *Tait's Edinburgh Magazine* n.s. 22 (September, 1855), 531–39.
Unsigned review of *North and South*, *Examiner*, April 21, 1855, 244–45.
Unsigned review of "The Royal Academy," *Art-Journal* n.s. 2 (June 1, 1856), 161–74.
Unsigned review of *Two Years Ago*, *British Quarterly Review* 25 (April 1, 1857), 399–420.
Unsigned review of *Two Years Ago*, *Saturday Review* 3 (21 February, 1857), 176.
Urquhart, David, *The Effect of the Misuse of Familiar Words on the Character of Men and the Fate of Nations*, London: Trübner & Co., 1856.
Usherwood, Paul and Jenny Spencer-Smith, *Lady Butler, Battle Artist, 1846–1933*, London: Alan Sutton/National Army Museum, 1987.
Van Dyke, Henry, *The Poetry of Tennyson*, New York: Scribner's, 1920.
Vanden Bossche, Chris R., "Realism versus Romance: The War of Cultural Codes in Tennyson's *Maud*," *Victorian Poetry* 24.1 (1986), 69–82.
Waddington, Patrick, *"Theirs But To Do and Die": The Poetry of the Charge of the Light Brigade at Balaklava, 25 October 1854*, Nottingham: Astra Press, 1995.
Warner, Philip, *The Crimean War: A Reappraisal*, London: Arthur Baker, 1972.

Weingart, Winfried, *The Crimean War, 1853–1856*, London: Arnold, 1999.
Welsh, Alexander, *The City of Dickens*, Cambridge, MA: Harvard University Press, 1986.
Westwater, Martha, *The Spasmodic Career of Sydney Dobell*, Lanham, MD: University Press of America, 1992.
Whyte-Melville, George, *The Interpreter: A Tale of the War*, new edn., London: Longman's, Green, and Co, n.d.
Woodham-Smith, Cecil, *Florence Nightingale, 1820–1910*, London: McGraw-Hill, 1951.
  The Reason Why: The Story of the Fatal Charge of the Light Brigade, London: Penguin, 1958.
Woolf, Virginia, *To the Lighthouse*, foreword Eudora Welty, New York: Harcourt Brace Jovanovich, 1989.
Yonge, Charlotte, *The Young Step-mother*, 2 vols., Leipzig: Bernard Tauchniz, 1861.

Index

Aberdeen, George Hamilton-Gordon, 4th Earl of 2, 7, 9, 23, 61
Administrative Reform Association 9
adventure fiction 67, 81
The Adventures of Dr Brady (W.H. Russell) 38–42, 68, 235
  characterisation 41–2
  Crimean episodes 39–42, 227; problems of 40–2
  reviewed 227
Airey, Richard Airey, 1st Baron 45
Albert, Prince Consort 142–3
Allen, Matthew, *Essay on the Classification of the Insane* 253
Alma, Battle of the 8
  fictionalised depictions 39–40, 85
  newspaper reports 17, 27–9, 30–3
Anderson, Benedict 59, 231, 245
Anderson, Olive 18, 20, 21
Armstrong, Isobel 128–9, 155–6, 159–60, 161–2
Arnold, Matthew 1, 8, 69–70, 123, 158
Arrowsmith, Aaron 23
Aspinall, Arthur 18
Assad, Thomas J. 164
Athenian Mercury 228
Aurora Leigh (Barrett Browning) 69, 113–22, 240, 244–5
  authorial commentary 115–16
  composition/choice of name 242
  contemporary criticisms 118, 120–1
  treatment of gender 116–17, 121–2, 243
Austen, Jane, *Northanger Abbey* 43
Aytoun, W.E. 72, 118

Bagehot, Walter 162
Bainbridge, Beryl, *Master Georgie* 250
Baker, Ernest 67
Balaklava, Battle of 8, 10, 18
  see also Light Brigade, charge of
Ballantyne, Thomas 88
Baltic, naval conflicts in 8

Barlow, Paul 179, 197–8, 200–1, 202, 204
Barrett Browning, Elizabeth 63, 93, 166
  attitudes to War 243
  correspondence 113–16, 120, 237, 242
  recommendation for Laureateship 113, 242
  views on Nightingale 113–15, 118–19
  views on women's movement 120
  "Mother and Poet" 130
  Poems Before Congress 118
Barringer, Tim 173
Barry, James (artist) 108
Barry, James (Miranda), Dr 108–9, 120, 241
"The Battle of the Alma, as fought at Astley's" (*Punch* cartoon) 180–1
Baudelaire, Charles 174, 257
Beato, Felice 256–7
Benjamin, Walter 262
Bentham, Jeremy 237
Bentley, Richard 63
Blackstone, Sir William 18
Blackwell, Elizabeth, Dr 119–20
Blackwood's Edinburgh Magazine 2–3, 35–6
Blakeley, Captain (war correspondent) 27–8
Blakesley, Joseph Williams, Rev. ('A Hertfordshire Incumbent') 56–9
  academic qualities 57–8
Boer War (1899–1902) 6, 20, 216, 217
  see also First Boer War
Bolter, Jay David, and Richard Grusin, *Remediation* 169
Bosquet, Pierre-François-Joseph, General 142, 146
Boxer, Edward, Rear-Admiral 37, 227
boyhood/boyish nature, depictions of 70–1, 189–91
Braddon, Mary Elizabeth 109
Bratton, J.S. 255
Brimley, George 155–6
Bristow, Joseph 91, 106, 128
Britannia, images of 4, 104–6, 210–12, 240

Index

The British Expedition to the Crimea
    (W.H. Russell) 225, 226
  revisions of newspaper material 29, 37
Brontë, Charlotte *see Jane Eyre*
Brontë, Emily, *Wuthering Heights* 208–9
Brooks, Chris 203
Brougham, John, *Demosthenes* 56
Brown, Ford Madox 194–5
  Waiting: An English Fireside of 1854–5 246
Brown, Sir George, General 30, 39
Browning, Elizabeth Barrett *see* Barrett
    Browning, Elizabeth
Browning, Robert 243
  Men and Women 124
  The Ring and the Book 138, 248
  see also "Childe Roland to the Dark Tower
    Came"
Butler, Lady *see* Thompson, Elizabeth
Butler, Sir William Francis, Lt.-Gen. 216
Byron, George Gordon, Lord 90, 95, 210
  Don Juan 225

Callen, Anthea 215
*Calling the Roll after an Engagement see The
    Roll Call*
Cardigan, James Brudenell, 7th Earl of 7, 68,
    141, 146, 230
  pictorial depictions 142–3, 184–6
Cardwell, Edward/Cardwell reforms 213
Carlyle, Thomas 123, 139, 147–8, 149, 258
  *On Heroes, Hero-Worship and the Heroic in
    History* 3–4, 67–8
  "Two Hundred and Fifty Years Ago" 77
catch-phrases, use of 21–2
Cathcart, Sir George, General 46
"The Cavalry Charge" (Dobell) 143–7
  narrational voice 145–6
Chandler, James 6
Chapman, Benedict Lawrence 231
Charge of Light Brigade *see* Light Brigade,
    charge of, Balaklava, Battle of
"The Charge of the Light Brigade" (Tennyson)
    14, 124–5, 140, 151–4, 157–8, 161, 249
  commentaries 5, 60
  comparisons with contemporaries' works 134
  copies sent to Crimea 2–3, 62, 165
  details of vocabulary/syntax 152–3, 158
  distancing of authorial voice 151–2
  genesis/first publication 2, 123, 153–4, 155
  impact on popular culture 8, 10, 141, 147
  influence on contemporary fiction 84
  links with *Maud* 148, 156–7, 164
    (*see also Maud*, 'war ballad' passage)
  as public piece 154–5
  quoted in later works 66, 143–4, 248

  responsibility, treatment of 162–4
  revisions for successive publications 153–4, 159,
    162, 250, 252
  sound recording 165, 167, 254
  structure 164–5
  style/vocabulary 23
  target readership 152, 252
  Tennyson's comments on 153, 250, 254
  Times coverage 140, 141, 143, 145, 146, 153,
    157–8, 159
Charles, Godfrey Douglas 216
Chenery, Thomas 16, 23, 24, 58
"Childe Roland to the Dark Tower Came"
    (Browning) 159–61, 162
children, depictions of 192–4, 203–7
  playing at war 188–91
  see also boyhood
chivalry, ideal of 4, 79, 117, 124, 149, 235, 238
  grotesque reinterpretations 161–2
Chobham camp 257
  see also Leech, John
cholera 3, 29
  in London 91
Chorley, H.F. 113
Churchill, Winston 4–5
civil war, dangers of *see* social unrest
Civil War (1642–9), referencing 93, 237
civilian public
  commentaries on war 49–59
  wartime attitudes *see* incompetence, war,
    fantasy investment in
Clarke's Travels 50
class, attitudes toward 83, 92, 213, 263
  attitudes towards aristocracy 4, 95, 145, 185, 234
    (*see also* private soldier, social unrest,
    soldiers)
'cliff-hangers'
  Russell's use of 26–7
Clifford, Henry 63
clothing (for troops), manufacture/supply 55
  see also uniforms
Clough, Arthur Hugh 63, 89, 93, 123, 236
  Amours de Voyage 145–6
Codrington, Sir William, General 20
Coldstream Guards 3
Colley, Linda 5
Collins, Wilkie 36, 102
  The Moonstone 39
Collinson, James 194
  Home Again 188–9, 191
commercialism, movement of society towards
    97–8, 126, 159
'condition of England' novels 69, 73, 77, 88,
    91, 117, 122
Constantinople 8

Index

Cook, Sir Edward 107
Cooper, Helen 243
Copley, John Singleton, *The Death of Major Pierson* 197–8, 202, 207
Corfu 95, 108
correspondents *see* newspapers, war coverage, Russell, William Howard
Craik, Dinah, *A Life for a Life* 235
Crealock, Henry Hope, Captain, "The Heroes of Balaklava Fighting their Battles Over Again" 142
Crimean War
 commercial attitudes to 97–8
 fictional representations *see* fiction
 historical context 1–2
 impact on literary developments 102
 impact on popular memory 6–7, 8
 justifications 138
 leadership 1 (*see also* incompetence)
 pictorial representations *see* paintings
 poetic representations *see* war poetry
 progress of hostilities 7–11
 protests against 245
'crowdsourcing' 58–9
Culler, Dwight 165

Dallas, E.S. 68
Dallas, Frederick, Captain 12–14, 19–20, 37–8, 42, 43–5, 46, 66, 171–2, 230, 233, 253
Daubeny, Mrs 112
David, Deirdre 119, 244
David, Jacques-Louis
 Napoleon Crossing the Alps 169
 The Oath of the Horatii 188
Davis, Elizabeth 53–4
Delane, John Thaddeus 16, 44–5
Demidoff, Nikolai, Count 50
Dereli, Cynthia 90, 110
Dickens, Charles 9, 43, 84, 90, 202
 compared with Russell 36–8
 correspondence 87
 friendship with Russell 36
 influence of Russell on 36
 All the Year Round (ed.) 90
 Bleak House 12
 Great Expectations 38
 Hard Times 37, 63, 116, 244
 Little Dorrit 12, 36, 38, 63
 Martin Chuzzlewit 103
 see also Household Words
Dickinson, Lowes 194–5
Digby, Kenelm Henry, *The Broadstone of Honour* 79
disease 9, 48–9
 see also cholera

Dixon, Franklin W. 71
Dobell, Sydney 247
 England in Time of War 132–4
 "An Evening Dream" 132–4, 136
 "A Hero's Grave" 144, 249
 see also Smith, Alexander, "The Cavalry Charge"
doctors, as heroes 32, 41, 136, 235
Donizetti, Gaetano, *La Fille du Régiment* 201, 202
Doyle, Richard 197
dramatic monologue, use of form 124, 155–6, 246, 251
 see also Maud, as monodrama
du Maurier, George, *Trilby* 183–4
Duberly, Frances Isabella 230, 253, 257
Dürer, Albrecht 117

Earle, General 216
'Eastern Question' 7, 91
Edison, Thomas 165
Edward, Prince of Wales (later Edward VII) 210
Eliot, George 144, 234
 Adam Bede 72, 234
 Middlemarch 108, 241
 The Mill on the Floss 60
Ellesmere, Francis Egerton, 1st Earl of 146
"Enthusiasm of Paterfamilias, On Reading the Report of the Grand Charge of British Cavalry on the 25th" (Leech) 60–1, 142, 186–92, 195
 comparisons with Millais 194, 196
 female figures 187–8, 261
epic 4, 41, 89, 107, 123, 225–6
 in *Westward Ho!* 72–6
 in *North and South* 110, 112
 in *Aurora Leigh* 118
Errol, Lady 112
Eton *see* public schools
Evans, George, Pte, letters from 45
eyewitness observation 17, 173, 182, 189, 191, 206
 see also war poetry, problem of poet's distance

facial hair, fashions in 257
failure, as form of success 159
Favret, Mary A. 229
Fenton, Roger 33, 170, 176, 202, 256–7
Fforde, Jasper, *The Eyre Affair* 239
fiction, Crimean War in 1–2, 63–4
 in background of English settings 86–9, 94–8, 99–100
 direct descriptions 81–2, 83–6
 indirect referencing (through other war scenes) 75
First Boer War (1881) 215

Index

Flint, Kate 170, 171, 193–4, 203–4
'Flyers, F.' (newspaper correspondent) 47
Forster, John, correspondence with Tennyson 153, 165, 250
Foucault, Michel 103
France 1
Fraser, George Macdonald, *Flashman at the Charge* 233
French Army
    conditions/regulations, compared with British 24, 30
    contributions to military successes 10
Friel, Brian, *Translations* 7
"A Friend in Need" (*Punch* cartoon) 180
Fripp, Charles Edwin 216
Fussell, Paul 5–6, 28

Gallipoli 30, 33, 39
Galton, Mrs 112
Gaskell, Elizabeth
    correspondence 87, 93–4, 95–6, 98, 103, 109, 112, 238, 241
    views on Nightingale 111–12, 114, 117, 118
    Ruth 111, 242
    see also *North and South*
Gaskell, Meta 241
'G.D.N.' (*Times* correspondent) 57–8
Girouard, Mark 79
Gladstone, W.E. 150, 166, 250
Goethe, Johann Wolfgang von 79
grapes, (anecdotes of) soldiers' eating 27–9
Great Exhibition (1851) 6
Greg, W.R. 15, 20, 22
Griffiths, Eric 167
Groseclose, Barbara 231
grotesque see under chivalry
Grotius, Hugo (Hugo de Groot) 93
Gurney, Archer 151
Guys, Constantin 257
    "Carrying the Frost-bitten to Balaclava" 175
    "Carrying the Wounded to Balaclava" 175
    "Turks Conveying the Sick to Balaclava" 174–5

Habermas, Jürgen 14, 18, 47, 61
Halliday, Michael 180
Hamley, E.B., Captain 2–3, 48–9, 62, 126, 128, 137, 139, 140
Hancher, Michael 195–6, 197–8, 199, 201, 203, 205, 208
Hardy, Thomas, "Drummer Hodge" 216
Harrow see public schools
Helgerson, Richard 5
Hemans, Felicia 128
Henty, G.A. 71
Herbert, Percy, Hon., Colonel 37

heroes/heroism
    ancient *vs.* modern 129–30
    changing perceptions of 158–9
    female 4, 88, 102–3, 106, 112, 115, 121–2, 214–15, 255
    literary explorations 41–2, 66–9, 77–9
    literary/popular conceptions 3–4
    male, 3–4, 33–4, 41–2, 65–6, 79, 261
    see also manliness, 'muscular Christianity'
'A Hertfordshire Incumbent' see Blakesley, Joseph Williams, Rev.
"Highland Officer in the Crimea" (*Punch* cartoon) 207
Hitchens, Christopher 6, 219, 220
Holman Hunt, William see Hunt, W. Holman
Holmes, Rachel 109
Homer
    Iliad 2–3, 62, 115, 223, 225–6
    Odyssey 95
honour, treatments of 96–8, 100, 149
Houfe, Simon 180
Houghton, 1st Baron see Milnes, Richard Monckton
Household Words (ed. Dickens) 90–2
Houston, Natalie 135, 137, 138, 139, 145, 249–50
Howard, Henry R., Captain 261
Hughes, Linda 159, 166
Hughes, Thomas 71, 72–3, 153
    The Manliness of Christ 234
    Tom Brown's Schooldays 71, 233
'human interest' stories 89–90, 111–12, 236–7
Hunt, W. Holman 179, 220
    travels/public image 182–3
    comments on Millais' *Peace Concluded* 194, 195, 201, 208
    The Scapegoat 183
Hunter, J. Paul 36, 47, 228

Illustrated London News 170, 191
'imagined community' (Benedict Anderson) 59, 188, 231
imperialism 6, 220
(see also epic, national identity)
incompetence (of government/military leadership) 4, 9, 123
    featured in news reports 28, 49
    public outrage at 181–2
    soldiers' complaints of 12–13
'Indian Mutiny' 6, 41, 228
information
    speed of transmission see newspapers, immediacy
    unreliability 37
Inkerman, Battle of 8, 48, 133
    newspaper reports 42
    participants' descriptions 45–6

Index

Internet 61
The Interpreter: A Tale of the War
(Whyte-Melville) 65–7
Iraq War, online commentaries 61
ironic modes 5, 28, 124, 145, 151, 154, 191
 burlesque 2
 farce 12
 satire 195, 196, 202–3
Italy, unification movement 115, 130

James, Henry 112
Jameson, Anna 113–14, 115, 116, 121, 242, 243
Jane Eyre (C. Brontë) 76, 102, 107, 116–17
 (alleged) borrowings from 113, 242, 244;
 social/literary impact 102–3
'J.B.D.' (*Times* correspondent) 49–50
journalism *see* newspapers
Judd, Catherine 103, 107–8, 241
'just war,' concept of 93

Kay-Shuttleworth, James Phillip 90
Kaye, J.W. 121
Keller, Ulrich 6, 142–3, 173, 184, 185–6, 213, 240
Kinglake, Alexander 35, 141
 The Invasion of the Crimea 225
Kingsley, Charles 68–9, 101, 173–4, 241–2
 comments on Tennyson 124, 153, 249, 252
 correspondence 71, 72–3
 Alton Locke 69
 "Brave Words to Brave Soldiers and Sailors" 72
 The Heroes; or, Greek Fairy Tales for My Children 71, 158–9
 Hypatia 70, 233
 Yeast 70
 see also Two Years Ago, Westward Ho!
Kingsley, Henry 68–9
 see also Ravenshoe
Kipling, Rudyard 132, 213
 "The Last of the Light Brigade" 165
Knightley, Phillip 20, 222
Kronstadt, strategic significance 8, 10

Lalumia, Matthew 6, 15, 171, 197, 213, 263
Lamb, Charles 166
Lambert, Andrew 221
Langbaum, Robert 124
Lawrence, G.A. 68
 Sword and Gown 72, 234
Layard, Austen Henry, MP 97
leave (military) *see* 'urgent private affairs'
Lecky, W.E.H. 97
Leech, John 59–60, 168–9, 172–3, 174–80, 183, 184–92, 256–7
 friendship with Millais 178–80
 personal views of war 191–2

relationship of works with Millais' 195, 197, 200, 207–8
"Another Night Surprise at Chobham" 176–7
"General Février Turned Traitor" 259
"How Jack Makes the Turk Useful at Balaclava" 175–6
"A Little Dinner at the Crimea Club" 177
Mr Briggs' Sporting Tour 200
"The New Game of Follow My Leader" 195
"No! Don't" 231
"Nothing Like Knowing the Country" 176
"One of the Horrors of the Chobham War" 177
"The Plunger in Turkey" 195
"Well Jack! Here's good news ..." 177–8
see also "Enthusiasm of Paterfamilias ..."; "A Trump Card(igan)"
letters, from serving troops 42, 102
 complementing newspaper reports 45–6
 literary/journalistic influences on 46–7
 original narratives in lieu of 48
 publication 19, 42–7
 variations in tone 46
letters, to newspapers *see* newspapers, *The Times*
Light Brigade, charge of 8
 (apportioning of) responsibility 141–2, 162–3
 fictional representations 66–7, 78–9, 84, 183, 234, 250
 historical facts 140–1
 pictorial treatments 142–3, 183–92
 poetic responses 125, 140–1, 143–8, 248
 popular responses 4, 7, 158–9
 see also "The Charge of the Light Brigade" (Tennyson)
Light Brigade Relief Fund 165
literacy levels 44
Longfellow, Henry Wadsworth, "Santa Filomena" 4
Lootens, Tricia 44, 128, 137, 140, 149, 159
"Lord Raglan and the Weather" (anonymous poem) 51
Lovelace, Richard, "To Lucasta, going to the Wars" 96, 100, 239
Luard, John D'Albiac 182, 183
 A Welcome Arrival 3, 170–2, 197
Lucan, George Bingham, 3rd Earl of 140–1
Lushington, Franklin, "Alma" 158
Lushington, Henry, "La Nation Boutiquière" 144

madness, treatments of 75–6, 82–3, 85–6
 by Tennyson 156–7
magazines
 featuring of war-related material 90–1
 military quarters decorated with 170–2
Malakoff redoubt, assault on 17

manliness 71, 78, 86, 98, 260
  artistic manliness 182–3, 199–200
  see also 'muscular Christianity' and heroism, male
Mann, R.J. 150, 165
Marston, Westland, *The Death-Ride: A Tale of the Light Brigade* 249
Marx, Karl 2, 4, 61, 219, 231, 236
Massey, Gerald, *War Waits* 147
Maud (Tennyson) 97, 101, 124–5, 148–51
  autobiographical elements 155
  comparisons with contemporaries' works 128, 131, 134, 159, 160–1
  composition 250
  contemporary reviews 124, 126, 150, 155–6
  as monodrama 150–1
  narratorial voice/personality 155–7, 160–1; distinguished from author's 150–1 (*see also* madness, suicidal impulse)
  responsibility, treatment of 162
  revisions 163–4, 252–3
  structure 164–5
  Tennyson's comments on 150–1, 156, 166
  Tennyson's reading of 115, 165–7, 252, 254
  versification 164
  war, treatment of 1, 93, 94–5, 150–1, 157
  'war ballad' passage 149–50, 154, 160, 164, 167, 250, 251
Maude, George, Captain 48
McGann, Jerome 149, 151, 152, 254
Meredith, George, *Beauchamp's Career* 250
Meynell, Alice 217, 264
Meynell, Wilfred 213
military *see* soldiers
Mill, John Stuart 119–20, 240–1
Millais, Effie 196, 201, 204
Millais, John Everett 168–9, 172–3, 182–3, 191–2, 214
  Autumn Leaves 261
  The Black Brunswicker 168–9, 170
  The Blind Girl 203–4
  Bubbles 200
  L'Enfant du Régiment 201–2
  News From Home 207–8, 228, 261–2
  The Order of Release, 201, 208, 257
  Portrait of a Gentleman 200–1
  The Proscribed Royalist, 208, 196–7, 262
  The Rescue 261
  sketches 178–80; "Ingenious Protection Against Midges" "Pre-Raphaelite Sketching: inconvenience in windy weather" 179–80; "This is the Protection a Plaid Affords…" 257–8
  see also *Peace Concluded*
Millais, John Guille, *Life and Letters of Sir John Everett Millais* 196–7, 257–8

Milnes, Richard Monckton 56, 106–7
Milton, John 41–2
Mitford, Mary Russell 113
monodrama *see* dramatic monologue, *Maud*
"The Moral of this Year" (anonymous poem) 91, 247
Morawski, Stefan 169, 170
Morning Advertiser 223
Morning Chronicle 21, 27–9
Morris, James 8, 221
Morris, William, *The Defence of Guinevere and Other Poems* 161–2
mothers/mother-figures, poetic depictions 129–30
Mulock, Dinah *see* Craik, Dinah
Mulready, William, *The Convalescent from Waterloo* 188
Münnich, Burkhard Christoph von, Count 57
'muscular Christianity,' fiction of 67, 68–9, 71–3, 77, 224, 235

Napier, Charles, Admiral 56
Napier, E. Elers 56, 58
Napoleon III 169
Napoleonic Wars 3, 16, 17, 54, 229
Nation, national identity 4–5, 59–60, 73–4, 112, 126, 131, 134, 191, 218 (*see also* 'imagined community')
Nelson, Horatio, Lord, Admiral 54
Newbolt, Henry, "Vitaï Lampada" 189–91
The Newcomes (W.M. Thackeray) 63, 95, 205, 238
  characterisation 199–200
  relationship with Millais' *Peace Concluded* 197, 198–200, 202–3, 207
newspapers
  censorship 20
  foreign news coverage 15–18
  freedom in reporting 18
  immediacy 2–3, 17–18, 25, 223
  influence on literary forms 139–40
  role in popular culture 15, 59–62
  value to enemy 19–20
  war coverage 1, 2–4, 13–37
Nicholas I, Czar 2, 7, 20, 31, 161, 259
Nightingale, Florence 4, 16, 24, 25, 53, 55, 56, 86–7, 104–12, 123, 210
  attitudes to gender/women's movement 120, 243
  contemporary criticisms 111–12, 113–15, 118–19
  correspondence 94, 95; publication 230
  impact on popular culture 4, 6, 9, 68, 88, 104–6, 121, 214
  influence on literary characterisations 98, 103, 109–12, 116–17, 119, 241
  literary tastes 62, 103, 111, 242

pictorial depictions 261
poetic tributes 135, 246
self-image/vocation 106–7, 108, 117, 234, 240
views of medical profession 119–20
Cassandra 4, 15, 68, 109, 117, 120, 121, 240–1
Notes on Nursing 107–8
see also nurses/nursing
Nightingale, Parthenope 87, 108, 120
"A Nightingale in the Camp" (anonymous poem) 106
Nolan, E.H., *Illustrated History of the War Against Russia* 226
Nolan, Louis, Captain 141, 162
North and South (Gaskell) 62, 65, 69, 86–112, 119, 212, 236, 240
  contemporary reviews 101–2, 240
  journalistic influence 89–91
  social content 94, 96, 110–11, 117, 122
  treatment of character/gender 98–102, 104, 109–12, 115; contrasted with others' works
  treatment of military life 94–5
  treatment of passion 100–2
Norton, Charles Eliot 93
novel(s)
  competition with newspapers 89
  contemporary debates on 67
  copies sent to troops 61–2, 111
  suitability as vehicle for ideas 64–5
  see also 'condition of England' novels; fiction; 'muscular Christianity'; realist fiction; 'sensation novels'; sentimental novels
nurses/nursing 44, 53, 54–5, 113–15, 119, 205, 214, 241
  nursing heroines 40, 65, 81, 86, 103, 235, 241, 242
  see also Nightingale, Florence

Oliphant, Margaret 68, 101–2, 104, 240
Omar: A Tale of the War (Reynolds) 64–6, 67–8, 109
Omar Pasha, fictional representations 64–6
"One of the Gallant 93rd" (*Punch* cartoon) 180
Ottoman Empire 7
Ouida, *Held in Bondage* 234
"Our Artist Goes to Nature" (*Punch* cartoon) 180
"Our Artist in the Crimea" (*Punch* cartoon) 181–2
Owen, Mrs W.H. 255
Owen, Wilfred, "Strange Meeting" 31

pacifism *see* peace
paintings, of Crimean War scenes 1–2, 3, 15, 168–209, 228
  narrative tendencies 169–73
Pallas, Peter Simon 50, 57–8
Palmerston, Henry John Temple, 3rd Viscount 7, 9, 10, 56, 57, 61

pamphlets, supersession by newspapers 15
paraquotations 169–73
Paris, Peace of (1856) 10–11, 221
Patmore, Coventry 120–1, 155
  The Angel in the House 4, 98–100, 117, 119, 120, 244
peace
  advocacy of 93–4
  as killer of passion 101
Peace Concluded (Millais) 15, 63–4, 192–209, 228
  (alleged) preliminary sketch 196–7, 260
  genesis/alternative title 194–5, 205
  intertextuality 197–203
  links with other works by Millais 200–8
  problems of interpretation 195–9, 209
  symbolism 203–7
Peace Society 93–4
Peck, John
  on Gaskell 87
  on the Kingsleys 70, 72, 73, 75, 80
  on Russell/realism 27, 29, 32, 33–6, 38–9, 89
Peel, Robert (son of PM) 25
Peirson, Francis, Major 197–8
Pelissier, Aimable-Jean-Jacques, General 64
'people's war,' Crimean as 15, 51–3, 53–4, 136–7, 222
photographs, of war scenes 170, 256–7
physician's villa, description of (by Russell) 32–3
Pinero, A.W., *Trelawny of the "Wells"* 256
plot-driven novels *see* adventure fiction
poetry
  prewar debates on 123–4
  see also war poetry
Poovey, Mary 104–5, 110, 239
poppies, as emblem of doomed youth 133, 247
Pre-Raphaelite Brotherhood 169, 173–4, 180, 188
  criticism/mockery 179, 205–7
  visual characteristics 203
Prince (transport ship) 9, 75
private soldier(s), contemporary depictions/commentaries 4, 96, 132, 228
Procter, Adelaide Anne 91–3, 124, 128–30, 136
  "The Lesson of the War" 91–2, 129
  "The Two Spirits" 92–3, 129–30, 189–91
  "Waiting" 91–2, 129
promotion, (criticisms of) system 37
public opinion 1–2, 18–19, 136–40
  relationship with *Times* coverage 22
public/private perspectives, mingling of 44–5, 48, 137, 155–6
public schools, rivalry between 189, 233
Punch 197
  cartoons 33–4, 59–60, 169, 174–82, 184–92, 195, 205–7, 207–8, 210–12, 231
  criticisms 176

284   Index

Punch (cont.)
   poems 4, 68, 96, 105–6
   satirical commentaries 126, 159, 195, 226–7, 228, 258
Pusey, Edward Bouverie 233

Quakers *see* Peace Society
"The Queen Visiting the Imbeciles of the Crimea" (*Punch* cartoon) 195

Rabbe, Alphonse, *History of Russia* 58
racial/national 'outsiders,' narratives by 54
Rader, Ralph Wilson 155
Raglan, FitzRoy Somerset, 1st Baron 10, 13, 28, 140–1, 186
   death 78, 195, 225–6
   newspaper reports 225
   pictorial representations 64
   popular commentaries 51
Raglan, Lady 225–6
Ravenshoe (H. Kingsley) 13–14, 67, 82–6, 89, 261
   compared with other works 70, 81, 88
   narrative failings 84
reading rooms (for troops) 61–2
realism, in art 173–4, 183, 186–7
   compared with literary 203
   relationship with masculine persona 182–3
realist fiction
   domination of novel genre 67
   Russell's reports compared with 27, 32, 33–7, 38–9, 89
Redan fortification, assault on 10, 17
Reed, John 234
remediation 169–73, 186, 194
Reuter, Julius 17
Reynolds, George W.M. (ed.), *Miscellany* 232
   see also Omar: A Tale of the War
Ricks, Christopher 158, 162
   see also Shannon, Edgar
Robertson, James 256–7
Robertson, Thomas William
   Caste 168
   Ours 168–9, 170, 255
Robinson, Henry Crabb 16, 222–3
Roebuck Committee 9
Rogers, Edward, Col., *The Modern Sphinx* 109
The Roll Call (Calling the Roll after an Engagement, Crimea) (Thompson) 210–15, 262
   contemporary reviews 212, 214–15
   enactments 216–17, 263–4
   'manliness' 214
   popular response 210–12
   subject matter/composition 212–13

romance *see* adventure fiction
Romanticism 125
Rose, June *The Perfect Gentleman* 241
'Rosie the Riveter' 24–5, 104
Rossetti, Dante Gabriel 166, 252
   "The Woodspurge" 204, 261
Rossetti, W.M. 128
'Royals' officer,' letters from, 45–6
Ruskin, John 159, 161, 202, 205
   Academy Notes 204, 207, 214, 263
   Modern Painters 169
Russell, William Howard 13–14, 16–18, 25–37, 38, 46, 53, 54, 58, 126, 146, 157–8, 159, 169, 185–6, 225, 236
   characterisation, lack of 32, 34–5
   column space 25–6
   contrasted with rival reporters 27–9, 48–9
   criticisms 48–9; for ignorance of military matters response to 61
   guilt at non-combatant status 41
   influence/referencing in contemporary fiction 64, 89
   literary characteristics 27–37, 53, 227
   (*see also* realist fiction)
   memorial (in St Paul's) 222
   as novelist *see The Adventures of Dr Brady*
   private correspondence 44–5
   public commentaries on reports 47–9
   satirised 226–7
   self-corrections 49, 224
   self-representation 33–6, 42, 182
   serialisation of reports 26–7
   war experience outside Crimea 223, 228
Russia 1, 7

Sadleir, Michael 83
Sala, George Augustus 214–15
Sambourne, Edward Linley 210–12
Sanders, Andrew 95
Sant, James 142–3
Sassoon, Siegfried 4–5
Savin, Maynard 168
Schama, Simon 188
Scutari Hospital 23, 24
Seacole, Mary 14, 38, 53–4, 243
Sebastopol, siege of 8, 9–10
   newspaper coverage 26–7
   premature announcement of victory 17
Second Boer War (1899–1902) *see* Boer War
Sellar, W.C., and R.J. Yeatman, *1066 and All That* 7–10
'sensation novels' 39, 40–1, 68–9, 81, 86, 102, 109
sentimental novels 45
"Servant and Baggage of the British Officer in the East" (*Punch* cartoon) 176

Shakespeare, William 2, 146–7
　Henry V 5
　Romeo and Juliet 121
Shannon, Edgar, and Christopher Ricks, "*The Charge of the Light Brigade:* The Creation of a Poem" 152–3, 155, 158, 162
Shaw, George Bernard 168
Shelley, Percy Bysshe, "Ozymandias" 145, 146–7
Shore, Arabella
　(and Louisa Shore), *Collected Poems* 246
　(and Louisa Shore), *War Lyrics* 124, 131–2
　"The British Soldier" 131
　"The Maiden at Home" 131–2, 133
Shore, Louisa
　"War Music" 127–8
　see also Shore, Arabella
Simpson, Sir James, General 45, 195
Simpson, William 207, 256
Sinfield, Alan 246
"Sketching from Nature" (*Punch* cartoon) 205–7
Smiles, Samuel 258
Smith, Adam 237
Smith, Alexander, and Sydney Dobell, *Sonnets on the War* 6, 124–5, 132, 134–40, 141, 154, 249–50
　confusion of intent/effect 138–40, 143, 144–6, 148
　diversity of narrative voices 134–5, 136
　"The Army Surgeon" 135, 253
　"The Cavalry Charge" 143
　"The Crystal Palace" 135
　"Miss Nightingale" 135
　"Murmurs" 135
　"Rest" 147
　"Self" 140
　"A Statesman" 135
　"Worthies" 135
　"The Wounded" 135–6, 138
　see also Dobell, Sydney, "Vox Populi"
Smith, Alison 204
Smith, Goldwin 126–7, 150, 245, 250–1
Smith, Malvern Van Wyk 5
social unrest, events/depictions 88, 93
soldiers
　poetic honouring 138
　as poetic narrators 247
　(shift in) popular perceptions 95–6, 189
　see also private soldiers
sonnet form, significance of 146–7
Soyer, Alexis 53, 54, 172
'spasmodic school' (of poetry) 81, 124, 244, 247
spectaculars/panoramas 259
Spencer-Smith, Jenny *see* Usherwood, Paul
Spenser, Edmund, *The Faerie Queene* 71–2

Stephens, Frederick 205
Stewart, Garrett 198–9
stocks *see* uniforms
Strachey, Lytton 106
'A Sufferer by the Present War?' (*Times* correspondent) 54–5
suicidal impulse 156–7, 159–61
　war as expression of 157–8
Sussman, Herbert 82, 182–3, 239, 258
Sutherland, John 39
Sweden 10

Tate, Trudi 60, 142, 152, 154–5, 165, 188, 192, 248–9
Taylor, Tom 214
telegraph 1, 17–18, 223
Tennyson, Alfred, Lord 56, 113, 116, 231, 247
　views on Crimean War 150–1, 154, 156, 161
　"The Charge of the Heavy Brigade" 156, 167
　Dream of Fair Women (Queen Eleanor of Castile) 196, 260
　Idylls of the King 149, 162, 235
　"The Lady of Shalott" 77
　"Mariana" 91–87, 128
　"Ode on the death of the Duke of Wellington" 155
　"To the Reverend F.D. Maurice" 126–7
　see also "The Charge of the Light Brigade"; *Maud*
Tennyson, Emily 158, 250
Tennyson, Hallam , 166–7
Thackeray, William Makepeace 9, 36
　"The Due of the Dead" 127
　satirical contributions to *Punch* 226–7
　see also The Newcomes
'thin red line,' coining of phrase 236
thirst, suffered by soldiers 29, 30, 31
Thompson, Elizabeth, Lady Butler 4, 210–18, 221
　public acclaim 210–12, 214–15
　The 28th Regiment at Quatre Bras 214
　Autobiography 216, 217–18
　Balaclava 215
　The Colours: Advance of the Scots Guards at the Alma 216
　The Return from Inkerman 215
　Scotland for Ever! 215–16, 218
　see also The Roll Call
Thomson, James, Assistant-Surgeon 32, 33, 34
The Times 15, 86, 170
　appearance in paintings/cartoons 63–4, 186, 192, 199, 207, 225
　circulation 20–1, 223
　collection of soldiers' letters 45–6
　criticisms 22

The Times (cont.)
  influence on progress of war 20, 58
  influence on public opinion 139
  leading articles 13–14, 19, 21, 23–5, 42–3, 47, 54–5, 95, 97–8, 141, 143, 224, 237
  letters to 23, 47, 49–53, 54–9, 55–9, 61–2, 137
  'private editorial' voice 55–9
  prose style/techniques 21–5
  referenced in fiction/correspondence 78, 88–9, 115
  Russian reading 2, 19–20
  'sick and wounded' Fund 23, 25, 54–5, 58
  size/layout 25–6
  supremacy over rival publications 20–2
  as 'voice of the people' 22
  war reports *see* Light Brigade, charge of; Russell, William Howard
Todleben, Eduard 9
Tolstoy, Leo 9
travel literature, influence on war reports/fiction 35–6, 65
trenches/trench warfare 1, 9
  artistic depictions 207
Trollope, Anthony, *The Warden/Barchester Towers* 20, 205
"A Trump Card(igan)" (Leech) 184–6, 207–8, 259
  effect of unreality 185–6
Tucker, Herbert 149, 155–6, 162–3
Turkey 1
  see also Ottoman Empire
Turkish forces, depictions of 174–6
Two Years Ago (C. Kingsley) 67, 77–82, 91, 124, 173–4, 235, 247
  characterisation 80–1
  comparison with other works 86, 88
  conflict of plot with intent 79–80, 81–2
  reviews 234–5
  subplots 79, 81
Tyrtaeus of Sparta 126, 252

Uglow, Jenny 86, 111–12, 242
uniforms, criticisms of 30, 43, 47
'urgent private affairs' (catchphrase/pretext for leave) 194–5
Urquhart, David 22–3, 136, 137, 138–9, 139–40, 224
Usherwood, Paul, and Jenny Spencer-Smith, *Lady Butler, Battle Artist* 210, 215–16, 262

Van Dyke, Henry 166
Vanden Bossche, Chris R. 161
Varna 8
Velazquez, *Don Diego de Acedo* 200

Victoria, Queen 10, 11, 22, 91, 113, 210
  iconic significance 104
  pictorial depictions 240, 260
Victorian era
  attitudes to national identity 5
Vienna Conference (1855) 10
Virgil, *Aeneid* 247
vox populi, as popular slogan 137
  see also public opinion
"Vox Populi" (Smith/Dobell) 137–40, 145

Waddington, Patrick 143
war
  as arena for heroism/redemption 66
  'fantasy investment' in 60, 188, 192
  modern responses 5–6
  negative impact on participants 84–6
  playing at *see* children
  role in national identity 4–5
war poetry 91–2
  criticisms 126–7
  focus on those waiting at home 128–32
  imaginative action, theme of 131–4
  poets' self-criticisms 127–8
  problem of poet's distance from action 125–8
  unifying function 123, 129, 136–7
water supplies 58–9
Watts, George Frederick 235
Waugh, Evelyn, *Brideshead Revisited* 83
weather 8–9, 176–7
  meteorological tables 50–1
  newspaper debates 49–53, 56
Weingart, Winfried 221
Weld, Charles Richard 166
Wellington, Arthur Wellesley, 1st Duke of 155
Welsh, Alexander 97, 238
Westward Ho! (C. Kingsley) 5, 76, 173, 215
  characterisation 71–2, 75–6
  comparison with other works 77, 79, 80, 86, 103, 110
  conflict of plot with intent 73, 74–6
  ideological/propagandist basis 70, 71–3, 233
  treatment of female characters 73–4, 76
Whewell, William, Prof. 93
Whyte-Melville, George, military career 65–6
  see also The Interpreter: A Tale of the War
Williams, Henry 58
women
  accompanying officer husbands 112
  artistic status 114–15, 116–17
  characterisation in drawings/paintings 187–8
  (commentary on) wartime situation 54–5
  domestic/'angelic' role 98–9, 108, 114, 118, 119, 214–15
  empowerment 55

literary depictions 65, 67–9, 73–4, 76–5, 86, 98–112
poets 128–34 (*see also names of individuals*)
popular images/conceptions 4
portrayals, as waiting for loved ones' return 128–34
social evils suffered by 115–16
women's movement 120, 121–2, 243, 264
Woodham-Smith, Cecil, *The Reason Why* 238, 248
Woodville, Richard Caton 216
Woolf, Virginia 240–1
  Freshwater 165–6
  To the Lighthouse 165, 167, 252

Wordsworth, William 45, 87, 93, 113, 212
  "The Ruined Cottage" 33
World War One 1, 20, 24–5, 67, 154–5, 217–18
  poetry 123, 125, 133
World War Two 24–5, 59, 104, 222
wounded, treatment of 30–3
Wright, H.P., Chaplain 61–2

Yonge, Charlotte M. 78–9
  Heartsease 78
  The Heir of Redclyffe 78
  The Young Stepmother 78–9
'A Yorkshirewoman' (*Times* correspondent) 55
YouTube 61

CAMBRIDGE STUDIES IN NINETEENTH-CENTURY
LITERATURE AND CULTURE

General editor
Gillian Beer, *University of Cambridge*

Titles published

1. The Sickroom in Victorian Fiction: The Art of Being Ill
   MIRIAM BAILIN, Washington University
2. Muscular Christianity: Embodying the Victorian Age
   edited by DONALD E. HALL, California State University, Northridge
3. Victorian Masculinities: Manhood and Masculine Poetics in Early Victorian Literature and Art
   HERBERT SUSSMAN, Northeastern University, Boston
4. Byron and the Victorians
   ANDREW ELFENBEIN, University of Minnesota
5. Literature in the Marketplace: Nineteenth-Century British Publishing and the Circulation of Books
   edited by JOHN O. JORDAN, University of California, Santa Cruz and ROBERT L. PATTEN, Rice University, Houston
6. Victorian Photography, Painting and Poetry
   LINDSAY SMITH, University of Sussex
7. Charlotte Brontë and Victorian Psychology
   SALLY SHUTTLEWORTH, University of Sheffield
8. The Gothic Body: Sexuality, Materialism and Degeneration at the Fin de Siècle
   KELLY HURLEY, University of Colorado at Boulder
9. Rereading Walter Pater
   WILLIAM F. SHUTER, Eastern Michigan University
10. Remaking Queen Victoria
    edited by MARGARET HOMANS, Yale University and ADRIENNE MUNICH, State University of New York, Stony Brook
11. Disease, Desire, and the Body in Victorian Women's Popular Novels
    PAMELA K. GILBERT, University of Florida
12. Realism, Representation, and the Arts in Nineteenth-Century Literature
    ALISON BYERLY, Middlebury College, Vermont

13. Literary Culture and the Pacific
    VANESSA SMITH, University of Sydney

14. Professional Domesticity in the Victorian Novel: Women, Work and Home
    MONICA F. COHEN

15. Victorian Renovations of the Novel: Narrative Annexes and the Boundaries of Representation
    SUZANNE KEEN, Washington and Lee University, Virginia

16. Actresses on the Victorian Stage: Feminine Performance and the Galatea Myth
    GAIL MARSHALL, University of Leeds

17. Death and the Mother from Dickens to Freud: Victorian Fiction and the Anxiety of Origin
    CAROLYN DEVER, Vanderbilt University, Tennessee

18. Ancestry and Narrative in Nineteenth-Century British Literature: Blood Relations from Edgeworth to Hardy
    SOPHIE GILMARTIN, Royal Holloway, University of London

19. Dickens, Novel Reading, and the Victorian Popular Theatre
    DEBORAH VLOCK

20. After Dickens: Reading, Adaptation and Performance
    JOHN GLAVIN, Georgetown University, Washington DC

21. Victorian Women Writers and the Woman Question
    edited by NICOLA DIANE THOMPSON, Kingston University, London

22. Rhythm and Will in Victorian Poetry
    MATTHEW CAMPBELL, University of Sheffield

23. Gender, Race, and the Writing of Empire: Public Discourse and the Boer War
    PAULA M. KREBS, Wheaton College, Massachusetts

24. Ruskin's God
    MICHAEL WHEELER, University of Southampton

25. Dickens and the Daughter of the House
    HILARY M. SCHOR, University of Southern California

26. Detective Fiction and the Rise of Forensic Science
    RONALD R. THOMAS, Trinity College, Hartford, Connecticut

27. Testimony and Advocacy in Victorian Law, Literature, and Theology
    JAN-MELISSA SCHRAMM, Trinity Hall, Cambridge

28. Victorian Writing about Risk: Imagining a Safe England in a Dangerous World
    ELAINE FREEDGOOD, University of Pennsylvania

29. Physiognomy and the Meaning of Expression in Nineteenth-Century Culture
    LUCY HARTLEY, University of Southampton

30. The Victorian Parlour: A Cultural Study
   THAD LOGAN, Rice University, Houston
31. Aestheticism and Sexual Parody 1840–1940
   DENNIS DENISOFF, Ryerson University, Toronto
32. Literature, Technology and Magical Thinking, 1880–1920
   PAMELA THURSCHWELL, University College London
33. Fairies in Nineteenth-Century Art and Literature
   NICOLA BOWN, Birkbeck, University of London
34. George Eliot and the British Empire
   NANCY HENRY, State University of New York, Binghamton
35. Women's Poetry and Religion in Victorian England: Jewish Identity and Christian Culture
   CYNTHIA SCHEINBERG, Mills College, California
36. Victorian Literature and the Anorexic Body
   ANNA KRUGOVOY SILVER, Mercer University, Georgia
37. Eavesdropping in the Novel from Austen to Proust
   ANN GAYLIN, Yale University
38. Missionary Writing and Empire, 1800–1860
   ANNA JOHNSTON, University of Tasmania
39. London and the Culture of Homosexuality, 1885–1914
   MATT COOK, Keele University
40. Fiction, Famine, and the Rise of Economics in Victorian Britain and Ireland
   GORDON BIGELOW, Rhodes College, Tennessee
41. Gender and the Victorian Periodical
   HILARY FRASER, Birkbeck, University of London; JUDITH JOHNSTON and STEPHANIE GREEN, University of Western Australia
42. The Victorian Supernatural
   edited by NICOLA BOWN, Birkbeck, London; CAROLYN BURDETT, London Metropolitan University and PAMELA THURSCHWELL, University College London
43. The Indian Mutiny and the British Imagination
   GAUTAM CHAKRAVARTY, University of Delhi
44. The Revolution in Popular Literature: Print, Politics and the People
   IAN HAYWOOD, Roehampton University of Surrey
45. Science in the Nineteenth-Century Periodical: Reading the Magazine of Nature
   GEOFFREY CANTOR, University of Leeds; GOWAN DAWSON, University of Leicester; GRAEME GOODAY, University of Leeds; RICHARD NOAKES,

University of Cambridge; SALLY SHUTTLEWORTH, University of Sheffield and JONATHAN R. TOPHAM, University of Leeds

46. Literature and Medicine in Nineteenth-Century Britain From Mary Shelley to George Eliot
    JANIS MCLARREN CALDWELL, Wake Forest University

47. The Child Writer from Austen to Woolf
    edited by CHRISTINE ALEXANDER, University of New South Wales and JULIET MCMASTER, University of Alberta

48. From Dickens to Dracula: Gothic, Economics and Victorian Fiction
    GAIL TURLEY HOUSTON, University of New Mexico

49. Voice and the Victorian Storyteller
    IVAN KREILKAMP, University of Indiana

50. Charles Darwin and Victorian Visual Culture
    JONATHAN SMITH, University of Michigan-Dearborn

51. Catholicism, Sexual Deviance, and Victorian Gothic Culture
    PATRICK R. O'MALLEY, Georgetown University

52. Epic and Empire in Nineteenth-Century Britain
    SIMON DENTITH, University of Gloucestershire

53. Victorian Honeymoons: Journeys to the Conjugal
    HELENA MICHIE, Rice University

54. The Jewess in Nineteenth-Century British Literary Culture
    NADIA VALMAN, University of Southampton

55. Ireland, India and Nationalism in Nineteenth-Century Literature
    JULIA WRIGHT, Dalhousie University

56. Dickens and the Popular Radical Imagination
    SALLY LEDGER, Birkbeck, University of London

57. Darwin, Literature and Victorian Respectability
    GOWAN DAWSON, University of Leicester

58. "Michael Field": Poetry, Aestheticism and the Fin de Siècle
    MARION THAIN, University of Birmingham

59. Colonies, Cults and Evolution: Literature, Science and Culture in Nineteenth-Century Writing
    DAVID AMIGONI, Keele University

60. Realism, Photography and Nineteenth-Century Fiction
    DANIEL A. NOVAK, Lousiana State University

61. Caribbean Culture and British Fiction in the Nineteenth Century
    TIM WATSON, University of Miami

62. The Poetry of Chartism: Aesthetics, Politics, History
   MICHAEL SANDERS, University of Manchester
63. Literature and Dance in Nineteenth-Century Britain: Jane Austen to the New Woman
   CHERYL WILSON, Indiana University
64. Shakespeare and Victorian Women
   GAIL MARSHALL, Oxford Brookes University
65. The Tragi-Comedy of Victorian Fatherhood
   VALERIE SANDERS, University of Hull
66. Darwin and the Memory of the Human
   CANNON SCHMITT, Wayne State University
67. From Sketch to Novel
   AMANPAL GARCHA, Ohio State University
68. The Crimean War in the British Imagination
   STEFANIE MARKOVITS, Yale University
69. Shock, Memory and the Unconscious in Victorian Fiction
   JILL L. MATUS, University of Toronto
70. Sensation and Modernity in the 1860s
   NICHOLAS DALY, University College Dublin

Printed in Great Britain
by Amazon